AN UNCERTAIN FUTURE

An UNCERTAIN FUTURE

Voices of a French Jewish Community, 1940–2012

THE JEWS OF DIJON

Robert I. Weiner & Richard E. Sharpless

UNIVERSITY OF TORONTO PRESS

Library and Archives Canada Cataloguing in Publication

Weiner, Robert I.
    An uncertain future : voices of a French Jewish community, 1940–2012 / the Jews of Dijon ;
Robert I. Weiner & Richard E. Sharpless.

Includes bibliographical references and index.
Issued also in electronic formats.
ISBN 978-1-4426-0558-9 (bound)
ISBN 978-1-4426-0559-6 (pbk.).

    1. Jews, French—France—Dijon—Interviews. 2. Jews, French—France— Dijon—Social
life and customs—20th century. 3. Jews, French—France—Dijon— History—20th century.
4. Jews—France—Dijon—Identity. 5. Dijon (France)— Ethnic relations—History—20th century.
6. Dijon (France)—Biography. 7. Oral history—France—Dijon. I. Sharpless, Richard E. II. Title.

DS135.F85D54 2012   944'.426004924   C2012-903826-1

We welcome comments and suggestions regarding any aspect of our publications—please feel free
to contact us at news@utphighereducation.com or visit our Internet site at www.utppublishing.com.

North America
5201 Dufferin Street
North York, Ontario, Canada, M3H 5T8

2250 Military Road
Tonawanda, New York, USA, 14150

ORDERS PHONE: 1–800–565–9523
ORDERS FAX: 1–800–221–9985
ORDERS E-MAIL: utpbooks@utpress.utoronto.ca

UK, Ireland, and continental Europe
NBN International
Estover Road, Plymouth, PL6 7PY, UK
ORDERS PHONE: 44 (0) 1752 202301
ORDERS FAX: 44 (0) 1752 202333
ORDERS E-MAIL: enquiries@nbninternational.com

The University of Toronto Press acknowledges the financial support for its publishing activities
of the Government of Canada through the Canada Book Fund.

Typesetting: Em Dash Design

Printed in Canada

To the Jews of Dijon

CONTENTS

ACKNOWLEDGEMENTS

Our work in Dijon would have been impossible but for the continuous warm community response author Robert Weiner received over the years, as well as the welcome extended to Richard Sharpless. For the willingness of so many individuals to grant informal and formal interviews that often revealed both personal and painful aspects of their lives, we extend our deepest thanks to: Jean-David and Ariel Attal; Gaby and Miriam Barda; Gislain Bensoussan, Annie Edelman, Bébé Edelman, and Deborah Bensoussan; Henri-Claude Bloch; Michel and Cathie Bussidan; Nadia Kaluski; Izy and Luna Cemachovic; Jean-Claude Dahan; Alain and Isabelle Danino; Bernard and Marcel David; Malou Dressler; Alain and Gaby Grynberg; Gérard Hachmoun; Élie and Danielle Hadida; Marguerite Haas; Albert and Myrna Huberfeld; Georges Huberfeld; Mark and Sylvie Knopher; David and Yvette Laufer; Jean-Claude and Marlène Meimoun; Lucien Mestman; Alex and Babette Miles; Sœur Odile; Max Orlik; Roger Partouche; Lucie Picard; Elie and Marie-Ange Sadigh; Haim and Hannah Slonim; Simon and Annie Sibony; Marc and Jennifer Taieb; Denis, Françoise, and Charles Tenenbaum; Marcel and Leah Tobis.

We are grateful for the generous support from Lafayette College that provided summer and travel grants, sabbaticals, and funds for EXCEL scholars (student research assistants); this project would have been more difficult without their assistance. In particular, we thank two bilingual students, Maria Mitova and Vanida Narrainen, who translated most of the interviews and *Mazal Tov* articles. Jessica Farrell and EXCEL Julie Depenbrock of Lafayette College contributed their technical skills in the final editing of the manuscript and receive our appreciation.

We extend thanks to our selfless departmental secretaries Kathy Anckaitis and Tammy Yeakel, and to Natalie Fingerhut, our supportive and capable acquiring editor at the University of Toronto Press. We thank Betsy Struthers for her suggestions and meticulous editing.

Robert I. Weiner and Richard E. Sharpless

PREFACE: WHY DIJON?

This book had its origin in the early 1990s when Robert Weiner became involved with the Jewish community of Dijon, a major provincial center in eastern France. His interest in this relatively small but unique society evolved into a long-term study. He knew that most published works about French Jews focused on the large Jewish population of Paris, yet nearly half of all French Jews live elsewhere in France. It was Weiner's purpose to provide insights into the lives of these "others" by immersing himself as much as possible in a community that had all the attributes of Jewish identity, that was representative of non-Parisian Jews, and yet that was distinctive in its own way.

This contemporary oral history, based on interviews and recorded observations made over an 18-year period, is the first of its kind, at least in English. The interviews, some repeated with the same subjects years later, provide a portrait of how this community evolved over time in response to challenges, both internal and external, and of the tensions that have brought about changes within it. These tensions include, to provide some examples, those between Jews who emigrated from Eastern Europe and North Africa; the traditional community and newly arrived Lubavitch Jews; Jews and non-Jews, including recent Muslim immigrants; the older and younger members; and intermarriage within and outside the community. Indeed, the interviews cover virtually every form of Jewish identity found in Dijon. They are complemented by several excerpts from the community journal, *Mazal Tov*, which provide the reader with an additional perspective.

The book will be of interest to the informed reader interested in contemporary Jewish life as well as to the student of Jewish and European history and sociology. Most issues that impact the modern world, from the effects of economic change to the ongoing problems of ethnic conflict and anti-Semitism, are discussed in the interviews. More specifically, such questions as how to be both French and Jewish and how to be loyal at the same time to a secular nation as well as a separate spiritual homeland are asked and answered quite differently. In sum, the book provides fascinating personal accounts of those who experienced the renewal of a community from the catastrophe of the Holocaust through integration of a new culture to optimistic growth and expansion followed by division, slow decline, and uncertainty about the future. It is the story, written small, about other European Jewish communities and perhaps those elsewhere.

Weiner's interest in the Dijon Jewish community began somewhat informally in 1993 when he led a group of Lafayette College students on a

semester-abroad program affiliated with a French language institute associated with the University of Burgundy in Dijon. He was aware, of course, that
in the late 1980s and early 1990s there was a revival of interest in France in
the Jewish experience and a resulting substantial production of both popular and scholarly writing.* Most of this output, however, focused on Paris.
Though understandable considering the role that Paris has in the highly
centralized nation, Weiner believed that Parisian Jewish realities and identity could not be equated with that of French Jews who lived elsewhere in
the country—unless proven to be so.

The Dijon Jewish community, defined as those individuals who identify
themselves as Jews and participate to some extent in "Jewish" activities,
lends itself well to a study of this type. It numbers approximately 225 families within an urban population of about 150,000 (the metropolitan area
contains another 100,000). Though relatively small in relation to the general
population, the members of the community played, and continue to play, a
significant role in the commercial and professional life of the city. Thus, the
community is small enough, yet dynamic and important enough, to enhance
our understanding of "provincial" French Jews.

Weiner discovered in that spring of 1993 that he had arrived at a unique
moment in the community's history. Unlike most Parisian synagogues, or
even synagogues in other larger cities, the synagogue center in Dijon represented virtually every major current in French Jewish life, except for the
most recent immigrants from the former Soviet Union and Lubavitch Jews
(who would, in any case, soon arrive). This blend, combined with a youthful,
growing, and active population, resulted in a creative and dynamic atmosphere that marked a significant change from the previous decades of cautious
rebuilding after the war and adjustment to newcomers from North Africa.

A major factor in creating this atmosphere was Simon Sibony, the community's rabbi since 1977 and himself a Moroccan immigrant. Although the
synagogue was part of the French Central Consistory system, established
in the nineteenth century to oversee and represent national Jewish affairs,
Sibony resisted the increasingly conservative tendencies of the Paris-based
Consistory Council. He remained open, tolerant, and moderate. To cite one
example, he permitted women to sit on the main floor of the sanctuary—
though behind the men—and encouraged them to participate in non-religious

---

* Robert Weiner, "French Jewish Images of America: The Case of Dijon," *Proceedings of the
  Western Society for French History: Selected Papers of the Annual Meeting* XXV (1998): 79–87;
  Robert Weiner, "On Interviewing French Jews: The Case for Oral History," *Proceedings of the
  Western Society for French History* XVI (1989): 316–25; and Robert Weiner, "Perspectives on
  French Jewry in the 1980s: Crisis and Renewal," *Proceedings of the Western Society for French
  History* XIII (1986): 251–60.

leadership positions within the community. These practices were departures from those prevailing in most Consistorial synagogues.

Another fact that made Dijon distinctive was that, except for the absence of a full-time parochial day school, there existed by the early 1990s a virtual full service community for Dijon's Jews. They had almost every organization that might be found in larger synagogues and even in larger cities. Anyone, including curious Christians, with a desire for religious or secular activities could find something of interest, from serious Talmud study to youth groups, public cultural events, communal trips, B'nai B'rith, and even a Jewish radio station.

This period of growth and activity in Dijon was the result of the conjunction of local and national developments in French Jewish life. At the national level the processing of Holocaust memory and related Holocaust issues was still important, but in other ways a Jewish cultural renaissance was in progress. Parisian Jews and the national organizations they headed were finding public voices and defending the right to be different as a legitimate minority presence in France. Combined with this was the struggle against persistent anti-Semitism and anti-Zionism in the country, as well as support for Israel.

These issues resonated clearly among many Dijon Jews, especially a group of prominent professionals and business people with young families. Creative and active, they joined with older members to energize their community, founding the France-Israel Association (1991), the B'nai B'rith lodge (1991), and Radio Shalom (1993). Their collective goals were to monitor and fight anti-Semitism in all its forms and to support and explain Israel and its difficult and complicated problems to a wider public. They also sought to raise public awareness of the Jewish presence in Dijon, in particular among local officials and politicians.

At this juncture Weiner had not yet decided to begin an oral history of the community. He merely sought to collect data for articles that he might write. For that end he began attending as many religious services and secular community events as possible and keeping a journal of his observations. Since he already was a cantor, trained in the United States, he soon became an active participant in religious services. He then widened his contacts throughout the community, first with Jews with Eastern European backgrounds like himself, and eventually with more recent members with origins in Africa and the Middle East. Following that first extended stay in Dijon in 1993, he visited at least once annually, and occasionally more often, over the following 18 years, including another extended stay in 2000. He became, in effect, an adjunct member of the community, with a wide circle of friends and acquaintances, and was accepted as a trusted insider.

Weiner's early interviews were more free-flowing and somewhat less directed than the later ones. Most were chronologically based, allowing the subjects to speak about their family backgrounds, childhood, education, etc., before moving on to more directed questions about their Jewish lives, experiences, and views. It was in one such 1993 interview, for example, that he quickly learned that intermarriage was an especially touchy issue and best approached through casual conversation rather than as an interview question.

Weiner's questions covered a broad spectrum: political and religious preferences; perceptions of, and experience with, anti-Semitism; attitudes toward Israel, Zionism, and the United States; and relations with Gentiles, especially with Muslims. He also sought opinions about France's future, particularly about the future of French Jewry. Additional biographical material was included when an individual had an unusual background, such as birthplace, Holocaust experiences, or a known family history stretching back centuries.

Transcribed and translated by a number of talented French-speakers, the tapes of individuals sometimes yielded as many as 120 typed pages, though the norm was usually 40 to 50 pages. The information, as noted above, formed the basis for several academic journal articles as well as conference papers and class lectures.[*] Fortunately, Weiner's annual visit to Dijon and his extended stays in 1993 and 2000 gave him the opportunity to conduct a number of two- and three-session interviews of about two hours each. The close relationship he maintained with a number of interview subjects allowed him to return to question the same individuals he had first encountered in 1993.

Delays in putting the interviews into print turned out to be fortunate, because significant changes have occurred in the Dijon community in the last few years. The energy and sense of purpose that characterized the early 1990s have given way due, in part, to internal divisions but also because of changing local, national, and international conditions. As a result, further interviews were deemed necessary in order to provide a more complete and inclusive account of the contemporary Dijon community.

Weiner turned to retired Professor Richard Sharpless, a long-time friend and Lafayette College colleague, for assistance. Prior to his academic career, Sharpless had worked as a journalist and editor; although familiar with Weiner's work in Dijon, he provided a useful distance from the project. It was agreed that he would do all of the editorial work, especially on the 3,000 to 4,000 pages of transcribed interviews. Because of the structural problems

---

[*] Weiner, "French Jewish Images of America"; Robert Weiner, "Pour le meilleur ou pour le pire: The Jews of Dijon in the 1990s, A Memoir," *Proceedings of the Western Society for French History: Selected Papers of the Annual Meeting* XXIX (2002): 68–75.

involved with the copious earlier interviews (a topic on page 11 reappeared again on page 29, etc.), it was decided to abandon a question-and-answer format for a narrative by each interview subject. Sharpless then reorganized and closely edited the original transcripts and wrote the narratives as they now appear. Every effort was made to retain the voice of the interview subject and the accuracy of what was said.

A decision was made to divide the interviews into three groups that reflect the ways in which Dijon Jews characterize themselves. The first group is composed of members of the synagogue-center community, by far the largest category, which includes a gamut of religious views from traditional orthodoxy to secularism and much in between. Today, this group is comprised of some 170 to 180 families, mostly middle-aged and older.

The second group of about 15 families is the Lubavitch. They also include a range of religious orientations, from Hasidic Lubavitch Judaism to a rather secular couple who placed their son in the Lubavitch school—the group's greatest attraction for young couples.

The third group is comprised of unaffiliated Jews, perhaps 40 to 50 families, who have chosen to remain separate from the established groups for a number of reasons. Generally more assimilated and more liberal, this group even includes several anti-Zionists.

In terms of the general organization of interviews within each group, except for the leaderless group three, we have chosen to begin with leaders, since they offer the best global introduction to each group's functioning, nature, and overall goals. This will afford the reader a coherent and engaging pathway into each group's development, structure, and functioning.

In addition, more sharply focused short interviews were conducted in Dijon during 2000–07, many with previously interviewed subjects. These were designed to update attitudes and opinions about the evolving community. These interviews were ably transcribed and translated by Maria Mitova and Vanida Narrainen, bilingual Lafayette College EXCEL student-scholars. They also completed the tedious task of reviewing the accuracy of the earlier interviews.

Several excerpts from the community journal *Mazal Tov* complement the interviews. Published several times a year, and continuously—though under various names—since 1978, the journal is an eclectic, excellent source of history and information. It contains articles about topics brought up in the interviews, occasionally written by the subjects themselves. There are opinion pieces, reviews, recipes, announcements, reprints from other Jewish publications, and letters. Though overseen by an editorial board, the views of the editor usually predominate. The current editor, Cathie Bussidan, has established and maintained high editorial standards while struggling to keep the publication going during difficult times. It remains an excellent source for study of the community. Numerous longer excerpts from translated copies of the *Mazal Tov* interviews are published in an E-book format.[*]

Drawing upon copious notes he took during his various trips to Dijon, Weiner co-wrote with Sharpless the historical Introduction and Afterword. Weiner also provided the chronology, glossary, and bibliographies, as well as co-writing the brief biographies that introduce each interview. These, along with a map of the city, provide the reader with a complete picture of the Jewish community of Dijon.

---

[*] It is hoped that the first selection of a two-volume anthology of translated *Mazal Tov* articles will be available by fall of 2012. A second selection of articles, from the late 1970s to 2000, should be available by the fall of 2013 at http://dspace.lafayette.edu/handle/10385/845 and http://dspace.lafayette.edu/handle/10385/846.

INTRODUCTION: MEET JEWISH DIJON

The majestic synagogue of Dijon stands where the medieval town of the Dukes of Burgundy and the modern city of post-revolutionary France converge. It shares a street with weathered nineteenth-century townhouses and bland twentieth-century apartment buildings, while on its north side the fortified walls of old Dijon once stood guard. The building, completed in 1879, mirrors the decorative style of the early Third Republic, along with a hint of Byzantine and even Islamic architecture in its high dome and corner towers. The synagogue is a fitting residence for the historic and varied traditions it has hosted.

Built by the generosity of less than 200 families, few of whose descendants have survived, the temple is a symbol of their wealth and importance during what historians have called the "golden age of French Jewry." Today their grand synagogue, witness to a terrifying and conflictive history, provides a home to a reconstructed but shrinking community facing an uncertain future.

Uncertainty has always characterized the experiences of Jews in Dijon and France. The earliest arrivals that came in the first European **diaspora** lived in constant transition. Forbidden in most of late Medieval Christian Europe from owning land or engaging in accepted crafts and trades, they were forced to survive at the margins of feudal society, captive to the changing whims of Christian rulers. If allowed to settle, it was usually in segregated areas. Regarded as religious outcasts, they were subjected to harassment and persecution. Always they were the objects of suspicion and fear.

Dijon was originally founded as a Roman military camp, but by the later Middle Ages it had evolved into a regional trading center and the administrative seat of a bishopric and the Dukes of Burgundy. Historic records indicate that a number of Jews, often identified, traded there. Their origins are unclear, but they possibly came from the larger Jewish settlements to the east in nearby Alsace or, since they were traders, from southern France. They loaned money to Church and secular officials, but their status made them susceptible to forced contributions, high taxes, and loan defaults. Nevertheless, the community continued to grow in number and to diversify economically. They undoubtedly had links to their kinsmen and co-religionists in other centers, notably those in the south who controlled much of the long-distance commerce in spices and luxury goods from the eastern Mediterranean.

The small community of Dijon would have read the **Torah** and practiced and observed, to the best of their abilities, the rituals, requirements, and festivals of the Jewish calendar. According to the archives, they met for religious ceremonies in various places within the old city. But, as always, security was unobtainable. The fevered religious fervor of the Crusades (from the eleventh to the thirteenth centuries) combined with the later charges of poisoning wells during the Black Death decades (1348–51 and after) resulted in the expulsion of Dijon's Jews in the late fourteenth century. They joined other uprooted French Jews in seeking refuge farther east. Only New Christian converts in southwest France and scattered groups in Alsace and Lorraine remained. Jews would not return in any number for almost 300 years.

Jews found their way back to Dijon in the early 1790s during the emancipation phase of the French Revolution. They were required to relinquish their medieval corporate identity as a distinct ethnic and legal group; within the new republican framework they became French citizens with individual rights and responsibilities. This marked the beginning of Jewish assimilation into the larger French nation, though it came not without resistance. And, like other religions in nineteenth-century republican France, Judaism received official sanction when a Paris-based Central Consistory to oversee and supervise Jewish institutions was established in 1808 under the direction of the Napoleonic Ministry of Religions. These developments eventually undermined the various regional customs and differences among Jewish groups in France.

By 1803 there were about 50 Jewish families residing in Dijon, mostly of Alsatian background. Though these first **Ashkenazi** immigrants probably spoke German, and possibly **Yiddish**, and were quite traditional in their beliefs and religious practices, their descendants by mid-century embraced the fact of French citizenship and culture. Like their co-religionists throughout France, they generally prospered during the tolerant nineteenth century as artisans, merchants, and property owners. The grand synagogue, inaugurated in 1879, is a monument to their success. By then their community numbered some 550 members.

During the last decades of the nineteenth century and the first years of the twentieth century Jewish immigration to France from Central and Eastern Europe increased significantly because of both religious persecution and worsening economic conditions in the Russian and Austrian-Hungarian empires. Most of these newcomers settled in Paris and the larger cities, where they joined the ranks of the working class. They were attracted to France not only because of the nation's reputation for religious tolerance but also due to opportunities created by the expanding industrial revolution. But their increasing numbers, and the fear that they were displacing French workers, resulted in growing animosity and anti-Semitism. This anti-Semitism was fueled by the alleged roles of the Rothschilds and other Jewish bankers and investors in several financial scandals and by the increasing public role assimilated French Jews were playing in all areas of French culture.

French anti-Semitism of this era had contradictory views: socialists, who nominally claimed to support the working class, saw Jews as capitalists; capitalists, on the other hand, regarded the mostly working-class immigrants as socialists. Conservative Catholics believed that Jews—and Freemasons—were destroying the soul of Catholic France. The "scientific" racists of that time claimed that Jews were the scourge of humanity and either a race of superior, but evil beings or an altogether degraded race. All this would find its final expression in twentieth-century European Nazism.

Dijon was not a major industrial center and did not attract large numbers of Eastern European immigrants. Those who did settle in the city were usually from Alsace and Lorraine, provinces annexed by Germany after the Franco-Prussian War (1870-71), but there is evidence that those who did settle there were not greeted with open arms. By now many—if not most—of Dijon's Jews were members of the middle class, or at least aspired to it, and tended to look down upon the newcomers. The immigrants, like those in other French cities, tended to cluster in the poorer, more crowded neighborhoods of the Old City.

The trigger that set off a wave of anti-Semitism and violence in France was the Dreyfus Affair. Captain Alfred Dreyfus, a talented Jewish army officer and member of the French General Staff, was charged with high treason in 1894 for supposedly passing military secrets to Germany. Though originally convicted based on false evidence and illegal procedures, Dreyfus eventually was pardoned in 1900 and exonerated in 1906, re-entering the army and serving in World War I. The incident bitterly divided French political and cultural elites. France's reputation for tolerance was damaged, and for many Jews complacency over their security and place in France was questioned.

Dijon's native Jews in the first decade of the twentieth century reacted with both uncertainty and concern to the national developments that would ultimately affect them. First was the 1905 law separating church and state, thus in large measure undermining the role of the Consistory. Second was the emergence in the wake of the Dreyfus affair of the anti-republican and proto-fascist organization Action Française. But of more immediate impact was the influence of the immigrant Jews, who represented a new departure for French Jewry. Proud of their own ethnic, cultural, and religious traditions, but poor and Yiddish-speaking, they challenged the authority of France's native Jews. Often faced with indifference or even hostility by the native Jewish elite, these newcomers founded their own religious organizations and established self-help associations, Yiddish newspapers, cultural organizations, leftist political affiliations, and trade unions. They gradually built separate communities. Their cultural weight, including openness to **Zionism** and all forms of ethnic diversity, impacted on traditional French Jews, such as those in Dijon, who were rethinking their Jewish identity as ethnic and racial nationalisms were appearing throughout Europe.

These local concerns were immediately overshadowed by the outbreak of World War I in August 1914. The Jews of France, native and immigrant, rallied to the defense of the nation. Approximately 40,000 of the more than 200,000 Jews in France and Algeria (an annexed French colony, where Jews became French citizens in 1870) served in the military; 7,500 gave their lives. Dijon's Jews also served and sacrificed proportionately. But victory came at a terrible cost: literally an entire generation was wiped out. The French government recognized the Jews' contribution to the nation's survival and final victory. Even ardent nationalists and some notable anti-Semites found reasons for praise. As a result, serious anti-Semitism in France became less of a problem in the immediate postwar years.

There was, however, little respite from political trauma. The collapse of the Russian and Austrian-Hungarian empires, the Russian Revolution, and the independence of Poland and other openly anti-Semitic states in Eastern Europe, plus continuing economic turmoil, resulted in another great wave of Jewish refugees sweeping into France. These eastern Jews were joined in the 1930s by German and Austrian Jews seeking to escape Hitler and the Nazis. On top of this came the Great Depression, bringing with it desperation and the resulting radicalization of French politics, xenophobia, and increasing anti-Semitism.

Dijon's Jews responded similarly to their co-religionists in other regions of the country. Some worked to help the newcomers who, counting those who had come before the war, now formed a majority of the local Jewish population. Prosperous members of the community contributed financially; others, usually the native Jews, remained indifferent or aloof. Some supported the Zionist enterprise in Palestine; others were embarrassed by it. Younger Jews in particular supported the Popular Front government in 1936 of Socialist Léon Blum, France's first Jewish prime minister; many older Jews were terrified that his election would lead to more anti-Semitism. And for all those who wanted France to defend itself against an increasingly aggressive Germany, there were others who preferred to make concessions in order to avoid war—for which they would ultimately be blamed. As one historian of that time, Paula E. Hyman, observed:

The French Jewish community remained fragmented and disoriented on the eve of World War II.... For both immigrant and native Jews, their previous experience in France left them ill-prepared to recognize, and respond to, the full extent of the danger that they confronted in the four years 1940–1944.[*]

On the eve of World War II, Dijon was a conservative, bourgeois, middle-sized city of some 100,000 inhabitants. The Jewish community numbered approximately 500, mostly of Alsatian background, plus a number of Eastern European Jews who arrived in the two decades after World War I, and a dozen or so families who had fled Hitler's Germany. The largely assimilated Alsatian Jews, very much **"Israélites"** and no longer adhering rigidly to traditional religious practices, had a condescending attitude toward the others and yet demonstrated a willingness to provide some financial aid to the newcomers and help in various other ways.

Following the collapse of Blum's Popular Front government in March 1938, xenophobia and anti-Semitism increased dramatically. The city and the region were a haven for various right-wing extremist groups, and as war approached, the atmosphere became increasingly toxic. The recently arrived refugees were warned by community members not to congregate in large groups or to speak German loudly in public.[†] By the outbreak of war in September 1939, the Jewish community was deeply apprehensive as well as divided.

Because of its location in eastern France and the presence of nearby Longvic, a major airfield, Dijon was an important objective for the Germans, who occupied the city on 17–18 June, 1940. The occupiers then made the city an administrative center for a number of surrounding districts. A Gestapo headquarters was established.

Dijon's Jews, natives and immigrants alike, suffered the same bitter experiences. Some served and died in the French military. Approximately 150 community members, a much higher percentage than French Jews nationally, perished at the hands of the Nazis. Their numbers included the popular and very active 36-year-old Rabbi Élie Cyper, a Résistant for whom a street adjacent to the synagogue was recently named.

Most of Dijon's Jews went into hiding during the war years. Those who could fled to southern France to what they thought was the relative safety of

[*] Paula E. Hyman, *The Jews of Modern France* (Berkeley, CA: University of California Press, 1998) 158–59.

[†] Rita Thalmann, *Tout commença à Nuremberg* (Paris: Berg International Éditeurs, 2004) 63.

the puppet Vichy regime, headed by the World War I military hero, General Pétain. Many were protected by "righteous Gentiles," sympathetic Christians who risked their own lives by doing so. Some served in the Resistance against the German Occupation in one capacity or another. The more established French Jews were usually fortunate in having most of their family members survive, sometimes even as a result of collaborating with Pétainists (Vichy authorities). The recent arrivals from Eastern Europe, however, were targeted by the Vichy authorities and frequently lost the majority of their families to the death camps. A few, dispersed elsewhere, simply never returned.

The synagogue did not meet the same fate—destruction—as others in German-occupied Europe. It survived due to the trickery of a member of the municipal council, Chanoine Kir, who persuaded the Germans that it would serve as an excellent warehouse. The Torahs and other sacred objects were removed and hidden by Kir and members of the Jewish community. After Dijon was liberated by advancing French forces (followed by Americans) in September 1944, the synagogue was used for **Yom Kippur** services. Several hundred military issue American mini-prayer books were left behind and still remain in a storage bin in the building.

As elsewhere, the postwar years were tumultuous. Reuniting of families, recovery of lost or stolen property, rebuilding of lives—these were the priorities. But not all were welcomed upon their return, although the recovery of most property in the city went relatively smoothly. Suspicion and resentment remained. This caused some Jews to drift away from the community, while others, notably from the Wormser and Meyer families, worked with great determination to recover what had been lost. Rita Thalmann, a writer and returning visitor to the city in the early 1950s, noted that the general atmosphere certainly was different after the war, but she found the community to be much the same as before, except for the significant number of those who were missing.[*]

Dijon's Jews, like most French, just wanted a return to normality. This began with the economic recovery of the late 1940s and 1950s. The synagogue became once again the center where people enjoyed meeting, especially since the war years had given them more of a shared experience. Essential community functions returned to life: religious services, a choir, scouts and summer camp for children, and the Women's International Zionist Organization (WIZO). Children received instruction, and **bar mitzvah**s were celebrated. Rabbis came and went, sometimes supplemented by a visiting rabbi from nearby Besançon or a religiously educated layman. By the early

---

[*] Thalmann 222.

1960s a moderate, traditional, reasonably integrated community of about 120 families enjoyed the normality they sought.

In 1962 Algeria's torturous independence struggle against France ended successfully, following the less violent experiences of Tunisia and Morocco in the mid-1950s. What followed was a mass exodus of Jews—eventually reaching some 450,000—from the former French North African colonies. They were propelled, in part, by the Arab belief that they were pro-French and in part by growing anti-Jewish and anti-Israeli sentiments throughout North Africa and the Middle East, especially following each Arab-Israeli war. About half of these refugees, many holding French citizenship or at least an affinity for French culture, went directly to France.

Jews had been resident in the North African French colonies since at least the Middle Ages and co-existed, generally peacefully, with the Muslim Arabs and Berbers. Under French colonial rule, the minority Jews were at times subjected to the same repressive policies as the general population and to French anti-Semitism as well, although Algerian Jews were emancipated by the 1870 Adolphe Crémieux Decree. This did little to lessen the anti-Semitism of French *colons* (settlers), especially during the Dreyfus Affair. By the outbreak of World War II, Jews were principally located in urban centers as shopkeepers, artisans, and tradesmen; they generally held a somewhat higher socioeconomic status than Muslims and were more adapted to French culture.* During the war, anti-Semitism was fanned by Vichy French authorities, who also sought support among pan-African nationalists against the Allies. This sometimes carried over in the postwar period.

The arrival of North Africans in Dijon began an era of tumult, trial, and transition. The newcomers and their settled brethren did not take to each other all at once, since backgrounds, styles, and life experiences were so very different. These were demonstrated especially in the one thing they shared—the synagogue. When the Ashkenazim prayed, it was in the calm, measured style of the rational French. The rabbi led and the congregation followed, but softly. Among the North African **Sephardim**, however, prayer was loud, passionate, and participatory—and by people who knew their stuff. This made for some interesting contrasts. Some never closed the cultural-religious divide. Only shared challenges and experiences, including mixed marriages, have managed to do that over time.

At first, the Ashkenazim controlled the synagogue's Board of Directors and existing committees. They also paid most of the dues. Eventually, given

---

* From 1862 onward the large number of Alliance Israélite Universelle educational institutions was especially important in forging cultural links between North African Jews and the French.

their numbers, the Sephardim began to dominate religious services. They preferred to give the community monetary gifts for honors, rather than paying set dues. "They pray and we pay," was the way some Ashkenazim expressed it. Or, less generously, they accused the newcomers of "acting like Arabs," only to earn the retort that the Ashkenazim were "assimilated Gentiles."

Not surprisingly, then, the 1960s and 1970s saw numerous disputes within the community. These were not only between Europeans and North Africans but between the different North African clans as well. They argued about rites, rituals, melodies, and distribution of honors. For a brief time a group even withdrew from the community.

Nevertheless, growth and revival continued. In the 1970s there were about 180 families in a stronger and more open community. The rapid economic and educational integration of the newcomers was successful.

The Arab-Israeli wars of 1967 and 1973 also galvanized Dijon's Jews into greater activity and increased their sense of common purpose. Ashkenazim felt renewed pride in their Jewishness mixed with anger over France's adoption of pro-Arab positions. For the Sephardim, ethnically more Jewish to begin with, concern with the welfare of Israel was intensified because they had close family ties there. Significant numbers of North African Jews had settled in Israel following their flight from Arab lands in the 1950s through the 1970s.[*]

Community members now not only had a synagogue to maintain but a powerful external referent of common identity around which to unite. Indeed, they joined others in France in support of an annual United Israel Appeal from 1973 on, with Dijon's Dr. Lucien Mestman serving as head for many years.

Dijon's Jews were reminded of a tortured past by the revival of anti-Semitic activities in the late 1970s and 1980s. Neo-Nazis made threatening telephone calls to community leaders. Swastikas were painted on store windows. Anti-Jewish pamphlets appeared in high schools. Local leaders, such as Mayor Robert Poujade (1980–2002) and Roman Catholic Bishop Decourtray, however, were good allies. Local efforts at Jewish-Christian and Jewish-Christian-Muslim dialogue began. The local branch of the International League against Racism and Anti-Semitism (LICRA) became increasingly active.

A source of stability was the appointment in 1977 of a young Moroccan-born rabbi, Simon Sibony, to the post that he still holds. Sibony conducted

---

[*] Although not formally expelled, the North African Jews were frequently traumatized and otherwise had very good reasons to leave while the getting was still good.

religious services well, despite limits as an inspiring teacher. His moderate orthodoxy, tolerance, and kindly nature were good for a community as
diverse as Dijon's. He and his wife, Annie, made people feel comfortable in
the synagogue and added strength to the community. Sibony was excellent
in dialogue with Christian and Muslim leaders and brought a small group of
helpful Christian sympathizers to communal events, including the Hebrew
classes that became a distinctive feature of the community.

Nineteen seventy-eight saw the first publication of an ambitious quar-
terly communal journal, which has become an important community link
and voice. Now called *Mazal Tov* ("Good Luck"), it has appeared almost
uninterrupted over the years under a variety of names. Its pages contain
everything from institutional reports and exhortations, notices of upcoming events and reviews of past ones, opinion pieces and historical narratives,
to recipes, jokes, and announcements of births, deaths, and other personal
events. It also informs its readers about, and offers, a specifically Dijon Jewish
framework for analysis of historical and current events related to Burgundy,
Dijon, and the wider Jewish world, including Israel and the United States.
It provides an excellent record for historical investigation.

During these years the community added a number of important physical structures and programs. The former were the addition of a ritual bath,
or **mikveh,** and a community center attached to the synagogue (1982); the
latter included the renewal of the local Jewish scouting movement, the
opening of a nursery school in 1983, the expansion of the Hebrew school
as the number of young people increased, the provision of Hebrew courses
for adults, and the founding of a seniors' club.

Another development was the increasing role of women, especially in the
area of education and in the affairs of the community. While their collective accomplishments engendered a real sense of pride, questions over their
place in the sanctuary resulted in a series of incidents during the late 1980s
and early 1990s. These created a temporary disruptive element in a period
of relative congregational stability.

One steady and unmistakable source of strength was Henri-Claude
Bloch, a merchant-scholar whose ancestors helped re-establish Dijon's
community during the French Revolution in the late eighteenth century.
During his presidency of the synagogue (1984–96) the postwar community
achieved its major accomplishments. Bloch was adept at obtaining small
subventions from local government sources and organizing large religious
and cultural manifestations of Jewish patrimony. He was also a prolific
contributor of historical accounts and opinion articles to the community's journals. He authored a two-volume *History of the Jews of Dijon and*

Burgundy in the Middle Ages[*] and prior to his death in 2008 was researching the community's modern history.

The major sources of success and unity during these years were the members of the community, which by now numbered some 220 families. Among them were successful, relatively young professionals of both Ashkenazi and Sephardi backgrounds with growing families. They brought energy, drive, and dedication to their work. But, as often was the case in post-1967 France, their activism was also stimulated by their desire to combat the negative forces that were then reappearing.

Economic dislocation and high unemployment resulting from industrial decline in the 1980s was accompanied by the resurgence of ultra-nationalism in the West. In France this took the form of Jean-Marie Le Pen's National Front movement. Though sometimes strongly denied, Le Pen's anti-immigrant rhetoric was tinged with anti-Semitism. Threats and acts against Jews increased during these years, including bombings and damage to synagogues and other property. The atmosphere was further poisoned by publicity surrounding the so-called Holocaust deniers, the sensationalism of war criminal Klaus Barbie's trial in 1987, and the Israel bashing that came with the beginning of the first Palestinian Intifada of that year.

A response came from community member Nadia Kaluski, who began giving talks based on letters sent by her younger sister, Louise Jacobson, from the deportation center at Drancy before she was sent to Auschwitz. These letters became the basis of a powerful play performed in France and several other European countries and, edited by Kaluski, were published as *Les lettres de Louise Jacobson* in 1997.[†] Until her death, Kaluski continued to speak at schools, universities, and public forums about the Holocaust.

Anti-Semitic activities also stimulated community member Bernard David to help organize the Dijon chapter of the France-Israel Association in 1991. The purpose of the group was, and is, to strengthen relations between the two countries by sponsoring public events and disseminating information about the Jewish state. In addition, a local **B'nai B'rith** chapter was founded in 1992. Apart from its normal function as a fraternal organization, it provided a place where serious discussions about community problems and their possible solutions could occur. Some members of the community saw the chapter, with its additional dues and Masonic-like regulations, as elitist and unnecessary,[‡] but it did have an immediate and noticeable impact on the community.

---

[*] Henri-Claude Bloch, *Histoire des Juifs bourguignons* (Dijon, France: Ed. Erem, s.d., 1989).

[†] Nadia Kaluski-Jacobson, *Les lettres de Louise Jacobson et des ses proches, Fresnes, Drancy 1942-1943* (Paris: Robert Laffont, 1997).

[‡] B'nai B'rith is now inactive.

B'nai B'rith member, Dr. Françoise Tenenbaum, helped by others, successfully pushed for the establishment of a Jewish-oriented radio station. Radio Shalom began service in 1993 and, under her direction, it provided the community with a public voice for the first time. When Tenenbaum became an assistant mayor of Dijon in 2001 under Socialist Mayor François Rebsamen, her husband Denis assumed the directorship of the radio and joined another local station in nearby Besançon to offer regional outreach.

Nineteen ninety-three was a premier year for the community. Attendance at religious services was high and enthusiastic, the Sunday school and other religious activities were working well, and the synagogue was sponsoring several adult study courses. There were two functioning youth groups, with the new B'nai B'rith youth branch offering different types of activities from that of the scouts. Encouraged by B'nai B'rith, the community for the first time invited major legislative candidates to address it in a pre-election gathering. As Dr. Denis Tenenbaum remarked to visiting American scholar Robert Weiner, "You might have come here at the best moment in the community's history." Naturally, President Henri-Claude Bloch and Rabbi Simon Sibony expressed satisfaction with the progress.

The following years, however, presented significant challenges. First, a major financial burden occurred when costly repairs to the synagogue were required. But the expenses involved with maintaining an old building became the least of the community's problems. No one in Dijon expected the scope of the anti-Jewish harassment and violence that followed in the wake of the second Palestinian Intifada in 2000. What worried Jews most was the paralysis that seemed to grip French authorities when confronted with rising Muslim militancy.

The Muslim disturbances that erupted in Paris and other major French cities during the first decade of the new millennium, particularly in 2005, finally forced the government to react. The national election of 2007 also signaled a harder line against Muslim extremists. Yet, the increased presence of armed police guarding synagogues and the placing of physical barriers to thwart bombings at their entrances, while reassuring to some degree, did not entirely allay the underlying anxiety that many Jews felt.

Dijon was fortunate in avoiding the riots that afflicted other cities, though minor incidents did occur and still do. Nonetheless, insults were sometimes heard on the streets, and teachers and students experienced discomfort in the schools. Even riding public transportation, for example, one could sense the hostility of Muslim passengers, who often chose to segregate themselves.

But the most immediate serious problem facing the Dijon community was not from the Muslims, who in any case were also a national concern.

Rather, it was the arrival in 1993 of a young **Lubavitcher** married couple who intended to reconstruct Judaism in the city. They came either as the result of a decision by their group's headquarters in Paris or at the behest of several increasingly religious and unhappy members of the Dijon community. The effect of their activities was to present a significant threat to Jewish unity and finally to cause a division.

The Lubavitch movement sponsors a worldwide **Hasidic** Jewish missionary program that endeavors to "renew" Jews according to the standards of eighteenth-century Lubavitcher rabbis. The most modern methods of proselytizing are used. The missionaries, usually young married couples, are dispatched wherever the leadership decides they would be successful. They are well trained for their tasks, dedicated true believers, and far more selfless than others might imagine. They are prepared to be gentle, loving, and non-judgmental, but they can be tough and courageous in achieving their goal of a more joyous but strictly observant Jewish practice. Although their worldly purpose is to save Jews and earn a living, they live segregated lives as much as possible in order to insulate themselves from the dangers of secular culture and what they see as the negative aspects of modern civilization. Yet, they also practice public Judaism (displaying **Hanukkah** menorahs during the Christmas season, for example). Their stated concern, however, is with Jewish self-respect and not what Gentiles think of Jews.

Lubavitchers often give far more than they take, except possibly from the wealthy donors they frequently manage to attract. Their financial support comes from various sources, including their work, local donors and adherents, the affluent, and subsidies from their Parisian center or even from New York City. Once they establish roots in a community, they are usually very difficult to compete against, especially if the community already has members unhappy with the level of observance or the local rabbi.

That is exactly what Dijon experienced from the second half of 1993 onward when Haim and Hannah Slonim arrived. Both were of Lubavitcher lineage. Hannah's father had been the dean of Parisian Lubavitcher scholars; Haim's family had roots in Jerusalem and New York. The couple proved to be exceptional community servants but also, eventually, community dividers, though that certainly was not their intent.

Faced with Haim Slonim's challenge of bringing a more total, but narrow, Judaism to Dijon, Rabbi Sibony and the communal leaders were clearly thrown off balance. There already existed a handful of disgruntled members seeking a more intensive religious experience, as well as a number of others who were curious about other forms of Judaism. Both groups were utterly taken by the sweet solicitations offered by the energetic young couple.

For the next dozen years the community dealt with frayed nerves, tensions, and occasional displays of bad tempers on both sides. There were disagreements over the use of communal space, the place of women in the sanctuary, timing of the services, repetitions of Torah readings already done by Rabbi Sibony, and even criticism of the city's one remaining **kosher** butcher, who was accused of not being kosher enough (he eventually closed shop).

Along with bad words and hurt feelings, some friends became distant, while former close acquaintances had less to do with each other. Numerous attempts were made at reconciliation, but ultimately these all failed. In 2003, the Lubavitchers separated from the synagogue in a formal schism, though members of both communities occasionally continued to participate in joint ventures, communal institutions, observances, and family celebrations. The community, though now divided, was at least temporarily relieved. Calm was restored.

The Slonims and their adherents worked tirelessly and built well. They acquired space for a **Beit Habbad** in the city as a drop-in center and place for teaching, worship, and other activities. Next came the establishment of a summer camp for young children. And in 1996 they founded a parochial elementary school, the Lubavitch School (EDEL), with the help of private donors, especially Gaby Barda.* The Slonims taught separate classes for men and women in addition to outreach activities for individuals and families who were sympathizers or who had special needs. In 1995, they converted the Beit Habbad into a larger and more attractive prayer space and modernized and expanded again a decade later.

The Lubavitcher group became what in the United States is referred to as a havurah, that is, a close-knit Jewish extended gathering of some 15 families that practices its religious activities and rites of passage together. The Dijon havurah sponsored numerous events, including Sabbath and holiday celebrations and, perhaps the most controversial, the construction and public lighting of a large Hanukkah menorah in the center of the city during the Christmas season.

The synagogue, now led by President Israel (Izy) Cemachovic, also expanded its activities. Most notable, in 2002, was the legal separation of the synagogue and community center into two separate entities for the purpose of obtaining public funds in support of secular cultural events. Though the Cultural Center of the Jews of Dijon (CCJD) was now technically divided from the Religious Association of the Jews of Dijon (ACID), community members might hold

---

* A prominent but disaffected community member, Gaby Barda, became increasingly orthodox and has continued to help fund Lubavitch activities in Dijon even after relocating to Paris.

positions on both directing boards. Having a separate cultural association also made it possible for less religious individuals, women, and interested Gentiles to participate more fully and hold leadership positions. Over the years the group sponsored numerous successful cultural events and assumed responsibility for publication of *Mazal Tov,* under the editorship of Cathie Bussidan.

A mundane event, however, became a metaphor for what was happening to the community in the first decade of the new century. The closing in 2005 of the downtown men's store *Albert,* owned and managed by Albert and Myrna Huberfeld, represented a consequential change in the demographics of Dijon's Jews. The store had served as an unofficial drop-in space and information center for over 30 years because the Huberfelds have been and continue to be at the center of nearly every community activity. Their retirement was representative of the aging of the Jews of Dijon and the decline of the community's population.

Changing economic conditions and political uncertainty produced results: most of the children of the previous two decades, upon maturity, sought their futures in Paris or elsewhere. A number of important families also relocated to Paris, while others went on to Israel, Canada, and the United States. In addition to fragmentation and demographic decline, there was also the long-term effect of intermarriage. The Dijon community, like most others in the Western world, was not immune to the impact of that trend. Nor, like small communities elsewhere, whether urban, religious or rural, was Dijon able to solve the problem of young people leaving for larger cities.

Nonetheless, the small Lubavitch havurah and the larger synagogue community still have substantial resources in terms of talent, dedication, and creativity to carry them forward. Barring a general demographic recovery, however, problems of scale and finance will tax them to their limits. As with so many diaspora communities, their immediate future still remains in their hands, but it is a future freighted with growing uncertainty.

Dijon's recent Jewish history has much in common with that of other provincial Jewish communities, and with that of the Jews of Paris and other large cities. In spite of the deep shadow of the Holocaust years and the continuous need to guard against enduring forms of anti-Semitism and anti-Zionism, most French Jews are deeply attached to France and have lived meaningful lives in this fascinating and beautiful country, to which they have contributed so much.

Now, however, they are once again on guard, hoping that France's and their best years are ahead, but uncertain if this will occur. We will, of course, listen to their voices, while recognizing that their future and ours may have more in common than we might like to admit.

CHRONOLOGY

Late Roman Era	Jews are present and active in commercial enterprises in the southern Roman provinces of present-day France in the fourth and fifth centuries.
500s	Small communities of Jews reside in Marseille, Narbonne, Orléans, and other trading centers.
700s	Under Holy Roman Emperor Charlemagne, Jews gain residency rights and economic and religious opportunities. The Jewish population expands, and communities experience normal growth. Religious practices and traditions are observed.
800–1000	Jews in Lyon, Rouen, and other cities are prominent in commercial activities because of their education, expertise, and international contacts. The synagogue at Rouen becomes a center of religious studies that attracts Jews from throughout Europe. Champagne also experiences the growth of Jewish communities.
1000–1100	The first widespread persecution of Jews in Normandy and other locations in present-day France occur as outrage over Muslim conversion of Christian churches into mosques in Jerusalem spreads. Jews are blamed for encouraging the Muslims. Jewish communal and intellectual life continues, along with immigration from Spain and central Europe despite anti-Jewish riots and massacres during the era of the Crusades. In Troyes Rabbi Schlomo Ben Isaac (Rashi) and his students have a major impact on Jewish learning through analysis of, and commentaries on, the Torah and Talmud.
1182	King Philippe Augustus first expels Jews (1182) and confiscates their property before recalling them in 1198 because he requires their financial and other services. He makes them his personal serfs, an initiative followed by other nobles.
1215	Pope Innocent III mandates distinctive clothing for Jews. In 1269 King Louis IX imposes the wearing of a distinctive sign, the *rouelle* (wheel).
1306	King Philippe confiscates Jewish properties and expels them from his kingdom, which includes about three-fifths of present-day France. An estimated 100,000 are affected, with most settling in lands bordering the French state, including Provence, Alsace, Lorraine, Spain, Italy, and the Germanic states.
1315	King Louis X recalls the Jews to France, pressured by demands for their financial services. He promises guarantees for personal security and property. Few, apparently, respond.

1348–1395	Jews are blamed for poisoning wells and contributing to the Black Death (bubonic plague) that sweeps Europe. In 1394 Jews are again expelled from France and in 1395 from Burgundy and Dijon. Only small communities of "New Christians" (Jews who convert to Christianity) in southwestern France and traditional Jews in Alsace and Lorraine remain (Alsace and Lorraine were not then in France). Montpellier continues to have a Jewish community, largely involved with its medical school as doctors and apothecaries. The New Christians probably come to places such as Bordeaux in the mid-sixteenth century. (In 1394, Bordeaux was also not yet under French jurisdiction.)
1498–1501	Jews are expelled from Provence (annexed to France in 1481) and, except for the New Christians and in the papal enclaves of Avignon and the Comtat de Venaissin, are effectively gone from France until the seventeenth century.
1650–1700	Because of their growing commercial importance, New Christians in Bordeaux and Bayonne are able to establish themselves legally as a corporate group with the rights to create synagogues, cemeteries, and communal organizations.
1700–89	Larger, well-organized communities develop in Metz and all of Alsace, with a slow but steady expansion of the Jewish population in Lorraine as well. In 1770 a Sephardi synagogue opens in Paris, followed by an Ashkenazi synagogue in 1778. The Jewish population of France and its annexed territories is estimated at close to 40,000. As Enlightenment thought spreads across Europe, the argument for religious toleration intensifies.
1790–91	"Emancipation" of the Sephardim in 1790 and the Ashkenazim in 1791 during the French Revolution is seen as a means of assimilating Jews into the French body politic. All Jews now have individual rights as citizens rather than as members of a corporate "nation" within France. Some Alsatian Jews establish themselves in Dijon in the 1790s and especially after 1800.
1806–07	In 1806 the Emperor Napoleon calls an Assembly of Jewish Notables, followed by a rabbinic Great Sanhedrin the following year. The latter ratifies the findings of the Notables, who formally split the religious and ethnic elements that defined traditional Jewish identity. Jews are judged to be limited to voluntary membership in a religious community alone. Jews' nationality is declared to be equivalent to their French citizenship. They now are often referred to as "Israélites."
1808	Napoleon establishes Jewish Consistories on the national and regional levels, under whose auspices religious life is to be organized. Unlike Catholic and Protestant administrative bodies that are funded by the state, Jewish groups are to be supported by additional Jewish taxes until 1831. Napoleon also decrees a

ten-year series of economic restrictions on Alsatian Jews (the most numerous) intended to counter "usury." A hated special judicial trial oath for Jews also is imposed; it is finally abolished in 1846.

1815–70   Conditions for Jews gradually improve. Under the Emperor Louis Napoleon III (1849–70), Jewish banking houses, notably Rothschilds, Péreires, and Foulds, play important economic roles. Jews enter all fields of government service, the military, journalism, education, culture, and the economy. Many claim to be "happy like God in France."

1850s   A series of educational, self-help, and self-defense agencies are founded. The most important, the Alliance Israélite Universelle (Universal Israelite Alliance), is established by the Jewish elite to counter acts of anti-Semitism and later to foster the "Frenchification" of Jews in the new colonies of North Africa and elsewhere in the Near East.

1859   The Central Rabbinical School, founded in Metz in 1830, is transferred to Paris, thus providing French Jews with a training center for their own rabbis and teachers and underlining the importance of Paris as the center of Jewish religious and intellectual life. A distinctly moderate, orthodox Judaism begins to develop in contrast to the more radical reform Judaism emerging in Germany and, especially, in the United States.

1870–71   France suffers a humiliating defeat in the Franco-Prussian War. About 15,000 Jews demonstrate their loyalty by leaving the province of Alsace and the part of Lorraine that are annexed by Prussia.

1878   An exodus of hundreds of thousands of Eastern European Jews that continues into the second decade of the twentieth century begins, fueled by economic distress, violent pogroms, and anti-Jewish laws in the Russian Empire. Many find their way to France. Largely rural, very traditional, and Yiddish-speaking, they adjust only gradually to an increasingly urban, industrial, and rapidly modernizing France.

1879   Large, magnificent synagogue inaugurated in Dijon.

1880s   France is rocked by a series of financial scandals in which Jewish banking interests are involved. Jews increasingly come under attack by conservatives as the primary beneficiaries of the vast transforming, but also dislocating, economic and social changes taking place. Some Socialists and others on the Left accuse Jewish capitalists of enslaving France.

1892   The failure of the Panama Canal venture and resulting financial collapse, which involves Jewish financiers and politicians, undermine public confidence in the Third Republic.

1894–1906	Captain Alfred Dreyfus, son of a wealthy, German-speaking Alsatian Jewish family that had relocated to Paris after the Franco-Prussian War, and who is the first Jew to serve on the French General Staff, is accused of passing military secrets to the Germans. Following his conviction on fabricated charges and imprisonment, the case against a second officer who is actually guilty is covered up by the military. Outraged politicians, officers, and intellectuals, among them the writer Émile Zola, expose the fraud. In 1906 Dreyfus is exonerated and restored to duty, but the "Dreyfus Affair" of trials and re-trials, accusations and counter-accusations, lasts for more than a decade and exposes the anti-Semitism and deep political divisions within France. However, the Republic finally emerges even stronger from this values-clarifying experience, sometimes called the second French Revolution.
1895	Austrian journalist Theodor Herzl, responding to the public humiliation of Alfred Dreyfus and of the French Jews, writes a fiery reaction titled *The Jewish State* that calls for the establishment of a Jewish homeland as an answer to anti-Semitism. In 1897 he organizes the First Zionist Congress in Basel, Switzerland. Herzl is recognized as the founder of modern Zionism.
1900–14	The Marais-St. Paul areas of Paris are home to some 40,000 Jews, mostly immigrants from Eastern Europe, with their own religious and cultural traditions. They found Yiddish-language newspapers, religious congregations, self-help organizations, and, eventually, separate associations in support of the French labor movement, socialism, and Zionism. In 1913 they form the Federation of Jewish Societies of Paris. Their activities represent a cultural divide with the French Jewish elite.
1905	The formal separation of church and state becomes law. The Consistorial monopoly over normative Jewish religious affairs ends. In 1907 the liberal Copernic synagogue, representing the newly established Union Libérale Israélite (Union of Liberal Israelites), is founded.
1914–18	Forty thousand of the 150,000 Jews in France and the Algerian colony serve in the armed forces. Approximately 7,500 die. Their contribution to the survival and victory of France is widely recognized and applauded.
1919–39	Thousands of Jews displaced by war and revolution in Eastern Europe and, later, by anti-Semitism in Nazi Germany flee to France, causing additional fractures in a community and nation already beset by economic depression and deep ideological conflicts.
	In France as elsewhere, many organizations expand, including the youth group Les Éclaireurs Israélites (Jewish Scouts) and the

self-defense Ligue Internationale Contre l'Antisémitisme, or LICA (International League against Anti-Semitism), later becoming LICRA, against Racism as well.

1936   Léon Blum, leader of the Socialist Party, becomes the first Jewish prime minister. He heads the short-lived Popular Front government. Blum's election results in more violent anti-Semitic acts, including in Dijon where a toxic atmosphere prevails during the immediate pre-war years.

1940–44   Following the French defeat, the newly established pro-German puppet Vichy government in the southern third of France issues 160 anti-Jewish laws and decrees affecting all areas of Jewish life.

Jews in occupied Dijon, a major German military and administrative center, experience all manner of humiliations, property theft, and deportation, similar to that experienced elsewhere in France, at the hands of the collaborationist Vichy regime and the local Nazis. Although Jews are denounced by some collaborators and opportunists, many are aided by French Christians; some Jews and Christians join the Resistance as well.

Jewish resistance to the German occupation and aid for its victims grows. New groups include the Central Commission of Jewish Assistance Organizations (1940), the Jewish Army (1941), the Zionist Organization of France (1942), the Contemporary Jewish Documentation Center (1943), and the Representative Council of the Jews of France (1943–44).

1942   In July, French police in German-occupied Paris round up 13,000 Jewish men, women, and children for eventual deportation to concentration camps. With Vichy's collaboration the Germans transport 75,000 Jews from France, including Dijon, to concentration camps by war's end. Of those, 42,000 are sent to death camps. Less than 3,000 survive.

September 1944   Dijon liberated. High Holiday religious services held in the synagogue.

1945   At the end of the war there are about 250,000 Jews in France. That so many survived is due, in part, to the generosity and courage of many non-Jews who hid, sheltered, or otherwise aided them.

1945–48   Reconstruction efforts involving the reunification of families, recovery of hidden children, and return of lost or stolen property raise moral and legal questions and increase public tensions. Support of the American Jewish Joint Distribution Committee (JDC), however, aids recovery. In 1948 the JDC helps organize the Fonds Sociales Juif Unifié (FSJU), a fundraising and planning body that becomes the most powerful French Jewish organization.

1948   May 14, declaration of the founding of the State of Israel.

1956–68	Nearly 250,000 Jews from Algeria, Tunisia, and Morocco move to France (including to Dijon) following the decolonization of North Africa and the Arab-Israeli wars of 1956 and 1967. Half of the immigrants hold French citizenship, and most are partially French culturally, but their arrival causes dislocation, stress, and enormous expenses for established French Jewish communities.
1967	The Six Day War, June 5–10, between Israel and the combined forces of Egypt, Jordan, and Syria ends in an Israeli victory. Israel gains control from its vanquished Arab opponents of the Gaza Strip, Sinai Peninsula, the West Bank, the Golan Heights, and East Jerusalem, leading to future conflict and the Palestinian insurgencies.
	French President Charles de Gaulle characterizes Jews as "an elitist people, self-assured and domineering" following Israel's victory in the Six Day War. French foreign policy is reoriented to pro-Arab positions. Many French Jews protest these actions, occasionally on the streets, but using available media as well, a first in French history.
1973	Yom Kippur War, October 6–25, begins when a coalition of Arab states, headed by Egypt and Syria, launches a surprise attack against Israel to regain possession of the Sinai Peninsula and Golan Heights. After initial setbacks, Israeli forces enter both Egypt and Syria; a United Nations-brokered ceasefire ends the war. Through negotiations named the Camp David Accords, Israel returns the Sinai Peninsula to Egypt and in 1979 Egypt signs a peace treaty with Israel, the first Arab country to do so.
1973–85	The Yom Kippur War, resulting Arab oil embargo, and the Lebanese conflict (1982–85), require French Jews to actively defend and support Israel. From 1979 the Jewish Renewal Movement takes the lead and encourages immigrants and young people to become actively involved in public affairs.
1975–85	The growing body of Holocaust literature, film, art, and memorials elicits a denial or revisionist reaction in certain political and academic circles. Anti-Semitic acts increase. Jews and their allies respond to these outrages.
1977	Moroccan-born, Rabbi Simon Sibony becomes rabbi of Dijon Jewry, encouraging an era of growth and accomplishment.
1987	Outbreak of the Palestinian First Intifada (rebellion) leads to greater criticism of Israel and to more attacks upon Jews and their property.
1990–2000	North African immigrants play increasingly important roles in all aspects of Jewish life. Most French rabbis are now of North African backgrounds, including Chief Rabbis (from 1980 to 2008). Many mainstream synagogues become more traditional in practice. Lubavitch Hasidic Judaism grows in influence and adherents.

Israeli-Palestinian negotiations, creating real hopes for peace and a "two state" solution, lead to an improved climate for French Jews.

1993	Young Lubavitch couple, Haim and Hannah Slonim, set up residence in Dijon in order to "revitalize" Judaism, leading to increasing tension and eventual schism in 2003. Habbad parochial school founded in 1995.
1995	President Jacques Chirac accepts French blame for Vichy's policies and collaboration with the Germans during World War II.
2000–03	The outbreak of the Palestinian Second Intifada (2000), the attack on New York's World Trade Center (2001), and the American invasion of Iraq (2003) fuel Arab nationalism and radical Islam worldwide. French government and Jewish leaders fail to respond effectively until 2003. In France, anti-Semitic acts increase, often committed by members of the large resident Arab population, but also by Africans. Israel is criticized severely and unfairly in the French media, leading to angry and desperate Jewish reactions, including leaving France for Israel and North America.
2005	Mass protests sparked by Arab grievances break out in cities throughout France. In response to increasing violence, Jewish communities tighten security arrangements, request local police support, and form self-defense groups. Jewish parochial schools are expanded to meet the demand of students leaving troubled public schools.
2006	The torture and murder of a young North African Jew, Ilan Halimi, by a group of Muslims horrifies the French. The government reacts more aggressively to provide increased protection on all levels and to initiate more effective and severe judicial responses to hate crimes. Israel attacks Hezbollah in Lebanon, again leading to more criticism.
May 2007	Nicholas Sarkozy, who is a pro-Israel and "law and order" candidate, is elected French President. He is part Sephardic Jewish on his mother's side, an example of intermarriage in his mother's generation and of Jewish assimilation in France.
2008	A global economic crisis occurs, impacting an already weakened French economy.
	Ashkenazi Gilles Bernheim is elected Chief Rabbi of France in a highly contested election. Many hope he will initiate more moderate policies, although that has yet to occur, except for his more public persona.
	Barack Obama, supported by most American Jews, is elected first African American President of the United States. This results in a changed emphasis in American foreign policy, with greater sensitivity toward Muslims worldwide.

2008–09	In response to continuous Hamas shelling, Israel invades Gaza, resulting in high civilian casualties; Hamas is more restrained thereafter. Severe, near universal, criticism of Israel ensues.
	Anti-Semitic incidents spike, despite efforts to protect Jewish persons and property. The critical United Nations Goldstone Report places more emphasis on Israeli attacks on civilian areas than on Hamas's incitements.
2009–10	President Sarkozy inaugurates and then closes a national debate on French identity and expels many Roms (Gypsies) from France.
July 2010	Israel clumsily boards Turkish-led boats attempting to break the Gaza blockade, causing deaths among Muslim and Christian sympathizers.
2011	Goldstone retracts many segments of his report that are most offensive to Israel, despite Muslim objections.
	"Arab Spring" uprisings throughout much of the Arab world and North Africa bring government changes in Tunisia, Egypt, and Libya. Reforms in Morocco and Jordan, as well as repression in Bahrain and Syria continue. Palestinian demonstrators approach Israeli borders, leading to civilian deaths. Huge Israeli demonstrations call for cheaper housing and food and expanded social services.
	Socialist Party candidate Dominique Strauss-Kahn, a Jew, is arrested on rape charges in New York City. The criminal charges are dropped, but allegations of sexual misconduct in France are made. His political career is likely irreparably damaged, and Socialist Party unity is undermined.
	New National Front leader, Marine Le Pen, eschews her father's anti-Semitism, but retains populist racist attitudes toward immigrants of color, especially Muslims.
	Financial weaknesses in the Western European economies and American debt problems result in another global recession.
Spring 2012	Arab unrest continues and intensifies. In France violent anti-Semitic acts increase, including the murder of four Jews in Toulouse. In May elections Socialist François Hollande is elected President.

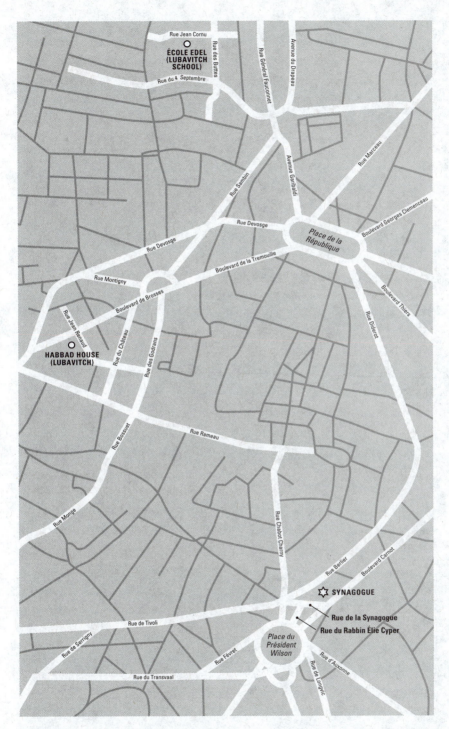

Map of Central Dijon with Major Jewish Sites

Speaking About Jewish Life in Dijon: Interviews

The
SYNAGOGUE CENTER

This group represents the majority of Jews in the Dijon community. Its members are diverse in ethnic background, religious practice, culture, and socioeconomic condition. They are religious and secular, liberal and conservative, and young and old. Among them are Holocaust survivors and community leaders.

COMMUNITY LEADERS

Rabbi Simon Sibony

As rabbi of the Dijon synagogue since 1977, Simon Sibony remains the central figure in the community. He is a good-natured man of warmth and generosity. His open-minded approach to individuals and groups, religious and secular, has gone far towards making Jewish life more acceptable and secure in the city.

May 1993

I was born in 1945 in Meknès, a city like Dijon, of perhaps 200,000 people, the majority of whom were Muslims. It is in Morocco, a country where there was tolerance and friendship for Jews. I was born into a large family; we were 13 children, and that was the normal size of Jewish families. My mother—may her memory be blessed—was a woman very attached to her religion. My father was the same way, and he was very strict with me about Judaism. But he also was tolerant and open-minded. I try to follow his path.

There were 26 synagogues in Meknès. It was an important community, with about 50,000 Jews at the time.* They lived in the Old and New Mellahs [districts], which were separated from each other. There was a French district that was recent and modern. The Muslims lived in their district, the Medina. Although we had a separate life, like in a ghetto, we had good relationships with our neighbors. My father worked with Arabs; he made caftans, Muslim clothing for ceremonies. He worked in the Medina and walked there every day. The Muslims respected him. Thanks to his business, we would be in contact with Muslims all the time.

In the Mellah we really celebrated the **Shabbat**. At least everybody wore the prayer shawl in the morning and came to the synagogue. People wore the **kippa**, or skullcap, in the district. We did not have any problems there and were free to wear it. We had many kosher butchers, kosher restaurants. It was a kosher city.

We could not imagine Meknès without its religious life. It was lively. People did not have to work on Saturdays, a sacred day. Starting from Friday, the chief rabbi and another rabbi would walk around telling people to close their shops. Even Muslim shops that were in our district had to close. On Fridays, the synagogue was full. The holidays were amazing. We would build

---

* In 1951, Meknès had the fourth largest Jewish population in Morocco, with about 15,000 Jews.

our **sukkah** in the street for the festival of **Sukkot**. Those who were rich and had a garden put theirs in the garden. Those who didn't have much money would build theirs on the streets.

There were different kinds of schools. We had Jewish day schools for 2,000 students where Hebrew translations and prayers were taught. I learned Hebrew until I was eight or nine years old. After that we had the Alliance school where I learned French. I left when I was 12, when I was recruited for the **Yeshiva** of Tangier. It was there that I did my bar mitzvah.

We were 100 students at the Yeshiva and we had a great time. It was the best seven years of my life. There were youth movements, some religious, some less religious. We would go camping in the forests. In summer we went to the beach, but we went early in the morning before anybody else got there because we were not allowed to see women. We had three weeks vacation during the summer, but usually we stayed at school except for the sukkot festival, when some of us would go home. Meknès was only an hour away, and we could go there for holidays.

My parents were not wealthy, but the Yeshiva was helped by American Jewish aid. At the Yeshiva we had rabbis from England, France, and Switzerland. All of the rabbis were Ashkenazi, even though it was in Morocco. The head rabbi was Ashkenazi. We had Polish rituals. We had our Sephardi books, but during holidays we had both Sephardi and Ashkenazi services. We did not have any problems with that because the rabbis taught us the Torah. The rabbis at the Yeshiva were very Orthodox. We were not allowed to see girls even when we were 17 years old, and we were not even allowed to go to the movies. We had to wear the skullcap in the streets, but we were afraid to wear it in the Muslim districts, so we wore hats.

Of course, it was kosher. The Torah was studied day and night. We woke at six o'clock in the morning for the six-thirty service. Afterwards we had breakfast. Then we studied in a classroom with 90 people or so. That was communal study, and we prepared the text from the **Talmud** until eleven. From eleven to twelve o'clock we had study lessons in groups. At one o'clock we ate, and in the afternoons we had recreational hours when we played games such as soccer. That was followed by a **shiur** of laws and a shiur of the Bible. In late afternoon we had French lessons. Dinner was followed by services and homework.

We spoke mostly Hebrew and Arabic. At the Yeshiva, there were many kinds of people. People from the north spoke Spanish. We talked to them in Hebrew because we didn't speak Spanish. Others came from Marrakech, Fez, Rabat, Casablanca, Meknès. We spoke Arabic, a little Hebrew, and sometimes French. Hebrew was my second language, and at the Yeshiva I learned classic Hebrew. We had to learn French for our future, although I really did not speak it well until I came to France.

Mohammed V, the king at that time, had protected the Jews against the Germans during the war and against Vichy, whose laws he refused to enforce. But my father did not talk much about the war, probably because he did not know much. The Germans never really came to Morocco, and we did not suffer from the war, not like Europe. It was worse in Algeria. They had a Vichy government. Afterwards, when the Algerians fought for their independence, they fought against Jews too because the Jews in Algeria were French citizens.* In Morocco, the Jews were Moroccan and that was important.

Of course, we heard horrible things about the **Shoah**, but we did not know exactly what happened. We did not have enough information. I personally learned what happened because I read many books before coming to France. I read books like *Mila 18*.† I saw films that shocked me. I didn't learn the details until I came to France because my parents never talked about it—but of course they did not know much.

We knew about the 1948 and 1956 wars from the radio and the news in Morocco. Of course, the Moroccans took the side of the Arabs. Our community supported Israel, but we could not express it. But when Morocco stood against French control, the Jewish community was considered part of Morocco, so we did not have any trouble. When the king came to visit, we would not go to school; the rabbis would welcome him and tell him that we were good citizens. And he responded. Morocco had had bad times, but they protected the Jews. We never talked about Israel in public. Even at the Yeshiva we never talked about it. We read the newspapers, and we talked about it in private.

I decided to go to France in 1966. There was no future for us in Morocco, and also the situation in Israel was getting worse and we were scared. We thought that as long as King Hassan II was alive, the Jewish community would be safe, but what if something happened to him? Of course, there are Jews who stayed there. There are still [in 1993] many Jews in Casablanca.‡

I was not French and I did not speak the language very well, though I understood it. I did not have much money, but I came to Paris because I thought that I could find something interesting. I wanted to teach, to be in charge of a community. I had taught in Morocco for a few months. I studied at the Yeshiva for seven years, but I was not a rabbi in Morocco. I studied

---

* The Crémieux Decree of 1870 enfranchised Algerian Jews.
† Leon Uris, *Mila 18* (New York: Doubleday, 1961).
‡ Several thousand Jews reside in Morocco today.

in France in a seminary. I decided that I didn't want to be in a system like the Yeshiva all of my life. I preferred to work in a community. I wanted to work outside of the Yeshiva system so that I could get to know different kinds of people.

I did a year at the seminary. Then there was a community in Périgueux, somewhat near Bordeaux, that needed me in 1967. There I taught the Torah and helped the community. I left after a year because I wasn't paid enough to support a family. I returned to the seminary in Paris and remained there for four years on scholarships. During the time I was at the seminary I also completed my secular studies. I became a rabbi in 1974. At first I worked in small communities, including Beauvais, not far from Paris, where I started a community. In 1977 I came to Dijon.

My parents left Morocco in 1967 right after the Six Day War because my father, who worked in the Medina, heard the Arabs say that they were going to kill the Jews. He was scared. It was a time when **aliyah** was prohibited in Morocco. It had become almost impossible to leave, but some Jews migrated to Israel anyway in the 1950s and 1960s. It also was a time when you could not get a passport to go to France. But my father used to work for important people in Morocco, so [he was able to get the family] to Israel. I first visited them, and Israel, in 1968. I spent my vacations there with my family. Israel was a dream for me.

My older brother is a rabbi and teaches at the Jewish school in Pavillon [France], but the rest of my family is in Israel. I decided to live in France because I already had a knowledge of French culture and also thought that France was better for me as a person. I always thought that French culture was rich and impressive. It was my dream to move to France. I didn't choose Israel because, with the wars and everything, I thought that it was not an easy life. I did not feel like fighting, perhaps because of my kids.

While I was at the seminary and teaching at a center where young people met, near the Latin Quarter, I met my future wife, Annie. The center was like a second home for me. Everybody went, and they were happy to meet there in a religious atmosphere. We had Sabbath meals. In the mornings we had services. In the afternoons I gave Talmud and Bible lessons. And that is where I met my wife because she used to go there too. At the time she was a student, studying to be a lawyer. Some of the girls came to our Shabbat lessons because they were interesting. I knew her for two years, and we were married in 1974 after I finished my studies. She is an Ashkenazi, but it isn't a problem. Annie did not have any concerns, either. Many Sephardim came to France, especially after 1962—first, the Algerians, then the Tunisians, finally the Moroccans.

Three years later in 1977 we came to Dijon. At the beginning it was an Ashkenazi community here, but small. During the war, unfortunately, about 80 per cent of the community was decimated. I'm not completely sure how many families were here before the war, maybe 180. In the synagogue there is a list, but it accounts only for people who came back and includes the names of members of their families who died. The list doesn't account for everybody because entire families were decimated.

Our community has a long history. As early as the twelfth century there was an important community located in the center of the city not far from the synagogue. Behind the synagogue was a cemetery. There also was an academy. The leaders were **Tosaphistes** who lived during Rashi's time and usually did not agree with him. Dijon's rabbi wrote a commentary that was kept by Cîteaux's abbey because they were on good terms. I think that at the end of the fourteenth century the Jews of northern France were sent away, and we have nothing left from that period.

Before World War II, the Ashkenazi community was internally divided because people came at different times from different places. Some came from Alsace-Lorraine. They are called the Old Ashkenazim, but few are still here. Some came from Poland at a time when there was a lot of anti-Semitism there. During the 1930s many people came from Germany because of Hitler. Unfortunately, many are not here any longer. A few of their children remain.

After the war the community was very much smaller. Maybe 30 families returned.* There was a small community but not a religious one. When I came in 1977 some people, maybe 20 or 25, came on Friday nights or Saturday mornings, but not always. During that period young people did not come often. There was a vacuum after the war. There was no structure, no religious life, because the Jews were concerned with other vital things. After the war many of the marriages were with non-Jews. Finally, thanks to the arrival of people from North Africa beginning in 1962, the community began to grow. Today 80 per cent of the community is Sephardi as a result. At first some people did not like those coming from North Africa. Even though initially there were some problems, after awhile everything was fine. People understood that they really did not have any choice. They had to live together as a community.

So, fortunately, this has not been too much of a problem in human relations and understanding, and this is really important. It's a situation that doesn't exist elsewhere. For example, in Paris there are many communities. If you are Polish, you go to a Polish synagogue. If you are from Alsace, there

---

* Although we do not know the exact number, it must have been larger than 30.

is a synagogue for you too. It's the same among the Sephardim: some are from Algeria, others from Morocco. They each have their own synagogues.

There now are 300 families here [probably some 250 families], and we are really close. We have to be together, so we try to live together. For example, Friday night our ceremonies are practically Ashkenazi; Saturday morning is more Sephardi. For major holidays it's the same: half Ashkenazi, half Sephardi. It's an experience you can only have in the provinces, in small cities like Dijon, where you have this type of community. I think that everybody is happy with it. You can see that from the number of attendants on Fridays and Saturdays [and their enthusiasm].

Our community is a dynamic community in comparison to others in France. We have important structures even if we are a small group of people. We have prayer services on Mondays, Thursdays, **Rosh Hodesh**, Saturday afternoons—all religious events. We have two shops that sell kosher food, which is good if you consider that in Strasbourg they only have two for 1,000 families.* Our synagogue is imposing. The people who built it 120 years ago were few in numbers, but they probably thought that the number would get larger. And without the war our community would have numbered 700 or 800 families.

I must mention that every Rosh Hodesh, when we use two Torah scrolls, we use a **Sepher Torah** that was given to us by the Americans at the end of the war. When the [concentration camp] prisoners returned to Dijon, they did not have a Sepher Torah so the Americans gave them one. I personally love to read in it because of the writing; it is beautiful. I get emotional when I read from it because it is part of the history of our community. During the war the Sepher Torahs were hidden, and now we have 20 or so.

During the war, there was an abbot in Dijon who later became the mayor [1945–71]. His name was Chanoine Kir. He saved the synagogue. The Germans occupied the synagogue and stored clothes there. They destroyed the furniture but did not destroy the synagogue as they did in other places.

At present, in addition to the synagogue we have the community center, which was recently built and where we hold our meetings. We have facilities for instruction, parties, and so forth. We provide the structures that give Jews the opportunities to practice their religion. In the **Talmud Torah** school there are 40 children. When I first came, I had only three or four. There also are classes for adults almost every night. For women, there are study classes and the WIZO [Women's International Zionist Organization].

---

* Strasbourg, with approximately 12,000 Jews in the 1990s, certainly had a wider array of kosher facilities than projected here.

For elderly people there is a Third Age Club and classes. We now have a B'nai B'rith group of 40 or 50 people who are really dynamic and do things such as providing aid for Israel and Jewish culture. In addition, there is an organization, the Fonds Social Juif Unifié [FSJU, French Jewish fundraising agency*] that organizes parties and collects money for Israel. Recently, we established a radio station that I believe is going to involve more people in our community and that can reach those who do not come to the synagogue, such as the elderly. We do publish a newspaper every two months, but I believe the radio is more important.

Of course, my job naturally includes weddings, bar mitzvahs, religious events.

I mentioned that when I first came not many attended the synagogue on Friday nights. During that period young people didn't come often; now there are more young people on Friday nights. They also come if there is something going on after school; they are involved in B'nai B'rith and the Scouts, and they have Hebrew classes. They all learn how to read in the Talmud Torah because I insist on that. If they know how to read, if only a little, I believe that they will feel part of the services. In the studies of the Talmud Torah, I emphasize the liturgy. Of course, in the first year they don't learn the translation. First year is mostly knowledge of history and religion; for the intermediate level there is deeper analysis. For kids preparing for the bar mitzvah we mostly do the **Chumash**, the translations, and prayers. I expect them to know some important parts of the service like the **Sh'ma**, the **Amidah**. All the kids know that there is a minimum that a Jew has to know. But, of course, they know more than that. My dream is to have a Jewish school here, but it's hard to accomplish; we need at least 30 or 40 more families for that.

There are some communities with more people, but they do not have the same structures we have. The mikveh is a good example. When I first came here, we did not have one; my wife had to go to Lyon, so we established one here. Before, families did not go to the mikveh; now at least ten families attend. My wife takes care of it, and she also takes care of the **gan**. Today in Dijon we have the structures of a big community without being one, and perhaps we have fewer problems because of that.

But what is happening in other communities is happening here: the community is getting younger. When I first came here, I had to deal with old people; that community disappeared, and a young new community is taking its place. Many Jews left for Paris because they could not find work here.

---

* The FSJU, founded in 1948, is the main French Jewish fundraising and disbursement agency.

The important moment occurred in 1979, 1980; every week someone died. By the middle 1980s many Jews were coming from North Africa. Today, we see more young people than old people. But many young people also leave to find work. It's hard to find a job here.

Fortunately, as I said, we have fewer problems. Our community has a sense of solidarity. We do not have Orthodox folks, Lubavitchers, Liberals, Conservatives, like in the United States. We all attend the same synagogue. There are some people who drive their cars on Shabbat, but they still come to the synagogue. We do not have the right to exclude them. We have to live together.

At this moment, I wish that young people in the community were more dynamic because they are our future. They have to get more concerned about their religion and about Israel. I believe that it is very important to support Israel. In the past the community was indifferent to Israel. That changed after the Six Day War. It was an important moment for all the communities in France. Of course, we have the same problem that all of the communities in France have: if we support Israel too much, we are accused of being citizens of Israel first, rather than of France. But I believe that it's possible to love both your mother and your father, to love both Israel and France. I think that for Israel there must be a constant fight, people must be concerned. We have to bring a message to the Catholic people. We all have to live together, as the Torah says.

Here we do have good relations with Catholics, in religion as well as politics. On Thursday nights we have a class with Catholics. Three or four priests study the Bible, the **Tanakh**. When I first came here, there were no relations at all. I helped in developing interactions, because we live in a mostly Catholic world and we are a minority. Now, I do have friends who are priests. We need friends, and if we do not establish good relationships, they might become enemies.

The bishop is really important to the community. Perhaps twice a year, I go to the Catholic church because it is important to be seen. It does not mean that I agree with them in a religious sense, but I have to be there for important ceremonies, like when Michael Colonie became Bishop of Dijon. There also are national days such as July 14 and Deportation Day.* Some ceremonies are in the church, so I have to go. The Catholics are happy [that I do so].

There are other events. For example, in Rashi's time there was an abbot whose memory we celebrated last year because he cared about the Jewish

---

* Since 1954, the last Sunday in April has been designated "National Day for remembering the victims and heroes of deportation."

community. His name is saint Bernard of Clairvaux. He was an extraordinary man who helped the Jews at a time of severe anti-Semitism. He was brave but, unfortunately, did not succeed. Still, he did a lot. He protected the Jewish community here and throughout Europe. He wrote and fought against the persecutions.

We also held a Biblical Exposition in 1991, and a large number of people came to see it. It was held in the museum and also in the synagogue. People came every day for a month. The most brilliant moment occurred on the centenary of the synagogue in 1979. It was an important event. We had a concert; the **hazzanim** were really good and had wonderful voices. There were more than 500 people in the synagogue, perhaps more Gentiles than Jews. Many churches advertised the event.

We do not have many contacts with Muslims, although some come to our kosher shops or to see me because they do not have anyone else to go to. We are not very involved with the mosque, but I hope that one day when there is peace with Israel the relationship will be different. I also am the rabbi for the prisons, and sometimes the Muslims ask me to visit them. I go because we have to establish good relationships for the future of our community.

We do have relationships with all of the 26 religious sects in Dijon except for the Adventists and a few other minority groups.

There is no organized anti-Semitism. We do not have physical attacks as in Paris. Sometimes there are phone calls or people write things. Here, they tend to insult the Muslims; we are second on the list. If the Muslim community did not exist, there would be more [hate] directed against us. That is why we fight against any type of aggression. We have the LICRA [International League Against Racism and Anti-Semitism] here. We have the B'nai B'rith. We fight against the extreme Right. But from what I know, our community hasn't experienced physical attack, not even during the war in Lebanon [1982–85]. At least at the local level we have political support. We had the mayor [Robert Poujade] here for a B'nai B'rith and community meeting and he was very comfortable. We have always had a good relationship with the authorities.

A big issue everywhere is that about 60 per cent of our marriages are interfaith marriages. I have read articles that claim that the Jewish communities will disappear. I don't believe so, but there is work to be done. I believe that it is a problem of education. As I mentioned before, there really was no community before 1962. There was no rabbi. The Jews that returned after the war didn't know what to do. So the people who grew up during that time didn't have the opportunities that we offer our children today.

Today we have children who come until their bar mitzvahs, and because their parents are not religious, they stop coming after that. Others stay away from the community for other reasons; because they married a Gentile, they feel they are not welcome anymore—which is not true. A Jew is a Jew even if he or she married a Gentile. The problem appears when they have to give their children a religious education.

For study I accept children of women who are not Jewish. I accept them in the Talmud Torah, and after that they can do whatever they want. When they are 14, I send their file to the **Beit Din** in Paris where they examine it, and then they meet with the parents. If everything goes well, they are admitted into the community. I teach them everything they need to know, and then it all depends on the Beit Din, which does not accept candidates before 14 or 15 years old. They think that the child has to be mature enough to accept the implications involved [in conversion]. And sometimes the mother is converted, too. But today the Beit Din is severe. They do not accept conversions for the purpose of marriages. In the past it was easier, now it is more difficult. I can accept them, but the problem is that I have to go through Paris, and some rabbis there are difficult. In the past 15 years, I have converted perhaps ten people. They come to the synagogue without a problem.

Of the young Jewish people who have studied, have attended the Talmud Torah, who continue afterwards to live a Jewish life, probably only 10 per cent will have an interfaith marriage. For those who quit after the bar mitzvah, possibly 50 per cent or more will marry non-Jews. Of course, the children of a Jewish woman who marries a non-Jew are considered Jews. But most of the time the children do not even get a religious education. In the North African group, if a man marries someone who is not Jewish, the woman has to convert. And if a man wants his wife to be in the community, there is nothing wrong with that. In that case, men determine the situation of the family. Men have more control, especially in the Sephardi community. We have to consider that for the future.

In terms of contribution to the community, probably about 50 families don't contribute [money]. They are mostly in mixed marriages. There are other Jews who don't participate because they came from North Africa and are not used to our system of paying dues to a community. But if one of them dies, I have to welcome the person into our cemetery. The religious ceremony has to be done; we have no choice. If they are poor, we don't ask for any money or we ask the minimum contribution. We try to reach an understanding, always try to come to an agreement.

Sometimes there are people who live outside the city who need us for that kind of situation. A person died recently; he was in an interfaith marriage. He lived 25 kilometers away, but we did it anyway. Another woman lost her child. She lives 20 kilometers from here, and she decided to bury the child in Israel. We did the service and only asked for a small communal donation.

I have stayed here for so long because people got used to me and I got used to them. I had a chance to go somewhere else, but I did not because a rabbi has to start over from the beginning with the people and it isn't easy. There are some communities with more people, but they don't have the structures that we have here. As I said, today in Dijon, we have the structures of a big community without being one. I am happy being a rabbi. I do not think that I would want to do anything else.

June 2005

My Judaism is not liberal. It's not like in the United States, where you have liberal, conservative, reform, so forth. I follow an Orthodox path, also called the Consistorial tendency in France, that is, Orthodox but open to the world, open to everyone in the community. This French Orthodoxy has changed a little in the past few years. It has become stricter due to the integration of people [from North Africa]. French Judaism today also is more "mystical," making it more radically Orthodox.

Actually, I am pessimistic. If the current leadership doesn't do anything, we will end up like in the United States, where with different tendencies there are different synagogues. This is perhaps okay in a large city, but in a small city like ours where you might have liberal, conservative, even Lubavitch tendencies, you cannot have this. That's my fear.

At this moment in our community, we have managed to maintain a certain unity in the synagogue. There are people who are religious, less religious, and non-religious. But it's mutual enrichment, and all are welcome. There are people who come once a year, for a funeral or something like that. The more religious ones influence a little the non-religious. But the non-religious also have important things to teach. And I believe that it works.

My fears about Judaism in France are not only national but also local. Several years ago a Lubavitch couple came to live here in Dijon. They created some problems to the extent that certain people were greatly disturbed. They created a mystical religious movement that caused a lot of trouble. Today the troubles are over because they have separated [from our community]. But back then we tried to live together.

In a way, they are open—they accept everyone, even though they are strict about the separation between men and women. They are strict about upholding their principles, but they are open in many ways, including about mixed marriages. They become very open when money is about to be donated.

Thanks to God, we somehow manage without them. We still have financial difficulties, of course. For example, in our school we had 15 students last year; next year we'll have less than ten. An entire generation has left Dijon. Our community has lost many of its young people. They left because they are experiencing problems common to all. But Dijon doesn't talk about them. I told the elected officials, "Listen. You are doing great things for the city. But you need to create more job opportunities."

I think that the national government got the message when the European constitution was rejected [2005]. People voted against the government because it wasn't doing enough to provide jobs for young people. Today a young person studies for 15 years in order to end up unemployed. This forces the young people to leave their hometowns, go abroad, or go to the Paris region—where there aren't jobs, either. So the situation is very difficult. You don't provide jobs, and the country is slowly growing older. This isn't good for the future of France.

For the future president, I will support Sarkozy.* He has shown that he is fond of Israel. He also is pro-American, and everyone knows that the United States supports Israel. He is somewhat different. Until now, all the governments, both Left and Right, have been pro-Palestinian. I think that it would be a good thing for France to move closer to the United States, which is not against Europe.

I am pro-American because the United States embodies freedom and the struggle for justice. It is not enough to say, "I'm for human rights." People should defend these ideas. The United States does it. World War II showed that even Europe needs the United States.... In these delicate situations, the Americans are here for Europe. They fight for the right things. Of course, the United States stands up and protects Israel. If Israel gets into a difficult situation, it can't count on anyone except the United States. And that's another reason why I'm pro-American.

I love France, I love Europe, but I also love Israel. No one can take away my love for Israel. It's because I have family there. It's because the State of Israel is the biblical Israel. Of course, it's not perfect, but I love it with its good and bad things. I like its leaders who were elected democratically, even though I think that sometimes they make the wrong decisions. I love spending my vacations there. It's a beautiful country, a country of great diversity, a rich cultural life, friendly to all people. I think that Israel is a country that can be an example for many other countries.

---

* Nicholas Sarkozy was elected president in 2007 but was defeated by François Hollande in May 2012.

But to return to the Dijon community—unfortunately, as I said, the young people are leaving. At the age of 17, they leave to pursue their studies, and after they graduate they remain away. Then the marriage problem appears. It's very hard for them to find a spouse here. So they go where they can find one more easily. We had a few weddings this year of people who went to Paris and married there.

Now I would say that the most successful activities we have here are the Sabbaths and the holidays. We have big celebrations. Teams are responsible for their preparations. Today we have the CCJD [cultural center] doing a fantastic job. There are very active people involved who do a lot of things, including conferences that are held here. Many of the ladies of the community are active in this.

A recent event that was a major success was hosting a chorus of 150 people who performed here [local choruses performed separately, then together]. People came from all over the country to Dijon. We welcomed them to the community and cooked more than 1,600 meals. The event was a major success for us. I think that people who attended realized that our Jewish community is very open, very tolerant. Some rabbis say that such a chorus should not perform in the synagogue. A chorus doesn't have much to do with prayers. However, the synagogue is the best place to hold such events. It's very important to get together in the synagogue, to hear the voices so that the people can open their hearts.

Very often the people who attend these events are very important to the community. They support the synagogue in the mayor's office, or else they make big donations. I believe that we have to encourage them further. Not holding these events in the synagogue would discourage all those people who stay and practice and perform. I don't want to do that. Moreover, we even have non-Jewish people who participate. This is something exceptional, to have a mixed chorus, for example. I don't think this affects our beliefs in any way. All these people appreciate our welcoming and the fact that we're open to everything.

I've always made sure that our relationships with others are very good. I mean with the Prefecture [government district office], the mayor's office, all the other officials, including the police. I have always tried to maintain good relationships between us. I will do this as long as it also doesn't interfere with my religious duties.

Within our own community, with the Lubavitch, it has been difficult. For example, I've been invited to the Beit Habbad. I won't go because I don't want anyone to think that I'm part of that group. I respect their ideas, but I don't support their policies because of the way that they create divisions within the community. I also don't like that they criticize our community. They say that our community is liberal when in reality it is open but not liberal. They confuse the meaning of words.

I respect every human being. Everyone has something to teach me, and maybe I have something to teach, too. On the larger community level, we interact with everyone at all levels—with Catholics, Protestants, etc. Our relations with them are excellent. And even in the synagogue non-Jewish people come [to events].

Over the last 15 years, relationships between Jews and others have changed on the personal level. It's true that people who came regularly don't come as often anymore or don't come at all. On the other hand there are groups like the Protestants who come more and more often. Maybe things have changed because I haven't encouraged them so much lately, or because I have been more concerned with my family problems. Also, we have lost several eminent members from the community. I should say, too, that attendance at our events by the larger community has been less this year. But I recognize that there is a greater need to care for our relationships with others. However, if we look at the activities of our cultural center, there are a number of non-Jews who attend their events often. This is true of the France-Israel Association as well. That movement is very active this year. With the B'nai B'rith youth group there have been some problems on both the personal and religious levels, but the senior group has about a dozen members who attend.

Radio Shalom's management is by our community. There is a certain amount of sympathy for the Beit Habbad. They produce some of the programs that are very interesting. But everybody works together on the radio.

Of those who use the ritual bath, six or seven [Lubavitch] show up regularly and five or six from our side, as well. It works out. Our community takes the lead, of course. My wife is one of the people in charge. She is a volunteer.

The Slonims [the couple who head the Lubavitch] are very nice and kind people on the personal level, but there are people around them who aren't very nice. They fight against some of the work of the community, and I don't like this at all. They fight this "war" on several levels. They don't pay their dues to the community. They don't come when they are supposed to. They don't participate in some important events. I remember that in one year none of them showed up. For example, at a recent WIZO event, none of them came. When there is a meal cooked and offered to the community, they don't come either. Neither the leaders nor the rank-and-file attend our services.

At one point, ten years ago, I was on the edge of a nervous breakdown. We had big problems. Some people in the committees thought that we could accommodate them [the Lubavitch]. I said "No!" I explained that because we have completely different ideologies, it's almost impossible for us to live together. It would be possible if they knew how to make an effort to accept us. There should be efforts to accommodate on both sides. In the synagogue they wanted greater separation between men and women. We tried to reach an agreement, but they wanted more. They wanted to have the community hall at their disposition when they wanted it, but they never helped in its maintenance. In terms of finance, they want to contribute with donations, but this is impossible. The community has always been ready to help, but there are some principles that the community simply cannot ignore or make an exception about. We don't want to discourage our most reliable supporters. We have to think about our women and about all those less traditional people who support us.

Today, there are actually almost 200 families in the community. About 20 of these families can be considered as active on the religious level. The other 180 are less active, but they attend all the holidays, etc. But they all support the community. And they bring other members in. I think that this will help us survive and go on, because there are new families that have joined in the past ten years or so. We have peace. For the past five years we have lived in peace.

In respect to Jews in France, several things have happened. Events in the Middle East caused confused feelings with respect to Jews and Israelis. The Jews here were seen as Israelis, which is completely wrong. French Jews are not Israeli. The war is there, not here. And this very serious misconception has been encouraged on purpose. This is a government that is Leftist—Socialist.[*] There is a tendency within extreme Leftist thinking that is profoundly pro-Arab, and this has continued to grow with developments in the Middle East. We look at this in an international context, taking into consideration the relationship between the United States and Israel. At some point people began assimilating the two sides, thinking that the United States and Israel act together. All this led to a new kind of anti-Semitism in the new generation, a kind of Leftist anti-Semitism. It is expressed here through damage to synagogues, attacks on Jews who are walking peacefully on the streets and are taken for Israelis. The media don't present the situation correctly because I'm sure they are directed in terms of misinformation to present a misleading presentation of current events. So all this has led to an anti-Israeli reaction in France, an anti-Israeli attitude—and, of course, an anti-American attitude as well.

---

[*] Until the spring of 2002, France had a "cohabitation" government, with a socialist prime minister (Lionel Jospin) and a conservative president (Jacques Chirac).

But I think that after 9/11 the situation changed for the Israelis and their connection to the United States. This was a change at a global level. Also, with [American President George W.] Bush, things changed a lot, too, in a good way. France, on the contrary, has remained anti-Israeli and pro-Arab. This can be seen through the anti-Semitism existing here. This anti-Semitism has always existed, and I'm afraid that it always will.

[The terrorist attacks of] 9/11 caused an important mental change. The United States came to realize that the only Middle Eastern country close to them is Israel. The United States directly experienced the hostility of the Arab world, especially of the Islamic extremists who openly displayed their anti-Americanism. The anti-Americanism in France is mostly due to French politics. French political leaders want to keep American influence here limited. France looks primarily to Europe because the focus is on protecting Europe. So after the attacks took place, France didn't want to be part of the American actions undertaken in reaction to the Islamic world because, geographically speaking, France is close to the Arab world, to North Africa. Moreover, France has always maintained good relations with the Arab world, including with [Iraqi leader] Saddam Hussein. No one questions this.

I believe that the desire of France and all of Europe is to have peace. We should get along with everyone. And when we talk of Europe, we should include Turkey. It's a Muslim nation, but it's part of Europe. I think the fact that we got close to Turkey had some influence on anti-Americanism here, especially in reaction to the American attack on Iraq. France wants peace, that's what it wants. The French think that the United States wants war; they see it as a warlike nation. What they don't understand, with their fixed idea of peace, is that sometimes people make stupid decisions. Having peace is great, but we should be able to make it happen. It was necessary to remove Saddam Hussein in order to have peace in the Middle East. The Jewish community saw him as a danger for Israel because the Scuds* could have carried chemical warheads. He also has done economic harm. His actions were very dangerous.

Now the real danger is Iran. And I hope that the United States understands this. Their responsibility is to reach a compromise with the Islamists in Iraq. This would calm down a bit the reaction against the United States in the Middle East. But I think that putting in power a mainly Shiite government in Iraq has indirectly strengthened Iran, because the Shiites are pro-Iranian. This could cause problems in the future, and not only for Israel, but for the world. Even in France we know that Iran can become a great danger for Europe.

---

* Missiles launched by Iraq against Israel in the Gulf War, 1991.

In France, the Islamists have developed two tendencies. There is moderate Islam, and then there are the Shiites and some Sunnis who constitute the radical movement. They are a great danger to the Jewish community and even to France as a whole. However, after the recent Muslim Council* election it became clear that this radical tendency was losing out to the more moderate. We hope that this is a sign of change in the Muslim community. I have seen a lot of this tolerant Islam here and all over Europe. I am not saying that there are no extremists; there are and there have always been. But, mainly, the Sunnis show a desire for this moderate Islam.

Five or six million Arabs are not a problem for France. After all, the country has a population of 60 million. But a lot depends on if this five million shows hostility towards France. If so, they might pose a danger. However, there are only several hundred thousand out of the five million who want to practice radical Islam. In this situation we cannot judge the entire Arab people by the behavior of a few. But there is no question that a radical movement exists.

The Muslims want to have mosques. Okay. This is normal; there are churches for Catholics and Protestants, etc. You know, in France there is separation of church and state by a 1905 law. Buildings built before 1905 receive upkeep money from the government; that is the case with the synagogue in Dijon, which was built in 1879. All others built after 1905 don't receive aid. Now, because there are a lot of mosques, the Muslims want to reform the law so that they can receive state aid, too. They want full integration into the country and support for their mosques, and I think that these are justified demands.

The separation of church and state is good and not so good at the same time. It's good that we have this separation because it provides for the liberty of the various faiths. For rabbis the disadvantage is that they are not paid by the state but by the community. But on the whole, the system works. I believe that in the long run the separation has turned out to be beneficial for religious life in France.

In any case, I'm optimistic about Islam in France. I'm optimistic because I've gotten to know Islam from the inside. I was raised in Morocco, and I know Islam very well. I know that all these radical movements won't last very long. Why? It's because we have a second generation Islam that doesn't see it in the same way as their parents. This generation speaks out; they

---

* When he was Minister of the Interior, Nicholas Sarkozy succeeded in creating the Conseil Français du Culte Musulman (CFCM) in December 2002. The goal, still in process, was to create more of a French Islam and for the state to have a meaningful interlocutor within the Muslim community.

weren't like their parents: preoccupied with earning a living and finding their place in the country. The second generation became the voice of their parents; they freely expressed what their parents couldn't say. They say out loud their concerns and their ideas. They have lived their lives in France and in doing so have come under the influence of the culture.

They don't support the exclusion of women, for example, or a form of Islam that excludes the "others" or France. This, of course, sometimes creates the kinds of problems we encounter with the Lubavitch. But with the Muslims [radicals], it's even more radical and politically oriented. With us, it more or less stays within the community. They are more politically oriented and express themselves in a not very democratic way. Obviously, this is not well received by either the French population or the government and the other religious communities, as well. Fortunately the moderate tendency in Islam, expressed from above [by the leaders], is gaining more and more adherents. The politics of the radical Muslims very often turns out to be racist and anti-Semitic. But neither French society nor the government approve of this. That's why these radical movements are declining in France.

If there is peace in the Middle East, this will calm things down even more. In France this will bring some changes. The French government will have to compromise on several things [with the Muslim community] and do its best to maintain the republican spirit that exists in the country. The Jewish community already has come to an agreement with Islam. Of course, we experienced several difficulties along the way, but we came up with compromises and reached an agreement, if you like, in the name of toleration. We [Jews] are only about 500,000, a number significantly less than the Muslims. So we don't want to give the impression that we are better than they are because we have been here for many generations. They have the impression that we have received a lot, and they haven't got theirs yet. So they are watching us, observing our actions. Therefore, we try to deal with them the best we can and help them, because they have the right to advantages. And I think that it works. I believe that we all should learn to adapt to the situation. The state should adapt to the Muslims, and the Muslims should adapt to the state.

For myself, I make a clear distinction between religion and politics, and this is seen in my relationship with the Muslims. When a member of the Muslim community demands something that has nothing to do with religion, I don't respond. And they appreciate this. I would not go and discuss those issues with them. On certain organized occasions, I do talk to them about politics. But if it concerns Israel, I don't go because I know that this will create tension. If the occasion deals with human rights, I go. For example, there are conferences involving Catholics, Protestants, Muslims—I always go and take part in the discussions. This is especially true if they are about killing and the role of religion. I go to very well-organized conferences where there are representatives of the Muslim community, and I converse with them on these topics. That's how I get to know them.

Once I hosted Muslim leaders of the Dijon community in my house. A local Catholic priest suggested the meeting. He wanted to get us all together at a bad moment at the time of the Intifada in 2000. We later had another meeting to discuss the peace conferences and other matters.

In 2001, we had a big meeting with the Catholics in the name of peace. We discussed tolerance among Catholics, Protestants, etc. Although the Protestants on the national level generally are Leftists and anti-Israel, people from here are not necessarily like those in Paris. This was not an obstacle in our dialogue.

There are different goals of these discussions here. Some of them are about peace, true, but others are simply about what the different communities in the city can do together. I even think that we should be having discussions with people who are anti-Israeli. The Muslims are anti-Israeli and we should talk with them, interact with them more. But in my house we have mostly religious and spiritual discussions. Usually there are about 20 people of all denominations.

I think that the people come here because of their faith, no matter if they are Muslim or not. I feel safe and comfortable, here and in the synagogue. I feel good and am optimistic about the future of France, and our community has a place in the future of France. I can say that. I have faith. France has a big future and will influence Europe and the rest of the world. I believe in France.

I love Morocco because I have lived there and because it was the home of my parents. I love Israel because our rituals come from there; my spirituality is built upon Israeli culture. So I adore Israel. But I love France for taking me in and giving me a place to live. I respect France for this.

It's not hard to practice your religion here. You can wear the kippa or not in the street; it's not obligatory, it's not against Judaism if you don't. If a Jewish man is in the army, he can practice his religion; he wouldn't have any problems doing so. A Jewish person working in a business has no problem taking time off for the holidays or even not working on the Sabbath. Everything is not perfect, of course, in particular with scheduling exams and such in the universities, but I'm sure that we'll succeed in dealing with this.

For me, a good Jew is one who is Jewish for himself, keeping kosher, observing the Sabbath, and so forth. It is a person who is Jewish at home as well, respecting the holidays, at least that. It is a person who puts on his **phylacteries** and prays every day but also participates actively in the life of the community. It is good if he is faithful to the community. So, it is a combination of the religious life and the community, because it [Judaism] doesn't work without that. Spiritually, we need to be good Jews, but occasionally we also need our batteries recharged. I think that all people need the community for that reason. They can't live as good Jews without it. They can still be Jews alone, but I doubt that they can be good Jews separate from the community.

What happens in Dijon after I retire? Well, there will be another rabbi who will continue working on what I started. It would be very good if the rabbi had a clear and firm orthodoxy. Hopefully he will be tolerant and open, as well.

Cathie Bussidan

As the editor of the community journal, Mazal Tov, *Cathie Bussidan is an effective recorder of the complexities and issues involving Dijon's Jews. She is much involved in cultural events and has been a strong promoter of efforts to make Jewish culture more widely known to the French public. She also is a keen observer, and sharp commentator, on the growing impact of the immigrant Arabs and Islam in France. Her opinions on the current state of French Jewry and their future mirror those of many of Dijon's—and probably other French—Jews.*

March 2000

I was born in Paris ten months after my father's return from the war. It was 1946. When I was two years old, we left and went to live in the countryside in Burgundy. I lived in a school where my mother was the only teacher in town. It was a very Catholic place. When I was little, I thought that everyone coming from Paris was Jewish. One day I didn't understand because my parents had friends visiting who were not Jewish. My parents were antireligious and forbade me from saying that I was Jewish.

I thought at the time that it was normal for my mother to be the teacher and for us to live in the school. Now I realize that it wasn't good. I also lived with the memory of those who had been deported. I used to kiss the picture of my aunt and my grandmother before I went to bed. For me, to be Jewish was not to be deported, and I did not know much more about Judaism. I lived in the middle of nature with my sister. Then, at ten years old, I went to a school that prepared future teachers. I was unhappy there because there were only girls. I began to gain weight. I was a good student, but the others made fun of me.

After I did my two years at the school, we moved to Chalons-sur-Saône, and that is where I studied languages. It was good for me; I earned my Bac*. My mother wanted me to continue scientific studies because she used to say that if the Nazis came back, I could survive by working in a chemical plant. Her sister had been deported with a friend who was a scientist. The friend returned, but the sister did not. That's why my mother wanted me to study science. She also told me that if I moved or had to go to another country, knowing science would make it easier. In the end, I studied languages. My sister, who was more artistic, became a math teacher.

---

* Baccalaureate, secondary school diploma.

My father was a factory worker and later became a salesman. But he wrote poetry. He also hated going to work. Politics was what he liked. He and my mother started a Family Planning Association in Chalons-sur-Saône. They also were in the United Socialist Party, but it didn't last long. They were active in the LICRA. Later they started the LICRA in Dijon when I asked my parents for their help there. My father used to say, "If I were a dictator, I would do this or that; if I was president, I would do this and that." He did the entire world. It was easy to control the world from the kitchen table. He only wrote poetry when he was unhappy, like when he was a prisoner of war or worked in a factory.

In high school I met other girls who were Jewish, but I didn't become good friends with them. All my very good friends were Catholics. However, I met Jews from North Africa—very nice people. I met people who observed the Shabbat. That was something new for me. I was happy to meet people to whom I could say that I was Jewish, even though I really didn't know what that meant. For me, during my entire childhood Jews were the ones who came back from the concentration camps. It was a heritage, a heritage of misery and sadness. My parents, however, had Jewish friends. My mother sometimes reminded me that it was Yom Kippur or the New Year. But it all was very confusing. One day, I told a friend that I was Jewish. Afterwards, all night long I was tortured with guilt because my mother had told me never to say that. The next day I told my friend that what I had told her wasn't true. She acted as if it wasn't important. I was 11 years old.

Two Sephardim that I met in Chalons taught me a few things. I learned that Jews were extraordinary. I knew that they suffered a lot. I knew that a rabbi could marry you. But that was about all.

I moved to Dijon when I was 17. I started my studies there—it was a disaster. But I met Africans. I met Arabs, whom I did not like very much. I told them that I was Jewish, but it didn't seem to matter. Then, in 1963 I had a wonderful year. I had many friends, flirting and all that for the first time. The African friends that I met liked politics like my father. They talked about Mao, Ché Guevara, other revolutionaries. I really didn't see them as different. In fact, my first love was an African. In 1962, when the **pieds noirs** came back to France, they came to our door for help, but my mother refused. My family supported the Algerians. They saw the "black feet" as fascists. In the end, however, I married a pied noir. But I am ashamed at how my mother acted then.

As I said, my time at the University of Dijon was a disaster. I simply didn't like it, I didn't like science, and I was lost. So I went to Paris to continue my studies, but the result was the same. I didn't pass the exams. Since it was easy to get a job, I went to work for Michelin as a chemist.

The war in 1967 was when I started to want to meet other Jews. I didn't know much about Israel, but the Six Day War had a very important impact on my life. My mother supported Israel, and in Paris I had friends who didn't talk to me at the time because I was Jewish. I was shocked. I realized then that I needed to start meeting more Jewish people.

A year later I moved to Dijon. At first I was lost because I didn't know many people. Then my parents took me with them to a conference where I met Michel Lévy and other wonderful Jewish students. I met everyone there, including my future husband. The first time I went to a synagogue was when I got married. And I was still anti-religious. It was 1968. I agreed to get married in a synagogue, but I told Michel that I didn't want my children to be brought up in the religion. I explained to the rabbi that I didn't agree with the place of women in Judaism and that it was unfair that a woman couldn't become a rabbi. He told me that a woman could not become a rabbi because she was not always pure. I told him that I read in the Bible that a man is impure after every ejaculation. Later the rabbi did not circumcise my son; I had an American doctor do it—without the prayers. When my children went to the Talmud Torah, they didn't like it.

But 1968 was one of the best years of my life. I got married. We finally moved into the twentieth century. Boys and girls at the university got the right to meet. People demonstrated because we didn't want de Gaulle. However, it wasn't as bad as in Paris. Compared to what my mother did during the Resistance, our political action wasn't much. She did things like making fake IDs with my uncle. They could have been shot for that.

My husband Michel grew up in a community that was completely different from mine. He grew up in Algeria in a Jewish community. He was from a very bourgeois French family that lived in Beaune. His father worked for the government. His mother came from a very poor family, but she had to stop working when she was married. If your husband was wealthy, you weren't allowed to work. Michel had a sister, but he was the only son. When I met him, he was very shy. He moved to France with his mother because he got involved with the OAS* and [his family] thought that it was dangerous for him to remain. [His family] wanted him to study medicine, but he was very unhappy. After he did his military service, he found a job in Dijon. We met, were married, and we have two kids, Hélène and David, born in 1971 and 1973. We stayed in Dijon because he liked his job, and it also worked out because I wanted to be close to my mother. I love my mother, though she is very possessive. I also wanted my children to have a grandmother. I didn't

---

* The militant, pro-settler, anti-independence movement in Algeria.

have one, so I wanted them to spend time with theirs. It was good to live in the same city and to see her frequently.

I remember that during the Yom Kippur War in 1973 there was someone who now lives in Las Vegas who was listening to the radio continuously in the synagogue. I thought that he should do it somewhere else. But we were scared during the war. We were scared for Israel. And we contributed a lot of money. At the time, old Ashkenazim controlled the community. They were old, and we were the young ones.

During the 1970s, I worked for seven years at a job I didn't like. I was bored, and I wanted a job where I could have more human relations. So I started teaching and passed my exams in 1976.

Dijon was a conservative city. There were the rich and the poor, and there were political power struggles. When I first arrived in Dijon, I spent a lot of time with Africans because the French people of Dijon were not open. I always said that it takes 15 years for a person of Dijon to open his door to a stranger. Unfortunately, even some pied noirs became like that. However, little by little, the city began to expand economically. And that had an effect on people. The newcomers had a positive impact on the community.

Not much happens in Dijon. It's a quiet city. A previous mayor [Robert Poujade] became the first national minister of environment, and he developed things that you can see: trees, parks, things like that. But one problem was that a lot of money was given to private schools. I didn't like that. They gave money to the Catholic Church and less for cultural events or youth. I have a friend who works in an association to help prevent violence against women, and she told me that they get less and less money.

When my father was president of LICRA, I went once in a while. After my father quit, I became more active and was eventually made secretary. Now I don't believe in it anymore. We made mistakes. Yes, we have to combat certain mentalities, but protecting certain people just because they were foreigners just wasn't right. However, the 1972 law against racism was an achievement of LICRA.

My work with feminism is different from my work with LICRA. Years ago, there were feminist collections of writings that had an influence on me. They explained that you were not born a woman but that you became one. It was very well explained. Girls have been treated differently from the beginning.

With respect to Judaism, I read Albert Memmi.* I read about interfaith marriages. I told Michel that we also were from different cultures and backgrounds, and that we had two different mentalities. I also read Roger Ikor

---

* Albert Memmi is a Tunisian-born Jewish author of more than 20 books and novels.

and Marek Halter.[*] In watching a program by Rabbi Eisenberg[†], I came to understand the study of the Bible by Jews.

When I was little, I used to read my Catholic friends' religion books, and it was funny. They said that God was everywhere and that He had no form or appearance. Then, in the next chapter, it said that God created mankind in His own image. I understood critically what I read, but my Catholic friends learned it by heart and understood little. But I loved learning about religion. I wanted to learn about other religions. When I met Michel I asked him if he believed in God and he answered that he had never asked himself the question. But for me it was very important. I began to realize that I needed to do something as a Jew. I needed to know what Judaism is.

In 1967, I started to ask questions; I began seeing Jewish people and got involved with Judaism and Jewish life. At the beginning, it was very slow going because I had been so anti-religious. I had never gone to the synagogue, nor did I want to learn about religions. I had read the Bible with my father, but that was different. In 1968, I finally approached the community. I also did it for the children.

Later I became involved with the newspaper [*Mazal Tov*]. At first, Michel Lévy was the head, but he made many grammatical mistakes. So I told him that I'd help him. I like working on the computer. But when Lévy left for Paris [early 1990s], the newspaper stopped. I thought that it was good for the community and that it should continue. Of course, I couldn't do it alone. Putting out the paper was a lot of work. Nor did I want to do it by myself because I didn't want people to see me as being personally responsible for it. However, little by little, as I learned the computer it became easier to work, and I was able to do more alone.

My philosophy about the newspaper is that it should be an expression of Judaism in every way. It should help Jews in Dijon communicate and understand the different aspects of [their religion]. Today Judaism is very much diversified. You know, even in a single family, there are different ways of being a Jew. For me, the responsibility is the heritage. It also is the obligation to be very humanist and tolerant. But I do not say that Jews are the most oppressed people. We need to accept others, but we also have to protect our heritage and see that it is not destroyed. It is not enough to pray. That's not enough.

---

[*] Two other prolific French Jewish authors who published books and essays about Jewish identity and many other subjects.

[†] Rabbi Josy Eisenberg is a noted rabbi and scholar who often appears on television.

June 2005

We were talking about Jews being open and tolerant towards others. Now, in France, we see a little separation between the communities, and we need to work on that. But, in the name of the Jewish Cultural Center of Dijon, I want to say that we are open to everyone and invite as many people as possible that are not Jewish to come and see what Jews do. For example, on 4 September, 2000, we held an open house in the synagogue on the Jewish Patrimony Day.* Then we had a choral concert that was open to everyone. We advertised it throughout the entire region.

We attempt to show who we are and to meet other people by all means possible. And, in fact, there are people in the cultural center who aren't Jewish. I would say that there are about 30 non-Jews. Among them is a Muslim, Morad El Hattab, a philosopher and author, who came to one of our conferences and whom I found to be absolutely wonderful. And we have "adopted" him. He is very intelligent and open-minded. He organizes conferences, speaks well in public, and shares things with the cultural center. I also have other Muslim friends who sometimes come to our conferences.

There are, of course, people who oppose this. It is difficult for all strongly religious people. The strongly religious Jews are close-minded and conservative just like the strongly religious Muslims. From the moment they decided to live and reproduce only among each other, hiding the truth, they cannot open themselves to the rest of the world. In exceptional situations they can co-exist, but they cannot talk to the other. Would Radio Shalom help to resolve this? Well, we don't really know if non-Jews actually listen to the radio. I used to believe that Radio Shalom wasn't very popular, but people have told me that they listen to it, especially because they enjoy the music.

But to return to Jewish Patrimony Day: about 800 people attended and around 100 [stayed] for the concert. And I am sure that there were Muslims present. Both events were held in the synagogue. People first visited the synagogue; afterwards they went to the auditorium where there was an exhibition of archives. Viewing paintings in the community room was next, followed by a buffet.

So that is what we do at the Jewish Cultural Center: protect our Jewish culture here in Dijon. In addition, we have courses in Jewish dancing, singing, and cooking. We organize conferences and show films. We sell Israeli wine. What else? We try to get the largest audience possible and bring Jews and non-Jews together to work with us in our association.

---

* The European Day of Jewish Culture, also called Jewish Heritage Day, is part of a wider annual European Day of French Patrimony celebration.

The Lubavitch, however, don't participate at all. Some came before, but little by little all of those who were part of the Lubavitch movement here ended their membership and participation [in the cultural center] and now ignore us completely. And, personally, I haven't attempted to improve relationships with them. I'm not really eager to try. I don't like people who keep themselves away from others. Well, if there are people who want to try and improve relations, they can do so. But I am not interested in sectarians. Just because they are Jewish doesn't mean that I have to deal with them. If they want to come closer, and if they want me to help them change their attitude and bring them closer to us, of course I would do it. But I don't believe that this will happen.

I nevertheless think that our diverse cultures are very interesting. For example, when one creates songs, it is done in Yiddish. When one makes dances, they are Israeli or Hasidic. The cuisine as well: we combine the cooking of North Africa and Central Europe. It's an enriching experience.

I don't agree that the French people don't accept diversity. On the contrary, I think that the French are very receptive to other cultures, even if they don't always show it. For example, here in Dijon, there is a festival where dances from all over the world are performed. Every night, there are shows in the theaters, and the places are always full. On our Jewish Patrimony Day, a lot of people came up to me and surprised me by saying that they hadn't dared to come [to the cultural center] before because they thought that they couldn't, but that they were very interested. There are people who won't take the first step of coming on their own, but who are willing to do so if we present them with the opportunity. You know, when we showed our Israeli dancers in the street during the festival, the street was always crowded. And what does it mean? It means that the people of Dijon are eager to see performances that are representative of other cultures.

The Israeli choral group that comes frequently is welcomed in an incredibly good way. They don't know about our customs, but they are ready to learn. You know, no one wears a kippa in Dijon, in the street, except the rabbi and the Lubavitch, and they wear hats on top. So when I gave the choral group a tour of the city, and some of them were wearing kippas, I told them that they could wear them if they like, but that it wasn't our custom to do so. And they simply took them off.

This is a city where one can see Muslim women wearing veils occasionally. But it shocks us to see that. We hate that people show their religious preferences through their clothing. In the schools, for example, it's prohibited. Fortunately, the French secular tradition does not put up with those people who, I would say, are disguising themselves. But my colleagues and I didn't really have more problems with the Muslim children than with other children. There were very well brought-up Muslim children and others who were badly raised. There were charming Muslim children and troublesome Muslim children. The only problems occurred when the schools offered Arabic courses. That doesn't work well with the mentality that governs French education. All of a sudden, the Muslim children were separated from the others. I was strongly against this. On the whole, however, any problems I had were with badly raised children. The ethnic origins of the children didn't play any role in that.

At the moment, in Dijon, one can say that there aren't any big problems within the Jewish community right now. Nevertheless, we feel that there is something among the Arabs that authorizes them to exercise their anti-Semitism. It is something that hasn't been present before. I feel that members of the extreme Right have the same attitude. For example, graffiti was found on the gravestones in a cemetery of a village near here. Someone removed the **mezuzah** from the rabbi's front door. I don't casually speak Hebrew in my garden, though my neighbors probably know that I am Jewish anyway.

I do wear the Star of David in Dijon, but I wouldn't in Paris, especially in the subway. One time I was in the train and two disgusting Arabs got on who were smoking. I just said, "Excuse me, but I think that you forgot to put your cigarette out." I would never have said that if I were wearing the Star of David because then I think they would have attacked me.

I do have a bit of a phobia about crowds. I don't feel safe in a crowd. I don't know if it's because I am Jewish or because of my phobia, but I will not go walking in certain neighborhoods. I live in a house that is right next to an essentially Arab neighborhood. I don't like to walk around there because I don't like the atmosphere. For example, there is a market where I used to go on Sunday mornings, but now there are too many bearded men and there are too many veils. I don't like that. Too many bearded Jewish men and too many Orthodox women wearing wigs—it's the same to me: I don't like it.

I don't know what the future will bring in France. I know that each century has experienced violent periods of anti-Semitism. For the moment, since 1945, we have escaped it. But will it return? I don't know. If it comes, it may be from the Left or the Right. Or the Muslims. Or the National Front. In my opinion, the National Front is less and less powerful, but that may be just an impression. I think that now the Muslims are much more dangerous, at least some of them. However, the majority of Muslims live in peace. But Jews have another problem in France.

France is a country where people assimilate. After two or three generations, one is French like everyone else. And now there is a situation that is totally foreign to this French mentality and that seems more like what you have in the United States. I have thought carefully about this, and I told myself that if people don't assimilate, it's because they are very numerous, like the Muslims, or because, again like them, that the media they receive from the Muslim world allows them to live within their four walls as in an Arab country where they can't be touched by French culture. In some families, they have the television tuned to Arabic stations 24 hours a day. In fact, I think that the failure of assimilation of the Arabs comes partly from the media creating this parallel universe.

What can be done with the "old" France? I don't know. I don't recognize that France anymore. I don't recognize the ethnic separatism and the liberalism of the economy. I don't recognize it at all. What we mean by liberalism, of course, is really savage [or unregulated] capitalism. We are in the process of resembling England little by little, and that worries me. It is harder and harder for us to take care of ourselves; it is hard for us to work. There are more and more people at the subsistence level. This is not France. And the Jewish communities are closing in on themselves more and more. This is not my France. It's not the France that my grandparents chose to live in. They chose France because at least here they thought they would have the opportunity to do something with their lives and to live safely. They said it was the country of the "rights of man." There is the League for the Rights of Man, but it is a little taken over by the extreme Left. That's because the moderate Left doesn't do its job anymore. Therefore, people turn to the extreme Left to rebel.

There is so much anti-Zionism in the extreme Left because some people are profoundly anti-Semitic in their culture and they justify themselves, justify their anti-Semitism. No, they aren't anti-Semitic when the Jews are the victims, they are anti-Semitic when the Jews are the victors. They can put up with the Jews in pinstriped pajamas, or gassed, or burned. For them, they have a lot of compassion. But they can't stand Jews in uniform [armed Jews].

Those are the Christians, especially the Leftist Christians. And France is a Christian country, a secular Catholic Republic. I have a Communist friend who completely agrees with me. She is not alone. There are a zillion people who belong to France-Israel who are Communists [meaning Leftists]. So it is not obligatory that Leftists be anti-Semitic. People are comfortable with Jews as victims, but not as victors—the Israelis, for example.

It is necessary that a victim have a torturer. If the Palestinians are the victims, then the Israelis are the torturers. The Jews think the opposite. They think that the Jews are the victims and the Palestinians are the torturers. Neither group is able to think that there are torturers in both camps. In any case, people who think binary—it's one side against the other.

However, as to the question of peace between Israel and the Palestinians, I think that they will make peace one day. France and Germany made peace. Israel and the Palestinians will make peace. It's impossible any other way. Not tomorrow, but it will come. We don't talk about it very often, but there is some good will on both sides.

Will that improve relations between the North Africans and the Jews here in France? We aren't there yet. I think that there will be good reasons to hate each other. There are always good reasons for people to hate each other. I just don't have blind confidence in human nature. We are always acrimonious. We have technological progress, yet.... I think that the problem of anti-Semitism in France is very exaggerated. From what I hear, there are people who think that we are in great danger. We are not in danger at all. [The situation] is a little worse than ten years ago, but it's nothing.

I don't have any immediate concerns. Not immediate. [The problem is] not so much the community, it's the economy. When I began to work, I snapped my fingers and three or four employers asked me to come. And now, my son is 32 and can't manage to live securely. He will have to work until 70 to have enough for retirement. It's unthinkable. We had jobs, we had security, we had comfort; our retirement and old age were secured, health care was assured, we had a good life. And all that is being lost little by little. I just saw the price of fuel that was announced today. It is twice as high as last year. How are we going to manage? What are we going to do? When you know that the rise in oil prices pays for the war in Iraq, that's scary.

Yes, I am against all wars, but I am absolutely against the war in Iraq. I believe that if it was necessary to have a war somewhere, the place wasn't Iraq. I totally agree that Saddam Hussein was a mass murderer, but he should have been attacked when he gassed the Kurds and not when we invented, so to speak, weapons of mass destruction that never existed. It's a war that started with a lie, a horrid lie, with a reason that doesn't exist. It's the oil. That's the actual reason. So I'm not at all in agreement with the war. And now there is too much misfortune. Al-Qaeda wasn't in Iraq. Now they are well established there, and it's a catastrophe for the world.

I don't have any hope at the moment, and I'm sorry for the younger generation because, for us, we had May 1968, and we still had hope. We were so happy when Mitterrand was elected [1981]. We still believed in all those things. It was very agreeable. But now, I don't believe in anything [political] anymore.

I would like to visit the United States. I have never gone. I have friends there. I have people in Boston, as well, my old Soviet pen pal. But I think that my French mentality is so different from the American that I could not enjoy living there. Those who came from North Africa lived in communities. They might find themselves better off in the United States than in France because they don't understand much about secularism. But I am profoundly secular—republican, French-style. So I cannot live anywhere but in France. I can't live in Israel either because I love the French language. I'm very comfortable with it. It's a language that was also my line of work, and I can't see myself living in a country that gives me difficulties with the language.

In Dijon one of the best things about the Jewish community is the conviviality. For those who go to services, there is something rather strong that ties them together. I hear that from friends who return from Saturday morning services. They are always talking about whom they met. They're happy. As for me, in what I do, we have small get-togethers. If there is a lecture, afterwards we get together. We have a drink, we eat, we chat. And I think that that is important. And then we invite each other to our houses. Or we go as a group to the cinema. We are pleased to get together for celebrations.

There was a period when we were really wounded by the break with the extremists [the Lubavitch]. As for me personally, I have rather liberal tendencies, so I would prefer if women were not placed on the side so much. But we have absorbed the split, we have adapted to it. Now things are much calmer. The only thing that I really regret in Dijon is that people leave. It is a community where there are no more young people, and there are more and more elderly. Unless there is a strong increase in numbers as in 1962 when the North Africans arrived, the future of the community is in question.

We have not had marriages for several years now. I announce in the journal this or that marriage, but none of them take place in Dijon. And we had, in issue number eight of *Mazal Tov,* six or seven deaths but no marriages. There was a birth notice of my grandson, but that's all. And he's not Jewish. His mother is a Catholic. At best, he'll be half-Jewish [laughs].

What kinds of things do I personally do now to help the Jewish community? I do cultural things. I do work on the computer, or I bring things from Lyon or Paris when I have the opportunity. I meet people. But I never go to services, except for Yom Kippur, when I go to say hello to friends. I'm not a believer, so I don't want to be hypocritical. I am a bit more involved now that I'm retired, and this makes me happy. Plus, at the cultural center there are new members who have given me a lot of new energy and ideas, a lot of joy. There are also those who help me with our journal. They type articles for me. That saves a lot of time. I don't have to do the work that's involved in trying to decipher texts. I receive them by email and only have to correct the spelling, punctuation, and syntax errors, and put them together on the paper.

There you are: it's the conviviality that I enjoy most of all.

Israël "Izy" Cemachovic

Born in Lithuania, cosmopolitan, articulate, and multilingual,
Dr. Cemachovic is the president of the Jewish Religious Association
of Dijon. He is a specialist in gastrointestinal medicine who received
post-doctorate training in the United States. Since 2000 he, along
with the rabbi, has been the public face of Judaism in Dijon.

June 2000

My father was 46 when he married my mother. They were married in Lithuania
in 1946 after the war. He had returned from fighting in the Red Army against
the Germans. When the Russians occupied Lithuania [in 1940], he was
deported to a Siberian labor camp where he spent 14 months, but he was
released into the Army. It was possible for Poles and other Eastern Europeans
to fight alongside the Russians against the Germans. My mother spent four
years, from age 13 to 17, in various [German] camps. She was not released
until April 1945. The experience was very hard for her, and she never spoke
much about it. Her three sisters, a brother, her parents—all disappeared.
When she married my father, she had no one. My father lost nine brothers
and sisters in the war. There were 11 children from two marriages, and only
he and a half-brother survived. If he had not been deported to Siberia, he
also would have died in the Holocaust.

I have only one sister, who was born in 1948. I was born in 1956 in Cotino,
Lithuania, a city not far from Drema, which was a major Jewish center in
Eastern Europe. My parents named me Israel, after my father's father. It
must have been a difficult decision to give me that name because of the anti-
Semitism of the Russians and others. My father's name was Rubin and my
mother's, Sarah, typical Jewish names, and because of that people laughed
at them in the street, shouted at them from the windows when they were
children. But I guess that they named me Israel because they respected tradition, even though they were not religious at all. My father almost never
went to the synagogue.

In 1957, the year after I was born, the Russians authorized Polish refugees
to return to Poland. Probably it was part of the de-Stalinization process of
that time. And although my father had a good life, he decided to leave and
go to Israel through Poland.

By occupation, my father was a furrier. Of course, there was no job like
that for him in Israel, so he had a difficult time, doing all sorts of odd jobs.
He told me that during the year and a half that they were in Israel he did
about 40 different jobs. He wanted to go to the United States, but he had

to wait for a visa somewhere else because they were very hard to obtain in Israel. Since he knew some people in Belgium, he decided to go and wait there. That's how we got to Belgium.

My mother was willing to stay in Israel. She spoke Yiddish like our parents and grandparents. She was very strong in her Jewish traditions, with her Jewish people. So of course she was reluctant to leave. And Belgium was not easy for my parents. They had to learn French. They worked very hard. But when the visa for the United States was finally approved, they decided to stay. Really, it was my mother's decision. She said, "No, we don't move anymore." And that's how I became a Belgian citizen at the age of 16.

My education was normal—elementary and secondary school, then medical studies at Brussels University. After receiving my medical degree I did two years as a resident in internal medicine. From 1982 to 1983 I spent a year at the Cabrini Medical Center in Manhattan. When I returned to Belgium, I spent the next four years working as a gastroenterologist at a small community hospital.

I spent the year in the United States because, as a doctor, I considered it necessary to have an American experience. In medical school in Belgium, the texts are in English; medicine is very much attuned to Anglo-Saxon practices. I was more interested in practicing medicine than in research. For that reason I didn't have the support of the chief of staff of the hospital where I worked in Belgium. In the United States, I went door-to-door in order to get an internship and said, "Here I am." I was able to get one because I already had two years' experience behind me. At first, I went to Chicago, where I knew a Belgian dermatologist. I was hoping to get into Mount Sinai. But I didn't much like Chicago. Frankly, I felt that I would be too isolated—too far from Europe and separated from the Jewish community.

Since I was a child, I was interested in medicine. I remember that when I passed the examination to become a doctor, the lady at the shop on the corner described me as being "high as three apples," as they say in French. My parents helped me. They worked so hard. It was very important for my mother—the goal of her life was that I become a doctor. She invested a great deal in helping me.... I was not the only child. I have a sister. She is seven years older than me and is very bright. She speaks seven or eight languages, but she wouldn't pursue university studies. High school was enough for her. It was very hard on my mother. Because my sister wouldn't continue her studies, my mother invested more in me.

My Jewish education began when I was three and a half years old. At the time my parents were working seven days a week, really hard, because it was tough, and they sent me to Jewish camps. There the teacher tried to teach the children Yiddish, she told Jewish stories, but I was the only one who spoke it. The Jews from Belgium wouldn't learn Yiddish. From age seven I was a member of various youth groups. We met a lot, had summer camps. In 1970, when I was 14, I started visiting Israel.

I began studying Hebrew in Belgium. There you choose your religion and the courses you want, and the government pays for them. So I had a private teacher of Hebrew. When I visited Israel, of course, I spoke with the family of my father's half-brother, who had arrived in Palestine in 1926. My family learned about them by accident in 1957 when they heard their names on the radio. We hadn't realized that we had relatives still in Israel.

I learned Hebrew very fast when I was in Israel for a time after the Yom Kippur War [1973].

It wasn't easy to have Israel as a first name. I was teased about it. Occasionally I was called "dirty Jew," but not often, I must say. I think it was worse in France. A French friend told me that when he was a child in Dijon, he got it [was called names] all the time, which was not my deal at all. In Belgium they didn't have an anti-Semitic tradition like the French.

My parents didn't go to the synagogue very much. I think that they don't believe in God, like a lot of people who suffered so much during the Holocaust. So they don't believe in God and are not close to the religion, but still they respect the traditions. For example, my nephews did a bar mitzvah, but I didn't do a formal bar mitzvah because my parents considered that it wasn't necessary. They always told me, "You are a better Jew than the others, since you speak Yiddish and feel more Jewish than the people who never get involved in Jewish activities." So I accepted this point of view because I think you can still be very Jewish, very concerned, while not being so involved in all the practices. I think there is a place for Jews who hardly practice or don't get involved in all the religious stuff. I consider myself a Jew despite the fact that I don't know that much about the religion.

I read a lot of books and articles about Judaism. I consider that I'm quite well informed about Jewish history. For me it's an ethnic and cultural identity. I don't need a religion to prove my Jewishness, to make it more profound. And I don't have to hide that I'm a Jew—anyway, it would be impossible with my name. People know that I'm a Jew and accept me as I am.

Why didn't I stay in the United States and practice medicine there? The fact is, medically speaking, it was very interesting for me to work there. But I felt that the hospital where I was working was very much oriented towards making money. Perhaps that's not true of all hospitals in the United

States, but it was where I worked. And I didn't feel that medicine should be so oriented towards making money. Even when I was a child, I was interested in medicine, not money. I didn't see why it would be important for me to stay just for the money. I did well, I guess. They gave me the "best on staff award for excellence in medicine." I was considered to be the best intern. A good future was outlined for me. I would become the chief resident. But I said, "I'm sorry, I cannot stay." You see, philosophically, I'm more European than American. Money is not my only interest in life. I knew for certain that I would earn a lot of money in the United States, but I'm not doing medicine for money.

The reaction was quite condescending. They said that in Belgium the streets must be paved in gold since I was so eager to get back. (There, again, is the money point of view.) One of them even said to me, "Oh, you'll come back for your paycheck, don't worry." All this confirmed for me that we weren't on the same wavelength.

But I don't regret it. Of course, I met other people. One was a cousin of someone I knew in Brussels. She was married to an orthopedic surgeon. She told me about her friend who was married to a medical researcher. She described the researcher as a nice guy, but he wasn't making any money. He was just a researcher. And she felt so sad about that. It made me think that if I stayed in the United States and didn't make a lot of money, I'd be considered to be nothing. And I said, "Who needs that!"

Here, I'm considered a good doctor by my parents, by my family, by my patients, even though I don't have a huge car, a huge house. And, you see, I live quite well. We cannot afford big vacations; we don't stay in four-star hotels, absolutely not. We have a lower standard of living in Europe than in the United States. But it's enough for me.

There certainly are many good doctors in the United States who are not so money-oriented. Still, when you're talking about medicine there, it's always related to money. "Yes, he's doing well. Yes, he's a cardiologist. Yes, he has this, he has that." It's all a little bit boring. We doctors here are happy not to be speaking about money all the time. And that's good.

What I know about the education system in the United States is that, until high school, the youth don't know very much. I mean, they don't learn much. The level is much lower than here. Then, when they enter college, they already know what they're going to do. They start to study and become very specialized in the field that interests them. But they don't have a general culture. They don't have the classical culture that youth receive here. Of course, youth here also don't seem to be interested much anymore in history or poetry. In that way, the cultures are becoming similar.

After my return I did two more years' internal medicine residency. Then I did two more years—four altogether—at the big university hospital in Brussels.

I met Luna, my wife, in 1986. It was March 30. I remember the date because it was my mother's birthday. My sister had arranged a meeting with Luna at a friend's house. Luna was a Greek Jew. She was in Brussels training as an interpreter in Greek, English, and French for the European Union. That's how we met. We got engaged in 15 days and were married in three months. Luna is from Chalkida [or Chalcis], the principal city on the Greek island of Evia. After Crete, Evia is the largest Greek island. It's north of Athens and very close to the continent. There has been a Jewish community there for over 2,000 years. Today, however, the community is very small. During the war many were hidden from the Germans in the marshes. Afterwards a lot of them left for the United States. In fact, I have a good friend from there with a catering business in Memphis.

The Jews in Greece are not really Sephardic. They were in Greece long before the expulsion from Spain. Originally they must have come from Turkey, but they are called Romaniot Jews because of the Roman Empire. They are really the third branch of the Jewish people. My father-in-law was the head of the Jewish community there and has written about it for *The Jewish Encyclopedia*. He also discovered the Jewish cemetery, containing tombs from the sixteenth century but obviously used for almost 2,000 years. After he discovered it, archeologists came from Israel. The Jewish community in Athens, which is quite wealthy, is contributing to their work and to the maintenance of the tombs. They're also starting to build a museum close to the cemetery.

The Jews in Chalkida survived because of family help and because they paid the Greek peasants monthly in gold to provide for their food and everything. It was a large amount. In Salonica the Jews were completely destroyed. There, they were very naïve. One morning, they were told to gather together in one place with all of their gold and money, and they simply disappeared.

Luna's parents were very much concerned that she would marry a Jew. They were scared that she would marry a **goy**. In Greece, as in other countries, as in France, there are a lot of mixed marriages. And there are only about 5,000 Jews left in Greece. In Chalkida, there are only 80. Despite efforts to encourage the youth to marry within their religion, it isn't working. That's the reason Luna's parents sent her to Israel. She was there for four years, from 18 to 22, working for her bachelor's degree in English and French at the Hebrew University in Jerusalem. She enjoyed it very much, but she didn't find a husband. After her return to Greece, she was sent immediately to

Brussels. The next year she and I were married. So her parents were very happy, even though she lived in Brussels.

In 1987, we went directly to Dijon. There were many physicians in Brussels, and it was difficult to establish a name for oneself. So there was really no place for me. And, anyway, I also was getting a little bit bored. Since I didn't want to go back to the United States, I took the practical step of looking at France. I had always been interested in what was going on in France, in French politics—I always read *Le Monde* [Leftist French newspaper]. It would not be difficult for me to be integrated as a Frenchman. Belgium is like a province of France; Brussels like a province of Paris. Anything that is interesting happens in Paris, in France. France is the cultural power.

I also knew a Jewish girl from Brussels, a physician, who had married a French doctor. They were in Dijon. They were why I selected Dijon.

In middle-sized French cities like Dijon, there are usually two big public hospitals and a number of private clinics. So I called each clinic and said that I was interested in working there. Now, my head of department in Brussels was one of the most famous gastroenterologists in the world, and I said, "I know how to do this; I know how to do that, and so on. Are you interested?" Only one said yes. So I became associated with an older gastroenterologist. We worked together for three years before he retired and I replaced him.

There weren't many difficulties making the adjustment. The language is the same. Only the names of the medications were different. The practice was different because I went from a large university hospital to a small private practice. You suddenly become chief of a small business. You have to be a manager as well. We doctors aren't prepared for that.

What's funny is that I had a very busy practice from the beginning. My friends, the woman from Dijon and her husband, were in general practice and they sent me many people. The other doctors couldn't understand how a guy from Brussels, absolutely unknown in the city, could have so much work. The medical community was really amazed. People were wondering who I was. It was a pity that two or three years later, the couple divorced and she returned to Brussels; her husband died of a heart attack only a year or two after that. So when they weren't there, my practice dropped a little. I had to build my practice again based on my reputation. The doctors from Dijon sent people to their friends, people who studied with them. There were only one or two in general practice, plus a surgeon, who worked with me on a regular basis. All my other patients came because of my name.

I do believe that my being Jewish had something to do with how I was accepted by the medical community. There is a tradition of anti-Semitism among the French bourgeoisie. In fact, I just finished [reading] a book that tells a story of anti-Semitism among physicians during the war.* And there are still anti-Semitic doctors in France. Indeed, I would say that there is anti-Semitism among the general population. There is a specific anti-Semitism among the French bourgeoisie that you don't find in other countries. This comes from the Dreyfus Affair and was consolidated between the wars by l'Action Française[†] and writers on the Right. And you still find it among the Catholic upper bourgeoisie. Most definitely.

You also find anti-Semitism in the medical field. Personally, I don't hear anything against me, but I know a pharmaceutical salesman who travels around among doctors and who tells me stories. When Simone Veil[‡] was Minister of Health, he told me that terrible things were said about her among doctors. Now, this was not rational. It was because she was Jewish.

You know, I'm considered a foreigner—three times a foreigner: I'm not French; I'm not Catholic; but I am Jewish.

As for the bourgeoisie, the Catholic bourgeoisie—it's possible that the attitude of the Church will change now, with this Pope [John Paul II]. He will have an impact, but later. There is never a direct impact. I don't think that Catholic people wait for the Pope to tell them that they can love Jews. They do or they don't. I know a Catholic doctor who told me that the Catechism still teaches that Jews killed Jesus Christ. I'm not sure that this is true.[§] But if it is the case, you'll have to wait for the next generation that isn't taught that before attitudes change. I find that Protestants are closer to Jews than Catholics are, from the theological viewpoint. They are less anti-Semitic than the Catholics. Perhaps it comes from the experience of also being a minority in France.

The landlord of my office told me that when he was a child—he's now 80 years old—he was told by his parents to spit on the sidewalk when they crossed in front of a Protestant church. You'll notice that all of the Protestant churches and Jewish synagogues here have gates and other barriers and are locked. Catholic churches are always open.[¶] My father-in-law told me that in Greece the [Eastern Catholic] Orthodox—who, as you can imagine, are

---

* See Bruno Halioua, *Blouses blanches, étoiles jaunes : L'exclusion des médecins juifs en France sous l'Occupation* (Paris: Liana Levi, 2002).

† Semi-fascist, but monarchist movement founded during the Dreyfus Affair in 1899 by authors Charles Maurras and Maurice Barrès, with its newspaper, *L'Action française*, appearing in 1908.

‡ Simone Veil, a Holocaust survivor and politician, was Minister of Health from 1974 to 1981 and was responsible for introducing a strongly contested law in 1975 that legalized abortions.

§ This is certainly not true after the Second Vatican Council's encyclical *Nostra aetate* (In Our Age), published in 1965, in which Pope John XXIII exonerated the Jews of the crime of deicide.

¶ Catholic churches are seldom "always open" except, perhaps, in larger urban areas.

more Catholic than the Catholics—still carry the icon of the Virgin outside in a procession during Easter. Until World War II, they marched through the Jewish quarter and then made a pogrom and broke everything. Today, they just have the procession.

Yes, I'm sure that a few of my patients are anti-Semitic. They have their opinions about Jews, but if they find that I'm a good doctor, it doesn't matter. I remember that when I was in New York City, a Philippine doctor said to me, "Israel, you're not Jewish. It's impossible." For her, you see, Jews in New York were of a certain type, and they did not have a good reputation. And since I came from Europe, I couldn't be a Jew. It was very funny.

We arrived in Dijon on Yom Kippur in 1987. We didn't go to the synagogue the first day; we didn't know that there was an organized Jewish community here. It was my banker who said that we must meet the rabbi from the community. I was given a name and I called. Actually, it was the president of the community; the banker simply didn't know the difference. Well, we met the same day and were invited for dinner. We were accepted immediately and made welcome. They were very happy to have us come.

At first, I was not very active. I participated in all the religious holidays, but I was not active from a political standpoint. As a matter of fact, I knew that there were disagreements among the [synagogue] board members. I was not asked to participate. They didn't consider me as having a place as a newcomer, which was acceptable to me. I had enough politics from reading my newspapers, my books. They didn't need me and I didn't need them. I thought that the community was doing fine without me. It was working well enough for the needs of my family. But there were very strong personalities [on the board], and the disagreements got worse. It became difficult for them to function, so they came looking for me. They told me, "Listen. We need somebody who is outside of all these battles that have been going on for years, someone who can maybe calm everyone down." That's why they asked me to become president.

It was an unusual situation, because I never served on the board before I became president. The man whom I replaced as president [Armand Sibony]* himself came to see me. He said that he couldn't do it anymore, that his wife couldn't stand to see him so aggravated all the time because of the fights. He had to retire. Anyway, he said that his work was taking him to Paris and that he couldn't manage the community from there. He told me, "We need somebody in Dijon who is well-respected, well-known locally. Also, you're Ashkenazi, you're whiter than the Sephardim." Now, he's a Sephardi also.

---

* No relation to Rabbi Simon Sibony.

But he also knows that he's "warm-blooded," as we say. He was becoming increasingly agitated.

Of course, I didn't expect any of this to happen. Then, there were a few other members who came to see me and told me that they agreed that it was a good idea. They said that they didn't see anyone else who could be in the position and be neutral. They said that I was the man they needed.

A major problem came up as soon as I became president. It was a personality problem. One of the members of the board always wanted to be president, and he was very disappointed not to be named—and probably won't ever be named. As a result, he put a lot of procedural obstacles in the way over the four years. It was difficult for me because the people who placed me in the position wanted me to do exactly what they wanted, like a puppet. They wanted me to expel this member. Although I agreed with their point of view, there was no way for me to legally expel him, but they couldn't understand that. They were upset because I wouldn't do exactly what they wanted. So I had to fight both sides. Not against them, but to try and explain to them. By now, I've learned how to avoid fights, and everybody's happy. I think that I did what was needed on the board to calm everyone down so that we can all play the game.

But the major problem of the community is with the youth. The community does not take enough care of them. They are not sufficiently well led. And if the youth don't get involved with the community, then eventually there won't be any community. I really think that for many years now the youth have been disregarded, left on the margins. Correcting this should be our main goal. That's why I created the Parents' Committee, which works to increase involvement.

One of the things the Parents' Committee has done is moderate the demands of certain tendencies within the community. For example, there were Orthodox parents who insisted on "racial purity," something that I absolutely reject. These parents said that there were kids who were not considered to be Jews [involved in our youth activities] and that they shouldn't be accepted into gatherings of Jewish youth. I categorically rejected this position.

Well, we had some fights, not very intense ones, but I had to explain myself very clearly. There are a lot of mixed marriages here, many more than in Belgium. And so there are a lot of cases of mixed Jewishness that we cannot avoid. Even if you look at it from the economic point of view, we cannot reject people. There's no way for a young boy or a young girl, who considers himself or herself a Jew before a bar mitzvah, or even after, who participates in Jewish activities, not to be accepted independent of his or her formal Jewish status. That's very important to me. The rabbi, of course, has to consider the Consistorial way. If the mother's not Jewish and she didn't convert, and the child didn't convert, then the child is not considered a Jew. But there's no question about a child who wants to study in the school. He cannot reject that child, if the child wants to learn Judaism.

So I think that the youth have to be taken care of. It's not just the responsibility of each family. They are the future of the community, and we have to care for them together. They have to know that we care for them and accept them. We have to support their projects, such as the theater, and help them financially. And we are helping them, just as they are helping us.

The Lubavitch are another issue. They are very single-minded. They believe that they know what's good for the Jewish community. They know what they want, and they won't accept other views. I consider them to be dogmatists. There isn't much difference between them and the Muslim dogmatists, except that the Muslim dogmatists are killing people and the Jews aren't. But mentally, they are the same. Their views are correct [according to themselves], and there is no discussion.

The problem is that the Lubavitch created a Jewish school. They wouldn't say it this way, but the fact is that the school's here mainly because they wanted a place to put their own children so they wouldn't be mixed with goyim. So they created this school for their own children, and they are attracting other children whose parents agree with their point of view. So there is this school here in Dijon that is a school of rejection of other people and of extraction of children from French society. It's a position that I cannot accept.

Jewish schools in bigger cities, in Brussels and Paris, are different because children are sent there to receive a Jewish education, to learn the Jewish religion, and not mainly to become separated from French society. But here, apparently, we see this principle of exclusion, of separation from the French community in order to preserve purity and avoid any mixing. I'm not supporting this, and most of the community isn't supporting this. So the Lubavitch and their adherents are very upset with the community because it isn't supporting them. But we don't agree with their principles, and we don't have money to give them. We don't think that there are enough Jews to support such a school.

There also was the matter of the religious services. The Lubavitch wanted to have parallel services in another room. We forbade it. They wanted to know why this was bothering us. I told them that we have a rabbi, we are satisfied with what he is doing, we are paying him, and we don't see why there should be a parallel service in another room. Then the rabbi—this happened in a general meeting—spoke and said that if we allow the Orthodox to have a separate service, we should allow the liberals to do so, and so on. He said that this is a small community, it isn't the Tower of Babel, and it has to be united. I personally agree with this point of view, so I collected all the keys to the community rooms.

You know, they were even grabbing people so that they had enough for their **minyan**. They were in the main room and were catching people [and taking them out to join] their services. That is unacceptable to us. They also wanted to segregate the women from the men; they wanted the separation, a larger **mechitzah**. We knew that the majority of the community, especially the women, didn't want that. The women have the right to see the rabbi, they have the right to hear and see what's going on. I don't think that it's a sacrilege if the women are watching. You have to accept certain things, even more so in French society today.

But the Lubavitch do bring positive things to the community. They are very active with the youth.... That's why I'm not rejecting them. We are trying to bring them together with us, but we also have our way of life, and we don't want to cut our ties with the French community. That's very important, and they have to understand that. If we wanted to cut the ties, we would have left for Israel. We want to live in France as Jews, and we don't want to be completely living in a ghetto. They have to accept that.

I always was concerned with Jewishness, with the Jewish people. I am very much concerned about Israel. I have asked myself how to be a Jew in an open society, how to fight against anti-Semitism, how to apply my ideas to action. This is not easy. How do I stay a Jew when not practicing religion or going to Israel? That's the question we are asking ourselves. How do you consider yourself a Jew when you don't go to the synagogue or go to Israel? It's a question I don't yet have an answer for.

Okay, I speak Yiddish with my parents, but when they aren't here anymore, with whom do I speak it? Hebrew, I speak only in Israel. That's the language of the country. It's not the language of the Jews. There is no more language of the Jews, as was true of Yiddish. So what does being Jewish consist of right now? What will it be for the next generation? Will it be only religion? These are difficult questions that I'm asking myself quite often.

I did not join B'nai B'rith, first of all, because I'm against all secret societies. They're like Jewish Masons. I don't like the secrets. Second, I think that if you have something interesting to say, it should be discussed openly. And discussed in sessions open to everybody, not in closed sessions. Third, belonging to the organization required time and work, and in the evening I was tired, I didn't want to go. Those are the main reasons why I didn't join.

I know that there are internal divisions in the organization right now. I think that the community of Dijon is too small for that kind of stuff. We need new people. That's what's making me afraid for the future. If there is no youth coming to Dijon from the mixed marriages, the future is bad. I don't think the religious or Israelis are too concerned about mixed marriages. Yet, I think that it's the main point for most Jews right now. If people are not getting married with "Jewishness," then everything is coming apart, [there's no future]. For me, it's important. But the number of mixed marriages in Dijon, in France, are more than 50 per cent. Officially, it's 50 per cent, but it's more. On the board now are people who are married to non-Jews. Their children won't take over [their duties and responsibilities] after them, that's for sure. However, there is an exception. One of the board members married to a non-Jew has a daughter who doesn't consider herself a Jew, but the son became a Lubavitch.

The thing is, you have to show the youth that it's interesting to be Jewish, to spend time among Jews, to speak about Jewish history, and not focus just on religion, because that can be counterproductive. I'm afraid that if they are offered only religion, they will reject everything. There must be other activities. One of those activities is to meet other Jewish youth from other cities. But there is a problem here in Dijon and in other communities that involves what I would call "Jewish hypocrisy": people won't travel on the Sabbath, and so they can't send their children away for a week [to meet with other youth]. But the hypocrisy is that they keep their shops open, they go to the markets and do shopping on the Sabbath. The youth here don't come together. There is competition between their groups. I have the sense that it was better six or seven years ago.

It's necessary to build links between the Jewish and non-Jewish communities. There are people interested in Jews, in Judaism, who don't know how to approach us. That is why, when the synagogue is repaired, I want to bring material from the Jewish museum in Paris and open the doors so that French people can come and see what a synagogue is, see Jewish artistic stuff. We also want to organize cultural events.

The role of the radio, I would say, is mainly to inform non-Jews rather than the community. Of course, Jews listen, but a lot weren't listening when it was on the air a few years ago. The problem is that it can't stay on the air without assistance. We offer rooms to Radio Shalom now and try to help as much as we can, but they can't expect money every month. That's impossible for us. The donations are going down from year to year, and when the parents die, the children don't take over the donations. Also, people from mixed marriages don't contribute.

I don't think that it's a good idea for politicians to speak on the radio. It gives the community too much importance for its size. There probably is self-satisfaction in having important people come, but, in fact, these people give us too much importance. It's not a good idea to maintain the impression among non-Jewish people that the small Jewish community of Dijon is so important. One of the main points of anti-Semitism is that the Jewish world is very powerful. Even my neighbors think that Jews have too much power in economic and financial fields. And when you invite political people, political personalities, they will tell you what you want to hear. And that's not so interesting. It's important to have good relations with them, but you don't have to give them the impression that what they say is really important. They are friendly with us because I'm sure that they think we have a lot of strength. That's why they are giving us so much money to repair the synagogue. It's true that it's a cultural monument, but they know that the community cannot exist without the synagogue. If they really didn't care, they would have left us with the synagogue closed and given us an apartment downtown, and that's it.

As for our relations with the Muslims, there should be contacts. But they are not as organized as we are. There are many tendencies within their community. If, one day, there is an organization and a reason for us to meet with them, certainly we will do so.

I cannot predict what the future of the Jewish community in Dijon, or even in France, will be. Nobody is a prophet. The religious people say that only religion is the way, and that is not entirely false. But for me that is too conservative. It is not the modern way of living. To keep the Jewish community alive with just traditional religion would be very difficult. And to do so with the mixed marriages will be very difficult. I'm somewhat pessimistic.

What influence does the proximity of Israel have? Probably 80 per cent[*] of Jews in France have never visited Israel. The French are very French, and sometimes they are more French than Jewish. They certainly are more French than pro-Israel. Israel is close, but if they don't have family in Israel, they wouldn't be interested in it. Now, you see, the people who go to Israel to live are only the religious. It's not a socialist Zionism anymore. It's only when you feel you can't live your religion normally that you go.

I think that, since Jews were always persecuted, they were always on the side of poor and lost people. We have a tendency to help people who need help; the Jewish philosophy is to go and help the weaker. And there was always a tendency among Jews to be Leftists, despite the fact that the world thought that Jews always were wealthy. But very rich Jews are a minority,

---

[*] Actually, the reverse is true: Most Jews in France have visited Israel. See, for example, Erik H. Cohen, *The Jews of France Today: Identity and Values* (Amsterdam: Brill, 2011, 191.

despite what people think. In Dijon the social level is not very high. There are a lot of civil servants, professors, and, of course, a few in liberal professions, like doctors.

I think that Jewishness is more a moral way of life rather than a confessional religion. Of course, I was shocked when my father told me about the Jewish bordellos in Vilna; for me, a Jewish man, Jewish women were morally perfect. And now, in France, we have Jewish gangsters. But still, we believe that Jewish people should behave differently from other people and show that they have a higher morality, despite whether they practice religion or not. We have a morality to do the best for people, to practice charity, and not to be so involved with our personal Jewishness and be closed in among ourselves, not to be interested only in our own problems. That's why I didn't move to Israel. But I am still a Zionist. I still consider that the place of Jews is in Israel. Yet, I think that when Jews are among themselves, they don't behave like Jews anymore.

Albert Huberfeld

*For many years, Albert Huberfeld has been at the center of Jewish
life in Dijon. An activist in the community, he has held leadership
positions in the synagogue as well as the cultural center. Until his
retirement several years ago his haberdashery in the city's central
business district was an unofficial gathering place, where news
and opinions were exchanged. He continues to have a major role in
community affairs, now serving as president of the cultural center and
treasurer of the synagogue center.*

Spring 1993

I was born in Dijon, but my parents came from Poland. My father migrated
to France in 1934 and began work as a tailor. My mother's family moved
from Poland to Germany, and from there everybody went their own way:
one uncle to England, another to Israel, a third to France. My mother was
living with her brother in England. She was very happy. Jews had a better
life in England where people are more accepting. But the family wanted my
mother to marry, so they found a Polish Jew and sent her to Dijon. She didn't
have a choice. It was an arranged marriage. That too was in 1934.

During the war, my family left Dijon and hid in the countryside near
Macon. We traveled there in a truck, hiding behind furniture. When we were
there, Catholic people helped us. I don't have many memories from that time
because I was too little, but I think that we were happy there. One big problem
was food, so my mother got involved in the black market, trading in clothes
and things like that. There were risks. My father hid at first, but then, since
he had acquired French citizenship, he joined the army. Because he knew
Polish and German, he worked as a translator. When my father returned, I
was six years old. I didn't know him. He was a stranger to me. Fortunately,
no one in my immediate family died. All of my mother's family were living
in other countries, but my father had 12 brothers and sisters, and only two
survived. One returned from Auschwitz, but his wife and son had disappeared.

After the war, my family returned to Dijon. My father felt that he belonged
to France and to Dijon. We got our apartment back and money for the furniture that had been taken. My father brought back a prisoner of war he had
met, a German who also was a tailor. He worked in the shop my parents
opened and became almost part of the family. Of course, my brother and I
also helped our parents.

In public school during the 1950s I didn't encounter any anti-Semitism,
but there weren't many Jews in school either. My parents' friends were

Jewish; everybody spoke Yiddish. We lived in a downtown neighborhood on the rue Berbisey. The French Jews, who were more integrated in society, considered themselves a higher class and didn't like the Polish Jews. They didn't mingle with the Poles except when necessary in the synagogue. Even the Russian Jews, who were better educated, were higher. Among all the groups, the Polish Jews were considered the lowest class. Later, of course, came the pieds noirs. Then Polish Jews and French Jews had more things in common.

In the 1950s I did my bar mitzvah with a very good young French rabbi. He was an Ashkenazi like the others during that time. Some came from the East; they were very strict. They taught us in the Talmud Torah. We also had a shammes who had a very strong Polish accent. He was a very good singer, but his accent was terrible. Even though we had a hard time understanding him, he was good for the community.

Back then, Polish Jews suffered a lot from the aftereffects of the war. They did not hold on to religion; they did not really believe in it anymore. They still prayed, but their belief was not strong, though they felt Jewish and lived among Jews. I remember when my uncle came back from the camp and could not find his wife and son. For him, religion did not exist anymore. There was no God. He became an alcoholic. When he married again, it was to a non-Jewish woman.

My parents were different, but they were a little like the other Polish Jews. They prayed when they went to the synagogue maybe three times a year. They celebrated Yom Kippur, but that was it. They did what they had to do, but they were not religious. We children felt more strongly Jewish because we heard so many times about the war and the atrocities. Even if we had never gone to Shabbat, we were Jewish. Gentiles called us Israélites, but we did not use that word.

When I finished school, my parents decided that I would go into the clothing business with them. We had the shop in Dijon, but my father wanted to expand. My father wanted my brother to work with him also, but my mother didn't agree. Georges went off to Paris to study dentistry. I stayed to work with my father. He bought a truck and we traveled, selling clothes. My mother stayed and worked in the shop in Dijon.

Early in the 1960s, I went to Israel expecting to do my military service there. At that time, France and Israel had an arrangement. Since I didn't speak Hebrew, I couldn't go into the army right away, so I lived on a kibbutz. I lived there for about a year. There were people from all over making their aliyah. People spoke French. They were from France, Belgium, Switzerland, and North Africa. The people from Morocco had to go to France first and do their **haksharot** for the aliyah. I found myself living with people like that. It was an incredible experience. And, at the time, it was not dangerous. There weren't any problems with Lebanon. We talked with Lebanese people on the border. Of course, at night, we had guards. I did my turn too; that's how I learned to use an Uzi [submachine gun].

When I was about to enter the army in Israel, I had to return to France. My mother had separated from my father, and now she was alone and ill. I went back to stay with her. My brother couldn't because he was doing his French military service. Later, I also did my French military service. Though it was during the Algerian War, I served in France and Germany. There, I met a rabbi from North Africa. He was very nice, but he couldn't drive, so I became his chauffeur.

I returned to Dijon after my service and worked selling refrigerators, washing machines, electronics, things like that. But I always was thinking about Israel. So, in 1965, I went back. I felt that I wanted to stay forever. I lived in a regular kibbutz [not one based on absorbing immigrants], and studied Hebrew eight hours a day for three months. It was during that time that I met Myrna. They [Kibbutz members] had found me a job in Tel Aviv, working in a shopping center. But it wasn't enough, especially with the tax of 150 per cent on the car I had brought with me. I decided that if I returned to France, worked, and earned more money, I could return to Israel later. So I went back.

Once back in France, I decided not to return to Israel except for a volunteer three-month period after the Six Day War because it was hard to make a living there at that time. It's a wonderful country, and I was happy to be there, but it was hard for a little Frenchman who is used to comfort to live there. I kept in touch with Myrna, writing in French and Hebrew [she was from South Africa and predominantly spoke English]. She could not understand me very well, and she thought I wrote asking her to come to France to get married. Well, I don't remember writing anything like that! But she did come to France, and we ended up getting married.

When I returned to France, I noticed that there were a lot of pied noirs at the synagogue. They were new people. It was difficult for us, the Ashkenazim, because now we were a minority. We had to get used to new traditions, new ways of praying. The rabbi was an Algerian, a Sephardi. And there was the risk of a schism because of differences between the Tunisians and the Algerians over the rituals and personalities. Most people weren't tolerant. Fortunately, because we were a small community, a split didn't happen.

I think that it was hard for the Sephardim to establish themselves. They spoke French and had their citizenship, but to Catholics they still looked like

Arabs. And many of them previously had comfortable lives, even if they did not earn very much. In France, life was different. But for us, the Ashkenazim, we discovered a new category of Jews. For those of us who were young, like me, it was easy to get used to them. They added something to the community. The community was expanding, becoming more important.

What made everybody remember they were Jewish was the Six Day War. It had a major influence on people. That entire month [of the war] was terrible. That was when de Gaulle made his statement about Jews.[*] At the time, France was helping Israel. Then, the French government's attitude changed. People here were very worried. They supported Israel, including contributing money, I assume. I'm not sure about all the support because I soon left to work in Israel for three months.

But, you know, despite de Gaulle, many French non-Jews understood. Some even gave money. Because even though there is anti-Semitism in France, there is a negative feeling towards the Arabs. That is why many Frenchmen helped Israel financially. They liked what Israel was doing. They were winning against the Arabs. And they were upset with de Gaulle because of Algeria.[†]

When I came back to Dijon after my three-month stay, I worked here for a time and then opened a little shop. It was 1968.[‡] While we were getting the shop ready, the workmen had to hide inside to continue their work because everybody was on strike and people were marching in the streets. Most of the big demonstrations, however, were in Paris. De Gaulle resigned after that. I didn't really care that he did. The Jewish community was angry with him because he didn't support Israel.

In the 1970s the old Ashkenazim still directed the community. They were the ones who re-established the community after the war. Otherwise, it would have disappeared. They also supported it because the Sephardim were not used to contributing money for events and for the rabbi's salary. It was hard for the Sephardim also because they were mostly workers and didn't have much money. In the 1980s things got better. They wanted to be in the community and understood the system. Some also held offices in the administration of the community alongside the Ashkenazim.

I got involved with the community in the 1970s, first with cultural events, then with almost everything. During my days in Israel, my position as a Jew had changed a bit. I became more Zionist. I was not very religious, but

---

[*] In November 1967, in a press conference, President de Gaulle declared that the Jews were "an elitist people, self-assured and domineering."

[†] Following a violent war of independence, Algeria became independent of France in 1962.

[‡] The year of student and worker demonstrations in many parts of France, especially large cities.

I was proud to be a Jew. We stay Jewish no matter what happens to us. Our obligation is to continue that. I feel stronger about being a Jew than about being religious. It is important not to hide that you are a Jew. And that is why I tried to be helpful in the community.

It started little by little. Myrna and I went to community events; we started to go to cultural events. We participated in dinners, and we also participated in exchanges with other towns. After the shammes retired, the community decided to change some of the rooms [in the cultural center]. I wanted to help with the construction, the renovation. At the time, we had a president who had many projects in mind but who never carried them out. He would bring up an idea and let others do something about it. We also had a lot of members who would participate initially, and then for some reason they would quit.

I was the one who stayed because I felt an obligation as a Jew and as a member of the community. The community could survive with only praying, but it would be better off with some cultural events, too. Suddenly, then, I found myself involved in many things, including an organization, the UGIF,[*] which raised money for Israel. After the UGIF I was asked to present myself as a candidate for the synagogue Board. I think I was asked because they wanted to balance the number of Ashkenazim with Sephardim. I was elected.

I was one of 12 elected members of the Board. There are elections every three years. One of the duties of the Board is to elect the president and two vice-presidents, who are the heads of the community. The Board members also pick the general treasurer. Women also, since the 1970s, have sat as elected members of the Board.

One very important event we organized was the centenary of the synagogue in 1979. We had to establish a budget and raise money because we did not want to use the communal funds. We held dances, a concert, an art exhibition, events like that. And afterwards, members of the cultural committee, including myself, would clean up. We used the money to repair the temple and for the centenary exposition. People came from all over. It was amazing.

June 2005

During our first interview 12 years ago, I said that there was discrimination against Polish Jews by Jews of French origin. Now I want to explain a little about what happened when the North Africans arrived. First, let me tell you that the Polish Jews who came to France were not well educated, even

---

[*] Union Générale des Israélites de France, The General Union of French Israelites/Jews. After the 1967 Six Day War, more French Jews began to refer to themselves as Jews rather than as Israélites, so that the current translation of UGIF would be General Union of French Jews.

in comparison to the Russian Jews. That is because the Polish Jews were excluded from schools in Poland, in particular the universities. So they were not well educated, and the reception to them was rather cold. They could not be assimilated easily.[*]

In comparison, the North Africans were rather educated. They spoke French perfectly. Among them were salaried folk, some civil servants, managers. The French Jews were also managers, professionals. So they had that in common. But what really made the difference was the numbers. Unfortunately, there were the deportations during the war, and those who survived were aging. So very soon the Sephardim dominated; the Ashkenazim were in the minority, though they continued to hold the offices until the 1970s. We can say that the community was unique: there was cooperation and participation between the two groups.

The Ashkenazim, in my opinion, were very tolerant in everything. They let the newcomers do things their way. On the other hand, the Sephardim at the time had to make more adjustments. There were problems among them because they came from different colonies—from Tunisia, Morocco, Algeria. They had different rituals, but they worked things out.

There was a period of calm in the 1980s and early 1990s until the Lubavitch family arrived. They came with the intention of rebuilding Dijon Judaism—and that brought problems. In spite of all our efforts to be within traditional French Consistorial standards, our attempts at common work, of common activities, of building a communal life, they found us not rigorous enough and wanted to impose their own practices. At first we tried to accommodate them, but we ended by making all the compromises. If we had done what they wanted, we would have lost 90 per cent of our members. These people in general are intolerant. In their eyes, we were not sufficiently Orthodox, or sufficiently religious, or too cool to maintain decorum during services. So the groups began to separate. By Yom Kippur of 2003, when separate services were held, the break was final. Now, they have their own services, their own school.

As for anti-Semitism, I see no signs of it, no signs of racism. The rabbi does a good job of representing us to the other religious communities. He is

---

[*] This statement is inaccurate. In 1920, nearly 25 per cent of university students in Poland were Jewish; that percentage—and the raw number—declined throughout the 1920s and 1930s, but Jews still formed 10 per cent of the university students in 1937–38. See J. Marcus, *Social and Political History of the Jews in Poland, 1919–1939* (Berlin: Walter de Gruyter, 1983) Table 19. Between 1919 and 1937 330,000 Jews left Poland, more than a third of them going to the Palestine Mandate, but a large number to France, too. Studies suggest that the roughly 500,000 Poles, both Jews and Gentiles, who immigrated to France from Poland in the period came from working-class and peasant families, which does explain the "not well-educated" comment.

on good terms with them. The media here is very open, too. Of course, there are problems in the large cities where there are important Jewish communities. The North African Arabs/Muslims who live in the suburbs import the conflicts of the Middle East, and that results in difficulties. Naturally, we all wish that the problems of the Middle East were solved. We all want peace. But I believe that peace will take more time than people imagine. Signing treaties is one thing, but changing mentalities after 60 years of friction will take a long time. And, though it may not be severe, there will always be a certain amount of anti-Semitism in France, on both the Left and the Right. This would be true even if the problem of the Muslims were solved.

There is a natural foundation of anti-Semitism in France. Even though the Pope decided to take a large step forward towards the Jews and even if he follows the lead of the young people, there will nonetheless remain some anti-Semitism. It is part of the French mentality. The politicians swear that they are against anti-Semitism, but that is a lot of talk. For example, between what politicians say and what judges in the courts often do, there's a difference. The troublemakers are arrested, then the judges release them, so as not to make waves. Everyone knows the national problem: it's that 10 per cent of the population is North African in origin. And that represents 10 per cent of the voters. And there is no politician who can ignore that fact.

After all his experiences, I think that no Jew can trust politicians as they are. Just look back through the years, through the centuries. What we must do, then, is to remain vigilant. Vigilant. Listen to what the politicians say, read between the lines, maintain constant surveillance, do not automatically believe all that is said. Because we all know that the goal of a politician is to be elected and reelected. Because of that, a politician can change ideas according to the times. Therefore, we really cannot trust them completely. That is why we say that a Jew must always have his suitcase on the bed, ready to be packed so that he can leave quickly.

However, at the moment we can say that we have a calm community in Dijon that functions correctly. We have a rather dynamic cultural center, with many activities open to the public. Judeo-Christian relations are excellent. This is thanks to the work of the rabbi. We would like a greater participation of our members, of our faithful, it's true, but unfortunately voluntary participation is down, and that's a problem for all associations now.

Interview update (June 2006)

In the past year we had elections, as we do every two years, and we now have a stable Board, well-balanced, that works easily. There are 12 elected members, including a president, vice-president, secretary, and treasurer.

Board members are now elected for four years, with half renewed every two years. In last year's election, we had nine candidates for six positions. All votes are by secret ballot. Officers, including the president, can succeed themselves. Meetings of the Board generally are held every six weeks or so.

The CCJD, the Jewish cultural center of Dijon—a new cultural association created to parallel the religious association—also has a similar governing board, with 12 members, including the secretary, who also is editor of the journal *Mazal Tov*. The journal presents the life of the community and is a tie that helps bind it together. The cultural program of the center is usually well done, with lecturers, films with Jewish themes, authors, and so forth. But since we have a relatively small active community, our resources are limited. With films, it is much easier. We pay for the cost of renting the film; with a lecturer, the cost is higher. Since there is no official fundraising for the cultural programs, the operating budget comes from dues the community pays. Included in the dues is a subscription to *Mazal Tov*. We always manage to fill the journal with news articles, press releases, reviews. Also, of course, articles written by the rabbi and members of the community. Of course, getting enough people to submit articles from such a small community is always a problem, but we manage.

You know, we accept non-Jews as equal participants in the cultural center. These are friends of the community, faithful sympathizers. One of them, Sister Odile, a loved and respected Catholic nun of Polish origin, militates for Jewish-Christian understanding and for support for Israel. Nearly blind, living modestly, in her seventies, Sister Odile writes texts for courses she still offers. Recently members of the Jewish community have come to believe that Sister Odile was born Jewish.[*] There also are a number of Christians who attend services in the synagogue from time to time.

Fortunately, we are able to run well-budgeted organizations because we have no debts. We have balanced accounts. We manage by increasing our dues annually, usually by about 2 per cent on average. There has been no debate about it. There are economically weaker members, of course, but we gladly accept what they can give. There really is no possibility of attempting to make them contribute more than they can afford. During holidays, we accept everyone; the synagogue is open to all. We do not charge for holiday services.

So, it has gone well for us this past year. The Talmud Torah is being taught, though the number of children is declining. The kindergarten functions, has

---

[*] Sister Odile indicated that this was not the case in a discussion with Robert Weiner in June 2010.

ten or 12 children and has classes on Wednesdays and Sunday mornings. The rabbi does the bar mitzvahs and marriages, though there haven't been any bar mitzvahs this year. The youth organization no longer exists, but the scouts and B'nai B'rith continue to function. The group for senior citizens, however, is not functioning well. WIZO is so-so. Fortunately, though, two women are elected members of the synagogue board, and most of the members of the cultural center council are women.

Radio Shalom is also doing well. It broadcasts from the synagogue proper. At present, there are three people working there, two under contract and the third hired as part of a subsidized government program to provide employment for young people. A core of community members volunteer their work, but we are always looking for more volunteers to create programs.

In regards to support for the national organization in Paris [the Consistory Council], there are possibly 50 or 60 donors from Dijon. That is from a community membership here of approximately 200 families. It is difficult, you know, to motivate donors, except when there is some sort of crisis. We do not have any really large donors in the synagogue. Neither for Israel, nor for anything else. Some members give extra, of course, for the **High Holy Days**. What this means is that all members of the community must contribute. Then, when there are departures, or deaths, they aren't replaced.

Therefore, the problem of the community is the lack of youth. We don't have to discuss this in Board meetings because it is obvious, and we see that there is no solution. We can advertise that life is beautiful in Dijon, but if there is no employment, even if life is beautiful, without employment no one will come. Families won't install themselves here if there isn't work. We don't need more dentists or lawyers. We lack industries, laboratories, factories. And the economy is getting weaker. When an economy doesn't grow, it declines automatically. So for the Jewish community of Dijon to continue, we need economic growth in the entire region.

The older members, the Ashkenazim, are dying off. Those families rarely attended the synagogue, but they were the large donors. From experience we realized that there are different motivations between the Ashkenazim and Sephardim regarding dues. Among the Ashkenazim, there is a tradition of support and contributions to the synagogue. It's a principle. Those people make the large donations, but they don't come to the synagogue. We rarely see them. However, in the Sephardi case, one comes to the synagogue often, makes small donations, gives small contributions. Now, the majority of the Ashkenazim are retired. They are only about 20 per cent of the community.

Even the Lubavitch are experiencing the same thing. I realize that they haven't grown much either. They have financial problems more serious than ours. I have been told that they have problems making the social security contributions to the state that they are required to make because of the people employed in their school. They pay their people's salaries but not their social security contributions. And, you know, the state doesn't give away gifts. One must pay the state, one way or the other. But I don't believe that their problems will cause them to unite with us. The Lubavitch Orthodoxy, which is rigid, cannot evolve to our side. It's the way the rituals are conducted. We are far more moderate religiously than they are. If we become more Orthodox, we are going to lose our faithful [the majority of liberal or secular Jews]. We have a traditional community. We are more open; we cannot go back to the past.

A problem for the future is the rabbi. He is now over 60. He can retire when he wants to do so. And perhaps now, another rabbi will have much higher demands. There are no longer a lot of candidates in the rabbinical school. Of course, we could use someone who did Jewish studies, who is not a rabbi, someone we call an officiating minister, but there are expenses and demands related with that, too. It may be a large problem, because here we don't often find volunteers.

Turning to Israel again, I also have confidence in the future, except that for me, the future is evolving. Obtaining peace is an evolutionary process. Peace with a capital "P" is going to take a long time. Well, in the meantime, there is the status quo, and the barrier fence is in place.* The security risks are lessened. Let's hope that, internationally speaking, Israel can retake its place among the nations, that is, if the government, after abandoning Gaza, demolishes the isolated settlements in the West Bank and the illegal settlements, too. Perhaps then Israel will be treated with greater respect.

But, of course, there is the mentality of the Arabs. With the Palestinians, Hamas, and the events in Lebanon, unfortunately that mentality will continue because everything is in the mind. When one has been told for 60 years that the Jew, meaning Israel, is the bad guy, is evil—a murderer—it takes a very long time to change one's mind.

I don't think that Iraq and Iran are issues for Israel. Israel is not on a war footing regarding them. It is not directly threatened. Iran, I think, is the equivalent of a scarecrow. They talk a lot more than they do. Even having the [nuclear] bomb won't change anything for them. Because the Iranian

---

* Established fence or a wall separating the West Bank from Israel's pre-1967 territory in order to hinder terrorism and control the movement of people across its border.

bomb would be a little like the Israeli bomb: it is there, above all, to intimidate. Of course, there is always the possibility that one of the radical terrorist groups could get a bomb, but that is, at the moment, remote. It is a frightening possibility, of course, but we can't think too much about that at the moment. There is speculation that the United States might attack Iran's nuclear sites, but I don't think that that will happen. There will be negotiations first. My preference is that the United States doesn't bomb Iran. That really should be the final, most extreme, solution.

As for the fanatics, there is only one solution: kill them. But, you know, the more you kill, the more of them there are. When life doesn't have any worth, when the youth don't give any value to life, there is nothing worse than that—when there is no respect for life. So whether it's Hamas or Fatah, or Hezbollah, Israel has to defend itself. Unfortunately, a future of peace is still far off.

Since we have last spoken, my opinions and that of my friends regarding the United States have not changed. I believe that the Jews are the best supporters of the United States because that country has used its treasure to support Israel. Even if Jews don't like certain American administrations, they continue their support because they know that without the United States Israel would be in a very difficult situation, internationally speaking.

Here in France, after the riots of the Muslim youth in the suburbs in the fall of 2005, and events in Gaza and Lebanon then still in process, and [Israeli President] Ariel Sharon's unilateral but uneventful withdrawal [from Gaza in 2005], I assume that among the French there will be a little less anti-Zionism and therefore, also, perhaps, a little less anti-Semitism. There is, of course, Muslim anti-Semitism. That is difficult. And that is a question mark. It also is a question of economics. If the youth find work, if they can live, then they have less time to think of anti-Semitism. So this is also a problem of unemployment, of inactivity.

There is also the Arab mentality, represented by the kidnapping, torture, and killing in Paris of a young Jewish man this year. When Ilan Halimi was kidnapped, tortured, left to die, apparently with the knowledge of neighbors not directly involved, this caused a great outcry among Jews and the French [Chirac] government. It is shocking that in the twenty-first century people can act in such a barbaric way. And they imagine that because we are Jewish that we are rich [the kidnappers expected a large ransom], that we are supported by everyone. What this demonstrates is a narrow spirit that is serious, dangerous.

I know that, especially in Paris, there are families that are planning to leave France or who have older children they want to leave. This is not true yet in Dijon, I think. But in Paris there are neighborhoods where it is dangerous to go out with a skullcap or a beard or showing the Star of David. I understand that there are Jews in those neighborhoods who plan to move to Israel. There are a lot of racist acts, acts of anti-Semitism not only in Paris but in other big cities like Lyon and Toulouse. But most of the anti-Semitic acts occur in Paris, of course, where there is the largest concentration of Jews, about 350,000.

My role is to remain here and serve the community. I serve the community daily as a volunteer. I do not consider it work. I am immersed in management of the finances, maintenance of the properties, taking care of the repairs, and so forth. I regard what I do as my Jewish duty. Yet, I feel 100 per cent French. I am a citizen of France. True, I am of Polish ancestry, but I was born here. And I have as many non-Jewish friends and social relationships as I do with Jews. My wife and I live in the city; we have a public life; we are not marginal. We see everyone. Of course, if it were a question of Israel against France in international sports competition, I would have a problem. But I probably would support Israel, because if it's David and Goliath, I support David.

In any case, I have retired. I have passed the age for moving to Israel. I will stay in Dijon with my family members, my friends and acquaintances. Life here in Dijon is decent. The city is agreeable, most beautiful. So why not stay? I am a Dijonnais from birth.

In the past, there was a Burgundian mentality, a regional way of looking at things. Now, with the influx of Italians, Spanish, people who were displaced from Africa, others, there no longer is a regional mentality. This certainly makes Dijon more interesting. And we have the good luck to be in the center of France, connected by highways, TGV [high-speed] trains, an airport. Now we have a Jew who is assistant mayor, Françoise Tenenbaum, of whom we are proud. Though I am not always in agreement with her political ideas, I know that we all support her. It's a good thing to have a Jewish representative who is not ashamed of her origins. I am glad that we have such a personality in City Hall. She is dedicated and extremely hard-working, an efficient and very dynamic person.

Before I conclude, I will give my opinion of mixed marriages because the issue is connected to the question of the future of French Jews. I must say that I am not for mixed marriages. In my opinion, life together, in view of the existing difficulties of current life, in view of the number of divorces, even among Jews, is hard enough. Under the circumstances, if one hopes to have the luck of having one's marriage survive, it's of utmost importance to marry someone of one's own religion. Now, of course, mixed marriages are not tragedies, either. Rather than remaining unmarried, rather than seeing young people alone, then so be it. But first, I am a proponent of Jewish marriages.

Allow me to speak about my attitude towards our daughter. We have done everything to provide her with examples of our community engagement. If one day she gets married to a non-Jew, she is still our daughter and we will love her as much. We will not have too many regrets. We may be somewhat saddened by this mixed marriage, but we would reproach ourselves less than if we were in a very strict religious community. This is my opinion.

In France as a whole, there is some disaffection in our synagogues, in our organizations. What is felt is the growing risk of mixed marriages. It's a problem for the future. Fortunately, in Dijon, we have a rather open community. So we gladly accept sympathizers, converted or not. For the majority of us, someone who has converted is a Jew. He made the effort, knowing that to convert in France, in the Consistorial way, is particularly difficult. So, bravo! We can embrace the Jew who has converted.

You see, conversion in France is now more difficult. The Consistory Council is strict. But the problem is very complex. I understand well the reasoning of the rabbinical Consistory court that prefers fewer Jews perhaps, but good or, in any case, serious Jews. Therefore, conversions are not easy. They believe that conversions in mixed marriages are often only a matter of convenience. Then there is the issue of the children of such marriages, and perhaps it should be easier for them.

Our rabbis, our wise men, think that reforming the law is not an ideal solution. All the religions that have reformed themselves, in general, have not disappeared perhaps, but they have done poorly, meaning that they have lost some of their core beliefs. Once reforms begin, often there aren't any limits. However, I personally would make conversion a little easier, especially for mixed couples. We definitely should make it easier for children of a mixed couple.

A long time ago I visited the United States. I have continued to read, and it is said that the United States is a country of liberty. It's true, there is a democratic spirit, and we see Jews there, more or less mixed, create new movements. We see that a lot in the United States, and these movements [within Judaism] adopt rules according to their members taking from one position, taking from another. They create particular communities with religious laws taken from a [conservative] position on one side and from liberal Judaism on the other. And in the end there is a question: Do so many movements within one religion weaken or dilute what remains of the basic religion?

I had once thought that the United States would return to a more Orthodox practice of Judaism, would come back to a religion a bit more traditional.

This problem, of course, does not exist in Israel. In Israel, one is generally obligated to respect the religious laws despite what one thinks. One respects the Shabbat; one respects the dietary laws. Whether one wants to or not, one is obligated to respect religion because Judaism is the religion of the state.

Of course, I do think that life in the diaspora will continue.* The Jewish population will become smaller, however; growth is minimal, except among the ultra-Orthodox families. We have already discussed the impact of mixed marriages. At the same time there may be some increase in aliyah.

---

* Jews the world over who live outside of Palestine/Israel, and who are, therefore, in exile from the Promised Land; a position no longer accepted by most non-Orthodox Jews.

Françoise Tenenbaum

Dr. Françoise Tenenbaum, the Deputy Mayor of Dijon for Solidarity and Health, is another public face of the Jewish community. She works tirelessly for the welfare of the people of Dijon and Burgundy, especially on issues of immigration, women's rights, and education. She is a founder of Radio Shalom, remains active in Jewish community activities, and publicly defends her community against anti-Semitism. She also is an elected member and vice-president of the Regional Council of Burgundy and the head of its Cultural Commission. She has been on the municipal governing body since the Socialist Party won both local and regional elections respectively in 2001 and 2004.

Spring 1993

My father's name was Levy, but he changed it during the war. He was a conscripted soldier who was imprisoned in the German Stalag XII B, a prisoner's camp in Frankenthal [Palatinate, Germany]. There, one of the French soldiers denounced my father by telling the Germans that he was Jewish. My father fortunately managed to escape the stalag with a friend, and they made their way back to France. He went to Lyon and began collaborating with the Resistance. That was when he decided to change his name to Lefebvre. After the war everyone knew him as Lefebvre, so he eventually kept the name. Separately and without knowing, his uncle did the same, but he changed his name to Lefort. They ended up having different names.

Before the war my parents lived in a French region called Alsace. Jews had been living there since the Middle Ages. During the war the Vichy government ordered the Jews to find out for how long their families had been living in France. My father found evidence dating back to the eighteenth century.

My father was born in Mackenheim, and his family lived in Scherwiller [both in the Lower Rhine]. My mother was born in Marckolsheim [also Lower Rhine]. My mother's maiden name was Woog. The history and origin of this last name is difficult to track. We know it is a rare name, possibly Dutch, and probably comes from Spanish Jews who migrated to Holland in the fifteenth century. Both my father's and my mother's families have been living in France for a long time. I therefore know that besides me being born in France, I am French. I am also related to the family of the famous Michel Debré who wrote the 1958 French Constitution—this is the 5th Republic Constitution and up to this day still rules—and also to the famous Laurent Fabius who, like Debré back in the late 1950s, has also been a French prime minister. I do feel French.

My parents met when they were children but lost track of each other during the war. They met again in Lyon and got married in 1945. They moved to Paris three years later.

It is difficult to get information about my family and what happened to them during the war. I do know that my father had a brother. Their parents—my grandparents, Sylvain Levy and Mathilde Ach Levy—were in their fifties when the war started. The Germans killed my 57-year-old grandfather on a road in Alsace because he refused to give them his bicycle. The Germans had their own cars but nevertheless killed him, took the bike, and left him dead on the side of the road. My grandmother then went to hide in a small town called Le Bugue in the French region of Aquitaine [southwestern France] with other Jewish as well as non-Jewish Alsatian families. My uncle, Georges Levy, was also made prisoner by the Germans. He was held five years and was forced to work on a farm in Germany. When he returned after the war, he had developed a heart problem. He came back sick, but at least he came back.

My mother also had a brother. His name was Felix Woog, but I do not really know his story. He probably was not a soldier because he was too young when the war started. My mother's father died from an infectious disease at the beginning of the war [there were no antibiotics at the time], and she and my grandmother moved to the French Vosges mountains where my mother was able to work for some time as a teacher. When the Germans arrived there, my mother, Jeanne Woog, moved to Lyon along with Cécile Borach Woog, her mother. She was not allowed to teach anymore because she was Jewish. She worked for some time in a department store, but after awhile they did not want her anymore, and things became complicated. My grandmother, who had worked with her father and afterwards with her husband in Alsace, was not able to work by herself during the war. Her world had disappeared.

Early one morning a German soldier knocked on their door. They were able to see who it was through a small hole in the door and did not open, because it was a soldier. The soldier finally stopped knocking and talked instead to a neighbor. When he left, the neighbor brought them a letter from an uncle who was in a concentration camp and was befriended by the soldier. The soldier came back next day to pick up a parcel. This time my grandmother and mother opened the door. The soldier said he was risking his life for this man. Unfortunately, the uncle never came back.

While my father was in Lyon at this time, the Germans found out that he was Jewish. He was requested, like all other Jews, to go to the Hôtel de Ville [City Hall] to register himself as a Jew. At the office there was a man working who was also in the Resistance and who said, "André, it is very nice of you to visit, but as you can see it is a busy day, so please come back another time." That saved my father's life.

My mother's family had a couple of houses in Alsace. After the war the houses were still there but without any furniture. Everybody in the town had trespassed and taken something, so she went around trying to get her belongings back. But other members of her family were hurt much more badly. My mother had five aunts and uncles who disappeared in the Shoah, although one of them, Arthur Borach,* had been holding office as deputy mayor of the town of Neuf-Brisach in 1934.

After their marriage my parents stayed a short while in Lyon and then moved to Paris. There my father worked with his uncles in the haute couture trade, selling fabrics such as silk and velvet. It was not a business in which his parents were involved. They were very poor cattle traders in a little town in Alsace. My father had to start working at age 14 because they did not have enough money to survive. After the war he got in touch with his uncles, whose parents had started a fabrics business in Paris in 1870 after the war with Germany because they wanted to remain French. Indeed, Alsace had at that time been occupied by Germany and as such became a German territory. Other members of their respective families stayed behind in Alsace under German occupation. In Paris, the uncles started out selling little pieces of textiles from a small shop under a porch. Eventually, the business grew. Since none of the uncles had sons to take over the business, my father and one of his cousins worked hard and eventually bought out the uncles' business by paying them until they died.

That side of the family was well-known and had a position of some status in Paris. They, for example, are among the financial founders of the famous French department store Les Galeries Lafayette. It is the same side of the family that Michel Debré comes from, as well as Laurent Fabius; Robert Hirsch, Résistant and senior official; and also Claude Lévi-Strauss, the famous cultural anthropologist. On my mother's side can also be cited Claude Bloch, former Director of the Nuclear Physics Institute [in Saclay, Essonne]. These persons studied in Paris's top universities and schools. For example, they and most of their sons graduated from the École Polytechnique de Paris. They all are from the part of the family that left Alsace in 1870. Those who stayed behind were poorer and not so well educated.

---

* Arthur Borach, born on December 20, 1894 at Neuf-Brisach (Haut-Rhin), died on 12 March 1944 at Auschwitz (Poland); see JORF 0198 (28 August 2009): 14256, text 67. His official position did not prevent him from being deported.

I had a brother born in Lyon, named Michel. He died shortly after my parents moved to Paris. It was very hard for my mother and she never really recovered, even after I was born in 1950 and another brother in 1953. Unusual for women in those times, my mother had a Bachelor's degree. In Alsace she had wanted to study dentistry, but her father did not allow her to go to Strasbourg, which was 50 kilometers from Marckolsheim, to study for it. She did not work outside the family business because it was uncommon at the time. However, she had many interests, especially art. She studied at the Louvre for some time.

My father did not have a degree, something that he always regretted. But he took night classes and managed to learn good English. His business grew, and eventually he had 70 or 80 employees. He started trading with Japan, selling them silk. He was also one of the first to reopen trade with Germany after the war, as well as doing business with the United States, United Kingdom, Canada, and the Middle East. He also sold French silk and velvet to Japan and began traveling every year to Kyoto and Kobe. He went there 30 times to show his collection. He invited me to go with him, but I unfortunately did not take the opportunity. When his cousin and partner retired in 1975, my father also quit and opened a smaller business that he called Velours de France [Velvet of France]. During his years in the business he was also an international trade adviser and one-time president of the Chambre Syndicale du Textile. He was in every sense a self-made man.

I spent my youth in Paris. I lived there until 1974. Our home was on the edge of the Paris Marais area, very close to the Beaubourg Museum, which was being built at the time, and also close to Les Halles, where my mother and I would go every Thursday morning to shop for fruit. I liked it a lot. Sometimes in the evenings we would go there to buy flowers. Vegetables, fruits, and flowers were fresher and cheaper there than anywhere else.

Naturally, I went to the public elementary school in the neighborhood. It was the time of the Algerian War. I remember that during the war only children were allowed to have milk. I also remember that during the Algerian coup* my father was in Holland. That was in 1960. He came back to Paris with tulips for my mother, who was very worried about the situation in the city. It was a time of trouble; sometimes I was afraid. My high school was in the Marais neighborhood close to the Carnavalet Museum. Since that time the Marais has changed. Now it is absolutely beautiful. The high

---

* An abortive military rebellion against the Fifth Republic that broke out in Algeria and was crushed by President/General Charles de Gaulle.

school, Victor Hugo, is located in front of Auguste Comte's house.[*] It is a very interesting place.

The Victor Hugo was an all-girls' public high school. The students were the daughters of people who worked in the textile industry, for which the Marais was well-known. And yes, I realized there I was a Jew. I remember, in particular, one episode. My parents had suffered a lot from the war but still celebrated the holidays, since my mother was religious. Every year I would take off from school for Rosh Hashanah, Yom Kippur. The year I was in sixth grade, I missed school for Rosh Hashanah, and my mother wrote an excuse saying that I had to go to a wedding. I turned in the note at eight o'clock, and at ten they called me back and asked me to bring my mother. When my mother arrived at the office, they told her, "We know why your daughter missed school, you suffered enough and you should not lie." And after that we always wrote the truth. My mother at the time did not dare say that it was for a Jewish holiday. We were afraid to say that we were Jewish. In fact, the word "Jew" did not even exist for us, we would instead say "Israélite."

But yes, there were a few other Jews in my class. There were others in my neighborhood, many immigrants from Eastern Europe, especially from Poland. I felt close to my Jewish classmates. I also had a Catholic friend with whom I walked to school because we lived in the same building; she lived on the floor above us. She is like a sister to me. I was also protected by my maiden name, Lefebvre, which is typically French. But I have never felt the need to hide my religious beliefs.

During those years we never talked about the war, just as we never talked about my brother Michel who died. We never talked about Michel— my second name is Michèle in his memory—because it was too much pain for my mother. As for the war, I asked my father about it; he never spoke of it because he did not want us to feel like Jews did not do enough. I think they just wanted to forget about it and start a new life.

I did receive a religious education. Every Sunday I would go to the Talmud Torah. I also did my **bat mitzvah** in the first group of girls who did it. That was at the Synagogue La Victoire, one of Europe's biggest synagogues built at the time of Napoleon III on rue de la Victoire in Paris. My parents used to go to another synagogue, Nazareth Synagogue, near the Place de la République. They sent us on holidays with a group of Jews, thanks to the Victoire, which had a youth organization. Then I pushed my parents go to the Victoire Synagogue where my friends were and where there was a special Shabbat eve service for the youth. Since it was the biggest synagogue in Paris, there

---

[*] Nineteenth-century French father of science-based positivist philosophy.

were more young people and more activities; the community there was made of settled French and Alsatian people, as well as Poles and families that had recently come from North Africa. In addition to my religious education, I learned things in the kids' camps. I used to go with my brother to a Jewish vacation camp sponsored by the Victoire Synagogue.

I was 17 during the Six Day War in 1967. It was my dream to go to Israel even though I did not speak Hebrew. We knew what was going on because we would bring radios to school. It was not allowed, but we nevertheless did it. At the time we did not have a television because my father was worried that my brother would never study should we have one. The very day after my brother graduated, my father bought a TV. He still has it.[*]

The following year, spring 1968, because of the students' and workers' rebellion, we did not have class for a long while. It was just impossible to take the written exams. Instead there were only oral exams, and we were not prepared for them. I remember that the day I took them was very hot, the exams were hard, and the professors were not focused. There was a demonstration against De Gaulle's government of almost 7,000 or 8,000 people marching from the Place de la Nation to the Hôtel de Ville. There was also another demonstration, this time in favor of de Gaulle on the Champs-Élysées with a lot of people. My father was singing the *Internationale*. He was a liberal although not enrolled in any party. He was a liberal for philosophical reasons: he believed that liberals are more open-minded, take more care of human rights, and are kinder to the Jewish community, not only to the Jews of France, but in general. As for Israel, my father was sympathetic but he never felt he had to settle there. He and my mother did go there in 1967 at the time of the Wall's liberation.[†] I went for the first time in 1970 with a group of young Jews.

In May 1968, I saw demonstrations and attended some of them. I went to the Sorbonne meeting in the grand amphitheater, and we held some meetings in my school [Pharmacy]. It was amazing. I really felt that we were doing something good. People were full of ideas. It was serious, too. We had hope; we were accomplishing things. But there were hard times as well. Once when I was taking an environmental class, the young woman professor came to class in tears. Her car had been burnt during a demonstration with her handwritten thesis in it; she had no copy.

---

[*] Tenenbaum's father died in 1997 (four years after this interview) aged 81. He passed away sitting on his sofa and watching TV after a dinner at a Paris restaurant with a friend.

[†] Protective Western Wall surrounding the Second Temple. East Jerusalem was reconquered by Israel from Jordan during the June 1967 Six Day War.

At this time it is impossible to say that the Shoah was present in our thinking. [Neither was] Israel, but we were more positive about that. We knew that anti-Semitism existed in France, even though perhaps we had not experienced it. Yes, and Vichy was a taboo subject that we did not talk about. We did not talk about it, but we knew the details. We are Jewish, and we have always been proud of it.

During that time when I was at the university, I did my first two years of pharmacology, and then I did environmental studies in the Science Department at Jussieu University in Paris and also in cartography at the National Geographic Institute. The people at Jussieu supported the Arab cause, as they called it. I would take down posters that were against Israel. They knew that I was Jewish, but I was not involved in any organizations. I knew Jews who were part of various Left groups, but I did not have time for those things. I never had time for myself because my mother was ill and I had to take care of the house.

I remember that when I was in high school, some people were organizing a demonstration for Vietnamese children. Of course, I was interested, so I went to the meeting, which took place in a café in the Marais area. They had drinks, and when I asked for a Coke they said that I could only have a Pepsi because Coke was American.* I left. Although I acted more privately, I did get into many of those discussions at school.

I met my husband Denis while on vacation in the Alps in 1971. His sister is married to my brother. They met before we did, and they asked us to go on vacation with them. That is how I met him. I don't know if my brother arranged it on purpose, but it worked out that way. We were not yet married when we all gathered at Denis's parents' house in Nancy for Yom Kippur. We got the news about the Yom Kippur War while at the synagogue. Somebody had heard it on the radio. Later, when back in Paris, we talked about it in the Victoire group.

In fact, my Jewish education had come to an end. Only for the High Holy Days did I go to the synagogue. I did not have much time. I tried to learn Hebrew, but that did not last long. I was a student in the so-called Latin Quarter of Paris, and I used to go to the Edmond Fleg Center for Jewish Students and also had lunch on a daily basis at the kosher restaurant open to students in front of the Luxembourg Garden. Of course, I still had friends from the Victoire and continued to go to the meetings and activities of Les Éclaireurs Israélites de France [French Jewish Scouts' organization]. I was also in charge of a youth section in that organization for a while.

---

* For many years Pepsi boycotted Israel, while Coke was sold there; as a result many Jews would only drink Coke.

After our marriage in 1974, Denis and I went to live in Metz for two years because he had obtained an internship there. He had finished his medical studies but had not done his medical thesis [MD] yet. While we were living there, I started working on my thesis; the subject was hospital planning in Lorraine. I had a degree in environmental studies and in geography from Paris VII University and the National Geographic Institute [Paris], but it was not possible to do a PhD thesis in environmental sciences, which was a problem. I also had to choose something that was possible to do in Metz. My adviser came up with the idea of public health since nobody had worked on the subject before. It is what we call in France "La carte sanitaire"—i.e., "hospital mapping"—the purpose being to study the geographical distribution of health services and then adapt it if needed. This method is still in use today; I was a pioneer.

Dealing with hospital mapping is both socially crucial and politically strategic. While the essence of the work depends on precise scientific data—e.g., statistics about life expectancy, demographics, or local distribution of health professionals—you end up facing strictly political choices that might change people's everyday lives for better or for worse. I also discovered that any efficient health policy should take into account traditions and past historical events in order to account for local habits that science only could not explain. There was, for instance, a small town in the Lorraine region from which people would rather travel a longer distance to go to a specific hospital than go to the nearby city hospital, therefore having to cross the country border line where Germany occupied France between 1870 and World War I. I also realized that wherever there is political influence, there is money available to run the local hospital in term of capacity, investments, or staff.

I started my thesis in 1975. Aurore, our first child, was born afterwards on 1 September 1975. Then, in 1976, we moved to Dijon for the first time because Denis was appointed there for an internship in the just built regional pediatric hospital. That is where Charles was born on 14 September 1978. Immediately after his birth, we went to Nancy where Denis worked at the regional pediatrics hospital while I finished my thesis.

I obtained my PhD in June 1979. I was the first in our family to become a doctor, even before any of the boys of the family. My mother-in-law,[*] could not stand it. Afterwards we returned to Dijon for a year, where Annabelle, our third child, was born on 30 June 1980, before we left for the United States on Columbus Day in October 1980.

---

[*] Janine Tenenbaum; her family, the Salomon-Lamberts, settled in Lorraine some centuries ago and is part of the upper-class bourgeoisie in Nancy.

In those years, the 1970s, I had Jewish friends and was in Jewish groups. We saw each other on Saturday evenings in Paris. While I was studying in Paris in 1973, I was sent to Hungary to analyze why forest trees were attacked by a certain kind of insect, but I also visited synagogues. When we were in Nancy, Denis was also in a Jewish youth group so we had Jewish friends. He was in a choir, and it was very important for him. The choir came to Paris for our wedding in July 1974.

I did not travel to Israel with Denis in 1970. I went with a Jewish group that year and then again in 1972 when I spent a summer learning Hebrew and Jewish history and culture in Givat Ram, the Hebrew University in Jerusalem. Denis went with his parents, and we saw each other there. I remember how proud and happy we were in 1970 to be in Israel! The youth group spent a few days in the Gaza Strip where we worked in a military kibbutz called Nahal. I worked on the land—weeding grass!—and I remember that during a tour we were in a jeep that suddenly stopped. When I asked why, I was told that the area was dangerous and that they were checking for possible bombs. Because there was a plastic bag in the middle of the road, the driver had to take it away before driving along.

In France in those years attitudes, including the government's, were in favor of Arab states' political discourse—for economic reasons like oil. These attitudes were especially pronounced during the Yom Kippur War.

In 1980 we left for the United States. It wasn't my first trip. For my baccalaureate in June 1968 my mother had organized a trip to the United States for me. I spent eight weeks and went by myself, which at the time seemed dangerous for a girl of a good family. I spent four weeks with cousins in Texas and then traveled to Washington, DC, New York, and Cape Cod, visiting my cousins' children and friends. I loved the trip. It influenced my ideas. I felt good in the United States, as a woman, a Jew—everything. I felt the same way when we went back to the United States the second time.

Denis wanted to see the world, so we took our three kids and went. I did not want to leave France because my mother was sick. But Denis wanted to go, so it was hard. We stayed in the United States for two years, and my mother died while we were there. I found Jewish life in the United States different, more open. It was very hard to live in Dijon. First of all, the kids were young, so I was very busy. And I was preparing my thesis. Denis was working hard at the hospital and worked at night to make more money for our everyday living. He also was preparing his thesis and publishing scientific articles. We didn't have free time. We didn't know anyone. We used to go to Nancy for the High Holy Days to stay with Denis's family. We didn't really know the Jewish community of Dijon. But after coming back from the United States we participated more and got more involved in different associations.

In the United States life was easier. Maybe I saw it that way because my father had been very strict. I felt that everything was easier, simpler [there]. We could invite friends over without notice. Aurore was in a Quaker school. We went to Conservative and Reform services since the two synagogues were near our home. We could talk about Judaism more openly. And on top of it, in Providence [Rhode Island] there was a neighborhood with kosher shops—Dijon had only two butchers at that time and has nothing nowadays.

When we came back [to Dijon], I applied for a teaching position at the university, but nobody knew me in the Department of Geography because I hadn't studied there. Also, they weren't interested in either human geography, environmental studies, or teaching geography in English. At the Department of Health there were no jobs open. They told me to go instead to the regional headquarters of the social security [service] because they needed somebody for hospital planning. Social Security hired me, and I started working in May 1983.

At this time the Jewish community was changing. Before our departure to the United States no other structure or service existed beside the synagogue and the butchers. I think that it really changed with the creation of B'nai B'rith. It was something different. The intellectual work was interesting and gave us a chance to meet a lot of people in a bigger organization. Originally we were members of the B'nai B'rith of Sens and Auxerre* because there was no B'nai B'rith in Dijon. The meetings were held in those two towns and in Dijon. For two or three years we traveled back and forth, and it was difficult. In Auxerre they needed us because there were not enough members there. But it gave us the opportunity to go to meetings, workshops—and I think it helped us.

We really wanted to do something. We wanted structure. We wanted to fight anti-Semitism and to improve our relations with Israel, the economic relations. The search for relationships between Burgundy and Israel was very interesting. This kind of interest did not exist before. All this had to do with the fact that Jewish identity in France had changed, but it was also very political. The elections were coming up, and the French B'nai B'rith wanted us to look for candidates to stand for office.

I think that it's important to be heard as a Jew. We are what we are, and we have to present ourselves accordingly. We did not do that before, not at

---

* Travel time between Dijon and these two cities is approximately one and a-half and one hour, respectively, each way.

all. I come from a family who suffered from World War II. We did not hide ourselves, but we did not live in the same open way. It is like hooking the **mezuzah** on the door. Many people do not put it on the outside but rather on the inside. It was like that in my parents' house. They told me, "We do not want to disturb people outside." They did not want to be questioned. They did not want to deal with these things.

Now politicians are invited to talk to us as Jews. They have to respect us for what we are. It is our right. We are French. But for many people we are still a mystery, hard to understand. Although fewer and fewer people believe that "the Jews killed Jesus," they do not understand how we live, and, on top of it, it's impossible for them to think that we do not celebrate Christmas.

In search of building bridges between us and other people, to break down anti-Semitism, B'nai B'rith was developing different actions. One of them was to start a radio station. We were in Auxerre, and the B'nai B'rith at the time had an arrangement with Radio Shalom in Paris. The president of our association in Auxerre asked us to find a way to get some programs on air on a Dijon radio station. "Go and see Radio Shalom in Paris," he said. We went to the B'nai B'rith meeting, and I remember that day I did a presentation about Jewish medicine. We were wondering who would head the commission for the radio, and Denis said: "Françoise." It started there. He really thought that it was something for me.

Longvic is a little town near [Dijon], and they had a local radio station. One member of our group contacted them, and they responded, "No, there are no problems. We already have a band of young musicians. It would be a great idea if you did an on-air show here. We are interested in that kind of thing." The rabbi and I went and talked with the town's mayor and his chief of political staff, who were responsible for radio stations. The mayor was very nice. As welcoming gifts, he offered us pewter glasses engraved with his town name. He also told us, "Listen, it is not possible because if we give you permission to run a program, we will have to accept the Arabs as well. But for you, Mrs. Tenenbaum, you can speak anytime you want! No, it is not possible [to run a regular Jewish program]. It would lead to problems. I could find myself in trouble." He was being very polite but racist.

"But of course you, Mme Tenenbaum, if you want to produce a radio show, it would be our pleasure."

"I thank you, Mayor," I replied, and left.

There were already three local radio stations in Dijon: a Catholic radio called "Radio Parabole," the "Voice of the Immigrant Worker," and a student radio called "Radio Campus." Why not a Jewish radio?

The following day I had a meeting with the committee of B'nai B'rith, and we created a [governing] association for a radio station. A month later the association started working. After that we had to wait six months to obtain an official authorization. This is a regional and national procedure because radio frequencies are distributed by the government. They are given to be used after an application for which one has to list the association members as well as the programs to be aired. The objectives of Radio Shalom are to make everybody aware of Judaism, to understand our community, and to make it possible for everyone to understand Israel, politically as well as economically, as well as issues specific to the Middle East.

Of course, I realized that this could bother other people outside and inside the community, but I thought that it was something necessary. Especially in times when racism and anti-Semitism are present, there is a need for us to be able to speak our minds. If Mr. Le Pen [leader of the extreme Right party] says something anti-Semitic, then we must have a way to reply through broadcast. Others had tried radio shows before, but they did not have the same goals. They were doing it only for people inside the Jewish community. I wanted something more. I always thought that others would listen to our radio as well. In my mind, sharing cultural, economical, or political points of view is a way to break down walls and reach civil peace, here in France as well as in the Middle East.

Albert Mallet, who was at that time Radio Shalom/Paris president, helped us start the project. To find money to run the radio station, which needed a lot, we asked Mr. Bansard for help. He, at that time, was president of the United Jewish Appeal Campaign* and was visiting all of the communities in France. He invited me to visit him in Paris, and there he agreed to purchase the equipment for the radio station and loan it to us. Jean-Claude Meimoun, a businessman who is a member of the Dijon community, provided us with a studio place. He even had a soundproof room built. Technicians came from Paris to help us set it up.†

Jean-Claude represents Radio Shalom before the Community [Center] Council. We work well together. Though I am president of Radio Shalom, I don't represent it in the Community Council, probably because I am a woman.... When the Council needs to talk to me, they invite me to come—such as on the day Mr. Bansard came. I think that there are a lot of religious people who are not used to talking to women. Once Jean-Claude told me

---

* Yearly French fundraising campaign for Israeli and French Jewish needs.
† Meimoun's family now lives in Paris, and Radio Shalom is housed on the second floor of the older communal space attached to the sanctuary.

that he talked with Gabriel Malka [a prominent local surgeon] about future shows for the station. I was happy because Malka was one of the persons who initially didn't want the radio station. I wondered why Malka and the Sephardim didn't talk with women. It's a real question. Of course, the Ashkenazi men also have problems concerning the position of women. The French do, too.

There is something else: the first bat mitzvahs. I did mine at the Victoire in Paris. In Dijon they did not celebrate them, but when Aurore was 13 years old I wanted her to have a bat mitzvah. The rabbi did not agree. When the Chief Rabbi of France came, Denis and I took the opportunity to talk to him about it. He had nothing against bat mitzvahs, and he then discussed it with Rabbi Sibony, who then said "yes." So, Aurore was the first little girl in Dijon to have a bat mitzvah. That was in 1988. We invited the entire community, and we had a reception afterwards in the synagogue garden. From that day every girl in Dijon had a bat mitzvah. I think they gave more people a chance to participate in the community. And thanks to the bat mitzvahs, the girls study and get involved.

I hope that things are beginning to change regarding women not only in the Jewish community. Giselle Halimi, a well-known Jewish lawyer, participated in a UNESCO conference in Paris on women and democracy. She also is the one who has worked since the 1960s to promote access to contraception for all in France. I am interested in the place of women in society, in democracy, at work, etc. The idea of quotas doesn't interest me, but I fight for my rights and human rights, including women and children. It is a little bit like Judaism. We have the same rights as others.

To return to B'nai B'rith, it is true that it is a small group and that it is isolated. It is not like in the United States. Not everyone can be in the organization, and it is more hierarchical. There are people in the community who have problems with this. They say that it is not democratically correct, that a small group runs things. Some people, those in mixed marriages, don't want to be a part of it because their families cannot be involved. There are also some Jews who don't belong because others cannot join. I agree that this is not democratic. This has to be discussed. I think more people don't join because they don't have the right information. It also costs about 1,300 francs [about €198] a year for a couple. This is not expensive, but it can seem so. People are not used to spending much, and it is true that the community is not wealthy. If the community wants to build projects, we'll have to increase the contributions for everyone, except for those who can't afford it.

Israel? Yes. I went twice like I said, in 1970 and 1972. My deceased mother has a cousin there. The cousin has kids, and I also have my own friends there.

The relationship between French-Jewish identity and Israel, did it change? Yes, I think that it has. I think that having the State of Israel helps French Jews, even with the war in Lebanon and the Intifada.

French Jews maintain this position: they are loyal to the idea that [Israel] is a Jewish country, even if they do not always agree with its politics. But they do not say that it is *our* country. Maybe religious people think differently, but French Jews think about it as a Jewish country. I think that French Jews do not get involved that much with political life in Israel. The important thing is that Israel exists. I think that in our minds is the idea that, if in the future, we have to leave [France], we will have a place to go.

You ask why we might have to leave: it has to do with history; it is something that goes from generation to generation. There is Vichy, Le Pen, and terrorism. I think that there certainly is the idea that we might be persecuted again. Perhaps it is not reasonable to think like this. I think that it is not reasonable, but Jews always think that they need to have their luggage packed and ready to leave. It has been like this for centuries. So, yes, we should be ready to leave. The Jews in the United States do not have this problem.

I know who would stay and who would not.

Every day I meet people about whom I think, "You are anti-Semitic, you are racist, and there is nothing that I can do to change you." They know that I am Jewish, but I cannot change these people. One day, I was with a group of students and two professors with whom I talked about AIDS—part of my job is health education. It was very hard to make them understand the medical secrecy. It's the same line of thought. We realize that people have fears, but we cannot open their minds.

This also is related to the Lubavitch, who just settled in Dijon. First of all, I do not want to say anything [too critical about them]. I am going to wait. The radio is for everyone. I cannot take a stand. But I think it's difficult to have people who are too strict. They are different. They are missionaries, and others fear them. I agree that it is necessary to be very careful and keep talking with our religious friends with patience. This is important for the future of the community. If the leaders do not work together, nothing will work.

You can see why this community came back to life. The leaders came together with the B'nai B'rith, and then other things started working. The WIZO is beginning to do different things. The FSJU is also beginning to do something.

What are the major problems of the Jewish community in Dijon? Well, it's difficult to tell because the Jewish community in Dijon, in France, is not rich like the communities in the United States, where people are also more active and more involved. In Dijon there are some very rich Jewish people who are not involved at all. Their children made interreligious marriages. They do not want to hear about the radio. They give money for Israel but not for the community. They do not want to get involved as Jews.

There are Jews without jobs, there are mixed families, there also are the ones who are more religious. There are Jews from North Africa who brought some spice to our community but also some violence. Even the public schools are sympathetic to Catholicism, although they should not show any religious preference. There is more anti-Semitism here compared to the United States. It's not easy to talk about Judaism with people who are not Jewish. It would be better if Jews in France had more freedom to speak.

Look what happened to my son Charles's report about the Resistance [which did not win a contest]. I had a discussion with my father, and he told me, "It is normal that Charles's report was not accepted because it talks about Jews. In a work about the Resistance you cannot do that. You have to talk about the Nation." He also asked why I started the radio, which created a lot of work, cost a lot of money, and might bother non-Jews. I hope he only feels this way because he's from a generation different from mine.

My mother-in-law came for a visit, and she also didn't agree with what I was doing because I am a woman. I took [my in-laws] to see Radio Shalom, and she wanted to leave. She never understood why I worked in the first place. She doesn't want to see all of this because, in her mind, a woman has to stay at home. Fortunately, my father accepts the fact that I work, but he thinks that the radio station is too much and also dangerous. Denis's father, Dr. Jean Tenenbaum, who came from Chelm [Poland] with his parents at the age of six and became a radiologist, was, on the other hand, always proud of my work and political engagement.

There also are positive things about the Jewish community. We try to learn about authors, music, and culture, and even organize performances. There is analysis of thought and also reflection. There is dynamism. It is a very interesting life.

June 2005

In 1993 my three children were still pretty young, and I had founded a Health Education Public Service which I directed. I had made well-known National Health education programs as, for example, "Better aging with balance sport activities" to prevent the elderly from falling. I voluntarily left in 1998 to participate in the creation of the URCAM [the Regional Center for Social Security in Burgundy] and take responsibility for a Public Health Strategic

Plan, coordinating all systems concerned with public health. There, I created all the strategies and prevention methods in Burgundy.

At the end of 1999 or the beginning of 2000 I was asked by François Rebsamen if I would be a candidate on the Socialist list in the municipal elections of March 2001. It was an important decision for me to make, and I spent a lot of time thinking it over with my husband. I ended up accepting the offer, envisioning that it would give me more opportunities, more tools to do a good job for French society, and further developing my competence to work in the area of public health. I recalled that the World Health Organization had declared that if politicians didn't intervene, health care professionals alone couldn't deal with the problems involved. So I told myself that this is my opportunity, and I requested that I be given responsibilities in this specific field. I was asked not only because I was acquainted with public health issues but also because for the past 20 years I had been active in a field that is closely related to politics in the region.

But of course I was not offered the position only because of that. This was the first election in which the parties needed women. It was mandatory to have women. The Socialist Party was looking for popular women. And I had professional experience in my field; I was president of Radio Shalom, and founder and past-president of the Women's Lions Club [Dijon Marie de Bourgogne]. I think that my experience was considered by the people who called upon me.

I accepted the mandate with the Socialist Party because it has always been pretty much my [political] orientation. Moreover, my preference has always been to work in the social services sector. I want to help people and make sure that everyone has access to public health services. That's how I saw my goal then. And I am satisfied because I obtained new tools and I was able to create things. But, you know, the more that you do new things, the more problems show up. So there is always more to be done.

I was engaged in the preparation of the electoral agenda for the campaign, which included proposals that I personally made. One of them was to build "Dijon Ville Santé" [Dijon Health Town] and have it approved by the World Health Organization. That task was accomplished, and it was accredited in March 2002, only a year later. "Dijon Health Town" is a town where every decision is analyzed in terms of impact on its inhabitants and is also a town that acts to improve everyone's health. Furthermore, I wanted to build a nursing home for elderly people with special needs. It is currently being built and will open its doors in the beginning of 2007. Child care centers that I wanted to build are also under construction. And, on top of everything, I wanted to implement equal access to public services by making prices according to everyone's income—this aim took me ten years, but it has been done. As time passes, new needs appear, and I have to react quickly.

For the town elections of 2001, I was named second on the party's list, the one just after the head of the list, the future mayor of the town, François Rebsamen. At that time, I was not in a political party, so I ran as "non-affil-iated," as representing civil society. In March 2002, I joined the Socialist Party, of which I am still a member.

I have more work to do in the field of employment that concerns me a lot. There are many things that need to be done. Recently, I became President of the Regional Council for the Education of Women. It helps in educat-ing women and finding them jobs. In Burgundy and everywhere in France women, youth, and people over 50 are particularly hard hit by unemploy-ment. In addition, several months ago I was asked to become president of UNICEF for the Côte d'Or district.* So that is another responsibility. There are always new things that show up and require time and effort.

One of our greatest problems is financial. We have budget problems because the national government has drastically decreased its funding. The government sends us experts but less money. The government used to at least provide money to build child care centers, for example, but it doesn't do that any longer. This increases the financial and fiscal pressure on Dijon. Today there are requests for child care centers that we cannot meet. How do we do this since we cannot increase taxes beyond a certain norm and there are other requests to be met? Obviously, people don't care about these difficulties; they want to get what they need at the very moment. Still, we have to respond.

It is the same with unemployment. Last night there was a military cere-mony. After the ceremony a man came to me and said, "You know, Madame, I have fought for France and my daughter does not have a job." So he expects us to find her a job and a place to live. Things like this happen all the time. I think that to improve the situation we should first work on the economy. If we develop exports of French products, we will create more job opportuni-ties. And if we do this, a lot of problems will be solved. This is very important.

Then, of course, we are also expected to increase housing. Because these are old cities, there are issues with land shortage. The old buildings are small, and we need larger ones. People want places to live, but at the same time they don't want to destroy old individual houses for new apartment buildings.

---

* For administrative purposes France was divided into departments during the French Revolution. The Côte d'Or (Gold Coast) is the department of which Dijon is the capital.

In 2004 we had county and regional elections, and I was asked to stand for the county where I live. It is traditionally conservative, but I managed to increase the percentage of votes for the Socialists by over 20 per cent. I didn't win the county, but now I am much better known. But we won the region, and I became Burgundy Regional Assembly's Vice-President for Public Health and delegate to the health institutions. So I now work throughout the entire region of Burgundy.

The rural zones are deserted by the young people leaving for the cities— Dijon, Lyon, and Paris. It's a very serious problem because only old people remain in the villages, and they live isolated from one another. It is our responsibility to find ways to assure them a decent life and to provide them with medical care. All this of course costs a lot of money.

The National Front is not represented on the city council, but they are in the regional one. We have a sufficient majority to pass everything we need, but they are there, speaking out and sometimes saying atrocious things that are terribly racist and xenophobic. In the beginning I made a lot of noise, calling them racists and xenophobes. I was trying to silence them. The president [of the assembly] allowed me to talk without even asking, which is usually not allowed. Of course, this got in the newspapers. Just yesterday reporters who were present at the regional assembly meeting talked to me about this. On the other hand, the local media is Right-oriented, which the newspapers' articles clearly reflect. We have to keep in mind the political orientation of the media.

Often people tell me that they are following my work through the media. This surprises me a lot. The difference between now and my previous work in public health is that now people comment in the newspapers about my work. But in this way people know and see that we [the Socialist Party] are really working for them. It is very interesting. As for the future, everything depends on the elections, the popularity of candidates. But I am ready, and we will see.

On a personal level and as a woman, there is no problem. Everyone knows that I am Jewish. The National Front speaks out about it, but I act effectively and with confidence. In fact, I was attacked during one of the sessions of the regional assembly. So everyone knows it. It's quite clear. At the beginning of our municipal mandate in 2001, our principal opponent, the head of the opposition party, said, "The Jews are in power."* He really said this.

---

* The main opposition party was the UMP, Union pour un Mouvement Populaire, a conservative party.

This was reported, but I don't think that I am the subject of an open aggression or antagonism because of my Jewish origin. I was, rather, attacked more because I am Left-oriented and they are on the Right. There are people, let's say from the bourgeoisie, who don't really like having women in politics. Of course, I don't know for sure, but it's not openly anti-Semitic in all cases. For example, I have been criticized by the Rightist political opposition in the municipal assembly for giving allocations to the gay-lesbian organization in my field [welfare], but this is normal. Meanwhile, other organizations with Rightist leadership continue to receive allocations. After all, we were elected to serve all the people.

As for the Jewish community, they don't say anything when I work with the Muslims. The community is rather open to these things. But the community itself has changed. There is a deep division that was not there in 1993. The arrival of the Lubavitch divided the community.

The Lubavitch have their own school. In the municipal assembly I have always insisted that the municipality support secular people. For example, we were discussing the organization of the mayor's "end of year dinner" for the elderly, and the deputy in charge wanted to call this the "Christmas meal." I insisted that this be called simply "end of year meal." I also called to the attention of my colleagues that in the previous year there were no Muslims or Jews attending these festival lunches, and I am talking about 3,600 people. I said, "See. There are neither Muslims nor Jews [coming to this dinner]. It's called a 'Christmas meal,' and there is pork on the menu." I told them that if they wanted Muslims and Jews to participate they shouldn't call it the "Christmas meal" and certainly shouldn't include pork on the menu. So I hope that now there will be Muslims and Jews attending.

In 2001, I established the "Dijon Children's Rights Day," based on the "International Convention on the Rights of the Child" [UNICEF] and Janusz Korczak's works.[*] This has been working well ever since. Instead of being decentralized in all the neighborhoods, it takes place in the City Hall where I reserve all the conference rooms and we bring children from all the neighborhoods together. In this way, children get the idea that the City Hall and downtown are theirs as well. This is a way to encourage them to live with everyone in the city. But every year I have to fight with the people from the suburbs who come and tell me that they can do the same thing in their own neighborhoods. And I have to tell them that this isn't the way to do it, that it is up them to come and become part of the whole.

---

[*] Janusz Korczak was a famous Polish Jewish physician, educator, and author, who chose to accompany his young students to Auschwitz rather than save his own life.

Every year we choose a different topic. There is one day for the parents, for the professionals in the field, and the associations. They all do some work on the selected topic. At night there is an open conference, and we invite people from all the neighborhoods to come. The next day is for the youth, the children and the teenagers. We organize various activities that make them think, but we also have games.

This year there was a group of Muslim women who indicated that they wanted to take part in the Parents' Day activities. They said that after reflection and discussion they wanted to do creative activities, not cooking and baking, because "people always asked them to do this." I agreed, because that is exactly how I want things to go. I think that we should become familiar with each other's culture. I believe that my Jewish origins helped me see the importance of this.

I also changed the rules for gaining acceptance to the day care centers. The City of Dijon provides day care services for about 800 children aged less than three years old, but 500 mores spaces are needed. I'm working on welcoming 300 more children before 2008, although day care centers are very expensive for the city. Building one costs approximately €2.3 million, and the Dijon budget for babies is €10 million annually, without taking into account actual building construction.

I changed the rules to admit children whose parents are either unemployed or still studying. This did not go over well with some people who think that priority should be given to two working parents. But if one thinks that way, one will end up providing services to families with the best financial situation. What I want is that other people, particularly those who need to get education and jobs, get places in the day care centers. In this way parents can pursue their studies, and the children, who are to some extent isolated, will get the chance to freely socialize with others. So I changed the rules to promote these ideas, but it is very difficult to explain all this to my work team.

On this issue of cultivating understanding of cultures and state support, the churches know how to deal with their problems; the mosques also are doing pretty well. In my opinion, the synagogue has the biggest problem getting along in Dijon, because it has never asked the local government for assistance. They don't dare. Three months ago I organized a course for the community leaders to teach them how to apply for assistance. And two months later I was angry because they didn't ask the Regional Council in the correct way.

I think that in France it is important to be part of the idea of being secular on the outside while at the same time respecting everyone's faith. In this regard the Law of 1905 [separating church and state] created a very balanced and well-functioning system, implying that neither the state nor any religious body should interfere in one another's affairs.

There have been anti-Semitic incidents not far from here. There was desecration of a cemetery in a small community about 20 kilometers away, although there were no Jewish graves there. I think that the young offenders relied on the fact that the taboo against anti-Semitism in France is less strictly monitored. That is certain.

Besides this, there was the vote against Europe [the French rejection of the European Constitution in 2005]. That's another thing based on the same fears. In politics, solutions are not found based on nationalist issues but based on society. It is necessary that we work on the urban configuration. We need to knock out the ghetto neighborhoods. This is what we currently are working on in Dijon. Unfortunately, it's very difficult to do this—extremely hard. It costs a lot of money, and the culture works against you. Even so, you definitely have to do something about it.

Just across the street there is a small building that is under construction. It will be a social housing building. We try to build buildings like this everywhere. And in the difficult neighborhoods that we are renovating completely, we plan to build high quality apartments to enhance social diversity. Because otherwise some neighborhoods become poor, and the wealthier people from these neighborhoods tend to send their children to private schools. They don't interact with poorer people and immigrants in the neighborhood. In this way they contribute to ghettoization.

However, [since 9/11] I believe that things have become better. I believe so. I think that right now the representatives of the Jewish community and the politicians should be very careful to dissociate French problems from the Israel-Palestine problem. Every time the two problems get mixed up, it becomes a disaster. There was a conference here with the director of the Jewish Consistory Council who committed the huge error of mixing the two problems. He came to discuss anti-Semitism in France and instead talked about Israel-Palestine problems. The two issues must be separated.

In addition to social problems, much remains to be done. We need to deal with housing, education, and employment. But, no doubt, the school is the main and foremost integrating institution. The problem is that the schools don't know how to deal with these issues. For example, I was elected to the district coordinating committee responsible for 21 towns around Dijon, and I established an observatory for social health. We found that neighborhoods that have difficulties with integration also have different problems. For example, in the second year of elementary school [in those neighborhoods], 30 per cent of the students are behind, and at the baccalaureate level 10 to

12 per cent of the students cannot read. And, on top of that, the government cuts the number of teachers.

In 2002 there were pro-Palestinian demonstrations here and throughout France. Some of the assistants told me that I should join them in a demonstration because they knew I was very interested in what was happening in the Middle East. I told them that I had checked thoroughly to find out what this demonstration was about and that it was not for peace, it was only one-sided, pro-Arab, and therefore I would remain in my office. I told them to call me if they found out that it was really for peace. Later they called me to tell me that I was right.

After I got elected in 2001, I resigned from Radio Shalom Dijon in order not to mix politics and media. Denis, my husband, became and is still president of the radio.

SURVIVORS OF THE HOLOCAUST

Bébé Edelman

Bébé Edelman's story is similar to those of many Eastern European Jews who immigrated to France before World War II. A higher percentage of them were killed in the camps than native-born French Jews. She and her immediate family survived thanks to the help of sympathetic French Catholics.

Spring 2000

The first thing that I remember is seeing my uncle hit his wife against the wall. He had six wives, and they all suffered the same thing. He was in Paris, the first one to leave Russia. Like my father, he was from Odessa; my mother, too. They left because of the pogroms against Jews. They spoke Russian and Yiddish at home. I didn't learn French until I started school. My first language was Yiddish.

I was born in Paris in 1921; we lived there until the war. I had a brother and a sister. My father ironed in a dry cleaning place. It was the only work he could find. My parents had wanted to go to the United States, but after the third child was born, they decided to stay in France. We were not unhappy. My parents worked hard, and we had everything we needed. Later on, when I wanted to go out with boys, they would ask me all these questions: What does he do? Where does he live? What do his parents do? You see, my parents were very strict. They were religious.... We did not eat pork and things like that. If my husband had been raised the same way, I would have continued. I was used to it, but my husband didn't like it.

I started school when I was four. There was a school next to our street where all the Jews went. My father didn't want me to go to that school. He liked being Jewish, but he didn't want me to go to school with all those Jewish kids. I went to a school instead where there were few Jews. He also didn't allow me to speak Yiddish to him. He wanted to speak French. One time in elementary school a girl called me a "dirty Jew." I didn't know what that was, so I started crying. When the teacher asked me why, she put me in front of the class and asked me to show my underwear. She knew that I always wore clean white underwear.

When the war started and the Germans broke through to Paris, our lives became hard. And my parents had already been through something like that in Russia. When they saw what was happening, my father told us that we had to leave. At the Gare de Lyon [railroad station] there were so many people trying to get away, it was impossible to get through. We could not make it, so my father decided to stay. But we had to find a way out.

When the Germans occupied Paris, my father sold them rubber. Then he found a way to go down south. But we had to pay. He went to Lyon; my mother sent me when he found a small place. My mother sold everything to get money to leave. She came and we moved into an empty store that had a kitchen and was big enough for us. There my parents tried to run a dry cleaning business.

Everything in Paris was gone except a piano that I was learning to play. After the war, when we returned, my mother found that piano and a couch in a store where there were confiscated goods. My mother brought both of them home.

When my mother came to Lyon, my youngest aunt was still in Paris. She was in a forced marriage that had been arranged for her, and she wasn't happy. She had two daughters. After her husband was arrested and the Germans came for her and her daughters, a neighbor told her to leave the girls with her. But my aunt wanted the three to stay together. Well, they were separated anyway at the Vel d'Hiv camp.* A Catholic friend of my uncle went to the camp and found the girls. My uncle asked the French police if she could take them but was refused. She was allowed to bring them food, and she went every day for a while. One day, she went and found no one. She was told that the girls were probably on a train going to Germany. It is possible that the oldest saw their mother when they were on the train. She found a piece of paper and wrote [a letter] on it and put my uncle's address. It was delivered. My cousin Maurice told me this story. After the war, I found the Catholic woman who told me it was true. I knew during the war that my aunt and cousins would not come back. The letter my cousin wrote to my Uncle Henri told us that.

Before the war started, we knew what was going on in the camps. The Jews did, and so did the French, but they didn't want to believe it. I think that they closed their eyes. I knew what was going on because I met a Jewish couple that had come from Germany with their son. The son was about my age and he told me that they had left Germany because the Jews were being killed.† This was before the war when we were still living in Paris. Marshal

---

* The Velodrome d'Hiver, a cycle racing stadium, where rounded-up Jews were quartered before being sent to Drancy or elsewhere, especially in July 1942.

† Some Jews were killed in Germany during the late 1930s, and many were brutalized and sent to camps, especially during Krystallnacht (Night of Broken Glass, November 1938). However, the mass murder of Jews did not begin until the German invasion of the Soviet Union in June 1941.

Pétain knew what was happening. He helped the Germans get rid of the Jews. Vel d'Hiv is an example of this.

During the war I met Sam, my future husband. I met him through a friend who was staying with a very generous woman who helped refugees. Sam and I traveled on a bicycle into the countryside to find food. My mother was very happy with that.

For a while, Lyon was free. But when the Germans came [1942], we had to be careful. Fortunately, Sam knew the back roads. We also went camping even though my mother didn't want me to, but I learned a new lifestyle. I fell in love. I was already [almost] deaf, and when I told Sam that he only said, "So?" I think that our marriage was based on true love. Of course, we had little fights like everyone else. Later, when he was in the hospital, he told Evelyn [their daughter] that he had loved me very much. I cannot forget him. True love exists. He wanted me like I was.

We were married during the war, and when the Germans occupied Lyon we hid. But when you are young, you take risks. Sam tried to find a job and found one as an electrician. His boss was a great person who once warned him that the Germans were coming into the store. The boss helped Sam escape. There were not many people like that. Sam hid in the opera house where I visited him every night. I could go out because I had an identification card.

We were married after the liberation of France, but when the war was still going on. We got married in his parents' apartment. His parents didn't like the marriage. When Sam went away to work at times, he always sent me his news. His parents would send someone to me to ask about their son. Sam wouldn't see them unless they accepted the marriage. After the marriage, we stayed in Lyon. Sam worked very hard. Nine months after we were married, Annie* was born [laughs].

I remember when the Americans came to Lyon. Sam left to fight on their side. He went with a Resistance group into the countryside. I decided to find him because I was afraid that something would happen to him. I took my bike, and while I was riding, I met a jeep with four Americans in it. I told them where I was going. They wanted to help, but they were busy, so they gave me food. Later, there was a party for the Americans who contributed coffee for everybody.

In Lyon, after the war everybody was working. We had little money. Sam didn't have a work permit, but I did, so we sold used clothes. We sent Annie to live outside Paris with nice people. We would go to see her.

---

* See Annie Edelman's story in the section on "Community Members," p. 153.

Sam was Polish, and that's why he didn't have a work permit. He wanted to become a French citizen. When he got his French nationality, we threw a party for him. When he voted for the first time, we took photographs.

We didn't have a Jewish life after the war. Sam wasn't interested. We bought ham and things like that; we lived like the other French. My parents went back to their old lifestyle when they returned to Paris, though.

I didn't know what to do with the holidays. Once, when we went to someone's home for them, I was criticized for not going to the synagogue regularly. Sam simply said that it wasn't worth going. I didn't have any explanations for my children. They knew, they learned about [the Holocaust and Judaism] at school. I simply was not good at explaining things.

Sam went from job to job, eventually working in pharmaceuticals. He wanted to do more and have more, but he didn't succeed. We had a good life though. My children had everything they wanted. So we were happy. At one point, they were building very inexpensive houses in Chenôve. We asked the children if they would like a house there. They had to choose between a house and vacations. They chose the vacations.

Annie was a good student. She studied psychology. I never really asked her if she was happy with what she was doing. At first Evelyn wanted to become a physician; she did a year and decided to become a nurse. Pierre, I think, is very happy. He did not get his Bac; he wanted to work. I told him that he should finish high school, and he told me something that I never forgot: "Mom, would you be ashamed to have a son who is a worker?"

As for my grandchildren, they are fine. They get along well. At least Sam got to see his first grandchild.

The only thing I wanted for my children is that they get along, and I think that they do. I don't like giving them advice, but if there is something that I could teach them, especially my grandchildren, is that they have hope. Hope.

Marcelle David

Marcelle David's harrowing story of survival as a child during World War II unfortunately is similar to those of many others whose lives depended upon the courage and goodwill of ordinary French people. After several narrow escapes from the Germans, she returned to Dijon with her surviving family after the war and helped rebuild its Jewish community.

Spring 1993

My parents came from Łęczyka, a place 50 kilometers from Łodź, in Poland. Thanks to a factory work contract, my father was able to come to France in 1930 and work as a tailor. As an alien worker, he eventually was able to bring his mother; they joined four brothers and sisters who were already here. In the same year, in May, my mother, who was engaged to my father, also came. They got married in August 1930 in Belfort [in northeastern France], where my father was living and working.

They were married by a Jewish mayor. For my mother, only a Jewish mayor could marry them. After that, they were married by a rabbi in a religious ceremony. The wedding didn't take place in a synagogue because my grandmother was very pious; it was held at home. My cousins still remember it because they had to carry two small candles.

Since my mother was the daughter of a tailor and knew the business, she began working right away at a big store and earned a good living despite the hard times during the Great Depression. My father also was doing well because he frequently worked overtime.

I was born ten months after the marriage, in Belfort on 7 July 1931. They named me Marcelle after my grandmother. It's very important for deceased grandparents to be represented by a new generation. My grandmother always lived with us. She took care of me while my parents worked. We all lived together happily in Belfort. Fortunately, we had everything that we needed: an apartment, a car ... my parents had everything for six years.

Then we started hearing about what was going on in Germany. My mother had a sister who had lived there since 1920 or 1921. She lived through the rise of the Nazis. Before getting married, my mother had gone to Germany. She saw the beginnings of Nazism. The Nazis went about in uniforms; they began throwing stones through the windows of Jewish shops. It became quite somber there. An aunt and uncle who lived in Kassel left Germany quickly in 1933. They were given only 24 hours to get out. They had an apartment, a comfortable life, but they had to leave everything behind, carrying only their suitcases. They arrived in Belfort in a state of shock even though the entire family was there to welcome them. Eventually, they moved on to Dijon, where there was an important colony of [German] Jews.

When the war broke out in September 1939, my mother was expecting to give birth that month to her third child. He was born on September 12 in Dijon because Belfort was close to the border with Germany and we had been asked by the government to move. So we had gone to live with my mother's sister. Since this was the third child, my father was discharged from the army so that he could support his family. He had joined to support the war effort along with many of the Jews from Belfort. They were assigned to the Foreign Legion because they were not yet citizens of France. My brother and I were the only French citizens [in our family] because we had been born on French soil. My French birth certificate later played an important role in my life.

The Germans came in 1940. Everything was cut off, and the [Vichy] anti-Semitic laws went into effect. That meant that my father couldn't work any longer as a tailor. He had to turn in his trading license, and his name was erased from the list of tailors. Afterwards, he disappeared. We thought that he had been arrested. We went many times to look for him. At that time they took only men; they didn't yet care about women and children. We learned that he had fled with others from Dijon. When he crossed the demarcation line [between Occupied and Vichy France], he was arrested. That was in 1940 or 1941.

We had to wear the [yellow] star. Everyone had to except my brother Michel who was less than three years old. We went to school wearing the stars on our clothing. It was very disturbing. Inspectors of Jewish Affairs came to the school to check on us. I found it a little weird that men were paid to make sure that children wore stars. In the entire school, only three kids had to wear the star. We didn't have the right to go to the playground. It was forbidden to Jews and dogs; the public parks were forbidden to us. We couldn't go to the movies either.

We also had to give up our radio. We had had that radio for a long time, we were happy with it, but we had to give it up. Then after Dad was gone, an inspector of Jewish Affairs came to take away his merchandise. At the time, my parents had two garages, one for the car and the other for the merchandise. They absolutely wanted the merchandise, but Mom showed them the garage with the car instead. So they took the car and left. The merchandise was shared with my uncle, who took part of it. That merchandise represented capital, and since Jews were forbidden to work, it gave us some money to live on, to survive. I was 11 years old. I remember it very well. There are things that one never forgets.

The pressure began to be very intense. There was a person in the office of the Prefecture who told us, "I will warn you 24 or 48 hours in advance when there is round-up. There will not be time to ask questions. You will have to go right away and inform the maximum number of people that you know. You have to because everyone is on a list, and there is no way that you can stay at home."

The list of Jews was compiled by the Religious Association of Israélites of Dijon. They had no choice but to turn over the list to the authorities. We were on the list because when we arrived in Dijon there was a community there and, since we were very community oriented, we became involved in it. It was part of our family.

Well, we had some problems because my grandmother was 75 years old at the time. She was a little slow and did not walk a lot. Because she had health problems, she didn't want to leave with us. But Mom told her, "Either we all leave together, or we are all taken. You will have to take your responsibilities." Grandmother told her, "No, no. Let me stay at a neighbor's. Give them a little money." Then Mom insisted, "There is no way I will leave you. You come with us, or we're all taken together." Finally, Grandmother accepted.

When we were warned to leave, we had to empty the entire apartment in 24 hours. We split our furniture up between our friends and then went to meet the people who would smuggle us across the demarcation line. They were members of the Resistance, and the one who guided us was from an administrative office in the city. We were told to take a car to a certain place where we would be met. We then were taken to a hotel to wait. The hotel was filled with Germans, including officers, but that is where we hid. When we received instructions, we were told, "Come early in the morning. We will have a freight train stop for you. We will put you in a freight car."

Well, in the morning, my little brother didn't want to get up. He was tired, he was upset, he was crying. Grandmother walked as best she could, and then my mother, brothers, and I carried the luggage. Mom also carried a box of chocolates that was given to her as a gift. That chocolate turned out to be very important.

The place where we were told to go was along the railroad tracks out in the countryside. But none of the trains stopped. One, two, three trains went by. We were telling each other that no trains were going to stop, that our situation was impossible. Suddenly, however, a train stopped just where we were. About ten men jumped down and came running towards us. Two of them grabbed Grandmother, one took me, another took the luggage, and in about 30 seconds, we were aboard in one of the cars. It happened so fast! We were hidden in a small space at the end of the car, surrounded by beds, bedsprings, wardrobes, everything you want. Grandmother, who was very pious, immediately began to pray.

The train stopped at the demarcation line where there was a control point. German soldiers, including some officers, came into our car and searched it. I could see their boots through the cracks between the furniture. They almost brushed against us. I was thinking, "It's impossible. I can see them, but they can't see me." Fortunately, my little brother was asleep in Mom's arms. He had been stuffed with the chocolate. If he had made noise or cried, we would have been taken. I think my grandmother's prayers were effective. Maybe what also saved us was that the Germans didn't have any dogs.

We stayed there like that for an interminable hour. Then the train began to move, went five or six kilometers, then stopped again. At that point, we were taken out of the freight car and moved into a regular passenger car. The train had passed over the line, and we were told, "we are in France." My mother took out chicken that she had brought along and shared it among us.

My dad didn't know that we were coming. He was under house arrest in a small village called Salornay-sur-Guye about ten kilometers from Cluny, on the national road between Macon and Chalon. He had fled across the demarcation line and been picked up by the French police because he was there illegally. Had he been sent back to Dijon, he would have been taken by the Germans. There were many Jews of foreign origin in the village, also under house arrest. They didn't have the right to leave; they couldn't travel more than three kilometers from the village without special authorization and without a guard following them. They simply were not free.

We took a taxi to Salornay-sur-Guye and checked into the hotel. We sent word to Dad, "Your wife, your mother, and your children have arrived!" Our arrival was quite an exploit because no one expected us to make it, considering that we had an old woman and a child with us to complicate everything. So, of course, we all were very happy. The family was reunited.

It was expected that permission for us to stay in the village was a mere formality, but in the morning two National Guardsmen came to take us away because they said that we had come illegally. Mom tried to explain. She said, "The Germans came to take us away. We came here because we were in danger. Do you want the Germans to take us?" But the guardsmen didn't want to hear anything about it. An order had come from Macon to repatriate us. We were to be sent back to Dijon where the Germans were waiting for us. It was not at all funny! We had risked so much to get where we were. Soon, we were all crying. We were desperate.

They took us to Mount Saint-Vincent to catch the train for Dijon. It would come early the next morning, so we were put up in a hotel for the night. My father, of course, was forced to remain behind, so we were separated again. Then, in the middle of the night, Grandmother had a heart attack, brought on by exhaustion and the emotional stress of the trip. It really put us in a dreadful situation. Fortunately, the hotel manager took pity on us. She was an important member of the Resistance. She shamed the guardsmen. She spoke like a real Résistant and told them, "What did these people do to you? You know very well that the Germans will take them. These people are in real danger. As Frenchmen, you don't have the right to turn them over!"

Well, those guardsmen weren't happy with themselves. They telephoned back and forth to the Prefecture of Macon, and finally we were given the authorization to stay with Dad. We would be placed under house arrest with him in the same village. We returned to Salornay-sur-Guye and found a place to stay. What I remember most is that we were cold. But after we were settled, I began school. I went to the girls' school, and my brother went to the school for boys.

At the beginning, it was difficult. I was from the city, not the country. There was also a sort of jealousy, a kind of hostility. I arrived in the middle of the school year, and the other children didn't want to talk to me. They had a leader who told them not to talk to me. Every time that I tried to talk with one of the children, she was ordered not to answer me. I soon discovered that their leader wasn't very intelligent. Then I told myself that the best way to get back at her is to work harder than her.

So I worked hard, I learned my lessons by heart, really worked, did as the teacher said. I knew everything. But it also was hard for me. As soon as the teacher asked a question, I would raise my hand. Then the others wanted to know the answers, they wanted me to whisper to them. I decided that I wasn't going to do that; it was very important to me. Eventually, since the others saw that I knew the answers, and their leader did not, they came to me. Finally, the wicked leader became friendly, the most friendly. And that was how I became integrated into the school. After that, there were no problems. I made friends. Since my brother went through the same ordeal, we were the best students in our respective classes for three years. At least ten points separated me from the child who was in second place in class.

As I said, my father had succeeded in finding a place for us, but the owner's daughter, who was two years younger than me, was very cruel. While we were in school, she kept calling me "dirty Jew." Finally, I became very angry and punched her, knocked her down in the school courtyard. The teacher came and asked, "Marcelle, what happened here?" I told her that the girl was always calling me a dirty Jew and that I was tired of it. The teacher said that I couldn't be treated like that and that I was right. The teacher was very fair. She really was very nice. I felt that she was on my side.

My mother became pregnant, and since there were no baby clothes available, we had to make them. My mother didn't know how to knit; my grandmother knew but was very rusty. So I went to the teacher and said, "Mom is expecting a baby. I would like to knit clothes, but I don't know how. Would you teach me?" And it was the teacher who helped me make my sister's clothing. Since we didn't have much material, we had to use sheets to make the clothing.

Something else important happened in 1942. An aunt, an uncle, and their daughter and son had also left Dijon and were staying in Décines, near Lyon. They managed to visit us in July while we were on holiday from school. My mother and my aunt decided to switch children during the holiday; I went back to Décines with my aunt and my cousin stayed with my parents.

Just after we arrived, the next morning, the police decided to close the district. Then, they came to my aunt's house with a list. My cousin was on the list, but of course she wasn't there. So they took me to replace her. It was the French police and National Guard. There were no Germans there. They gave us 15 minutes to pack, 15 minutes. We were put in the back of a truck with women, children, some babies, old people. The women managed to bring some canned food. Everyone was comparing canned food, I remember that well. Then, everyone was crying because we didn't know what was going to happen.

Fortunately, before I left for Décines, my father had given me a certificate of naturalization. My cousin argued with the police, telling them that I was taken by mistake, that I was a French citizen. My cousin fought well for me, arguing my case. Finally, since I was 11 and didn't have any place to go, the police agreed that I could leave, accompanied by my aunt and one of the National Guards. He followed about 50 meters behind us, and after we went some distance, he shouted, "What are you waiting for? Run for your freedom!" That was something that stayed with me because I remember telling my aunt, "Let's go. We'll run and hide. They won't find us. They won't know where we went." My aunt refused because her son was being held as a hostage. She said, "Me, I cannot leave Boubi [Bernard]. You go and call your dad. He'll send someone to pick you up."

And that's what happened. I left my aunt, and she went back and was taken to a camp.

My father, of course, couldn't travel. The daughter of a hotel owner came instead, the trip paid for by my father. She took me back to Salornay. My cousin knew that her mother and brother had been taken and that the police would be looking for her. She went into hiding and in time made her way to Lyon where she found non-Jewish friends. They hid her during the entire war.

It was very difficult when Mom became pregnant. Marie Louise was born during a terrible time in November 1943, but we were lucky to be living in a village where there were many members of the Resistance. We were not denounced even though we were at the mercy of any denunciation. Every so often, the *milice* [fascist French police] came to the village looking for Jews, and the mayor would say, "Oh, there aren't any left here. They all went to Switzerland."

My father, however, was arrested. What happened was interesting.

One day, he was at the barber's when some National Guardsmen came to the house looking for him. He was to be sent to a camp for foreigners; they were not called concentration camps yet, they were called detention camps. When my brother saw the policemen in the house, he ran to the barbershop and told my father not to go home. So my father went to the mayor's house. The mayor was a Communist and also a member of the Resistance. When my father got there, he was hidden in the barn by the mayor's 19-year-old daughter, who also was in the Resistance and did a lot of work for them.

Of course, everyone knew that my father was in Salornay. While he was in hiding, a plan was made to help him. He was told of a doctor in Macon who was part of the Resistance network. A photograph of my father would be provided so that the doctor could identify him. The doctor would then provide a certificate telling that my father couldn't be sent to a camp because of his poor health.

Well, Dad didn't believe it. He would tell them, "Oh, la, la. It's not possible. I can't believe this!" Finally, the mayor, his daughter, and a Resistance network agent told him, "Max, don't worry. You're under our protection. You will get out of it. You have to trust us."

Then, he had a crisis of conscience to turn himself in. It was really dramatic. The day Dad turned himself in, the police were waiting for him when he came home. He said goodbye to everyone, and I heard him say to himself, "This is impossible. I will never see them again." He was taken to Macon and imprisoned. My mother went to see the doctor there. My grandmother accompanied her because my mother was nine months' pregnant and close to delivering. Mom showed a photograph of Dad to the doctor. "I beg of you," she implored him, "I'm waiting for a fourth child, you really must leave a father for these children." My grandmother was crying. There was a lot of emotion.

In prison, my father didn't eat for several days. I remember later that he was very pale, his face, his hands, you would think that he was deadly sick.

So when he went through the medical examination, the doctor signed that he was not healthy enough for a detention camp. Because of that certificate, signed by the doctor in the Resistance, my father came back home. The policeman who came with him kept telling him, "See, I told you, I really told you that you would be home tonight."

At that time, people didn't know about the Final Solution. We thought that the women and children would be taken and placed in labor camps. We thought that it was work that interested them. We did not think that it was a question of our lives. Never would we have thought of that; we could not imagine such a final solution! It was impossible to understand.

Immediately after [his release], Dad entered the Resistance. He went into hiding. There was a lot of resistance in the area around Cluny; it was a region of large forests. In the Resistance were both Partisans and members of the Free French.* There was some rivalry between them, too.

I remember in particular the "day of the parachutes." It was 14 July 1943 [Bastille Day], the middle of the day. We saw three planes coming. The first parachute they dropped was blue, the second white, and the third red [the colors of the French flag]. Everyone was shouting and waving. It was going on right in the middle of the day, under the nose of the Germans, who were ten kilometers away. By the time the police arrived later that afternoon, the parachutes and everything with them had disappeared. The goods and the parachutes had already been shared out. We didn't know about nylon until we saw those parachutes; then we began to make clothing from it. After that, when we saw young girls with nylon clothing, we knew that more parachutes had been dropped.

After Dad went into the Resistance, we didn't see him very often. We didn't know what was going on. There were fights between the Germans and the Resistance. In Cluny, there was a very serious battle. It was terrifying. There were tanks, artillery—I even saw the first German prisoners of the Resistance. It made me tremble. They were the first Germans that I saw as prisoners. Some of them were killed.

Dad took care of the parachute drops and guarded Germans, as well. He spoke perfect German. In addition, he spoke French, Yiddish, Hebrew, and Polish and understood Russian. He could write Hebrew, too, and so could Mom. Dad did his duty as an enemy of the Nazis.

---

* The Partisans were members of the internal homegrown French Resistance, while the Free French were those controlled by General Charles de Gaulle from London. The two groups became united during 1942-43, when de Gaulle's agent, Jean Moulin, succeeded in combining them.

When it was time for my little sister to be born, my mother didn't want to go to the hospital in Macon. She knew that she would be in danger there. On our ration cards, there was a stamp for Jews. When the midwife saw that my mother was Jewish, she put her name on a separate list because the Germans required them to do that. These lists were put together in schools, clinics, hospitals, everywhere, and especially in the maternity hospitals and retirement homes where there were many old people. Everybody and everything that was Jewish was on a list. So Mom knew that she was in danger if she delivered in the maternity hospital. When Dad said to get her suitcase ready to go to Macon, Mom said, "No, Max. I'm staying at Salornay and want to give birth here." When Dad didn't agree, Mom said, "There's no way that I'm giving birth in Macon. I'm not going there for any reason." Arrangements were made with a midwife for the birth in Salornay. For the first time, Dad had to help with the birth, which was his fifth child. I was very proud of that.

After the Liberation, we returned to Dijon. We didn't have a place to live since someone else was in our old apartment. Finding a place was very difficult. Dad managed to rent a room and a kitchen for us. Seven of us had to live in that room and a small kitchen. It was unbelievably crowded. We managed to get back some of the furniture that we had entrusted to our neighbors. The judge who lived on the first floor of the building had our dining room stuff. We also got some living room furniture, but not a lot. We had to buy many things when we got back, but the most important thing was that we all were alive. Eventually, we managed to find a room for Grandmother. She was 80 years old then; my brother and I were in charge of taking care of her. As conditions improved after the war, we moved once, twice, three times. At the beginning, the apartments didn't have much comfort; there was no water, no toilet, no comfort at all. But slowly things got better.

During the war, we had ration cards for food and clothing, perhaps for other things, too. We even had to use the textile ration card to get the yellow star that we were required to wear in the German occupied zone—I didn't wear it in the free zone where we lived. Since everyone in the family had ration cards, we had enough so that we wanted to help the members of the family that were in hiding in the occupied zone. Because the people of the village of Salornay were very nice to us, we asked the local baker if we could send some of our ration points to our family. He agreed. I remember that he was cute and really brave.

After we were settled in Dijon, we went on a search for Mom's and Dad's family members. We were very anxious because we found out about that time what really had happened. We started to count those who were missing, afraid that they were gone. Then, we realized that no one had survived. No one! About 75 people among Mom's and Dad's relatives! Close family members taken and killed by the Germans. There were no more families. Nothing. Everybody disappeared.

Around that time, after the war, I was 14. And I understood what had happened. I understood everything. There are things that one never forgets. Whoever forgets the past is bound to live it again.

In 1968, I went to Poland with my father and my daughter. He returned because he wanted to know what really had happened. He said, "I should absolutely go to Łęczyka," his family's native village. Getting there was really complicated because now it was in part of the Soviet Union.* But we succeeded and asked the questions we wanted answers for. There were some nuns, widows, who said that no one could be saved, not even a baby, not even a child, no one. It was impossible. To try and save someone, you took the risk of being denounced. They would have been denounced because the Polish people are extremely anti-Semitic.

Then we went to Auschwitz. I prayed a lot because it was really important [to remember]. It was 1968, soon after the Soviet invasion of Czechoslovakia. Everything was mixed up. In one way, I was reliving the past; and then, in another, I was living the present, which also was hard.

In 1945, [when I was 14] I went back to my old school in Dijon. I had left my school friends from several grades below. Then we all got together again in sixth grade. Since the sixth grade was on the second floor, I walked up to find my class. All of my friends were very happy to see me back. Everyone was wishing me well. It was a good time, I was happy. Then the headmaster of the school, the one who used to call me into her office, and who was still headmaster, saw that the lines [of children waiting to enter the school] were uneven because I was saying "Hello" to people. She came towards me, and she slapped me. She slapped me just like that in front of everybody. When I asked her why, she said, "Because you are disturbing the lines." I realized that she was not pleased that I had returned. The slap was her welcoming present.

I had come back filled with happiness. But after that slap, I figured that she was anti-Semitic. I understood that I had to deal with a bad woman. I didn't want to stay in that school. But I stayed long enough to pass the Certificat d'étude exam [exam taken at age 14, marking the end of primary studies; no longer given]. I did not have anti-Semitic problems in the class-room. I had been asked to tell my story, and afterwards the teacher, whose

---

* Łęczyka is in central Poland and was never part of the Soviet Union. However, Poland was part of the Soviet empire.

husband was a major figure in the Resistance, gave a moral lesson to the students. She told them that they had to treat me justly. That teacher always protected me, which was very important to me. That was not the case with the headmaster.

My parents had to start all over again after the war. It was very difficult. We didn't have a store. My parents went from market to market, selling clothes. My mother found some distributors in Strasbourg and managed to get some material. She made good pants, blue pants for peasants, velvet pants, clothing like that. Thanks to her, we restarted. After I received the Certificat, my parents needed me in the markets, and I worked, too. I worked in the markets for nine years. It was only later that we were able to have a store.

Like my parents, I was a member of the Jewish community after the war. I liked to hang out with the Jewish youth group; curiously enough, we didn't like to talk about the war years. We were so happy to be alive. Each of us had his or her story, and we did not want to think about those tragedies. We wanted to live life because it was terrible during those years: we were at the mercy of those who would denounce us, of raids, at the mercy of everybody. We did not want to talk about it, we were just happy to be with each other. We were alive. That was what mattered.

The community was broken by the war. Many people from the synagogue died. Those who succeeded in leaving Dijon for the free zone in the south survived; those who stayed were taken. Many had been in hiding.

Since I was among the young men and women who were associated with the synagogue, my parents gave me permission to attend its activities. That was the only time that I had permission to go out. My parents were very strict. They didn't want me to marry a Gentile.

In any case, I didn't want to marry a Gentile, although there were some Gentiles who wanted to date me. They wanted young Jewish girls because the girls were well brought-up and very educated. They always ran after young Jewish women. For me, I was educated by my grandmother, a true Jewish woman. I knew what to do and what not to—there were 30 Jewish women available to be married in the synagogue at that time. Unfortunately, some of them married Gentiles.

Bernard was in the Jewish youth group. He was one of the leaders. He had noticed me, but I hadn't noticed him. His sister asked him, "Bernard, why aren't you going out with Marcelle? She's nice." He said, "Oh, she would never want to go out with me." Finally, during a Hanukkah holiday, while he was doing his military service, he came to the synagogue in his uniform. I looked at him. He had changed. He was slim, handsome. I looked at him differently. He danced with me later, and it was very good. The next day, a Sunday, we went to the Juras to ski. And, well, that's how it began; we started to go out. It was 1954.

I remember the day the State of Israel was proclaimed [May 14, 1948]. I was 17 then. Grandmother was still alive. She was very religious; she said on that day, "Now I can die. I have seen the State of Israel." For her, it was really important.

There were a lot of meetings at the synagogue at the time. It was really a time of great joy. That the State of Israel was proclaimed was a miracle, because the next day all the Arab states were going to jump on it. That was a dangerous time, and we were all very scared. A lot of young people from Belfort left for Israel. I had a cousin who ran away, who wanted to go to Israel to fight. She was arrested in Marseille, and her parents succeeded in getting her back because she was a minor.

My grandparents, my parents were Zionists, going back to the end of the nineteenth century. I have a photograph of my dad with a Zionist group in Poland when he was young. He had always been a Zionist. When we went to Israel, we recognized an avenue where trees were planted by the Jews of Łęczyka. Mom said, "Ah, this is something that remained from the grandparents."

Nadia Kaluski

Raised in a secular family with strong Leftist political convictions but attacked as a Jew, Nadia Kaluski joined the Resistance against the German Occupation during World War II. Her mother and sister, however, did not survive. After the war she worked as an elementary school teacher. Later she published her sister's letters from the French deportation center at Drancy and became an important French Holocaust educator. In failing health she ended her life in 2005.

Spring 1993

I was born in a small village in Seine-Loire, although my parents lived in Paris. It was six months before the end of World War I and Paris was under bombardment. My mother sought the peacefulness of the countryside, and that's why I was born there. But afterwards my mother moved back to Paris. At that time, I had a brother who was four years old. Later my younger sister, Louise, was born.

My father was a woodworker who made furniture. He was a Russian and a revolutionary. The czar's police had arrested him and detained him for two years, but he had wonderful memories of that time because he was with other intellectuals involved in plotting revolution. Yet after his release, he decided to leave Russia and emigrate to the country of Zola and Victor Hugo,* the country of freedom.

In France, he found work immediately. On his worker's wages, he could eat every day in a restaurant, have meat and wine on his table. He even acquired a bicycle. I have a photograph of him with three friends and the famous bicycle. For him, France was a wonderful country!

My mother also was born in Russia. Her parents owned a clothing store. They were more middle class, bourgeois. She never went to school because she had to help care for her six brothers and sisters. But she loved her youngest sister, Nadia, a great deal and wanted her to study. Thanks to my mother, my Aunt Nadia became a doctor. When my mother was 18 and had put aside a little money, she decided to learn how to read and write Russian. Around that time she also departed a little from her religion... there was a goy who was a perfect match for her, but he was a goy and, well, you know....

So she decided to leave Russia, to emigrate. She intended to go to the United States. But on her journey she stopped in France because she already had a brother there, Solomon, who was married and had kids. My Uncle

---

* Renowned, Leftist nineteenth-century French authors.

Solomon's wife came from the same place as my father, and so my father would often visit. It was there that my father met my mother. When they were married, my grandparents sent a little money for my mother's dowry.

My mother wanted my father to be more than a worker, and eventually he became the owner of his own business. But that wasn't easy for him because he was a Communist. He thought that becoming an owner was going over to the side of the enemy so he continued to wear the same uniform as the other workers. He worked hard, leaving very early in the morning and coming back late at night.

My mother always wanted me to study. She wanted me to become a doctor like her sister Nadia, whom I was named after. I first attended the Communal School in Paris, then went on to high school. But when the war came, things got a little complicated. I didn't want to study any longer. I became a teacher.

Regarding the 1930s, I have memories that demonstrate how irrelevant religion was to us. I had a girlfriend from school whom I had known for many years. Our high school was in rue des Rosiers, and there were many Jews in that neighborhood [the Marais]. One day we were walking there and saw an old Jew. My friend said, "Did you see that Jew?" She looked disgusted. I told her that I was a Jew too. "It's not true, Nadia, it's not true!" she replied. My friend went home and told her parents, "See, my friend Nadia is a Jew, and she is very nice." I used to visit her at her house, and her parents liked me. But when they found out that I was Jewish, they didn't want her to see me again. They were goys, Auvernians, anti-Semites. This was during the Popular Front government under Léon Blum. They didn't want her to see me because I was Jewish and my family was on the Left, politically, like the government. So we had to see each other in secret, and I still hear from her.

But we didn't celebrate Yom Kippur and the other holidays. Sometimes we were told about the **seder**, but we didn't do it. We didn't do Hanukkah either. I learned about it during the war. I didn't know about it before. I didn't learn Yiddish. My mother spoke to me in Russian, and I answered in French. When my parents didn't want me to know what they were talking about, they spoke to each other in Yiddish.

We did observe Christmas, with a tree. I know that surprises a lot of people. Even when my sister was in the detention center at Drancy outside Paris during the war, she wrote that they celebrated Christmas and that she received a present. After my sister's letters were adapted and performed in the theater and I was interviewed by Radio Judaica in Lyon, I was asked about it. They just didn't understand. I told them that, for us, it didn't have anything to do with the birth of Jesus, that it was more of a holiday for the children, that every child received gifts during Christmas, and so did we. It was a French holiday. I was French.

Although my father was a Communist and Léon Blum was a Socialist, my father respected him. Blum and the Popular Front were on the Left and they were doing good things, especially the social laws. What we were truly touched by was the Spanish war, the civil war. I had anarchist friends who went to Spain to fight. My friend's father died there. It was hard because things were actually pretty bad between Communists and anarchists.

I don't remember life during the 1930s very well. I do remember that my family lived a little drama because one of the workers had an accident. He cut his hand, and my father felt responsible. I also remember that there were anti-Semitic episodes in 1936. In the 1930s, there already were Jews who had emigrated from Germany.

I got married in 1939. We had to get permission because my husband was already in the army. He was stationed in the east not far from the Maginot Line. For a year, there was what we called "the phony war."* Then, after the fighting and the armistice, my husband was sent to Strasbourg and from there was taken to Germany as a prisoner of war. He had one year of war and five years of captivity. We were separated for six years. It's true that for a long time I did not receive any news, but when it was possible for my husband to send me letters during the war, he sent me many. He wrote with a pencil. He would write on one-half of a double page, and I would answer on the other half with a pencil. I know that the Germans read them because in one of the letters I received a note telling me to write more clearly.

In Germany, my husband had different jobs: he would cut ice, and he worked the land. He also worked with wine; he had to fill the bottles. Then he found an interesting job at an aviation factory—Zibel—as an industrial designer. While he was there, he wrote a lot of poems. He was not unhappy. They did not make him work too hard. He just had to look like he was working fine. If he wasn't, he would be sent to the Russian front. While a prisoner he fabricated a galena, a tiny radio, in a little box of matches. At night, he could listen to the BBC. He got the entire news, and the next morning he would share it with the entire camp. He was not considered Jewish. He was Jewish from his father's side, not his mother's. And his name—there are many goys who have a name with "iski," like Kaluski.

---

* The phony war was the period between the defeat and occupation of Poland by Germany in September 1939 and spring 1940 when the Germans launched an offensive in the west that culminated in the fall of France in May.

I received letters from him throughout the war. From time to time [mail delivery] would take a long time; for example, when I wrote to him about the arrest of my mother in August, he only mentioned it in November.

In May 1940, when the Germans invaded, everyone started to leave. I was given a mission with the kids to take them out of Paris. I took my mother and sister with me. We stayed two months in the Haute Vienne. We slept in classrooms. It was not very hygienic. My mother retained a horrible memory of those two months, because even though she was not religious, she would not eat pork, and that was all they would give us. When we moved back to Paris, I had to quit teaching. By October 1940, there already were anti-Semitic laws, and I lost my job. I had started teaching elementary school in 1938 when I was 20.

When we were forced to wear the yellow star and they began to arrest people, I told my mother and my sister that we had to get away. My brother and his wife already were in Lyon; therefore, my mother asked me to go ahead and find a place to stay. My sister did not want to leave without our mother, and that is when I said something I cannot forget to my mother; "If anything happens to Louise, it is going to be your fault."

Well, I left. I managed to pass into the free zone, and I found an apart-ment [in the same building] where my brother lived. I wrote to my mother. The French police had arrested them, but they actually were looking for me. Two French officers came to the apartment when only my mother was there. They did not find me; they could have left and said that they couldn't locate me. But they searched the apartment and found Leftist magazines. So they accused my mother and my sister. While the search was going on, my sister came back from school. She was not wearing the star. That is why they arrested and deported her. That was in 1942.

When Louise was in prison, she began to send letters. It was a help for her. They had put her with girls who were under 18. She was the only one there for political reasons. The others were prostitutes or thieves. She was 17 years old and the only virgin. She had to assert herself. She always made it seem like everything was fine.

I have a letter that I always carry with me. It is the letter before the last one she wrote to me before being deported. She made it sound like she was happy, almost like she was on vacation at Club Med. She wrote telling us how she did her laundry and how everybody was nice to her and that she had a lot of friends. She mentioned that she took classes; her philosophy teacher was a friend of mine from high school. She was always worried about our mother and Gilbert, my husband. She received a photograph of the family while she was in Drancy. She met incredible people there, a gentleman who had known Louis Pasteur and who would give lectures about him. She studied philosophy with her friend, Irma, whom she admired. Our aunt was also there at the same time.

Louise was deported in February 1943 and never returned. Her friend Irma was the only one who survived. I met her. She was ashamed because she had survived. She told me that when they were processed by the SS in the camp, they had to tell their profession. She told Louise to say "chemist." But Louise said "student." So Louise was sent to the gas chambers and Irma survived. She felt embarrassed to be in front of me. She was embarrassed because she was there and Louise was not. I was ashamed because she had lived through so many atrocities and because my mother and my sister had disappeared when it was me they were looking for.

My mother did not survive, either. After her sentencing, she was sent to Sens. She spent 14 months in prison. I wrote to the director of the prison begging him to keep her there. In November 1943, she was deported, and we never had any other news.

My father survived. My parents had been separated because they didn't get along. During the Occupation, he wore the star and nobody bothered him. Even in Paris. He ate in restaurants. He continued his small business under the management of the Germans. When the police called him in, he organized everything, including his will. He arranged for people to take care of Louise. When he went to the police, the official who talked to him was mad because my father had been writing letters using the official's name. My father told him it was only to save Louise. Finally, he was released and never bothered again. It is very strange because he remained a Communist, even during the war.

My brother, his wife, and I joined the Resistance, a Jewish component of the movement. It was called l'Union des Juifs pour la Résistance et l'Entraide. It was important to us that it was a Jewish movement. We did so because we were attacked as Jews, and therefore we wanted to fight in a Jewish movement. Yes, we were very assimilated, but we were attacked as Jews. There are a lot of people who said, "The Jews let themselves get killed." I cannot stand that idea. You know, even the most extraordinary people in the Resistance lost every kind of control they had once the Gestapo arrested them.

Back in 1936, I did not even have the idea to tell my best friend that I was Jewish. Then, suddenly, I am sentenced to death because I am a Jew. I realized then what it meant to wear a star. In the streets, people pointed at me. In the metro, we were only allowed to sit in the last car. You heard people saying, "Oh, look. How pretty. Isn't it too bad?" That was when I realized that I was not like the rest of the population. I had a neighbor with whom I was on good terms who one day saw me on the street when I was not wearing the star. "Why aren't you wearing your star?" she asked. I actually think that she was the one who denounced us.

When we were in Lyon during the war, life was hard, especially getting adequate food for the family. But there was work. I wasn't teaching anymore, but I learned to type and became a secretary. And, of course, there was the Resistance. I participated in a number of ways: I transported children. Also munitions. And I falsified documents, hundreds of them. My brother was in the Resistance with us. He was the head of our unit. His code name was "Lieutenant Denis." He trained people in the use of arms.

We really did not have any idea of what was happening to the Jews. We heard horror stories, but we couldn't believe them. Anything seemed possible except murder.

After the war, when I returned to Paris, I went to see a neighbor who had taken care of my mother and had stored our furniture. We had written to each other during the war, and she was incredible—she used to help my father prepare packages for my mother. Two of her daughters were nuns. One of them lived in Lyon. During the war, I went to see her and asked her to shelter and hide Jewish children, but she said that it was illegal and refused. Of course, that was not our neighbor's fault. She was the first person I saw when I returned to Paris and she was so excited. "You are back! You are back!" she kept saying.

Of course, our apartment had been occupied, and I had to find another place to live. I found a studio, and that is where my husband and I stayed for a while. But my husband was having a hard time, and I decided to take a teaching job again. We also had children then. I requested [a teaching position in] Saône et Loire, out in the countryside [east of Paris in Burgundy]. We went to Vigny-les-Parais, where it was very hard for us. Everything was very basic. Even the closest stores were eight kilometers from the house. The teaching was different because all the children were in one room and their ages varied from five to 14.

We were there about ten years. After the first four years, we finally got running water, and we also bought a used car. At that time, my husband was ill; he was paralyzed for almost a year. He recovered slowly but eventually was able to work again. My daughters grew up there and went to elementary school, where I taught them. They were smart and talented and pretty. When it was time for them to go to high school, they had to go to another town, so I asked to be transferred. That's when we left for Chalons-sur-Saône. After high school, when they enrolled at the University of Dijon, we moved with them, and here we stayed.

It was in the 1970s when I began to think about the Shoah, what had happened during the war. I started to think about it when people began to deny what had happened. I had avoided talking about it with my children. Yet, there always was a photograph of my mother and Louise on the wall. Before my daughters went to bed, they would give a kiss to Grandma Olga and Louisette. I did not explain all the atrocities, but I think they felt it. I had kept the letters from Louise and I would read them over and over again. I would cry a lot. Now it is impossible for me to cry. I used to get very upset when people began to deny the facts. We were the witnesses.

It was then that I decided to prepare a file with passages from my sister's letters. I sent the file to her high school in Paris. They never responded. I waited a year or two and started again. Finally, in 1989 I wrote to the administrator telling him that I was coming to Paris to visit him. He did not reply. I went to Paris anyway and checked into a hotel across from the high school. I went there, and the secretaries asked me what I was looking for. They were surprised when I told them because it all had happened in the 1940s and I had waited so long before doing something. I told them that for years people had denied what had happened and only now did I have a chance to talk about it, and for that reason, I wanted to see the administrator. But they told me he was not there.

I prepared a file for the national minister of education at the time and one for Serge Klarsfeld.* He told me that the letters were fabulous. He wanted to publish them. I was a little surprised, but I agreed. When I told him about my mother's letters, and my father's, he wanted to do something with the entire family, a Jewish family during the Occupation. But there was a couple who were not Jewish who were interested in the history of Jews during the Occupation, and they turned the letters into a play. It was performed in two theaters in Paris and [three times] at the festival in Avignon.† It is an intimate play. It is true and personalized, not about statistics. When you are told about six million victims, it makes you want to vomit. This play makes you want to cry because even though Louise's letters are not sad, we know what is going to happen to her at the end. It is the story of a young girl who was full of life, so smart and good-hearted.

I am going to tell you something about the word "Jew." I explained to Serge Klarsfeld that I was having a problem with the high school administrator who did not want to see me. Klarsfeld phoned him. The administrator

---

* Famous Nazi hunter and Holocaust scholar.

† *Les lettres de Louise Jacobson,* adapted by Juliette Batlle and Alain Gintzburger, and bearing the same name. The play was performed about 350 times in France, Italy, Belgium, and Holland, between 1991–98.

said that it was the secretary's fault, and of course he would like to see me. The administrator called me and explained that it had been a mistake and that he would see me.

Klarsfeld and I had agreed to make a commemorative plaque for Louise and other students who had possibly disappeared during the war. I took care of the research in Paris when a colleague of the administrator said that he was too busy to help. I found files, and eventually we had 13 names. Therefore, we did a commemorative plaque for 13 victims. There was a discussion about details like the dates. The administrator said that "Auschwitz" would be enough. I said that we had to put in dates, that people needed to know. Seniors in the school were asking during which war it happened. And the administrator was Jewish, his name was Soussan. I wanted to put on the plaque "because they were Jewish." He agreed to put "Jewish students killed in Auschwitz." That was okay, but it kind of implied that it had happened to students who were not Jewish also, and that was not true. They had killed them only because they were Jewish, not for another reason. The administrator did not want to change the inscription. There was a reception when the plaque was dedicated, and the administrator did not even mention Klarsfeld's name.

Another thing: we learned that people who died after deportation were not recognized as having died then. They were not even identified as Jews. They were listed as having died either at Drancy or Compiègne. It seemed that everybody had died in France. I requested my mother's and my sister's death certificates. They noted, "Dead in Drancy." I responded that they had died in Auschwitz. They had given me a deportation card with the date of departure from Drancy. My sister left on February 13 and died on February 18. I was told that I had to hire a lawyer to prove it.

I found these records in the Secrétariat d'État aux Anciens Combattants [Secretary of State for Veterans]. We started to send letters to deputies and senators, important people. They had to admit that these Jews were murdered. We received a lot of responses, many letters. Robert Badinter was Minister of Justice at the time, and he did not understand, he thought it was a sentimental thing. But it was about historical truth. An official act was passed on 15 May 1985. It corrected my mother's and my sister's papers. It corrected many records, but there are still many that are incorrect.

I learned about Israel during the war. I remember because my friend Freda left for Israel in 1943. She had been hiding in Lot-et-Garonne [a department in southwest France] with her family. They were Zionists. She came to see me in Lyon and asked for falsified papers so that they could cross the border into Spain. Louise was still in prison at the time. My mother was at the Petite Roquette prison. [Freda and her family] went to Spain and stayed in Barcelona for a year. They found passage on a ship to go to Palestine, and what is incredible is that the Germans protected the ship. After the war, we started to keep in touch again. I knew about everything that was happening in Israel. She died, but her children come to France often.

I have a hard time with criticism about Israel. I have become a Zionist. My identity as a Jew and a Communist changed. The Resistance movement was a Communist movement, but when the Communist newspapers started to come out, they were anti-Zionist. My husband used to say that between 1917 and 1945 there had been no radical change in the mentalities in Russia [which remained anti-Semitic in spite of being Communist].

My husband is not Jewish, but he began to feel Jewish when the Six Day War broke out in 1967. I was very upset about the war, and I wanted him to be concerned. He wrote to the Israeli Embassy and asked if he would be considered a Jew if he moved to Israel. They told him no because he was not born of a Jewish mother. He got angry. His first wife, from whom he was divorced, was Jewish. I was Jewish. Our children were Jewish. Maybe we would have gone had we found a positive answer to his question. Eventually, I traveled to Israel. I went there five times in the 1970s and 1980s. I liked the kibbutzes.

The 1967 war started right after we moved to Dijon. Freda and I were writing to each other. I remember those horrible songs sung by the Egyptian people. Then de Gaulle said something [that the Jews were a domineering people], and I thought that all the anti-Semites would come out of the closet. You know, for about 50 years, they were afraid to talk about Vichy. There is something wrong when we could not talk about a shameful past.

We came to Dijon in 1964. For two years I was a teacher. Then for ten years I was the head of a school. I discovered the secular lifestyle of the Leftist Jews. For me it was a new world. And it was a good world. I enjoyed it very much. We spent time reading about Judaism—the history of the European Jews and many other books, Sholem Aleichem,* of course. I learned about Hanukkah and **Purim**. I learned things like that.

We were not active and did not celebrate the holidays, but we knew that the holidays existed. In Dijon, there is a powerful sense of community. My link to the community is through our daughter, Cathie.† She was married in the synagogue. The wedding was very nice, but she was a little upset because she

---

* Prolific late nineteenth-century Hebrew and Yiddish author, born Sholem Rabinowitz (1859–1916).

† See the interview with Cathie Bussidan in the Community Leaders section above, p. 23.

had to go to the ritual bath. Slowly, she began to embrace the traditions, and now they celebrate Hanukkah. But they also celebrate Christmas. And now her husband Michel is secretary of the synagogue. Cathie is integrated into the community. She told me that I had been a Jew in the middle of sad Jews and that she was with Jews who were happy. "I want to be a Jew and happy and that is why I respect the traditions," she told me. I think that it's great.

My other daughter is with a gentile, but she does not hide the fact that she is Jewish. When we broadcast Louise's letters on the radio in Dijon, she told everyone that Louise was her aunt.

I am still a member of the LICRA; I am the Honorary President. I am involved because I continue taking care of information regarding the people who died after deportation. LICRA helped with Louise's letters. I am not involved in other organizations of the same type. But I am in France-Israel and the WIZO. I am no longer involved in political movements, but I am in humanitarian activities concerning unfortunate children.

Yes, I did think at one time that Hitler had won the war. I know now, however, that he did not totally win. But we should not forget. It may bother some people, but you can never remember the Shoah too much. I think about it, and I talk about it, and we should not forget. I am Jewish now.

Spring 2005

Yes, I have been making speeches. Talking in front of people is very interesting, isn't it? When they invite me to talk to students about my experience, I've gone. But I've not gone lately because of my illness. I cannot move around that much anymore. I have less confidence in myself, but I've had a very motivated, inspiring contact with a librarian. He and one of his colleagues— she also is a librarian—told me that they had listened to my speech when they were in high school. He said that he had great memories of my talk, and he wanted me to come and talk at his school. I told myself that I should try and do it. Another friend of mine, also named Nadia, who is not Jewish but who has always been [friendly] with the Jews, a very kind and generous person, I asked to come with me. So I had her along to help with the wheelchair. We arranged everything with the foundation that helps handicapped people. They were very helpful, especially with the transportation. My grandson, Mimi, managed to get out of work and came and listened. He's a wonderful man.

It took us 45 minutes to get there. The director of the institution welcomed me very nicely and let me talk as long as I wanted. And I didn't mumble, you know [laughs]. Then they presented me with a beautiful flower.... There were quite a lot of students; the attendance was not bad at all. They were about 17 or 18 years old. It was an interview-type talk and was recorded. I think that [my talk] was for that purpose as well as a lecture for the students. They asked me a lot of questions. I had to note them down because when I give testimony for my life in front of people I have so many things in my head. But everything went well, and I was pleased. The librarians enjoyed it even more. They said, "My God, this time was as impressive as it was four years ago when we first heard your talk."

So, for me it was wonderful. I believe that this has given me the confidence to do other things like this from time to time if it works out.

You asked me if I now have concerns about Jews in France. For the Jews, I don't think that it's very good. There are those who still make sick jokes and comments about Jews. They are people who make a show of this, and I think they are hideous people. I think that a way should be found to stop these people from doing it. So this is one of the things most troubling to me. Sometimes I wonder what is going to happen to the children....

Even during the Pétain regime and the propaganda that existed at that time, when we were obliged to wear the star, there were people who took risks to help the Jews. Actually, three-fourths of the Jews were saved thanks to these people. So when facing human beings, it's a matter of being a little bit conscious. So I am concerned. But, after all, the French people are not something contemptible to me. It's not that bad.

As for Israel, I think that there is hope for peace. I have always believed that the person who accepts the position of prime minister, the leader of a country so small but also so continuously jeopardized, this person definitely has a lot of courage. And even when I've heard very bad things about [then Prime Minister Ariel] Sharon, I think that in spite of everything, he has gained a lot of respect.

There were rumors of anti-Semitism in France, and he said, "Come to Israel!" [July 2004]. And this is why we need Israel. Because when we were facing those difficult years during the German Occupation, I was telling myself, "If we had a country, we could have gone there and escaped from this." No matter where, just an escape. Only if we had a country.

My father was a Communist and an anti-Zionist, but during the war I told myself that this was insane. People should have a country. It's absolutely necessary that they have a country. So when Sharon said, "Come to Israel" [July 2004], I believed that it was his job, his responsibility, to say that. He didn't mean to harm anyone. People need to have a country where they can find refuge when they need to escape from anti-Semitism.

The anti-Semitism in France might not have been severe enough to make people leave. Perhaps it is not. But Sharon didn't know that. He simply heard that there is anti-Semitism in France and told the French Jews to come. That's how it was at the time. There were a lot of Jews here who were angry with him, even some people whom I love dearly. They were not happy with Sharon. But it makes no difference. I like Sharon a lot. It's all in the name of our memories.

I love Israel and I love the people who have gone through great difficulties so that Israel continues to exist. After all, they are the people who protect us. But despite everything, it's not necessary to leave France. If someone wants to go—yes, but it's not necessary. I don't think it's right to consider Israel as only a place of refuge. But it's good to have another country.

COMMUNITY MEMBERS

Deborah Bensoussan

Deborah Bensoussan enjoys watching American films and TV programs and listening to American popular music, but like many young people in the affluent West, she also is seeking deeper religious meaning and experience. She is well informed of, and acutely aware of, the problems facing French Jewry, and though thoroughly attached to her country, also considers options. Deborah is an articulate voice of her questioning generation. She studied law at the University of Marseille and is now continuing these studies in Paris.

November 2006

My name is Deborah. I am 17, almost 18. I am in my last year of high school, before college. My high school major is economics. I have two sisters and a brother, who is much older than me. I am the youngest. My mother was a French teacher but is now retired. My father is a professor of microbiology at the university here in Dijon. My brother and sisters work in various sectors.[*]

I am half Ashkenazi and half Sephardi. On my mother's side, I am Ashkenazi; my grandfather's name was Sam Edelman, my grandmother's, Bébé Edelman. Both are deceased. His family came from Poland; that of grandmother, from Russia. They were merchants all of their lives. On my father's side, we are Sephardim. My grandfather's name was Albert Bensoussan. He died a few years ago. I didn't really know him. My grandmother is still alive. Her name is Marie Bensoussan. Her maiden name is Koubie. They did a lot of things in order to make a living, but I don't know exactly what. They did travel a lot.

On the Ashkenazi side, I have a very sad story to tell. It is about my great-uncle, the brother of my grandmother. His name is Henri Rabin. He lost his two little cousins when they were sent to Auschwitz, and every time we talk about Auschwitz he tells this story: he had been writing to them. He was in the free zone [of Occupied France] and they were in occupied territory. They sent him letters and he answered them, but they never received his letters. Sometime later they were taken by the French police and taken to the winter stadium [Vel d'Hiver] in Paris. Then they were deported. In their last letter to Henri, they blamed my great-uncle for not having answered

---

[*] See the interview below with Annie Edelman and Gislain Bensoussan, p. 153.

them. They wrote, "You are mean to us!" But, of course, he had answered them, but they were never given the letters. This was his last memory of his little cousins, and their last memory of him was that he had forgotten about them. I think that it's a very sad story.

I don't know exactly what my grandfather did during the war. I know that he did not wear the yellow star because he refused to. He helped Jews cross over to the free zone and to hide. He went back and forth between the two zones. I don't know what my grandmother did, or if they lived in Lyon. I think that they met before the war. You know, she was deaf since she was very young. When she was alive, I spoke more slowly; after she died, I started to speak more rapidly.

I think that I have heard stories about the war since I was young, but as I grew up there were more and more details added to them. When I was a child, they [her parents and grandparents] weighed their words carefully because the stories were too violent. They waited until I was mature enough to understand those things. My mother reminds me all the time that when I was nine or ten I asked why they did those terrible things to us. It was a question that troubled me during my childhood, and I think that it will trouble me all of my life.

When we were small, my sister Sarah and I, we liked it a lot when our father told us stories. But when we asked him to tell us a story before bedtime, it was never about Sleeping Beauty. We wanted stories of his life, of when he was a child. So he started to tell us that he was born in Algeria, that his parents went to live in France. He told us how he changed from one school to another. He registered by himself. Now when we change schools, it's my parents who take care of it. He was just ten years old, and he transferred his files. He also told us about how they went to live in Israel. It was during Algeria's War for Independence. When we went to Israel with him, we saw where he lived. Then, when they left Israel and returned to Algeria, it was at a time when they shouldn't have gone back. It was the worst time, with attacks, murders. So they came to France, to Marseille, and they stayed there for a while. I don't know how difficult my parents' lives were, but my mom and dad didn't have a lot of money, so it must not have been easy every day. I think that my sister and I are very lucky but that our parents didn't have such luck.

I learned a lot from my parents. I sometimes think that they taught me everything. They taught me the basics: simple things that we don't do at home because we are very close, but when we go to other people's houses we are very well-bred. We smile, we say "thank you," "good morning," "good-bye." I think that it's important to know [good manners] because it helps us adapt to a lot of situations. Also, my father, for example, transmitted some of his passions to us, like the desire to learn, to never just agree to things without understanding. Towards us, our parents were complementary. On one side, my father set the rules; and on the other, there was my mother who bent them to make us happy. I think that they make a good match.

My mother teaches me a lot, but not exactly everything. For example, I'm not yet very excited about cooking. But she taught us how to behave. Which I think is more important than cooking, right? It's important never to appear impolite.

My parents gave me my independence right away, but within rules they set. For example, I could go out until 10 p.m. One minute after ten was not permitted, but ten was good. So I went out until 10 p.m. and was happy.

I am not even 18 years old yet, so the most important thing is for me to get my Bac. I need to complete my studies and ensure myself of a stable life, how I will make a living. This is much more important than marriage. Later I will get married.

Yes, Judaism is very important for me. At home it is the most important thing. If today, someone told me that I am not Jewish anymore, I would not have anything left. This is the defining part of my life. [At home] we were culturally Jewish, that is, we talked about the war, the traditions. We never really celebrated the holidays. We did Passover a bit, Hanukkah and Yom Kippur a bit, but not more. It has been a few years since I started feeling that I want more, so for a while now, for example, I have stopped eating pork and shrimp. Recently, I stopped eating meat. It is important for me, but I do not want to impose my beliefs on my parents. While I am in their house, I adapt to what there is. When I am in my house, I will do things my way, but I will not break the ties with my parents. The most important people are my family. Religion will come after my family even if I really want to practice [Judaism]. Of course, if someone starts to become religious, there is a change in the lifestyle. We will start doing things that we didn't do five years ago.

I don't know why my religious belief deepened. It's internal. You can't really control it. It's an internal need. I really want to do it. I am not forcing myself to do it. I am not closing up either. My parents think so, but I think of it more as an evolution. I am happy to do this. It is about faith, I think, faith and culture. I believe in God and I need to get closer to Him.

I have a lot of friends who are not Jewish, but that hasn't changed anything. In fact, it shows that because I am leaning towards religion, I will not shut myself off from the world. It's just that is how I would like to live every day. But I live in France in a mixed society, and I will keep on mixing with people.

I don't know if God is closer to Jews than to other people. It is not about being boastful, but I think that Judaism is conducive to contact with God. I think that it is less so in Christianity. There is less of a sense of community. I think that it is important to have your own community even if you live with others, and when we are feeling bad, to get closer to our own community. Jews seem to understand each other better.

It is true that my father keeps books on Judaism and my mother knows a lot about Jewish culture. They are involved in the community, but they don't practice religion. We do know the importance of the cultural aspect of religion at home, but I wanted to add the importance of religion.

I only went to secular schools except for the two months I was in Israel, when I went to a Jewish school there. But I did feel different from others because I was Jewish. First, there are a lot of things that affect us differently. I think that one of the times when we realize that we're different is when we enter high school and we learn about the Hebrews, and we don't have the same perspective on things. When we learn about Moses, we don't feel like we know him, but at home we always talk about him. So we know more. Later in high school, when we learn about World War II, we are touched by it. We know a lot of things and we want to share them with our friends. And, of course, I did that, but in private. I didn't teach the history class over again, but I added additional things that I knew.

In school, I had some problems, such as anti-Semitic insults, because I was Jewish. But sometimes they were unaware of what they were saying. There is an expression that says, "Eat something in 'feuj.'" "Feuj" means Jew in French when you invert the letters. Doing anything in "feuj" means that one doesn't share with others. One time a friend of mine was talking about someone else and she used the expression. She said, "She ate the tangerines in 'feuj.'" My friend immediately apologized to me, but an expression like that now is a part of French slang.

As I said, when I started high school, I began being conscious of these things. Before that, I was simply too young. I think that it is things like this that make people get closer to the community. My best friend, Morgan Benhaim, is also Jewish and I'm glad. I can share anything with her. If, for example, I am feeling bad because of the situation in Israel, she will feel the same way, too. She is not indifferent to those things.

The Intifada did cause problems at school. Yes. I was returning from Israel. I had discovered Israel and I loved the country instantly. But when

---

* French slang dictionaries suggest that this term originated with teenagers of Arab descent in France; see, i.e., PROject MT, *Dictionnaires français de définitions et de synonymes*, Softissimo S.A. (1997-02), http://www.reverso.net.

I came back, they had conflated the Jews with the Israelis, and it seemed to me that they were mixing everything up. They were attacking a country that was very important to me; I didn't feel good about it at that time. After 9/11, we were talking about Bin Laden in class. My name is Bensoussan, so people began calling me Bin Laden. Obviously, I didn't like it. And they were French, not Arabs. The teacher made them apologize in front of the class, which I thought was good. Later, I talked to one of the guys who did it. I realized that he had no bad intentions and really didn't understand what he was doing. He called me Bin Laden like he could have called me "tomato." It was the same thing for him.

Now, I have fewer and fewer friends who are not Jewish. I was going out for about 18 months with someone who was not Jewish. He was nice, but we felt that there were some issues on which we could not agree—religion, for example. It was important for me but not for him. So, obviously, at one point, things were not going so well, and we broke up. He is sad about it, but I still talk to him. Unfortunately, it is hard for him right now because he found out that I easily replaced him with someone else!

I went to Israel for the first time in 2000. I went with my parents, just before the Second Intifada. I liked it there a lot. Why? I can't say exactly. Perhaps it's the beach and the sun. And I found it pleasant to be in the streets. If we were wearing the Star of David, we did not have to hide it because people next to us were wearing a kippa. It brings about a feeling of safety in a country that faces great danger. Here, I wore a star when I was very small, but I always hid it so I stopped wearing it. It's sad.

Another thing I liked about Israel was the Arab area in the old city [of Jerusalem]. It is very beautiful. It was before the war in Lebanon [2006], so I wasn't really scared. I walked alone. My parents knew about it and they were very worried. But looking back, I think that I was simply too young. I know that if I have to go back, I won't go alone.

I went to Israel to study, but I came back because I realized that I was not ready. I think that I was too young. I wanted to go, so I had to find out for myself. I realized that to live there for two weeks during the holidays and to live there every day are two different things. Israel is beautiful during the holidays because we don't have anything to do. We can go to Jerusalem, Tel Aviv. We have money. But in everyday life, you have to make a living, and it is very hard to make a living in Israel. So I think that I need to think really hard before making aliyah.

I have visited the United States twice. For me, it's the archetype of holidays. I think that I would find it hard to live there, but to spend three weeks or a month is totally fine. But for everyday life, everything is too big for me.

The houses are too big, the cars too. In France, if you go to the store you walk or take a bus. In the United States, you need a car to go. But I liked it a lot, and I can't wait to go back and see the West Coast. All the Americans that I met were very friendly. Also, in America, people are not ashamed to be Jewish. In American soap operas, there is always a Jew!

My being French didn't pose any problems. Yet, the French are very much against Americans. For the French, [George W.] Bush represents America, and since they are against Bush, they are against Americans—and, at the same time, against Israelis. For me, it's different. I am for Israel, America is its ally, and I know people whom I like a lot that live in America. I have always been for America, though not necessarily for Bush's policies. But he was elected by the people, and it is better to have a bad president who has been elected in a democratic way than to have a bad president who was not elected at all. I don't blame the Americans for having voted for their president. It is a democracy. Of course, there are things that I do not like about the United States, like the government's stance on abortion, and so forth. They seem to be lagging behind Europe on a number of issues.

I think that the French are so much against the Americans because of the media. I think that the media reflects the policies of the country. France is for Palestine, so the media will be oriented in that direction. The population will be for Palestine. I think that it is the same in the United States. Since they have an alliance with Israel, they will show the good side of Israel on the news. So, I think that the media acts to confuse and blind people. This is in every country and not only in France.

Why is France favoring the Palestinians? I don't really know. Perhaps it is because of what happened in Algeria, so the French thought that they would support them [the Arabs]. Maybe it is shame because of past colonization. I can't really say.

Still, you know, I like France. It is a friendly place. There are a lot of different landscapes.... You can go to different towns and you never find the same things. This is very nice. Nothing is standardized. You see, I am French and I love my country!

However, I don't really like Dijon because it rains a lot and the Jewish community is very small and, I think, not very welcoming. Now, at this stage of my life, I do not really plan on going back to Israel. I will definitely go during the holidays and maybe one day to live there, but right now, no. If the situation of the Jews in France deteriorates and I have to choose between the United States and Israel, I think that my choice will be Israel.

As for the Jewish community of Dijon, well, I try not to have a life in this community. I did not like the fact that they wanted to remove the youth center. I think that if we have one, this will allow the community to keep on living. There were problems that were unnecessary. As I said, I don't think that it is a very welcoming community. I have been to several others, for example, in Nancy. My best friend is from Nancy and I spent several Shabbats at her place. People ask your name, where you come from. In Dijon, each one is in his own world. There is no exchange. I don't think that it is a community that makes you want to go to the synagogue.

I want to be more religious and I love the synagogue because the building is beautiful, but I don't want to see people who are cold, unwelcoming, and not friendly. I think that the Lubavitch are much better on this level. Even though they are very religious, maybe too religious, they are friendly and very warm people. We can talk to them, and they take some time to answer. They are not snobbish.

I will not elaborate on the issue of the youth center because I don't think that it's interesting. But there were problems. And we did not get support from the community. A youth center with three adolescents is not possible, so we decided to stop. No, I don't think that it will start up again. I don't really care. It was a local group. But there is also a national branch [of a Jewish youth organization] in Dijon so I stayed in that. There was a time when I didn't go at all, but I went back recently because it was my youth center. I grew up in it. I know the people and it makes me happy to go. I have supervised children in a camp for kids and it feels good to share.

On the question of Islam, I think that there are two types: a moderate one to which my family is open and one that is not moderate and involves all those people who call for hatred. Just like my parents are not open to the type of Judaism that is hateful—even though we don't find many in France, there are some—when it comes to peace they are open to everything. If it is about war, aggression, conflict, they are closed. In France, I think that there are a lot of people who don't know what Judaism is about and who will be against it without knowing what it is. I think that there is a particular problem with the Muslims in France, but I don't know why. Now, it is with the Muslims. Sixty years ago, it was with the French in general.

I have hope about the future of France. But I don't know. Seeing how things are now, it will be difficult. Many of my close Jewish friends have become extremists. They have become more and more racist and less open. If you are not Jewish, you will not find that normal. When you are, it's not that you understand, but you know what drove those people to hate. It's a shame, because we all could have lived together. But now?

What will I do in the immediate future? Well, this is a question that should not be asked these days because the future is very uncertain. At the moment,

I am deciding among a lot of things like going into the theater, or doing law, or other things. I need to study my options. I do like foreign languages. I like speaking English a lot. I really would like to speak it better, because it's important for my studies, and English is used today in so many situations.

At the moment, however, there isn't anything in particular that is making me lean one way or the other. Right now, I am very uncertain. My parents are waiting for my decision, of course. They don't have any other choice. But I will make my decision by gathering information on the different study areas, and to what professions they lead, and in what places. I will see if there are things that suit me better elsewhere. I need to see what is possible.

Luna Cemachovic

Luna Cemachovic, the wife of synagogue president Izy Cemachovic, strives to stay aloof from the "politics" of the community while remaining involved. From a Greek background, and trained as a linguist, she is an independent thinker and representative of the younger generation of activists that invigorated the Dijon community in the early 1990s.

November 2006

All of my ancestors, as far as I know, were Jewish. They spoke Ladino.* My immediate grandparents spoke Greek, though my grandmother spoke to her family in Ladino. Unfortunately, my mother never wanted to learn it, though my grandmother wanted to teach her. So we missed out on learning that language. My father spoke Greek and didn't speak Ladino....

My family believes that not only my family but all the Jews in Greece go back to the Roman Empire. My father would tell you that we are not Sephardic, neither from Spain nor from North Africa, but that we are Romans.† We are older than the Sephardis who were expelled from Spain in 1492. We were part of the earliest diaspora that came to Greece from Israel and established a trading center here, not on Chalkida, but on the mainland. There are small sculptures of all kinds of traders made by Jews that show that.

I don't really know much about my family's background. As far as I know, my paternal grandfather was born in Turkey. He came to Greece after the exchange of population between Turkey and Greece following the war in, I believe, 1897. My maternal grandparents were born in Greece. Both sets of my grandparents lived through the war [World War II]. Gentiles hid them. My maternal grandparents were hidden in a sort of hut, made of stone from the fields. In the middle of the meadows, these small huts were used for the storage of grain, whatever. That's how they got through. My other grandparents were hidden in a village in the mountains close to Chalkida, the city where I was born and spent the first 18 years of my life. They lived on the top floor of a house, and I remember my grandfather telling me that when there was snow, the entire house would be covered and he would open a window and step outside.

---

* Ladino is a Judaeo-Spanish language spoken primarily among Sephardic Jews.

† Luna's claim to be Roman is somewhat confusing. There is a Greek community of Jews, called Romaniotes, but they do not speak Ladino. They speak a Greek dialect called Yevanic.

Both my father and mother remember the war, but they don't speak about it much. Not many of the [Jewish] community survived, except my parents and grandparents and maybe two other families. That was from a community of perhaps 100 families. The community I grew up in was made up of those who came after the war. What happened to the original community was very sudden. Some of the [Orthodox] priests tried to do something, but they couldn't really do much. My father told me that the mayor of the city tried to hide some people and tried to alert the Jews that something was going to happen so that they could escape. My parents were probably among those, but many were captured.

My parents didn't experience the camps, of course. The fact that they were hidden as children . . . they didn't have much to eat. It was really a bad experience for them, so they didn't tell us children much in order to protect us. At school we learned a little of what had happened. But I really learned about the Holocaust afterwards, just before I left for Israel.

My father's brother and sister and my mother's twin brothers got through the war with the family, but my maternal grandmother's sister had 12 children and all of them were in the camps. One of the sons later fought in Israel's independence war and died there.

[During the war and afterwards] relations between Greeks and Jews were quite good. Jews thought of themselves as Greek nationalists. They felt comfortable in Greece. But when Israel's first invasion of Lebanon happened in 1978, that was really hard. I distinctly remember my parents telling themselves that if this goes on we were leaving for Israel. It was really bad. There was graffiti all around; it was a bad atmosphere. Eventually, it subsided.

I don't think Greek Jews especially wanted to go to Israel because I have the feeling that they don't speak Hebrew, to start with. Not that you can't learn in Israel. But, for example, for my parents, who during the Lebanon incident started to think about going to Israel, all of a sudden they probably considered the language barrier and thought, "How will we survive without speaking Hebrew?" It was difficult for them. I don't know if Israel specifically was important to them as much as Judaism was important to them. You see what I mean? And probably then Israel, by extension, became as important. I'd say Judaism before Israel.

Anyway, as I started to say, I was born on 22 April 1963 in Chalkida on the island of Evia and spent the first 18 years of my life there in the same community and with the same people. My grandfather had been a peddler in fine linens before the war, and he sent my father to the School of Commerce afterwards. They then opened a shop in the center of town that sold ladies' clothing on the first floor and sweets in the basement. I remember it well.

On the first floor were dolls for sale and every birthday I received one as a present. As a peddler, my grandfather wasn't considered middle class. But with the shop, he and my parents became middle class. They probably became among the wealthier people in the community, which numbered about 50 families.

I went to school in Chalkida. I didn't experience any anti-Semitism or persecution or even comments from my teachers. I periodically had many teachers who very much admired Jews. They admired my parents because they knew them. Chalkida is a small city of about 40,000. There were people who were "modern" and of a certain culture. I myself didn't wear Jewish jewelry or symbols, but I had friends who did and they didn't bother anybody. It didn't create jokes or comments or anything.

I went alone to Israel in 1981. The reason I went was to study, that's all. It was not immigration. I was there to study languages. Children in Greece, generally, even nowadays, go very early into what we call "language schools." They study English, Spanish, German, Italian, or French. When I was a kid, French and English were in fashion. So parents automatically sent their children to these kinds of schools to learn languages. So at the age of four, I started English, and at the age of eight, French. I didn't study Hebrew in Greece. There was no Talmud Torah, although for the bat mitzvah we had a rabbi who came from Athens to give lessons. The poor guy was shy. There were four or five girls so women surrounded him. He was very shy, but he was adorable. At my bat mitzvah, we had mixed seating [in the synagogue]. Normally, at ceremonies, everybody was downstairs though the men were separated from the women. For the festivals, it was upstairs for the women.[*]

I enjoyed all the holidays. It was such a fantastic Jewish life that we had there. I still have photographs. My father was a leader of the community. Once he organized a play, and everyone wore turbans and dresses since it was the story of Esther. Next to the synagogue there was a small garden where my father planted vines. We made benches and put long tables there. All the ladies of the community would bring platters of whole fish and cakes and foods. All the community would come, virtually everybody. And all the festivals were like that. Sometimes several of us children would leave the synagogue and go to a nearby bakery where we bought cheese pies that we ate in a corridor outside. The ladies would scold us and say, "Shame on you!" I have fantastic memories of those years.

---

[*] There are variations in separating men and women in Orthodox communities. Often, for more important holidays, the level of separation is greater, with women sitting in a balcony.

During **Passover**, telling stories, my parents made a total abstraction of the Hitler years. They didn't want to talk about it. It was more fun for the kids around the table, kissing and hugging, and nothing political. The Seder lasted a long time. My grandmother cooked all of the specialties.

The community was very small, but we did not have that many relationships with our fellow Jews. The women of my mother's age gathered for meetings of WIZO. Beyond that, there were no relations. We didn't socialize with them. We socialized with non-Jews. Most of our friends were Gentile Greeks. My father said that there weren't enough Jews.

My decision to go to Israel resulted when my mother thought that, in the interval between the end of my studies and the beginning of the academic year in Greece, it would be a very good idea for me to go and learn Hebrew, since I loved languages. She said that I should go for a month or two and then come back and do my studies. At the time I was in Athens at the university, studying English literature. Well, I went to Israel for a couple of months and I enjoyed myself so much that I didn't want to return to Greece. But I think that somehow the decision to send me wasn't altogether innocent, either, meaning that they probably took into consideration the dating thing.

I stayed in Israel for four years, from 1981 to 1985. It was difficult, but wonderful. I was a student; I had no responsibilities. I lived in the dorms. I spent a year living in an apartment, which was not a very good experience, but it still was an experience.

As a Jew in Israel, I felt very comfortable. I felt good. Although I didn't have any problems in Greece, I felt that somehow these were my people. I thought that Israelis were okay but a little bit aggressive towards non-Israelis or non-immigrants. They were hostile to those who were not, in their opinion, good enough to live in Israel, because the state was paying for their studies—even though my parents also paid a lot of money for my studies. But it doesn't matter. They thought that we were just taking advantage of Israel's money, of politics. My boyfriend told me that. But at the time it was a very stressful atmosphere: the economy, the Lebanon War [1982–85]. I had the impression that people were just running around, all over the place. I remember leaving after four years; I went to Brussels and woke up in the morning and said to myself, "God, this is Paradise." People were walking, not running. In Israel I had the impression that people were hurrying somewhere all the time, for the bus, for the classroom, for everything. It was a stressful life. It's impossible to keep up with the pace of those people. I don't know how they make it. It's a life that only an Israeli can live. Although I guess that they must get tired of it, too.

But I stayed because I wanted to. I loved the atmosphere, the studies. I loved the university. I loved everything that was there. I especially loved the fact that I earned two diplomas in four years, in French and English languages and literatures. And I also learned Hebrew because I had to. I loved the fact that it was a very clean school, with intelligent teachers, with civilized people. I thought that I had a wonderful, fulfilling life from every point of view.

However, my contacts with Israeli society were limited because most of the time I was with foreign Jews. There were North and South Americans and lots of French people. I had a friend from Argentina who had a grandmother who didn't speak a word of Hebrew. She was such a wonderful lady. I had a Russian friend with whom I lived for a couple of years in the dorms. And since I had members of my family from both sides living in Israel, I spent the holidays with them, in Jerusalem. I still have contact with them, since I visit Israel every couple of years.

Of course, I also visit Greece once or twice a year. I have family and school friends there. My relations with my friends are wonderful. We are like sisters. Israel doesn't come between us. On the contrary, I have a [Gentile] friend whose mother is very pro-Israeli. She was my teacher of Greek literature and ancient Greek and philosophy in high school. She's a very cultured woman. She knows my parents. She appreciates them and Israel and Judaism. When I am back there, I feel secure. I have never felt threatened by anything.

When I finished my studies, I was supposed to return to Greece. Everything was set for me, meaning that my parents wanted to find a teaching job for me somewhere in Greece. If I had had the opportunity for further studies and work, I guess that I would have stayed in Israel. The prospect of teaching in the Greek mountains in a small school was not really thrilling to me as a young person. I already was 22, and it wasn't what I had in mind. When my mother told me about an advertisement she had seen announcing a competition in Brussels for a training course for interpreters, I decided to try for it, and I was accepted.

In Brussels, I didn't contact the Jewish community. But after three months there, I was invited to a wedding where I met an old friend [from Israel] who is Russian, married to a Russian. I discovered that she was working very close to the place where I was studying. So we started seeing each other again. Three months later, soon after we had our exams, she asked me to come for Shabbat. I was with her in the kitchen helping prepare the famous "frites Belges," [Belgian fries] when she told me that she had invited a friend of hers who was coming with her brother, a doctor. She added that he was 30 years old.

I thought, "Oh, my God! It's a set-up! Another guy with no hair, glasses, and short. How am I going to deal with it?" While I was in Israel, my mother's cousin tried to set me up with some guy who looked like that.

Well, we spent the evening laughing at the jokes this guy was telling, and I didn't realize until later in the evening that he wasn't the one I was supposed to meet, but the other guy—with glasses. It took me a while to figure it out. It was terrible. But three months later, we were engaged. We waited another three months for my training course to end to get married. We had a civil wedding in Brussels and the religious wedding a month later in Greece. I was 23. My parents thought nothing of the fact that my husband was Ashkenazi. The only questions that my mother asked were: "Is he Jewish? How old is he?" Nobody cared about the rest. My mother doesn't even know that Ashkenazis exist.

You know, I had no political consciousness. I wasn't interested in those things. I'm still not. I think it's so daft. My husband, Izy, is very much into it. He has always been like that. I listen to what he has to say, but that's about as far as it goes. I don't think we ever discussed politics. I was more occupied with theater, cinema, cultural things. My studies were of the cultural sort: literature, books.

After we were married, we lived in Belgium for three and a half years. I found life there rather dull, not very interesting. I thought that rather strange because Brussels is a larger city than Jerusalem but is less culturally oriented. In Jerusalem, there were always festivals going on. I went to many concerts there, to the theater. Israel is a cultural place.

It was great moving to France. It had never been my wish to live in a huge city. I come from a provincial city, a small city. Although Brussels is the capital and has lots of things to see, it is a small city. So Dijon was perfect for me. We came here in 1987 and became involved in the community right away. My father-in-law told us that whoever wants to make contact with the Jewish community goes to the synagogue for Yom Kippur. So we just went, and that was it.

I didn't yet have children, but that didn't matter. I was upstairs with the ladies, Izy was downstairs with the men. I don't know if he talked to anybody, but I spent my time as usual talking with the ladies up there. The first person I talked to was Anne Lucien. The first Jewish family we met when we came to Dijon were the Mestmans. Because the guy at Izy's bank told us that Mestman was a dentist and a rabbi, Izy was very much intrigued because he wondered how a rabbi could be a dentist too. But I think the bank guy confused rabbi with president of the community. Anyway, these were the first people who really welcomed us in their house in Dijon. Then we went to the synagogue.

As for being comfortable in the synagogue, let me tell you that as far as how the service is conducted, I didn't know anything about it. In Greece we never had real rabbis. The rabbis came [from Athens and other larger centers] for the big festivals, but that was it. I didn't think it was so different. To me it was just a service. But, that said, I immediately felt comfortable. That's really the truth. I felt the same way that I did in the community in Chalkida. It was home.

I think that for some people it doesn't matter whether they come from America or from Greece, some people just don't like living elsewhere. I can understand it. I had many friends here in France from Greece. They had a wonderful time. They came to study, but by no means would they stay here. My parents came for the bar mitzvahs [of my sons], but their mentality and that of my grandparents has not changed. Greeks are not big travelers, though they used to be. You settle in one place and spend the rest of your life there.

My first son, Rafael, was born two years after we settled in Dijon. The second was born three and a half years later. And the third one is now [2006] ten years old. They all speak Greek, better than I do. We speak it all the time. Izy took Greek lessons from a Greek teacher of French who lives in Dijon. Unfortunately, she focused more on grammar and less on what he really needed: vocabulary and conversation. He speaks it all the time, but when he speaks Greek to my father, everybody laughs because of his accent.

My life here has been very good. It's a family city. It's small, but it's good for children. You often can have them home for lunch. You can easily take them back and forth for various activities. You are close to the synagogue. You are close to everything! You can go anywhere you want in about 15 minutes. It's fantastic.

Cultural life here is okay. For a person who wishes to go and see something, there is plenty to do. The quality is less than what happens in Paris, of course, but it is a lot easier and cheaper than it is there. Had I been living in Paris, I would not go as often as I do here.

My views about the Jewish community haven't really changed over time. In the beginning, everything is very nice. Everybody is nice and kind and civil. Then, slowly, as you get into the life, you realize that not everybody is very nice and kind, but I think that as long as you keep a certain distance and, well, I guess as long as you do not get too involved and are tolerant, then you get along with everybody. And you can keep your personal views about anybody. But I still find it to be a very warm and open community. I'd say that I have more Jewish friends here than I had in Greece, but that's normal because the Jewish community here is larger. I do not always agree with what they do here and say, but I do not enter into politics and those kinds of discussions.

I am perfectly comfortable with this synagogue although it is more religious than the one I used to attend in Greece. In Greece, kosher food didn't exist. We had the **mashgiach** come once a year for Yom Kippur. It was kosher for the major holidays, but for Shabbat there was no way we could have that.

I am comfortable with a traditional synagogue, but certainly not Orthodox. For myself, I am not concerned anymore, because in a way I am finished with my Judaism. My Judaism has already done the work it was supposed to do, meaning that I am married to a Jew, I have children. But for my children I have a feeling that it is important to have some principles, some education until they get married. After that the job is over for me. Then it is their own job to figure it out for their own children. Whether I join an Orthodox, Masorti, or Liberal synagogue*—for me personally it doesn't matter so much. As for my Jewish philosophy or theology, I think that I work it out as the questions arise.

In Judaism, you cannot possibly say that you are Jewish without some sort of religious practices. And you cannot be a Jew by the practices and not the philosophy or the culture. Judaism is a whole. You cannot disassociate anything. It's a way of life. It's a way of thinking.

In the synagogue, I became active more or less as a result of the children. And I was definitely satisfied with their training. My children seemed fine with it, so for me it was perfect. They were happy with the process, though occasionally not with the teachers. But they did enjoy their bar mitzvahs, even though perhaps not the lessons. My children all attend public schools. I am satisfied with the educational system here. I compared it with the one in Greece, and I would not by any means send my children to study in Greece.

They have spoken to me about teachers whom they believe are anti-Semitic. In Dijon there have been problems with some teachers, though not specifically with my children's teachers. Sometimes they talk about how the history books don't always say what they should be saying. I remember one teacher being anti-American.... Probably their teachers were sensitive to the fact that they were Jewish. For example, during the war against Hezbollah in Lebanon this summer [2006] one of my first concerns was what was going

---

* By far the largest branch of French Judaism is Orthodox (the Consistoire), although Lubavitch ultra-orthodox Judaism has grown greatly in recent years. There are a handful of Masorti (American Conservative) synagogues and nearly a dozen Liberal (American Reform) congregations in France. In descending order of severity of practice (strict observance or interpretation of Jewish Law, affecting every aspect of life and religious observance, including gender relations), the ultras are most strict and the Liberals least strict, while often most creative, in terms of educational facilities, music, and artistic culture.

to happen to the kids when they returned to school in September. Nothing special happened. But again, there are many teachers who are more or less anti-American, who interpret and project opinions [contrary to those voiced in our house].

I have been more involved in community work. Despite the fact that not everybody loves each other, we are still a community, which is very important.

You asked about the radio station, but I don't want to get into politics again! I think that it's good because it keeps many people happy. Personally, I think that it's important only for those who work for it [developing programs, etc.]. Others don't care so much about it. On a national level, it's probably a very good thing. Locally, I don't think that it contributes much.

B'nai B'rith? It's just so much politics.

France-Israel? As long as it does good for Israel. That's what's important. My own view about it isn't important. Izy isn't the sort of guy who's interested in their philosophy. He is very Cartesian. He doesn't feel that he adheres to their way of thinking.

As for the rabbi, he is a very good man. I think that he has a great deal of knowledge. He has culture. The problem is that he is not charismatic. He can be boring. His sermons sometimes are too long, and he has a tendency to get lost in his own words. People stop listening. But his relationships with other religious groups are excellent. They admire him and he thrives on it. They admire him because of his culture, because of his knowledge. Now, diplomatically speaking, he has made mistakes during his career, and it has cost him a fan club. But he is a good, honest man. I think that he is a really kind man. I think that the kids like him, but I don't think that he is necessarily a good teacher. I cannot say that my kids learned enthusiastically. Apart from that, we are privileged because I don't think that any other rabbi would have stayed in our city, in such a small community, for so many years as he has. Yes, deep inside, he is a good man, a family man.

About the Lubavitch? The thorns in our community! I hear a lot about them. Ten years on, one sees things differently from in the beginning. They came, and everybody was outraged because they split the community and took people from the community. We didn't appreciate that.... Now, ten years later, I understand that the people who went with the Lubavitch, who were not happy with what we had, would have gone away sooner or later. I think that it's so much better [that they left]; it causes less trouble. Honestly, I wouldn't want those unhappy, dissatisfied people in the synagogue. Everyone is happy now. There is no problem. [Trouble] occurs only when those with the Lubavitch attempt to attract others from the synagogue. That I can never accept. I think that it is disloyal to your own community and to your

Jewishness. When they put up the public menorah during Hanukkah, Izy always gets angry because he doesn't like it. He thinks that Gentiles don't understand. I don't mind it so much.

I used to go with the children [to the Beit Habbad] on different occasions because they make so much of their festivals; we had the community, so why not something more? The children should see everything that's available. The problem was that the atmosphere became so disagreeable that the children didn't want to go anymore. One of my kids went to a small camping organization they had. The third time that he went he came home and said that he didn't want to go anymore. He said that they treated him badly and that everyone called him a Gentile.

A couple of years ago, after we had been to Israel, Izy, the children, and I went to the Lubavitch celebration of Purim. We wore Hasidic clothing. I was so happy. As we entered, Mr. Hachmoun [Dr. Hachmoun, a fervent Lubavitch participant] said to Izy, "Are you a Jew? Where do you come from? What are you? Are you really a Jew?" I wanted to slap him! Kill him! Wring his neck! There I am, next to my kids! Afterwards, he didn't even apologize. I don't know if he thought that we were making fun of the Hasidic traditions or not; I don't care what he thought. But such behavior is just unacceptable. I have nothing personal against the Lubavitch family, Mr. and Mrs. Slonim. I am not talking about them at all. They are very sweet and nice. I am talking about the people who go there. It is not the Slonims who were disagreeable to us; it's the others.

About Israel, my feelings haven't changed at all. We probably wouldn't be able to live there as a family. I am so scared that my children would have to go into the army that I probably wouldn't want to live there. But we love Israel. Our family is there. Our friends are there. Regarding the future, I think that Israel will survive, but at what cost I don't know.

This summer [2006] was terrible. Izy was on the verge of saying that it was the end. But then, as you mentioned when we were talking about the Jews, the intermarriages, and so forth, I have the feeling that the Jews will bounce back. My mother believes that Izy thinks that Jews are condemned. But I think we will bounce back. I mean, you have to trust us.

Nothing special happened to us during the summer, during the war. There was the occasional article and really trash news on TV. It was absolutely outrageous. The French didn't cover anything. They just commented, and it was really anti-Semitic and disgusting. Absolutely obnoxious. But that's French television. It's trash TV anyway. That's my opinion. The newspapers were the same. The newspaper Izy reads is Le Monde. And, of course, it makes him angry because they print the same horrible things that are being printed elsewhere. I read *Time* magazine. I cannot comment on the quality, but I thought that they made the effort to be more or less neutral. I think that they attempted to report rather than just comment.

During the November riots [2005] people from Greece called to ask if we were safe. I said, "Sure, what's going on?" They said that they saw the burnings of cars and things on TV, and that Dijon was mentioned. I said that I wasn't aware of that. I felt so stupid. But it happened. I don't know how many [were involved]. I think that the demonstrations here were just in solidarity with the others in Paris. We are concerned about the Muslim community here. It is expanding. They have, so to speak, invaded France. That is a pervasive feeling among us. The Jewish members of the community talk about it.

To finish, I must say that I am proud of what Izy is doing for the community. You don't stay 20 years with a guy without being a little bit proud of him, anyway! But I still stand up to him. I think that he really appreciates that he's not married to a mop! And yes, I am a feminist. I am a feminist because I think that a woman should have a life beyond the house and the fourth child. She needs to feel accomplished even if she doesn't work. Anyway, you can work and still be dependent.

I think that I cannot live with someone who is not honest and a worker. Some women don't mind, but I do. I hope that I can convey this to my children, that they should become like their father, whatever they do. Honesty should come before everything else. There is nothing more important. They should follow their father's example.

Alain Danino

Alain Danino is the son of Moroccan parents who immigrated to France after the Six Day War. He studied medicine in Paris, pursued further studies in Japan, and was a widely published member of the faculty of medicine at the Université de Bourgogne. Though raised in a traditional Jewish family, Alain has felt uncomfortable with established conservative French Judaism. In 2007, he moved to Canada with his family and serves as a member of the medical faculties of McGill University and the Université de Montréal.

January 2007

My family is a Jewish family from Morocco that came to France in 1968 after the Six Day War in Israel. I was born in 1968 in Morocco, but my parents had left the country when they were 18 or 19 and were back only to settle some affairs there so I was born there by accident. My parents were very young. My grandfathers were businessmen in Casablanca. Our name "Dannie" might be from the expulsion of 1492, the exodus of Jews from Spain to Morocco. My parents dreamt about coming to France because Morocco was a French colony and they spoke French. My father did business in real estate, and my mother studied and became a lawyer. My father was not a French citizen. In Morocco the Jews had Moroccan citizenship. The Jews of Morocco were protected by the king, Mohammed V, unlike the Jews in Algeria. So the Jews were the subjects of the king, and we were Moroccan.

My parents apparently sold everything pretty quickly after the Six Day War. My grandparents sold everything [also] and left for France. They had enough money to buy property in France, so they must have been quite affluent. They moved near Paris. That was my mother's parents. My father's parents left Morocco for Israel, so I have family in Israel. We received a French education at school along with a traditional Jewish education. We studied in the Talmud Torah. We went to the synagogue in the ninth arrondissement of Paris, [which has] the large boulevards and the Opéra and a lot of Jews. I received my Jewish education there, in Paris, at the Victoire.[*]

When I first started school I was in a Jewish school, and I didn't really like it. So I asked to be transferred to a public school that I liked and where I learned a lot. The Jewish school was narrow [in its curriculum], and I wanted to see more things.... My parents didn't have a lot of money at that time. They earned a good living, but they were very young. In the Jewish school,

---

[*] Flagship Consistorial synagogue in Paris.

the different social classes could really be felt, and I didn't like it. Then my parents made a lot of money, but I had already left the Jewish school. When I was in high school, I decided to become a doctor.... I liked literature, but I wanted to do medical study. I think that I spent my childhood in a Golden Age. There were no problems. The French felt very guilty at that time [with respect to the Holocaust and Vichy era], and there were no violent Arab movements yet....

The war in Lebanon in 1982 was during my bar mitzvah. Things were agitated at that time, but there was not any tension at school. We could talk about it. There were some Muslims even in medical school, but they were not yet aggressive.

We had a Jewish life. They were good times, but I am not very nostalgic. I feel very Jewish when it comes to the history, but Jewish practice was a problem for me very early. I didn't feel at ease in this world that was a bit closed. I also didn't feel at ease with the ideas.... I was more at ease with the "new" [more liberal] Judaism, but it was very limited in France. I don't know what was causing French Jews to be so closed; I really don't know. When I was six or seven, already I felt stifled in the big Jewish school in Paris. I asked my parents to get me out of there. I don't know why, but it is a closed community, and it doesn't reflect French Judaism. It is a big problem. The leaders of French Judaism do not reflect the diversity of French Jews.*

As for the political leaders of France, at all times and even now, we had leaders whom we liked. So we are very well integrated in France. Sometimes our government was the Left and sometimes the Right. The problem is that we don't have any [politicians] representative of French Judaism.

For me, the Lubavitch are more open in some ways than the Establishment because the Lubavitch have a foreign tradition that is not French. They do honorable work. For me, this phenomenon is very ancient, and the French Jews have not been able to rise up to it yet. I think that 90 per cent of the Jews in France do not completely follow the tradition but think that the synagogue should remain like a museum, unchanging. I also think that the absence of women in the Establishment is the key to its downfall, because the synagogue is a man's world. So the men go with their friends, and the women remain with their children and their friends. There is no incentive to think.

[Judaism in France] can change. It must because people who are not currently religious think that they don't have the right to say anything. But

---

* Liberal forms of Judaism have expanded recently, mainly in large cities. In any case, many French Jews have more of a secular ethno-cultural identity than a religious one.

it's not true. All the Jews have the right to say something. So we should get involved in politics. This is why I got involved in the association in Dijon, because you cannot do anything from the outside. You need to be inside, part of the action.

I met Isabelle while I was doing microsurgery. We took a course together at medical school. It was hard to concentrate on the work. Of course, I didn't have any problem because she wasn't Jewish; nor did she. I didn't ask her to convert. She could do whatever she wanted. But we knew each other for six years before we married in 2001. My family took it well, but it was hard for hers. It was very tense. Her parents are not very open. They are nice people, but very closed. But, it's better now with her family.

I don't know when Isabelle decided to convert to Judaism. She decided, and she did it. And we studied together, taking the same course [for conversion to Judaism]. It was excellent. We went twice a week at night for a year.[*]

Even before Isabelle decided to convert, she was [involved with my] family, so she was aware of the Shabbat. We always had Jews and non-Jews over for the Shabbat at home. Her conversion was not necessary for me, but I think that she was right because [it made family life] easier. And it's simpler with the children. In our family, she has found an open-mindedness, a way of thinking, that she had not found elsewhere. At my parents' home she saw that we talk, that we have disagreements, and that everyone has an opinion. In her house it was not like that. It's the Jewish life: the discussions, the disagreements, the controversies. Sometimes Orthodox Judaism in France—not the Lubavitch, who are very joyful—forget that it's a celebration. So that's how she became Jewish.

I chose plastic surgery because I liked it immediately. I like to see the work. It's visible. When we fix an accident or a cancer, we see it. It's hard, but the technique is very interesting and diverse. So I immediately liked it. I went to Japan because my Parisian mentor had gone to Japan 17 years earlier and asked me to go. The team there was very close to my mentor in Paris. I went without Isabelle. We weren't married yet, but she came to see me. I stayed in Japan for two years. I was at the hospital of the Tokyo Imperial University, which has the same standards as here. I returned to Paris in 2000.

In Japan, there were Americans who led the synagogue, and I made good friends with them, and I really liked [going there]. For them, [the main thing is] the concept of Judaism and not the ritual. The ritual is there, but they try to understand Judaism's role in the world, in humanity, and this is very

---

[*] Isabelle and Alain studied with a noted Masorti (moderate) rabbi, Rivon Krygier, head of congregation Adat Shalom in Paris.

important because the message of Judaism is very powerful. If we get stuck in the ritual, well, at times I find it hard to forget about the ritual, but we have to discover the reasons behind it.

I noticed that things started changing for the Jews in France after 9/11.... They had probably started changing before, but we had not really noticed. There was joy in some [Arab] places about what had happened. Some ugly events occurred. We saw the theories become reality, theories where the United States, the Jews, Israel, and everything were mixed up. But the aggressiveness against the United States was closely linked to that against the Jews, and we also saw it in people with whom we were very close because we had fought against racism together. Suddenly, we realized that they were developing ideas that were in fact veiled anti-Semitism. A lot on the Left had ideas that became unbearable. And I was on the Left out of tradition. In France, the Right was tainted by collaboration with the fascists. So, traditionally, the Jew was on the Left. But now there was a great gap. We couldn't talk. Israel became a rude word.

[Anti-semitism] was less widespread among doctors because in medicine there are many Jews. But in the rest of the university, Israel was a rude word. At that time, I was head of a clinic in a university hospital in Paris. Fortunately, there were no problems. I wasn't happy with the situation, and I stopped reading newspapers like *Le Monde* and *Libération* [a Leftist journal]. So now we don't read much. We read the *Figaro* [a more conservative paper], but it is less enriching than *Le Monde*. So we changed as the Right evolved. It's not the same. The Left evolved as well. I think that we cannot really say we were on the Left and switched to the Right. It's not true. The Left today is more conservative than the Right, so it's reversed. Nowadays, it's easier to defend our conception of society as a Jew on the Right than on the Left—at least for me. The Left is pro-Palestinian. Leftists seemed to have some resentment against the Jews, but no one talked about it. Then, suddenly, it was as if someone had opened a door, and [the Left claimed that the fault lay with] Israel, which basically meant that we should leave [the Left].

The moderate Right appears to be pro-Israel, but it isn't really. Part of the Right is racist, that's for sure. But the business world has obviously given this entire issue some thought, and there is a more balanced view. With the war in Lebanon [2006], now there is more balance. Part of the Left has started to realize that there are problems [with its condemnation of Israel], and that's why I am not pessimistic. Perhaps [this moderation of the Left attitude towards the Jews] was because of the riots in Paris and, yes, international terrorism. There also are problems in French ghettos where women are assaulted and raped. The Left is forced to think about this. We have actually seen some Leftist newspapers actually defend Israel.

But I don't know where the anti-Americanism comes from. I think that it is complicated, that it probably comes from the past, from the time of the rivalry with the English. At one point of American history, the French were their allies, at the time of Lafayette. Then, we saw that the Americans were like the Anglo-Saxon English and that's [an] ancient [rivalry]. There are new reasons. France has a lot of wealth, but we are not as influential as the United States or China, and we cannot accept this. So there are two solutions. We either accept [our position] and become a very good country on the technical level and very practical—and this is what the Jews want, that we stop with the great global theories and that we become efficient, very efficient—or we don't accept it, which is what we are now doing, and we make it seem like we can play like [one of the major powers]. Since we are not actually able to do so, we become very aggressive. There are unexplained reasons for this that run deep. The French are irritated by what the United States stands for just as they are irritated by what the Jews stand for. For them, it's closely linked. For example, if tomorrow I need to go to the United States, everyone in my university will think that it's normal, that I am almost American since I am Jewish so the Americans will welcome me. It's not true. But everyone is sure that it is true. They will think that I have a lot of friends there and that I can do whatever I want, that I just need to make a phone call. It's not true, but it's clear that they think that way, even among my good friends. We don't talk about this, but I know that even my good friends think that we [Jews] are just powerful like that. And this feeling runs deep.

I have visited Israel since I was a child. It's very important for me to go there, very powerful. I wanted to relocate, but the problem is that Israel is a complicated issue for French Jews. I don't know if you are aware of this. Do you feel this? You read things about it? For example, I went to Israel because I had welcomed an Israeli surgeon here who had worked with me for a year. There was a job being offered at the university there for a professor. So he said that they should send me, because I am good and highly qualified and can contribute a lot. So I sent my résumé and got no reply. I am not saying that I should have gone, but when I see how North America responds to me, [this rejection] hurts. They [Israelis] have a problem.[*] I don't know what the problem is, but there is a difficult relationship. And yet the French Jews are very close to Israel.

---

[*] Other French Jews complain about this as well.

Maybe the problem is with Israel, maybe because Israel has a hard time situating itself in the Jewish world. That's how I see it. So we do not have the opportunities [there] that we should have, even when we want to. I have several examples. We organized a congress in Tel Aviv six months ago. It was during the war in Lebanon, and the French plastic surgeons said that they will go and offer their support: 50 good surgeons. Not me, but the old, very famous ones. They went, and the Israelis made us pay double [for airfares]. They took the money. But we went; we participated as friends. But there is a problem [in how the Israelis treat the French Jews]. We are not far away, and they are our family. Well, for me, it's my family, and I am very tied to that.

Isabelle Danino

As a convert to Judaism and not originally from Dijon, Dr. Isabelle
Danino is uniquely placed to provide distinctive views about the
community. She is an outspoken professional with the convert's
enthusiasm for her religion, but she is not at all certain that either
she or her religion have a secure future in France. Since this interview
Dr. Danino, her husband, and family have relocated to Montreal, Canada.

November 2006

We have always been from Alsace, as long as I can remember. And Catholic. During the wars of 1914 and 1939 all my family remained in Alsace. My paternal grandfather, who was born in 1902, has changed his nationality four times. He and my grandmother belonged to the petite bourgeoisie. About what happened during the war [1939] I think that they were simply trying to tread water, without collaborating or resisting.

My grandfather on my mother's side did not know his parents. He was an orphan and lived with one of his aunts. After he married my grandmother, they founded a bread factory together. But before they met, they lived through the war separately. He was a member of the Resistance; she was a secretary to a man who supervised the circulation of messages through the Alsace region. People were hiding important messages in their shoes, in their socks, or even in their hair.

My father was born in 1942; my mother in 1948. Both were born in Alsace. They were married in February 1971, and I was born in December. My brother was born in February 1974. Both [of my grandparents'] families were practicing Catholics, very religious. I mean, they were praying morning and night. They went to church every Sunday and, of course, on all holidays. So that's how my childhood went as well.

I started in a private school, switched to a public school, and then was sent back to a Catholic private school. I received my baccalaureate in 1989. After taking preparatory courses, I went to a school for veterinary medicine where I spent four years studying and two years interning. Afterwards, I worked in a private clinic for a year. So after medical school, I had three years' experience in consultation and medicine.

When I was a teenager, I had a desire, not even a desire but a dream, to do classic dance and to play the piano. So I have done five years of classic dance and piano. But I was a very shy girl.

Before university, I went to a private Catholic school, and if I met any Jews, it's possible that I either didn't know they were Jews, or I had little contact with them. I'm sure that I met one, but that's all that I can think of with certainty. Of course, I knew who the Jewish people were. After my conversion, which was a very traumatizing moment for my parents, I learned that I had a Jewish great-grandmother, about whom I will never be able to find out. I don't know who she is. Before university, I was a little ignorant of Jews, but then I learned. In veterinary school, I met a lot of Jews, students and teachers, but mostly students. My best friends in veterinary school were Jewish. We were very close. [For instance,] I had a special course in micro-chemistry, where we were studying rats. A [Jewish] student, Hélène, had a phobia about rats. So I did the microscope work for her. As the course went on, we became very close. That's how we became friends.

It wasn't a shock for me to be among Jews. [Judaism] has always been of interest for me. I wanted to see if they do things differently. Christians read both the Old Testament and the New Testament. But the Old Testament, which Jews call the Torah, has always appeared to me to be more complex than the New Testament. The former has some hidden meanings that are absent from the [latter]. The New Testament seems to me too straight-forward. The same ideas are worded differently and expressed in a too straightforward way. But I found out about this much later, after I took some courses. When I was 12 or 13 years old, I came across the Old Testament and found it more interesting. There are more things, more history. For me, it's a genuine culture there that I don't find in the New Testament. This is the first thing. And then I read the *Diary of Anne Frank*[*]. I was young, 11, 12 maybe. I read it several times, and it was a big shock for me. But [Judaism] was just something that we never talked about, and we still don't talk about it at home.

What I like most is the universality of Judaism. Wherever we might be in the world, whenever we meet, it's like a meeting of the family. We recently received an Argentinian here, and it was like having a cousin. He shared the same experiences that Alain and I had during our childhoods. As for the prayers, well, had I remained in Paris I would have been better at them, but the fact that there are no classes here and women are kept to the side contributes to that. But this is not to criticize the community. I have a hard time with the prayers, but for the rest, I think that there is warmth that's not present in Christian culture. There are the family values, the Shabbat....

---

[*] Together with Elie Wiesel's book, *Night*, the *Diary* is perhaps the most widely read book on the Holocaust. Anne Frank, *The Diary of Anne Frank* (New York, NY: Random House, 1956); Elie Wiesel, *Night* (New York, NY: Hill and Yang, 2006).

The rabbi I studied with in Paris was fascinating, exceptional.* He's a great thinker. Alain shares my enthusiasm for him, too. We were very lucky to have known him. I tried to learn everything, and I really looked forward to each class. I knew that each night would be great. We went, and he explained everything, and it all made sense. I went for a year. It was enough for me because I had read a lot and thought about it a lot and had already made up my mind.

I couldn't go to the [Catholic] church anymore. It became impossible. Everything seemed so false I became uneasy. At the same time, I told myself that I needed to reconcile what I was thinking with who I was. Since I couldn't remain in that uncertainty, it was better to take the final step and convert. Many people told me that I had converted because of my marriage. Maybe that's a good enough reason for others, but not for me. I have found a good balance. I don't feel out of place even if it took my parents a long time to accept my conversion.

I converted in 2000. I told my parents four months before I finally did it. It was very hard for them. It was a betrayal that left consequences felt until now. When it happened, my brother played the "perfect son." We had always competed, and he didn't do anything to improve the situation. Now he is very nice, and I have a good relationship with him, but at the time he played a bad role. Even after my parents had forgiven me, he said [critical] things in front of them. I have only my paternal grandmother alive, and she told them to let me do what I wanted. She helped me and so did my godmother, who also is my father's sister. She helped me even though she said that she didn't agree with my decision.

My parents thought that they'd never see me again. For the first four months, it was very hard. They made angry phone calls to me. My mother would cry on the phone. My father refused to talk to me. It was very hard, and I understand that it wasn't easy for them. With my in-laws, I think that at first there was a lot of tension, but I was kept away from it. But they have become very welcoming. My mother-in-law is wonderful, and I am very lucky. My father-in-law is nice, but he is very traditional. Even Alain's grandmother told him it was okay if I wasn't Jewish if I am a good person. I met them all when I was still not considering conversion, but everyone in his family was relieved when I converted.

Alain attended the classes with me, and he learned things as well. At the time, we were not yet married. He had proposed to me when he was in

---

* Rivon Krygier, Congregation Adat Shalom, is a highly respected Masorti (a traditional but non-orthodox rabbi and teacher).

Japan, but it took a long time after that. It took eight years to decide. Things happened that caused us to delay because we were supposed to get married earlier. In the end, we slowed down the process because I was changing too. Given the status of children born of a non-Jewish woman in Judaism—it's a bit complicated.* So I preferred to wait a bit and we got married after the conversion.

For a while after the wedding we lived in Paris. I moved to Dijon in September or October 2001 and Alain came in November. He had done a year in Dijon while waiting to get a job in Paris, and because of that, he was offered a practice here in plastic surgery. I fought as hard as I could for him not to accept it. But finally, I couldn't stop him in his career if that is what he really wanted. At the same time, I couldn't really imagine living here, and that's still the case.

In Paris, I'd worked in different clinics, one with friends. I also worked while at school, filling in at some clinics. Before that, I had a normal university student life with a lot of friends. I really enjoyed those years. When I first came to Dijon, I had my clinic. I found a place and started. Then I got sick and discovered that I was expecting twins. I contacted a friend and asked him to come, and he agreed. I told him that he could stay in Dijon and we could work together, but in the end he was depressed in Dijon and went back to Paris. But he waited until after the children were born.

We integrated into the community quite soon after coming. We had some contacts, since Mrs. Sibony [rabbi's wife] came to see me two days after I came. That night, I asked Alain if Sibony was a Jewish name and he asked why. I told him that I was visited by a woman dressed as a nun, with a wig and a hat,† and I was sure that she was Jewish. Later, I discovered that she was the wife of the rabbi. When I was hospitalized due to my pregnancy, she came to see me in the hospital.

When we first arrived, many in the community invited us to their homes. Their welcome was very warm. I have rarely seen something like this. The community we were a part of in Paris also was warm because we had friends there. Here it is like a family. They welcome you easily. The Sibonys are incredibly warm and welcoming. People here allow us to do a lot of things. If we have an idea, people help us make it happen. We can easily gather people for projects. For the radio program, 15 people gathered immediately. I didn't have to make 15 phone calls to convince them. People want to do things.

---

* According to traditional Jewish Law, only a child born of a Jewish mother is Jewish.
† After marriage, Orthodox women generally cut their hair short and wear head coverings, signs of fidelity and modesty, since women's hair stimulates sexual attraction.

But what was most surprising for me was the segregation of women [in the synagogue] and their lack of participation. They are required to stay upstairs in the synagogue. We cannot hear anything, and we do not understand what we do hear. Even the rabbi's wife, who sat next to me, talked to me during the services, and I didn't know how to ask her to stop because I wanted to follow what was happening below. Another thing, I'm glad that I had the opportunity to study in Paris before I came to Dijon, because I wouldn't have had the knowledge that I do have. The segregation of women is one thing, but the lack of adult classes is more serious. There are no advanced studies for anyone.

Yet, I love the rabbi. Honestly, I have heard people who are now with the Lubavitch say bad things about him. I cannot tolerate this because having had a Catholic way of thinking that believes that the Pope is always right, I cannot say that whatever the rabbi does is right. But he is very human, and we could have a more brilliant rabbi but one who is less warm. He's nice; he's very wise. But I sometimes typed articles that he wrote for *Mazal Tov* that I did not agree with and was not happy with because they were not deep enough. And he sometimes annoys me because he does not work hard enough or communicate enough information. But he is so warm and welcoming that his good qualities make up for the rest. Yes, I prefer Rabbi Sibony to some erudite rabbi who would impose strict rules.

I might have problems within the community if I stay long enough for my children to do their bar mitzvahs. I had hard times with some people, and one specific person whom I liked a lot and whom I invited to my house, but who said that my children would not be able to do their bar mitzvahs because I was not Jewish. So we had some heated arguments. I did not talk to him for several months. Finally, he apologized for what he said, so I forgave him. But my answer to all this is that my boys will not do their bar mitzvahs here because I want them to go to classes, and I also want my daughter to have her bat mitzvah. The reason for all this is because Rabbi Sibony is affiliated with the Consistory, and since I had not been converted within the Consistory I wasn't considered Jewish by some people here. And maybe the rabbi would have to go along with the Consistory.

The children should not have to go somewhere else. I am Jewish. I did everything to become Jewish, and I don't have to prove it to anyone. That's what I told them. That's why I didn't tell them at first that I was converted because I knew that that's what disturbed them. Since they do not consider those who converted to be Jews, I didn't talk about it. But in the end, it turns out that I will not do it for the Consistory. For me, the Consistory is a political body and not religious, and it isn't the group that will determine whether or not I'm Jewish.

I was angry at that time, but not at everybody, and certainly not at the rabbi because he never said anything. But I think that the rabbi will be confronted with a difficult situation and that he will have to say no to me. What's certain is that I won't put him in that situation.

In Dijon itself, I never hid the fact that I was Jewish, and being Jewish never caused me any problems. People are rather nice. Of course, we occupy respectable positions in society and that protects us. For the time being, the children are going to school in a neighborhood where there are Arabs. There is a Muslim market there. I won't let them stay in that school for long because they say that they are Jewish quite naturally. Reuben Danino is a common Jewish name, and I don't want them exposed to any risks that can be avoided. I think that it is quite risky to be Jewish in certain areas. Unfortunately, apart from the Lubavitch school, there are no Jewish schools here. I don't want to send them to the Lubavitch school because I would rather that they meet people of different origins. I think that would be more enriching.

I have contributed to the community by participating in several activities. I am involved with the radio. I have also assisted in making a movie for the Patrimony celebration. What is really surprising over the years is my growing concern for Israel, something I never had before. I told myself that it was not just a religion, but also a land, and that it was important to think about it that way. It is quite surprising, because at first I didn't feel connected to Israel.

Alain and I went to Israel twice before we were married. The children have gone five times; they go at least once a year. What surprised me at first was to see a very developed country. Unfortunately, on my first visit there was a garbage collectors' strike so it looked like a cross between the United States and the Middle East. But I love it there. I couldn't stop going. I feel more comfortable in Tel Aviv than in Jerusalem. I don't like Jerusalem. I feel tension there that is unbearable. Every time I go there, I get into a fight with someone. One time it was because I had on a sundress and was told that it was indecent, and this despite the fact that a woman in front of me was wearing shorts and nothing was said to her! I have a hard time in Jerusalem, and every time Alain tells me to stop because I am spoiling his visit. It's easier in Tel Aviv because a big part of the city is secular so I feel more at ease there.

Israel has become important to me because now I know [the country]. At first, it was just a country full of foreigners. I didn't have the feeling of being part of a family that I feel in the diaspora. Then I got to know the people, the beaches, merchants, all of it, and I realized that these people are as warm as any Jew anywhere, that they have a beautiful life, and that at the same time they are ensuring our security. But I am worried more than Alain about Israel. Besides the Americans, there isn't anyone who's supporting it. Europe has completely abandoned Israel.

Why? It's because Europeans cannot get over the Shoah. It is impossible for them to accept it. It is beyond their comprehension so they need to find a reason why the Shoah occurred. And there is a reason: "They [the Jews] had asked for it." So now they are going to try and find in the behavior of the Israelis the reason for the Shoah in Europe. It is a bit complicated. And maybe it's to prevent them from seeing themselves as beasts. They need to justify what their parents and grandparents had done.

As to the future of my family, I think that we will not stay in France. We probably will go to North America. I love Israel, but it is another thing to live there. I don't think that I could do that because of the children. I wouldn't be able to see them in the military for three years. My reluctance to move there is not really because of the terrorist attacks but the three years in the military. I know that it's not fair to let others do it for me, but if I need to find a country where I can have some stability, I know that I will not find it in Europe. We've had proposals for England and Italy, but I don't feel like investing in Europe again. If we need to leave, I think that we will go to North America. We already have contacts and probably will leave in about a year and a half.

Moving to North America is for the safety of the children, of course, but it's also for Alain and myself. I cannot see raising my children here where their future might quickly be compromised, not necessarily because of anti-Semitism, but for economic reasons. We do have anti-Semitism in the government that is reflected in anti-Israeli feelings. [The government] is against Israel and for the Palestinians. The policy favors the Arabs. I think that 20 per cent of the population [in France] is Arab,* even though those figures are not official. And the government supports them. The result is disaster for our economic policy and disaster for our foreign policy.

For me, poverty and the lack of opportunities [for the Arabs] are not enough to explain everything. For example, it is well-known that in certain neighborhoods cars are burned so that people become afraid and sell their apartments at the lowest price. Then the Arabs take over those apartments

---

* The percentage of Arabs in France is probably about 10 per cent, six million Arabs among 60 million French people, but the Arabs have a higher birthrate.

and build their own neighborhoods. It's a demonstration of power. But to be able to control those areas, the police must be able to intervene.

We can deal with the Arabs here if we don't have a collaborating government. There are ways to channel them. There are other countries that had very harsh Muslims. We can talk about England. In the United States, there are Muslims who are veiled but are peaceful. So they can be restrained, but not by a government that collaborates.

We cannot go on like this. I do not want to keep working in this country if I am going to be killed with the taxes that support people who are against us. But there is also a personal reason why I want to leave. It's because I can't see a bright future in this country. The trend here is more towards international studies nowadays, and if I stay here I would have to send my children to the United States for their studies. I don't want them to go. I want to be with them. It also pains me to leave my parents, but I know that they won't come with me. But I don't want my children to live somewhere [away from me].

You see, I don't think that people change much. They evolve, but they don't change. France did not act well in the last war [World War II]. For the most part, most French didn't do anything. The best formed a resistance. Otherwise, most French did nothing, or even collaborated. Eventually, they placed themselves in the winners' camp [joining the war effort], all the while hating the true winners—the United States and England.

We are not always grateful to those who have helped us. We often have a debt that is too big, especially when we haven't been very honest. I think that France has begun to hate the United States because of this. I also think that there is envy, and it is very complex. France still thinks that it's a superpower when that is not the case. They think that they can still make themselves heard by the superpowers. So they systematically go against whatever the United States says just to claim that they also have a say in the matter. And this is simply ridiculous.

As I said, France is facing economic problems. It's because there are so few people who pay their taxes. We are constantly expecting to receive assistance here. It's awful. I had a babysitter working in my home who after six months just left one day without notice. She said that she could collect as much money from the government without working as I paid her.

All the values have been reversed. The aggressor becomes the victim. When you try to defend yourself, you become the culprit. I make money. I have a beautiful house and a car, and I am immediately suspected. You cannot have a great house or car. You need to keep a low profile. Alain and I work hard. We have pursued difficult studies. I think that it's normal for me to enjoy my work. But I can't. I cannot even say that I'm going abroad on vacation. I cannot say that I am taking my children to Israel. We went to Greece this summer, but I could not tell any of those who work around me. When they ask, I say that yes, I have a family home. I almost am tempted to say that we are living in a trailer in a campground, because I'm afraid of showing signs of wealth and success.

I find no pride in being French. Leaving won't be hard because I was born here by chance. I could have been born elsewhere.

Maybe I will feel French in a foreign country, but I don't feel proud of being French these days. If we, French people, derive no pride in it, how can you understand an immigrant, whom we ask to become French? It's complicated in the ghettos. They are not really French, but at the same time they are told that they are integrated into the society. But they say what they think in their songs. There is a song that came out that said that France is a whore that you need to bed. It's very vulgar, but that's how they see France.* So I'm not proud to be French. It irritates me.

This is not right. I gave so much for my studies, my work. I wanted to do something, and I am prevented from doing it. But, okay. I will do it somewhere else. France has lost other people. I have friends who left. How many? When I ask around, it seems that people have already packed their bags to leave.

* The song, "FranSSe," by rapper Monsieur R (Richard Makela), was the subject of great debate when conservative members of Parliament accused Makela of inciting racial enmity with his lyrics.

Malou Dressler

Malou Dressler was too young to remember World War II, but she has perceptive knowledge of the entire postwar era and how Jewish life evolved through various stages in France. As a now retired secondary school teacher of English, she experienced firsthand the impact of educational policy changes as the nation grappled with problems such as the assimilation of its Muslim immigrants. She provides a cautionary view of the Jewish presence in France.

September 2007

In the 1950s, the mainstream values of an old Catholic country were very much alive in Dijon. That meant that being a Jew was not easy because we were viewed just after the war with the same ideas that pervaded France in the nineteenth century. I remember once, while in primary school, a young girl said to me, "You killed Jesus." I didn't know what that meant, so I wasn't traumatized. I simply didn't know anything about Jesus, and I certainly didn't know why she was being rude to me.[*]

The war had a bad effect on the health of Jewish kids, and so many, like myself, were sent after the war into the countryside to recover in a healthier environment. We lived peacefully in a very nice village. The lady who looked after us was called "La Juive," the Jewish Girl. But she was nice. She was very courageous because taking care of Jewish girls made her very different from the other villagers—because she had Jewish kids. There were seven or eight of us there, all around my age. We were very happy. That was in the late 1940s, the early 1950s.

In those years, when I was young, my family talked about the war and what had happened. It was impossible to convey the trauma to other people because nobody knew about Judaism, about Jewish people. But the prejudices existed, so we had to be as smart as possible. We couldn't really be Jewish on the outside. At home we kept talking about those who had been killed, and the result was that I had a childhood based on absence. We grew up with the memories of those who had died, so it was an empty thing.

I went to high school in Dijon. We had to comply with and conform to the curriculum, which meant that we couldn't talk about what we had experienced, what we had been through. We couldn't talk about our culture. What was Jewish was completely insignificant to Catholics at that time.

---

[*] Her comment that Gentiles claim that Jews killed Jesus is a recurring theme in several interviews.

Today, it is normal to speak Yiddish. People now know about Judaism, but at that time—nothing. For example, they didn't teach about the Dreyfus Affair, about La Commune.* They evaded all the rough subjects. They did teach about World War II, but in a very formal way and not as accurately as today. I didn't learn much about what had happened. The deportations were taught within the context of French history, of course. There was not too much about the Vichy period either.

Dijon at that time was a very old-fashioned city with strict Catholic values. I remember that I felt deprived of something because my friends would do their First Communion, whereas I was watching them and couldn't have the same white dress and all the gifts that go with them. I was frustrated.... When my friends asked me why I didn't do First Communion, I'd tell them that I'd do it somewhere else. They never caught on because they really weren't interested in those things. I didn't take off from school for Yom Kippur. I didn't have any Jewish studies at home, except that my mother taught me Yiddish. Of course, that was not academic; that was for within the family. What my mother also taught me was to sew.

We lived in the center of the city. Today it's a very posh area, but back then it was for the proletariat. Poor people lived there. There also were Spanish refugees.

I attended the university here in Dijon. Afterwards, I lived in England for a time, working in Manchester. That was 1966. When I returned, I started working in Nevers, in a junior high school teaching English. I think that I studied English because it sounds very much like Yiddish—the music of English sounds very much like the music of Yiddish. I began to study English in high school and majored in it at the university.

In 1967–68, I wasn't interested in politics. You must understand that young girls were not independent then. French society was very strict, and we were not independent. We were just waiting to be adults, to be free, to be allowed more independence from our parents. But in 1967, I did go to Israel for a month. We had relatives there and I wanted to visit them. So just one month after the war I went to the West Bank, Gaza, everywhere. My cousins, who had been to Gaza and Ramallah, talked about their experiences. Now I realize how important it was, but at the time I couldn't distance myself from

---

* The civil war that broke out between Leftist Paris and several other cities and the rest of rural France, following France's surrender to Germany in 1871 after France's defeat in the Franco-Prussian War. The Commune was repressed by the provisional government, under Adolphe Thiers, with thousands of deaths and executions, leaving a legacy of class hatred and revolutionary mythology.

what had happened. After 1968,[*] there was more of an atmosphere of freedom here. It was very nice. It was better because people talked to each other.

I spent several years teaching in Nevers. I traveled. Then I came back to Dijon to study. In 1984, I began to teach high school in Dijon, where I remained until I retired. In the early years, I enjoyed teaching, but I saw the evolution of teaching away from excellence. What I mean is that the kids became less interested in learning, to know what their forefathers had learned, to know about their past, to know about history.

In 1989–90, Prime Minister [Lionel] Jospin's ideas defined a new orientation for national education. Teaching skills grew in importance at the expense of the transmission of knowledge that was often considered as being merely "encyclopedic." They wanted the student to be the center of teaching, and little by little, transmission of knowledge was neglected. I am talking about what I saw. Little by little, we neglected the transmission of knowledge. We were emphasizing child creativity, which was great, but the level of difficulty dropped.

We did not have any foreign students at the school, but there were Muslims. I learned that on 9/11 when we were paying a tribute to honor the dead. All of the students stood up, but one of my colleagues told me that in one of her classes some Muslim students left the room because they did not want to render a tribute. After 9/11, I also heard one of my colleagues in the faculty room say that it was the CIA that had organized the attack. He did not say it in front of me, but he never said it again.

When I was teaching, people knew that I was Jewish, but I did not have any problems. The problems started when the children born of Muslim families in France, instead of taking French classes, started to take Arabic classes. It meant that integration was slowed down because instead of helping them to speak French, we let them remain stuck in the Muslim community. And Islam grew.

In the 1980s, I voted for Mitterrand,[†] like everyone else. Then, when I saw that the law on teaching was destroying the best thing that France had, I started to tell myself that the pedagogues who wanted this law were cynical because they were not allowing the children to benefit from the classics that they themselves had studied. The law on teaching of 1990 introduced "life" at school [subjects such as reproduction and family life], but I think that the students don't need life, they need to learn what they don't know.

---

[*] 1968 was the year of sometimes violent student rebellions, mostly in Paris. These events pushed French youth culture leftward, weakening societal norms and established authority; moreover, President Charles de Gaulle resigned in 1969.

[†] François Mitterrand, President of France, 1981–95.

Not all teachers agreed with me. [A few of us] thought that making 80 per cent of students pass the Bac was a mistake. We were considered to be reactionaries. We were called dinosaurs. Today, however, they all agree with us.

The change in France concerning Israel happened slowly. After the Six Day War, the image that we had of Israel was wonderful. Israel was very much admired by the students. But this began to change when Arafat started to handle things. Then there was the war in Lebanon in 1982, followed by the First and Second Intifadas.* Then, the fall of the Berlin Wall and the collapse of Communism changed the vision of French progressiveness. They always have to have a cause, and the cause of the poor Palestinians replaced that of the poor working classes and the struggle between the social classes. [Israeli President Ariel] Sharon became the laughingstock of the teachers. At the school, there were baffling comments about Israel. I heard a history professor say that Sharon had made a big mistake by walking on the esplanade of the mosque in Jerusalem. He did not know that before it had been the esplanade of the temple.

After the First Intifada, and with the development of the media, the blogs, the Internet, mobile phones, everything changed because the news became instantaneous. Then, I had to be very careful when I had students of Muslim origin. We did have some Muslim teachers, of course, but we didn't talk politics with them; we only talked about students. At this time, my political views changed and my attitude towards Israel as well. After my visit in 1967, I returned three times; 2005 was my most recent visit.

Now, it is getting harder to talk about Israel openly because we Jews are always accused of being subjective because of our origins. We realized that a lot of teachers are ignorant because they have set ideas and their only source of information is the television. The problem is that in classes some teachers make their own propaganda, and we cannot talk about Israel anymore. I started to realize this in about 2000.

After 2000 and the beginning of the Second Intifada and the death of the Little Mohammed,† the minds of the people were inflamed. Everyone was

---

* Palestinian revolts against Israeli occupation of the West Bank and Gaza, in 1987 and 2000, respectively.

† Mohammed Al-Dura was a Palestinian child who was supposedly killed by the Israelis on 30 September 2000, during the second Intifada, but who probably was either killed by Palestinian bullets or was acting a "pose" and is still alive. The emotional scene of his death, used to castigate Israelis for genocidal acts of cruelty, led to what became known as the Al-Dura–Enderlin Affair. Charles Enderlin, a Jewish French journalist for France 2 (France's main television channel), reported the Palestinian version of events on the air and in print. Suits and countersuits ensued, with Enderlin being supported by hundreds of journalists, citing the issue of freedom of the press versus Jewish communal pressure against those who would publicly criticize Israel. However, in December 2011 the attorney general, in

talking about it, and the French Press Agency played an important role in vilifying Israel. The journalist working for the Agency who sent the dispatches was the nephew of Arafat. The dispatches claimed that the Israelis who had been the victims were now the murderers. As a result, plus the degradation of education that I spoke about, the students became very confused. Then, without discipline in the classes, they said anything they wanted. It didn't happen in my classes only because I was very careful.

There was only one other Jewish teacher in the school at that time. He was philosophically Jewish, but he was not part of the organized community. He is more distant in regards to Israel. But you know, the craziness of the media, the death of the Little Mohammed, the inability to have an objective analysis—these were the things that scared me and continue to scare me. It's a lack of understanding and knowledge of politics. There was total madness regarding Israel.

The "genocide" at Jenin [a West Bank Arab town] was awful.* We had the impression that people were repeating what the least intelligent media were saying. The most objective ones were probably those who had humanist values and Christian values, and who tried to understand. But those were awful years.

I remember there was a march in 2002 in Paris. It was a huge march by the Jews of France. I was not going, but on television I saw Rony Brauman, who is a Jew, born in Jerusalem, and who always attacks Jews. I was so fed up that I decided to go along with friends on the march.† I tried to explain my position to my friends at the high school, but people told me, "Of course, you are subjective." But I will tell you something: a week before my retirement we were discussing the law about forbidding girls to wear the Muslim

---

responding to a ten-year long defamation case before France's highest court in which Charles Enderlin accused Philippe Karsenty of defamation of character, concluded that Enderlin's cameraman had lied and accused Enderlin of having invented Al-Dura's murder, now seen as a staged event. Karsenty had accused Enderlin of false reporting and his employer, France Télévision, as well, of hyping the reports. To this day, the Affair still has agency, and many Jews believe it has led to an increase in anti-Semitism in France. See Samuel Ghiles-Meilhac, *Le CRIF : De la résistance juive à la tentation du lobby* (Paris: Éditions Robert Laffont, 2011) 203–08; Jean-Patrick Grumberg, http://www.Dreuz.info; and http://karsenty2012.com/images/stories/ag_cour_de_cassation.pdf.

* In April 2002, Israeli Defence Forces attacked the northern West Bank city of Jenin, then under the administration of the Palestinian National Authority, in order to suppress attacks on Israel. During the battle and ensuing occupation, civilians were killed and injured, thus raising charges of Israeli genocide; however, the media repeated numbers that were grossly inflated.

† Brauman is perhaps best known outside France for his collaboration with Israeli film director Eyal Sivan on the 1999 docudrama *The Specialist*, which was based on actual footage from the Eichmann trial. Sivan re-cut the footage to create his narrative. Both Sivan and Brauman are ardent critics of Zionism. See Rony Brauman and Alain Finkielkraut, *La Discorde : Israël-Palestine, les juifs, la France* (Paris: Mille et Une Nuits, 2006).

veil in school. A lot of my colleagues were hostile to this law because of the "right to be different." So the right to be different is for the Muslims but not for the Catholics or the Jews? I told a colleague that the law banning the veil was good. And he responded, "What about the kippa?"* So every time I talked about the veil or about Israel, I was criticized.

I want to add something important. Since 2000, we have been placed in the same box, the Jews who have 2,000 years of history in Europe and the Muslims who have about 40 years of history here. Each time, it was the Jews against the Muslims, and we had the impression that our French nationality was being taken away from us. We were French, but as Jews we were constantly set against the Muslims, as if the French people wanted to denationalize us. We had to justify ourselves. We had to explain that we were French, that there have been Jewish people here since Roman times. We are not at all like Muslims who arrived in France 40 or 50 years ago. All the time, we had to justify ourselves.

So when my colleague asked me, "What about the kippa?" I asked him, in turn, "Do you see a lot of kippas?" And he didn't answer. So, the issue on the veil is that, if it is a Catholic girl wearing a veil, the teachers would tell her to remove it immediately—she doesn't have the right to wear it. But because a Muslim girl is wearing a veil, there is always compassion towards Islam.

There was one colleague who took my side, but she was very discreet about it. She took me aside and told me that she had a lot of sympathy for Israel. But she never said it in the faculty room. [The teachers] are afraid. They're not cowards, they're afraid. I think that we need to stress the fact that all the French Jews who were perfectly integrated into the society were French *and* Jewish. Now, all of a sudden, because of the Second Intifada, we are Jewish and French.

I had become more politically involved in the 1990s when I joined France-Israel. Now that I am retired, I am still active in the organization here. In regards to politics, we realize that the Socialists are the hostages of the extreme Left. And on the Right, there are often men and women who have values that are humanist. Their ideas are more practical and less idealistic. The Right is less ideological than the Left or the extreme Left. Of course, [President Jacques] Chirac, a man of the Right, has always been considered a friend of the Arabs. But in 1995 he did acknowledge the responsibility of Vichy in the Shoah.

* The 2004 French law banning public display of personal religious symbols does in fact include the kippa, as well as large crosses, Sikh turbans, and the Muslim veil.

As for my view of the future of the Jews in Dijon and in France, it depends on the day. When I see to what extent the media and the younger generation are influenced by Islam, to what extent the words of the young North Africans are taken into consideration, and to what extent the politicians have to be cunning and careful, I tell myself that the 1 per cent Jewish population will not be a match for the six million Muslims. I think that our future is at stake in France, and the six million Muslims might jeopardize our future because gradually their impact is expanding.

For example, if France had gone to war in Iraq along with the United States, France would have been torn apart. That's why it could not have happened. At least I think so. I also think that France considered its economic interests because Chirac was the one who wanted Saddam Hussein to have nuclear power in Iraq. The foreign policy of France favors the Arabs. I think that it has always been in favor of the Arabs. It goes back to the time when Palestine was divided between the English and French.* Then there also was de Gaulle's policy: he never forgave the Israelis for having used the weapons that they were given in 1967.

It is very difficult to change the mindset of people from earlier France. The young North Africans, for example, are influenced by the Internet, by blogs. There is official news, what they learn in school, and there is a network working at the same time, and that is beyond our control. When we see the international commotion caused by a few words from the Pope [concerning militant Islam], it isn't rational.† It is beyond logic. All the young people today, be they Muslims or others, have cell phones, send text messages, have Internet and cable TV, and we cannot do anything about it. They are all connected to Al Jazeera [Arab news station].

The [Muslim] riots last year [2005] were very dangerous because they took France hostage. And since we did not dare to repress them, we saw nine- or ten year-old children burning symbols of their integration, such as nurseries, stadiums, and schools—anything that could help them progress in life. I think that this is where education has failed. We should have taught them Greek, Latin, Plato. We should have pushed them to study and progress.

Of course there will be more riots. They have died out, but they could flare up again. I am very worried.

---

* Following World War I England and France reached agreement on the fate of the defeated Turkish Empire, agreements later sanctioned by the League of Nations. Palestine, which comprised present-day Israel, the West Bank, and Jordan (independant in 1946) was occupied by the British until 1948, while French-influenced areas included present-day Lebanon and Syria.

† The reference is to the lecture given by Pope Benedict XVI at the University of Regensburg in Germany on 12 September 2006. The Pope had quoted a negative remark about Islam made by a fourteenth-century Byzantine emperor.

Annie Edelman and Maurice "Gislain" Bensoussan

Annie Edelman, of Ashkenazi origin, has long been involved in the Dijon community's cultural life. She remains very much the socially conscious individual she was as a student in the 1960s. As a volunteer at Radio Shalom and a staff member of the journal, Mazal Tov, *she is one of the most informed members of the community. Along with her Sephardic husband, Gislain, she maintains an open and hospitable household where people of diverse backgrounds and identities are warmly welcomed. Now retired, she recently became a member of the Cultural Center's Board of Directors. The story of her mother, Bébé Edelman, is told in the Survivors section above.*

Maurice "Gislain" Bensoussan, is Annie's husband. He is a widely published researcher in food biology and Professor at the Université de Bourgogne. A former Trotskyite with a prodigious memory, he joins his wife in many community cultural activities.

Spring 1993

My name is Annie. I am 46 years old [in 1993]. I was born in France. I have been married twice, and I have six children and a grandson. My mother, who is still alive, was born in Paris in 1921 [see the interview with Bébé Edelman above, p. 84]. Her parents emigrated from Odessa, in Russia. My father, who was born in Warsaw in 1924, was two years old when his parents brought him to France. He had no memories of Poland, his native country. For him, it never existed. In addition to me, my parents had a son and another daughter, my brother and sister. They both are married and have children.

I was born in 1946 at the beginning of the "baby boom." As a child I moved around a lot with my family from Lyon to Paris, from Paris to Lyon. My parents had real financial difficulties after the war. My father's studies had been interrupted, and he had a hard time finding adequate work. He changed jobs frequently and did many things. My mother, who had no higher education, also worked, but the jobs came and went. Sometimes we had money for awhile, then for awhile there was very little. Money came into the house and left it as if there was no future. Sometimes we could not buy clothes. Then my father would find another job and it was okay again.

Of course, I was too young to understand that the situation was a consequence of the war. Yet, I was not unhappy as a child. Sometimes it was hard, but I was not unhappy. My childhood was not like Émile Zola's.* My

---

* Nineteenth-century French author of social realist novels.

parents ... my father had a positive personality, a good temperament. He was always smiling, making jokes. It was especially difficult for my mother because she had to feed and dress the kids, do everything. We did not have to do anything as children but simply live.

At school, I was a good student though I had a few minor disciplinary problems. I moved from school to school as we moved from neighborhood to neighborhood, but it caused me no problems of adaptation. It really was not very hard. I do remember having difficult relationships with some of the teachers. Then my mother would say, "She is anti-Semitic." It was her explanation for everything. At the time, I did not like that explanation at all. Now I realize that it was true most of the time. It took me a long time to understand that. You see, I had only non-Jewish friends. I was not raised in a Jewish community. The only Jews I knew were my family members: parents, grandparents, uncles, cousins. My friends were mostly Catholic. I knew nothing about Judaism. I only noticed that my mother lit a candle every year in memory of my grandparents. But I could not explain why, and most of all, I was not interested. I had not been taught anything about Jewish culture.

For a long time, I did not know what a Jew was. The only thing that I knew was that it was sort of dramatic being a Jew. I knew that they ended up in extermination camps and that they did not like the Germans nor did the Germans like them. I knew so little that at elementary school when my friends had their First Communion I thought that I didn't because I was Protestant. In our history classes, we talked about conflicts between Catholics and Protestants. It was at that point that I learned that I was not Protestant, but Jewish. I would say that I was about nine years old at the time. So you see, the only real meaning that I gave to the word "Jew" was that it implied something dramatic.

My "Jewish life" began when I was 14. The turning point came when I saw the movie, *Mein Kampf*[*].Thanks to the film, I began thinking about Judaism. I asked my mother what it meant to be a Jew. She did not have an answer. Or, rather, the answer she had was that it meant "the ovens." I decided to investigate for myself. We were living in Lyon at the time so I contacted the rabbi there, who turned out to be very impressive. Then I met some young people in the city who had a community house where classes were held. They were mostly boys, though occasionally a girl would attend. One day, young people of the Ha Shomer Ha-Tsair[†] came and convinced me to participate in their activities.

---

[*] *Mein Kampf*, a Swedish film, directed by Erwin Leiser and released in 1960, follows the rise and fall of Hitler from his life as a failed artist to his rise to power and eventual suicide after Germany's defeat in 1945.

[†] Leftist-Zionist Youth Movement.

So you see, it started little by little and eventually became an important part of my life. I tried to understand it all by myself because my parents did not know anything or did not want to know.

I did my first college year at the Catholic University of Lyon, then transferred to the university in Dijon for my second year. There I continued to learn more about Judaism. For a long time, I had worn a "Magen David" [star of David] in gold, and one day at the university's cafeteria a guy noticed it and asked me if I was Jewish. I replied that I was, and he told me that his name was Michel Lévy, that he was Jewish, that there was a synagogue in Dijon, that there was a community with people of our age, and was I interested? I told him that I was, and that is how I came into contact with the community of Dijon. It turned out to be easy to integrate into it because it was then rather small.

Still, there were difficulties. I had gotten married when I was very young and already had a child. And my husband was a Catholic. But he did not have any problems about me being Jewish. I was not a practicing Jew. My children were not part of any religious community. My integration was hard [for my husband] and was so until the day I met Gislain, my second husband. Then, problems of that kind came to an end. I had other problems too [with my first husband], but that is not the point. I met Gislain at the synagogue.

I had finished part of my studies when my children were born. I had two kids then and I raised them. At the age of 35, I reconsidered everything. I started my studies again, I worked, I learned to drive. I wanted to be independent even if it seemed to be too late.

I had never been involved in politics. Even in May 1968, when there were student and workers uprisings in Paris that nearly toppled de Gaulle and helped lead to his retirement a year later, I didn't participate but only observed. Then came the Six Day War, in which Israel defeated Egypt, Syria, and Jordan, who were supported by several other Arab states—at first, Jews worldwide had feared another Holocaust, provoking widespread great support for Israel and other Jewish causes. I was concerned and, as usual, followed the news because I wanted to know what was going on in Israel. Here in Dijon we held a meeting at the synagogue to collect money. I was always there because we had friends in the community. I remember really well, for example, photographs of Israeli soldiers in front of the Kotel.* Those images were really strong. But I did not understand everything; at the time, I was really busy with my children.

---

* The Western or "Wailing" Wall surrounding the second Temple; the holiest site for most Jews.

I do, of course, remember de Gaulle's attitude [about Israel and the Jews], the embargo,* all the politics, and, afterwards, Georges Pompidou, whom I remember even better. As the years passed, I became more and more concerned.

GISLAIN: Like Annie, I was born in 1946, but in Algeria, in the city of Mostaganem, located on the coast near Oran. It was at the time a small city of perhaps 50,000 inhabitants. I can say that I had a flawless childhood. There was a small Jewish community with a fine social life, like all the Jewish communities in Algeria. We had many "traditionalists," but not many real Orthodox folks.

My brother was born in 1951; when he was about six months old, we left Algeria for France. We lived in Paris where I started elementary school, the same type of school Annie attended. I too changed schools several times, since we lived in three different neighborhoods. Then, after Israel's 1956 war with Egypt, my parents decided to move to Israel, where we arrived in February 1957. Israel had joined England and France in an attack on Egypt, experiencing major military success while they moved slowly, although all conquests were later returned in the face of American and Soviet pressure. What I recall is that they sold everything we had in Paris but bought a refrigerator and stove, the kinds of things that were scarce in Israel. When we arrived in Israel, we were assigned a place near Akko in a neighborhood that was not yet completely constructed. We had one floor with a kitchen and a room. The bathroom was in the garden. There was water but no electricity. The little comforts that we had brought from France could not be utilized because there was no electricity.

I was a little older than ten and I went to school from February through July 1957. I can't say that I learned much. Still, it was a new style of life. We were Jews; at my house every Jewish festivity was celebrated.

We stayed in Israel only eight months because my father could not find a job. When we returned to Paris, I continued my schooling. I attended high school for two years near the Place de la République, an area where many Jews lived. In my first year high school class, there were four or five Jews of a total of 40 students. This was different from my first experience in Paris, when we did not have many community contacts and my school friends were not Jews. I also knew that the high school classmates were Jews because their names sounded like names from North Africa.

I was almost bar mitzvah age so I started to attend weekly Talmud Torah classes in the neighborhood synagogue. I was with other young men who

---

* France failed to deliver weapons already purchased by Israel because of the embargo.

also were preparing for their bar mitzvah. The classes were not well orga-nized; we just learned by rote without translating anything, repeating words again and again. Somehow, I managed to learn to read Hebrew.

In 1960, my parents decided to return to Algeria, to Mostaganem. It was during the Algerian War for Independence. But I continued school there and everything was fine. At 14, I still remembered the Algeria I knew when I was little. I have good memories of that period because at the time I did not understand the political situation. For me, it was simply the country of my childhood. Yet I remember looking at it with amazement because it was so different from France, especially from Paris. I'd say that my stay in Algeria was like a long vacation: the sun and visiting old places where my parents had lived before. And I had my bar mitzvah there. But I also saw dead people, and much destruction because of the bombs.

We left after a year and a half, in December 1961, about six months before Algerian independence. At the time, I was 15 and thought that I could take care of myself. As soon as I learned the name of the neighborhood in Marseille where we were going to live, I wrote to a high school there and was accepted by the Lycée Thiers.

We left Oran for the ferry to France on a Friday, and the following Monday, I was already taking classes at my new school in Marseille. I spent the next 20 years there, completing all of my studies including a doctorate in microbiology.

If you want to know why we originally left Algeria in 1952, it was for work. It has always been like that. Although life in Algeria was easy and inexpen-sive, maybe it was just tempting for young people like my parents to go and try their chances in France. For example, my mother had four sisters and two living brothers. Both of the brothers were in France, one working as a tailor and the other as an optician. My mother's sisters all lived in France, one before moving on to Israel. My father's three brothers also lived in Paris. Moving to France was the usual thing in most families.

We did not leave Algeria because of problems with the Muslims. We had Muslim and Catholic friends, although we all lived in different parts of the city. Things began to change when I was in high school and my brother was in elementary school. He had to learn Arabic, which showed the ending of French rule. Other things changed, too: Algerian and French youngsters attended the same schools.

It was not really hard when my family moved to France. My father made money; he worked with wood as a cabinet and furniture maker. It was not something that he did in Algeria where he was a waiter. He worked in other things too. Between 1952 and 1956, he worked in a Simca automobile factory. But we spent what we earned. It is not that we were poor; it is just that we were not rich. Perhaps if my parents had known how to manage money, we could have done better. My mother handled the expenses. She was not educated, but she had gone to elementary school. She was a good student but had to quit when she was 13 in order to help her grandfather in his pants business. She worked for him until she got married. She knew how things worked. She was aware of everything, how we could get loans and help from the town council and so forth. She got the town council to pay for my brother's and my summer camp. No, we weren't rich, but we didn't lack anything either.

When we came to Marseille, I found that there were Jews in the city; there were Jews in my school. But we did not have a community life except for the holidays. I saw the movie *Mein Kampf* at school and understood the relationship between the war and the Jews. But I had relatively little contact with Jewish problems until the Six Day War. It was at the start of my second year in university. In the cafeteria was a poster announcing that the Union of Jewish Students of France was organizing a general meeting so I went. I became a member and stayed until 1973 when I finished my studies.

During those years, I had a chance to talk with Jews about Israel and other things. I learned the history of Israel, the actions of the Labor Party, the role of the state, the political categories. When you are at university, you already have well-defined political inclinations. I tended to be on the Left although I never joined a political party—mostly because of Israel. But of course in Marseille the League of Jewish Students was always on the Left. I did have friends who were in movements like the Communist League. But when the biggest student organization in France at the time—an organization of which we all were members—joined with other Leftist parties in criticizing Israel and siding with the Palestinians, we sent in our membership cards saying, "This is the end!"

I was in the faculty of sciences. The majority of the people there were on the Left. The Jewish people I was friendly with were in medical studies and were in the League of Jewish Students. I only had one Jewish friend who was studying chemistry while I was studying biology.

We sometimes had discussion with Arabs; there were Arab groups at the university from Morocco and Algeria. They were against Israel and they supported Palestinians. Sometimes, people on the Left would support them because the League had participated in demonstrations against the Vietnam War, but the Arabs were kind of reluctant.

During my first two years at university, I had a scholarship. After that, I worked for six years between 1968 and 1974 in a high school as a student supervisor. For my doctorate I had to work in a laboratory, and for that I had a five-year research contract that allowed me to finish my first thesis.

By the time the contract expired, I had finished my PhD and had job experience too. I started looking for a job and ended up in Dijon by chance. I wanted to work in a university; in 1981, I engaged in the competitions and was accepted at the University of Dijon.

I arrived in Dijon in November on a Monday. A week later, I went to a trade fair, and there I met Michel Lévy, the person Annie first met. He talked to me about the community and pretty quickly I met everyone ... but I did not go to the synagogue. Some meetings were held in the synagogue and some in people's houses. During a meeting in January 1983, I met Annie.

ANNIE: At the time, I was a member of a community helping Jews in the Soviet Union, and every year we would organize an expensive ball. That year, during the ball, I talked to the people about the situation of Jews in the Soviet Union, but they did not pay any attention. The next day, I went to a community meeting.

GISLAIN: Yes, it was a small meeting, and I cannot remember why I was there.

ANNIE: I was angry because no one was concerned about the Jews in the Soviet Union. I had first become involved with the LICRA. I started with racism, not with politics. I can't remember the year, perhaps 1970. With LICRA, I met Jews who were members of the community and Jews who were not. I got involved in order to preserve human rights, not for political reasons. I always thought that one day I would try politics too, but I never did. I participated in political demonstrations because I was concerned about Israel and the fact that France has always been more on the Arab side. But the LICRA is not involved in politics. It deals with racism, anti-Semitism.

It is important for a Jew involved with the LICRA to deal with the worst kind of racism in France, that against Arabs. Arabs have been here for a long time, and they have nothing to do with the problems in the Middle East. They are workers who live in difficult conditions and we protect them, of course. Israel is another thing. The LICRA also shows to the Arabs that Jews are not always hard on Arabs. There are some Muslim members of the LICRA in Dijon. It is really integrated. In the rest of France, it is mostly Jews.

GISLAIN: Speaking of our relations with the Dijon Jewish community, I can say that we have friends in the community, but we don't really participate much in the religious events. Now, we participate more than in the past because of the kids. Sarah is in the Éclaireurs Israélites [Jewish Scouts]. She participates at Hanukkah and Purim. We want her to meet other Jewish kids. And she goes to the Talmud Torah. We pay community fees for the activities, the rabbi, [the] new community room. But we are not really religious; we do not go to the synagogue on Fridays or Saturdays.

It is a small community. There are 200 families. And sometimes a "family" is only one person. Therefore, there are only small opportunities. We did some things and activities; for example, one year, we had a movie club. We had some conferences. I really do not have anything negative to say. The community exists, and that is a plus. It allows us to meet people. But a major problem is that we do not have leaders.

Some people actually did things. We have a library, a community center, Hebrew lessons. The rabbi teaches in the Talmud Torah. People do try to help, but the young people leave. We used to have some League of Jewish Students, but they left.... We are responsible, and this concerns us.

ANNIE: We do not have a real organization. I am not criticizing, I am just observing. It is something that includes us and concerns us....

GISLAIN: We worked on the campus radio station, but independent of the Jewish community. People know that we are at the radio; they know the hours, but I do not know if they listen.

ANNIE: We worked at the radio once a week for two and a half years. We started it together. It is called "Shalom FM" and the program is 45 minutes long. We talked about everything. The radio at the university's campus is open to everyone. Some people from Portugal have a show; teachers come with students; young people have music shows. There are people from Thailand. There are all kind of things. One day, we noticed that there was a show for Palestine. We were not happy about that, and we went to see the president of the radio station who asked us if we wanted to do a show. We did our show to explain how Israel could be understood. We gave information about our community; we talked about Jewish communities all over the world.

GISLAIN: And we had music from Israel. We organized the program the day before. We would read the newspapers and then plan the show. We ended up expressing our own feelings.

ANNIE: By the end of the two and a half years, we were professionals. We had a lot of fun, too. I stopped because I was pregnant, and when Deborah was born, I could not do it again. We tried to find somebody who would take the spot, but nobody wanted to do it.

GISLAIN: I remember that we were at the congregational meeting of the community in January and Annie asked if somebody was able to take her place at the radio; no one answered. They told her that they would take care of Deborah while she would do the show.

ANNIE: I was really sad, but we stopped doing the broadcast. Deborah was worth the sacrifice.

GISLAIN: Concerning the relationship between my political thoughts and Israel, let me say that the domestic problems of Israel are Israeli. Since

I do not live in Israel, my opinions are more concerned with France and its reality. Of course, I can criticize Israeli politicians like Begin, especially when he tried to break the Histadrut.* But the people in Israel should deal with things like that.

I ought to mention here that I went to Israel in July 1968 with a cousin. We worked for five weeks in a kibbutz. We first had to convince them to accept us. Afterwards, we traveled through the country. My cousin returned to Israel to serve in the army, and now he lives there and is married and the father of four kids.

But on the subject of Israel. . . . I think that it probably is possible to criticize Israel when you do not agree with its politics. So, we can criticize its actions, but we cannot argue about its existence. However, here in the community they label you a Leftist if you say anything negative about it.

ANNIE: I do think that the community has changed in the last five years, maybe in its religious activities. I have the impression that more people participate. The cultural and intellectual life depends on the people and their willingness to do something. I have the impression that there are more religious activities than before.

Of course, in France, there is now the problem of Arab nationalism. People are scared, especially those who survived World War II. The first war in Iraq also had an impact. Right now, however, anti-Semitism is not a big issue. Now there are things that did not happen after World War II, things that were not allowed because of the atrocities that had happened. I live in Dijon and no one ever hurt me because I am a Jew. Right now, Sarah [Annie and Gislain's older daughter] has some difficulties with her teacher, but that is not something new.

It is hard to know if our Catholic friends understand our situation—being both French and Jewish. I have really good friends who accept me for what I am: blond, a little fat, a mother, Jewish. I also have a friend who is a Communist; we never talk about Israel because we have different opinions.

My Catholic friends do not participate in Jewish festivities, although there are a few Catholics who come to the Seder, the communal Passover meal, but I don't know them. We are not really religious anyway. We celebrate only because of the girls and in order to maintain tradition.

You know, there are no Jews in Sarah's class. There are three in the entire school. I do not think that the others know that she is Jewish, and she is too little to say it. I remember that once she ran into a friend on her way to the

---

* Menachem Begin was the conservative, nationalist Israeli prime minister from 1977 to 1983. The Histadrut is Israel's largest labor organization.

Talmud Torah and was asked where she was going. She answered, "To cate-chism." She must have thought that her friend would understand that better.

GISLAIN: It has not been a real problem to be a Jew in France.

Annie, June 2004

My relationship with the [Jewish] community of Dijon hasn't changed much. I hope that in the future I will have more free time and that I will be able to participate more actively. But my relationship is very good, though I haven't interacted with them as much as some of my other Jewish friends. When I go to those events that interest me, I eagerly participate. And my family does as well. Sometimes it is exasperating, of course, but I love them very much despite that.

It's regrettable that I'm not active in the national community. There is a lot going on in Paris that I would love to be part of. For example, the annual Jewish festival*—I would like to have the time and the possibility of partic-ipating in it. I did recently go to the exposition "Jewish Paris."†

We have had some problems in the community here. There's a lack of interest in our youth, a lack of an adult presence. Addressing this could perhaps keep them from leaving Dijon. It was my daughter Deborah who made me realize this. Of course, I'd heard about the problem from others before, but I wasn't concerned then.

Deborah's last trip to Israel changed her life. It was a trip of the **BBYO** with young Jews from all over France. It wasn't a vacation but had a cultural purpose. She got to know her identity, her history, and the lifestyle of Israel. She had participated in the Jewish Scouts here before, but the unit disap-peared because there was no leadership or direction. The older people just left. She was then too young to organize a group herself, so she joined a small existing group of the BBYO. She committed herself to these things in order to exist as a Jewish girl. But she showed an interest a long time ago, before she was ten. I think that she was eight or nine when she attended a lecture on the Holocaust, and she asked, "Why did they do this to us?" It was infor-mation about the Shoah and the stories I told her that gave encouragement. However, it isn't only that. In our family we always gave importance in our relationship to the community to Purim and Hanukkah. And you see photo-graphs in all these rooms of the family relationships that we talk about.

---

* Large annual gathering often held since the early 1980s at the Le Bourget airfield outside of Paris, with different central themes, presentations, Jewish music, etc.

† Exposition of pre–World War II Jewish Marais area, held in Paris's main City Hall in spring 2004.

Deborah was more interested in these issues than her older sister, Sarah. She [Deborah] began feeling a deeper connection to her roots. She started looking for different ways to make more of it. That is how she became more involved in the movement of Jewish youth. She wanted to become even more integrated, but she couldn't do it here. I don't think that by expressing herself she was affected by anti-Semitism or embarrassed in school. I don't want to be optimistic, [anti-Semitism is] not more serious than before, just different. I am talking about Dijon, not Paris or Alsace. In Dijon, I feel safe; I feel that my children are safe. Deborah has walked in the street wearing her Star of David. But she takes it off sometimes, depending on where she is going.

Sarah is more paradoxical. She seems not to be interested, yet she sometimes helps me out at the synagogue. When there was a choir festival at the synagogue, she went with me. That day the weather was great; there were pink lights on the synagogue, and Sarah pointed them out to me and said, "Our synagogue is beautiful." This made me think of Passover, you know, you have a child who is somewhat marginalized, who somewhat distances herself . . . is maybe less interested, but she is not out of it. There were incidents four years ago when she definitely had some conflicts. She faced a lot of comments on her Jewish origins while at school. She had selected a commercial business emphasis where there were many Muslim kids. My guess is that she endured remarks, and the school principal simply ignored the fact. He said that there were also anti-Palestinian and anti-Arab remarks going around too. But, institutionally, I can't say that there have been acts of anti-Semitism against either of my daughters.

But to return to my relations with the community, I will retire soon and there are a lot of activities. There is the choir; there is a committee dealing with celebrations; there also is the library. There are a lot of lectures. There is helping with the newsletter [Mazal Tov], which I was doing last Sunday. I can also help with the administration, more for the cultural matters, of course. I could even create something. I don't know. The radio is of less interest to me now. There is so much to work on.

Professionally, things are not going very well. It's hard to say why. Is it the Université de Bourgogne that has very little consideration for our work here [at the French language institute]? Maybe. For example, there are many Chinese students who come to study, but they're not accepted in the same way anymore. They wanted to create a pedagogic project, which is good. That's normal. But I don't know. Maybe the school needs to change its pedagogical methods, change its pace of teaching, and so forth. But for me, to be honest, it will be too late.

Personally, I was really interested in teaching literature. They had always refused to let me do it. It's hard to say why. Maybe it's because there are "gatekeepers" [protectors of academic "turf"]. Now, they are asking me to do it, but I don't want to do it anymore. It's a lot of work. And, well, like everyone, I've grown old. I feel it physically. But if I were to teach literature, it would be about the works of four authors: Gustave Flaubert, Victor Hugo, Albert Cohen, and Georges Perec. Why these? Flaubert's *Madame Bovary* is an exceptional piece of literature, a very deep work. One can feel that the author has thought about every word he wrote. And Hugo? Hugo is a master. He represents freedom, the Left, socialism, and I support the ideology of the Left, in my beliefs and in my spirit. Next comes Cohen. I can see my family in his work. When I read it I say to myself, "This is true, these are my feelings; this is my place in Judaism." Unfortunately, a lot of people don't read his work; he's a little too different. And Perec is not well read for the same reason.

Had I chosen to teach Perec, my colleagues would have made faces. It definitely would disturb them because it touched their feelings about the authors. As a whole, they are "ragged" by these authors. For Cohen, because he is Jewish, and they simply don't consider him a classic of French literature. Perec might be a bit easier because, after all, he was born in France. His ideas . . . for example, he has a good knowledge of Israel. He takes a firm stand. But he writes more about interior and exterior exile. Cohen, on the other hand, has said a lot about Israel and about anti-Semitism in France. I'm sure that my colleagues are not at ease with topics like that.

Sometimes one has the feeling of being in an anti-Semitic environment. But it is never a 100 per cent feeling. The story always goes like this: the person says, "I am not anti-Semitic. Some of my best friends are Jewish." At the university, sometimes one can hear remarks that are a little bit offensive. They are rather hypocritical, too. So it's hard to say, "Stop! You *are* an anti-Semite." Sometimes I feel that I would be glad to be confronted directly with a remark because then I would stand up, fight back, and defend myself.

I know many professors who are not ashamed of being Jewish. Moreover, I don't think that it makes a difference for their lives at the university. Everyone knows that I am Jewish. But such things as listing the Jewish holidays on the school calendar are not permitted. At the language institute where I teach, a former president refused to make mention of Jewish holidays. He asked me once, "Annie, is it going to bother you if a Jewish student needs information about the holidays and I send him to you?" I told him that I was glad to help out. Later, that president was replaced by another who said that the university was non-religious and that such activity must stop. So I and another colleague, who is a Protestant and whom I respect very much, had to stop and not bring the subject up.

I was asked if things had changed [since the last interview], and the answer is yes! There are things that are not discussed anymore. One cannot talk to certain people about certain things. There is a silence imposed on Jewish intellectuals. I'm not saying that I am necessarily considered a Jewish intellectual, but one needs a lot of courage to approach some of these questions. This is true, I think, since the start of the Second Intifada [2000].

The death of Arafat [2004] provides an example of how France is very pro-Palestinian. I was completely shocked and outraged to see how he was transported to France, how he was cared for here. They would not let him die. He was treated as if he was really a head of state. They completely forgot the blood he had on his hands, they forget all about the European allocations [of funds] that are missing. He left a lot of legal cases and difficulties for the Palestinian people. And even though I am not an expert, I can say that he never tried to help his people. He never used his money to help his people. And I was very surprised to see how fast he disappeared from our media when he died. [Stories about him] suddenly came to an end.

So since the Second Intifada I don't talk politics anymore, not with my colleagues. And it's the same with the Socialists. It's very difficult with the Left. There are Leftists who have a completely wrong conception of history. Look at the Algerians. [Because of the war of independence] the Algerians are seen as victims. They remain victims even though they are now in the third generation here in France and they carry French passports. Yet, for the Leftists, they will remain victims forever. Then somehow it seems easy to equate the victims of the Middle East with the victims in France. I personally find it a bit confusing, but that's how it is.

Returning to the subject of the Dijon community, I must say that, first of all, we are fortunate in having a gorgeous synagogue. That's not the case with most small communities in France. The expensive repairs made it even more beautiful. They were worth it. The religious life is taken care of by the rabbi, whom I love dearly. Why? He has maintained harmony among the people. And, while being very religious, he also is very open-minded. He truly believes. Moreover, he accepts us the way we are. He loves our children. So, I think that he is a good rabbi and I love him dearly.

Even though I'm not religious, I go to the synagogue from time to time, when Deborah wants to attend. But I try to participate in the organized activities as much as I can. I go to the synagogue with my family for Yom Kippur. My girls used to go for Hanukkah and Purim, but they don't go now because they're too old, I guess.

I'm just so happy to see the synagogue full of people. This is a gift for me. And there are plenty of activities, as I've mentioned. As a whole, I think that our community is very good.

Maybe it will be more interesting to talk about what we don't have. I can make a comparison: we lack a welcoming capability, I mean, the reception of new people who come, and their integration into the community. We don't have this ability. On the contrary, I have seen how this works with the Lubavitch. They obviously have more time and take care of this issue. We should understand that this process of welcoming and integrating newcomers is very important, especially for the young people. But it requires a lot of effort.

About the Lubavitch, I want to tell you how my opinions about them have changed because of Deborah. It's always Deborah who stands behind this kind of change. The family of her friend Morgan is very close to the Lubavitch, though they are not part of them. Deborah was invited to some of the Lubavitch parties and celebrations and also to a few weddings. And, of course, as they invite our daughter, they invite us as well. Not long ago, on the last day of Passover, I was invited to the Lubavitch home of Hannah and Haim Slonim and met her family, including her parents. They are very kind people. Hannah is a very sweet, easy-going woman. She said that she would like to know more about me, and so on. Haim talked to me and looked me in the eyes. I made note of this because one [a Lubavitch man] does not look the woman in the eyes when he talks to her. Hannah sat next to him and talked as well. Well, it's true that the topics of conversation were rather limited. For example, in the living room, they have a large collection of books, mostly of religious texts, and when I asked if he read books on other subjects, he said no.

Deborah participated in a lot of the activities they organized for the youth. She's always been very happy with this, with one single exception, maybe. During one of these occasions the girls had to be on one side and the boys on the other. And Deborah wanted to spend time with the boys also [laughs].

[The Lubavitch] have established a Hanukkah candle lighting downtown in one of the public squares, where they have set up a big menorah. Then they pass out candles to people who come. They offer coffee and tea. As I said, this takes place in the street, a public street. It is a public celebration of the holiday. They sing the songs and maybe one or two prayers. I attended for two years, but I won't go again. I think that it's too fancy, you know. I think that Hanukkah in Dijon and in France should be held at home, with family and friends, but not in the street. That's how I see it. Honestly, I don't like the idea. I am not ashamed of my Jewish origin. We always light candles on this day, since the girls were born, but always at home. We also put candles in the windows, so the neighbors can see. Of course, the candle lighting has public sanction because permission from the municipal authorities is necessary. Françoise Tenenbaum [the assistant mayor] was there. I think that she actually intervened to help them get permission.

I don't believe that the Lubavitch have done good work here. They have split the community. They have separated us. I think that a traditional community like ours has to fight for its goals by other means. The solution that the Lubavitch offer is "exclusion." And I don't think that that's the way to do it. But maybe it's more complicated than I can see.

[The Lubavitch] weren't satisfied with the work of the rabbi on Shabbat, and wanted to redo it. It's a shame because the rabbi has been doing it well. They go all the way to Lyon to buy meat because the butcher here is not sufficiently kosher for them. You know, the community is very divided right now, and there are people who see each other as enemies, not as friends. And this is very sad. We don't need this in our community.

[The Lubavitch] have a very closed lifestyle. They don't read anything other than religious books. I don't know if they read newspapers. I'm not sure that they vote. When their children reach the age of 11, they are sent away to school in Paris. Their private school here ends at age ten or 11. The question is, what kind of community are they looking for?

But I really don't have any concerns about the larger community in Dijon. As I mentioned before, I'm disappointed by the little interest they show in our youth. I have complained about this. I don't think that our president has understood some things very well. One has to understand that teenagers must have some relationships in which one should not intervene. One should help them from outside but not intervene directly. Parents are there to care, not direct.

About a potential conflict between Judaism and Islam, there is no problem in Dijon. There are problematic people in certain neighborhoods, but there is no big problem here. In the Paris region, there have been a lot of attacks, but one tends to forget also the profanations of the Rightist extremists. The situation is not only difficult for Jews [but for Arabs as well]. There is a lot of poverty, violence, and political incompetence.

Is all of this going to get better? I don't know. What I see is that after the death of Arafat, the point of interest of the journalists has shifted. One does not talk a lot about Israel anymore; the focus is mainly on Iraq. Every day is about Iraq, the violence, the victims. So I tend to think that they have put aside Israel, Palestine. And that's fine. When they forget about us, we're happy.

On the issue about wearing the veil [Muslim scarf], well, in France, you know, there are girls with covered faces. But you also see many Muslim girls [who dress] like Deborah, with belly buttons visible, tight tee shirts above, wearing make-up, trying to look attractive. Of course, there are people who want to wear the traditional veil, but when you go downtown on Wednesday afternoons [a half school day], where the kids walk around and play, you will see all these girls. Listen, Sarah has a friend who often says, "I don't want to go back to the customs of Algeria." And it's because she lives here in a modern society. I think that this actually is good.

In Dijon, we haven't come across the veil issue at all. I believe that they simply put it away because they could not find a solution. France is a secular country. There is religious freedom, but most religion is practiced at home. Ten years ago, when the first girls appeared in the schools with veils, they should have been told, "No. This practice does not conform to the French constitution. The law says no." Instead they were told, "Yes, but...." And that's when the problem started.

I still support the immigrants [from the former African colonies]. If France had said "No" to the immigrants, where would I be? I am definitely for the immigrants. Though it's been said that France cannot accommodate all the misery of the world, I don't think this is true. Because all the misery of the world doesn't want to come to France, so there is no point in closing the door. That's why I definitely support the immigrants, even if there are one or two million people. We have to help. We simply cannot leave them to die in their countries. France is a rich country. We have unemployment problems simply because we have problems with our politics.[*]

The prime minister[†] announced that we will have a job "death period" [probation period] for two years, which means that we are going to work for two years and after the second year, the boss can say, "Well, you didn't work out, so...." During the two-year period you can't be fired. But this period could be shortened, because who needs two years to figure out if a new employee matches expectations or not? If he insists on his idea, I think that he's going to face a very harsh reaction. The people will be in the streets. The syndicates [unions] will strike.[‡]

So, to be honest, I'm kind of uncertain, divided between the two sides of the problem. It's true that if I want to go to Paris for something important, and I'm told that the trains aren't running because the workers are on

---

[*] Prime Minister Michel Rocard (1988–91) said this.

[†] Dominique de Villepin, in office 2005–07.

[‡] This, in fact, took place and the new program was abandoned.

strike, I would definitely be pissed. But at the same time, they can organize a strike much more easily than I would. And sometimes I think that the railroad unions speak out for my needs. In a sense, they strike for me. That's why I support the Left. In France, as you say, when one organizes a strike, there are a lot of people who support it, even people who cannot move if it is a railroad workers' strike. What a wonderful country!

Now, this question about the reason for the hostile feelings between France and the United States can be answered by the Iraq War [2003].... But, in my opinion, it's the media that artificially intensifies the tensions. For example, if you talk to a young Frenchman and tell him about the United States, his eyes light up with amazement and enthusiasm. I think that the French people and especially the French youth show more enthusiasm about America than American kids show for France.

But the situation in Iraq is horrible. I simply don't think that the war has resolved the existing issues there. It's correct that the issues were there before the war, but at least then everything was clear. And the fact that they were clear made them easier to fight against. But at the same time, I don't think that we should make the mistake of many journalists who associate the solution to the problems of Iraq with the solution to the problems of the Middle East, namely Israel and Palestine. In my opinion, they are two completely different things, even though one will definitely have an impact of the other.

But I'm not angry at the United States at all. I think that there are some very bad people, horrible people, there but also incredibly good and humane people. If I could travel to the United States this year, I would go. No, no, I am not angry at America at all. I believe that America is a democracy. And this is very important for me.

I definitely have hope for the future of France and for the Jews of France. I never had a desire to leave; I've never said, "The situation is unbearable." I feel at home in my country; I'm French; I don't have the feeling that I'm threatened more than anyone else. I feel good here, and I want to stay here. I also want the children to stay.

When I retire, I hope that we are going to travel a little. And then, we want to write together. Gislain will invest time in our friends and in the community in Dijon, and maybe in another city. And me, I want to do some of the work I've never had time to do, maybe drawing. But it will be something that I can do, and then give it out to the people.

Gislain, June 2005

In the 12 years since I first discussed the conditions of Jews in France, I can't say that much has changed. As always there are local problems that can be explained by changes in certain parts of the population. But speaking for France as a whole, the most recent polls for which I can give you references showed a better acceptance of Jews, even up to the president of the Republic. But this does not mean that on the margins, among the less educated, amid those against the progress of French evolution, there are not problems. These are shown by certain government reports that indicated an increase of anti-Semitic acts. So I would say that there have been local changes, but nothing significant on the national level.

We should also note, however, the fact that, according to the statistics, the emigration of French [Jews] to Israel over the past several years has doubled. The average was about 1,000 annually; then it went to 1,500, 2,000, and 2,500.[*] It's a small number in quantity, but does it represent among Jews a certain uneasiness? It's possible. A great deal depends on the area where one lives, on one's professional environment—and, of course, everything depends on the anti-Semitic sentiment that in reality has never disappeared. But we cannot say, either, that on the national level it is encouraged. It remains a specifically local problem, although it is understood that it must be fought against.

In regards to anti-Americanism in France, it exists and it doesn't exist at the same time. Look at the American influence in society, in the food, the music, and lifestyle. At the same time there's fear of domination. While the Soviet Union existed there was a balance. Now there is no counterbalance. Europe, not being structured, cannot be a counter-power to the United States. Look what happened in the Balkans, in Yugoslavia, in Kosovo. France supported Serbia in the name of history. Germany supported Croatia. There was no common position by Europeans on the issue, no unity, no political will. Only the United States could act.

What French Jews see is that there is one ally. It is the United States. It's not an unconditional ally, and in the future the desire may be for it to be not as unconditional, but in the past it was the critical ally who was there. In Europe, we saw what happened at the time of the Second Intifada. There was the decision to financially aid the Palestinians. The result was the printing of schoolbooks, with European money, that were anti-Semitic, full of anti-Israeli allusions and untruths. And then there was the demonizing of [Israeli Prime Minister Ariel] Sharon, who, after all, has given up Gaza.[†] Yet, I think that it's better for Europeans to be involved in the Middle East. They

---

[*] The exact figures for 2002–10 can be found in David Shapira, *Les Antisémitismes français* (Lormont: Éditions Le Bord De L'Eau, 2011) 290.

[†] The Israelis withdrew from Gaza in 2005.

should be there because there are investments to make, but they shouldn't allow themselves to be blackmailed.

As a Jew, though, I think it's possible to trust French politicians. The politicians issue from the national society. In the Ministry of Foreign Affairs, at least since de Gaulle, the policy-makers ask, "What is Israel? It is five million inhabitants. What is the Arab world? Two hundred million inhabitants." But there may be other considerations. There are other opinions more open than that of the Gaullists. We will see what happens now with the disengagement [of Israel] from Gaza.

There are politicians of the first rank in the majority party in France who are pro-Israel: Chirac, de Villepin, and Sarkozy. The younger is Sarkozy, who has never hidden the fact that he is the son of immigrants. And that, I think, is a way to observe his difference in relation to the Gaullist Right. My wife detests him for his methods, but he was Minister of the Interior [security], and he took clear-cut measures on immigration, resisting illegal immigration. He also took a populist position on the sentencing of criminals that appealed to the extreme Right and was necessary to capture votes of the electors. He certainly is one of the possible future presidents.[*]

The Leftist media, like *Libération* [newspaper], are like childhood friends who are against Israel right now. We recognize their way of thinking, but we don't argue with them because we know that they evolve. They now represent *l'altermondialisme* [anti-globalization, the global justice movement]. I think that currently this is mostly among the young, the very young in the political culture. It is "human rights-ism." It favors the victim, whoever it is.

If there is another intifada, or increase in terrorism, well, it's not a problem with the Jews, it's a problem for French society. The government had the experience of the Second Intifada and what the consequences were. They have to protect lives and property. Interior Minister Sarkozy said it; the president said it. But now there's something new: there is in place a religious center for Muslims. It is a place for them to rally themselves. If they are republican, democratic, and Muslim—it's necessary for them to rally themselves. So if there is a Third Intifada, for France this means that the government now has an interlocutor.

There are fringes of the [Muslim] population that don't feel integrated into society. It's unfortunate that they don't feel integrated into France; they certainly aren't integrated into Algeria because they were born in France. It's a mixture of North Africans and Africans too. They were responsible for

---

* He was, in fact, elected in 2007 and then defeated by François Hollande in 2012.

demonstrations that often turned violent, with random violence [fall 2005]. Even members of the extreme Left testified about what they saw.

There are many problems in France: unemployment, education, and immigration, among others. Still, France, in general, is an extraordinary country. In the context of Europe, France was one of the founders of the European Union.... France has a very strong culture. But there are problems in France, Germany, England, and all European countries, in general, because at present, especially in Europe, we observe an overall desire to maintain a certain way of life, which protects the weak, the poor. However, the policy of liberalism on all accounts leads to more poverty and unemployment, because it costs more and we are obliged to close factories and employ workers at lower wages....

But altogether, I am optimistic. Yes, I am an optimist, because France has a privileged position on the European stage. Many countries do not. France is beautiful and rich. It is true that some of the population is poor; it is surprising that it has stayed in misery for a long time. However, the overall situation of France is relatively good.

However, we have got to integrate the Muslims. The youngest generation of the Muslim population consists of children who were born in France and whose parents came mainly from North Africa, Turkey, and even the rest of the African continent. The immigrants and their families live on the periphery of the city, where rents are cheaper. I believe that if France is truly a secular state—and the concept of secularism is hard to understand—there should be a real integration of the Muslim population in the French culture. The process started in 1970 with the integration of indigenous Africans, coming from Algeria. The integration was opposed by many civil and religious servants. However, looking at the statistics, the majority of the French population supported the integration process, which turned out to be profitable for the nation. Since the 1970s, already three generations of Jews have passed, and there have been many physicians, politicians, policemen, lawyers, custom officers, and so on. My grandfather, for example, was a tailor for the Arab population in France all his life. He had a special position in society. He spoke French, Hebrew, and Arabic. He was one of the people who managed to fully integrate among the French. At this time, the integration process was voluntary and France had been implementing it since the 1960s with the Algerian population, which returned to France after the [Algerian] declaration of independence.

We have to point out that since the beginning of the twentieth century there was a population coming from the Maghreb,* which played a major

---

* Region of northwest Africa, west of Egypt.

role in the integration process together with the immigrants from North Africa and, most specifically, Algeria. They mainly inhabited industrial towns, such as Lyon. The immigrants from the Maghreb have been highly rooted in French culture and language. The integration process of immigrants has never been a matter of the state itself, but of the community. For example, in the beginning of the twentieth century, there was an inflow of immigrants coming from Italy into South France. Initially, they were excluded, they were mocked at, and it took the French population one generation to actually start accepting them.

At the same time, the Algerian immigrants are not accepted as Africans anymore [in their historic land]. Moreover, the extreme expression of culture and religion among the immigrants does not have any future. It concerns only the old population, especially women, and a few young girls. You would barely see any veils or religious symbols worn in public [then]. As far as the language is concerned, they still speak Arabic, but it is a modified version of the official Arab language. The children of the immigrants go to French school with French [children]. Even at the level of superior education, I cannot say that there is a clear difference between the French population and the immigrants. France, as a country, definitely has a capacity for integration. The extreme and radical expression of religion and culture in public is not permissible. I would never allow a student to do that, and it has never happened to me. Extremism in beliefs and ideas is dangerous for society and must be avoided.

You asked about life here in Dijon. It has been considerably changing over the past 30 years. We have witnessed a shift from the Right to the Left. The Socialist Party has very strong positions in society. It is even responsible for the unions, for the militants, regardless of the fact whether they join the union or not. At present, the region is under the influence of the Left. In fact, 20 out of 22 French regions are governed by the Left. The coming of the Socialist Party has brought about dynamism in the region, which was dormant during the influence of the Right. At that time, there was a policy for the circulation of buses in the region, which was criticized by the majority of the population. The number of buses even decreased by 2 per cent per year, and even more people revolted against the regulation. Therefore, there was a need for a change in the policy so that people would use cars less often [which means] there is going to be less pollution. Another problem in the region was the decline of many industries. Thus, the region is mainly service-oriented. Over the past years, there have been attempts to increase and improve the provision of social services. IKEA, a shop specializing in the sale of furniture, was recently opened. This was one of the most discussed topics in the press and among the citizens of the region, because IKEA would attract many customers from all over the region and the approximate areas.

I do believe that the conditions of the region will improve. I do. Recently, the department of the government that is in charge of the promotion of European Union politics demanded all regions to submit projects for the development of the industries, the universities, and the services. Regions, such as Burgundy, have submitted four projects. The creation of these projects is very important, because each approved project receives full financial support from the state.

But to turn to more personal topics that I was asked about, let me tell you that I am preparing for my retirement. I am really interested in the life and fate of the Jewish population in North Africa. I am specifically interested in the preservation of their religion and culture in the region. The reason is that I am not really an optimist about the future of Judaism in France, because I believe that it is declining. It is not as strong as the one in Israel. And if there is a lack of strong religion and culture, there is an "a-religion," without any religion. This has been seen even with the Catholics here.

My concept of Judaism is that it is not simply a religion. It is more than a religion. And this is why I am interested in it. I am interested specifically in the origins of Judaism, of Christianity, of Islam. I am not that interested in the other aspects of religion. I am not that informed, because I do not have an education in religion. I believe that the texts of Judaism, which determine the nature of its practice, have been written by individuals who were inspired by the theme of divinity. We find such texts in similar civilizations, in the Mesopotamian region, for example, or the lands of the Persians. These individuals have decided to define the principles of life according to Judaism and, in that sense, also according to Christianity. There are marvelous television programs on the origins of Christianity. We learn the disciples of Jesus Christ were Jews and were part of a number of Jewish sects. They did not have the intention to create a [new] religion. I even saw a program that claimed that one of the sects, following the principles of Christianity, has similar beliefs as the followers of Islam.

I have been interested maybe because I am a Jew. I am not really religious, but I do not want to convert, I guess, because being a Jew is valuable. After all, we are a part of a minority. It's all about knowledge, knowing the history, knowing the religion, knowing the culture in general.

Finally, to speak of Israel—it has established itself as a force for 50 years now. It has embraced the principles of democracy and has maintained dominance in the Arab world. Now, the question is how the Israeli population will survive and evolve under the conditions of a region that is not necessarily amiable. Israel is highly connected to the Near East. An interesting aspect of Israel's foreign policy is its comparison to Armenia. The country is pretty much on good terms with its neighbors. It is not very rich. It does not have much petrol or resources. However, it has human capital, a population of intellectuals and workers.

Alain Grynberg

Alain Grynberg, son of Holocaust survivors and an acclaimed research scientist, describes his youth in Paris and at university as a period of Leftist radicalism combined with Zionism. He has largely abandoned those positions and now holds critical though sympathetic views of Israeli policies on the one hand and what he calls the "bourgeois" Jewish community of Dijon on the other. During a long residence in Dijon, he was a founder of the Cultural Center. He currently lives in Paris but maintains an ongoing relationship with the Dijon community.

Spring 1993

My life in Paris had two important aspects: my studies and my life as a Jew. My first approach to Judaism started when I was six years old. We did not get very involved at home because my father erased Judaism from his life after the war [World War II]. But he still thought that his son should know about his religion.

I started attending summer camps for Jews. This was in 1956, before the arrival of Sephardim in France. I went to a camp called *Foyer Ouvrier Juif* [Jewish Workers' Association], which is part of the *L'Art du Talmud à Poitiers*, an organization that helped orphans of the war and bought two castles to shelter them. The biggest castle was in Vervéry, in the department of the Oise, 60 kilometers north of Paris. The second castle was in Eure, 100 kilometers west of Paris. It was like a summer camp that brought together Jewish kids who did not come from wealthy families. I started there and stayed until 1975. I worked there and became a director.

When I went there, it was 12 years after the war and there were no orphans. The camp was for two months in the summer. There were sessions in July, August, and the first half of September. I virtually lived in that environment for 20 years. To this day, I have very good friends from there.

The Lycée Voltaire in Paris was my school. It was a big school with 3,500 students. Almost 50 per cent of the kids were Jewish. It was difficult at the time of the Algerian War. Every time there was a bomb alert, we would not go to school.

In 1960, something different happened: the Sephardim. We experienced the same sort of things as the people from Israel: the arrival of half a million people from another culture [Algeria] without jobs. They were poor. Of course, some of them had money, but not many. The Jews from Tunisia and Morocco were a little different. They did not all come at the same time.

I was about 12 at the time that the Jews from Algeria came. That immigration caused problems. There was no effort to integrate the two communities [French and Algerian] without taking into account the differences. At the time a youth program was established. It was the first to welcome the Sephardim in Paris like the Ashkenazi orphans had been welcomed after the war. I joined instantly. The program lasted until the late 1960s.

May 1968 opened the doors of politics, and for a while we lost interest in the youth movement. There also was the problem of the Six Day War, the difficulty of explaining it politically, the problems of the occupied territories.

I finished my studies and for a while was not very active. But later, I started again with the Jewish Center. After 1968, I was at the University of Paris, a student in sciences. During that time, I worked doing translations of scientific texts in English at the Center for Documentation of the Agricultural Industry. This helped me later on, too. I gave math lessons, mostly to Jewish families. I was successful because I am good in math.

I also helped people move. I had a friend at school whose father had a moving company, and I asked if I could work for him. Later, I found something else, too, moving pianos. That was interesting because it was a night job. They would tell me, "There are two pianos in Belgium." So, after classes, I would pick up the truck and drive to Belgium. It was a good job.

I had many jobs. One of them was for students who knew languages to serve as guides and take foreign clients out at night. It was exclusive. I went to the best restaurants and clubs and never had to pay. It is very good when you are 24. They could call me up and tell me, "Tonight we have three German people, go get the car and pick them up." I don't drink, and one night one of the clients got very drunk and got into an argument with me. I did not want to take him with me, so I left him. I was told he was still a client and had to be driven back. So that ended that job. I did not want to do it anymore anyway.

In any case, I finished my university thesis in 1977.

But let me go back for a moment and talk about my family background and something of my political beliefs. My father came from Poland; my mother was born in Paris. Her father was Russian and her mother was from Romania. My father came to Paris in 1929 during the economic crisis. At the time he was 20, although he had left home at the age of 15 to work in Warsaw. Like many others, he was a tailor. He lived with his employer who paid him two kopeks a week. When he came to Paris, he stayed with his brother who was a rabbi there. The brother was five years older. Unfortunately, he died in 1934.

My father told me that life in Paris for the Jews and non-Jews in the 1930s was fabulous. The Jews had a different attitude towards each other during those years. My father and my grandmother told me that they would support each other, give each other jobs. There was a purpose, a Jewish community. I didn't have a chance to know that era, but it's true that in my lifetime we still helped each other. I think that today things are different; there is a hierarchy and different classes, and this is starting in Israel too, unfortunately.[*] It is very sad because it represents the beginning of the end of the Jewish community. Once you start getting closer to a Gentile, because he has the same job you have, rather than closer to a Jew, this is the end.

My mother was born in 1915. As I said, her ancestors were from Romania, her mother born in Moldavia and her father in some small town whose name I cannot recall. Of my grandparents, I met only my maternal grandmother. She never learned to speak French. Everyone lived together, and we talked Yiddish in the house. And I might add that I never had any formal education in Hebrew when I was young. My father did not want me to learn it. It had to do with politics. He had been a Communist, part of the Jewish International. But my father seldom talked about this. After the war, he abandoned his political ideas and soon after, his religious beliefs.

I learned only a few things about my family during the Shoah. My parents had been married to others before the war. For both of them, it was a second marriage. My father's first wife died during the war. My mother's first husband died at the very beginning of the war. Most of my father's family died in Auschwitz. Of his ten brothers and sisters, there was only one brother who died in Paris and a sister who also died there in 1961. My maternal grandmother's family survived the Shoah. She had about 15 brothers and sisters, some of whom lived in the United States. One of the sisters who lives in Los Angeles is still alive. I have never met her. A brother lived in New York, and I got to know him well.

My father does not feel very comfortable talking about the Holocaust. He is actually more at ease talking about it with my wife. Everyone suffered from it. The French turned him in. It changed his vision of France. When he got his French citizenship after the war, I think that it was almost like an apology note. Of course, this had an impact on his identity as French. Even now, he does not speak about this freely. After he was deported, he spent four years in Auschwitz, from March 1941 to May 1945.

After the war, my parents met at a mutual friend's house in Paris. My father had a very good friend from Poland whom he met again in Auschwitz. My mother had a very good friend in Paris. These people had married before the war. After it, they all got together again and that was how my parents met.

---

[*] The gap has become worse since 1993. Consider the huge demonstrations in Israel during the summer of 2011.

I was born in 1950, a member of the postwar generation, the generation they thirsted for during the years they spent in the concentration camps. In the camps they were thinking about the kids they wanted to have. They were not a common generation: they had strength and a special attachment to life.

Israel was not important for my parents, even though it was for me. Don't forget that at the age of six I was singing Hebrew songs at the summer camp. The only idea I had about Israel was the vision of a golden temple. I did not know about politics yet. I believed in Zionism and I was happy.

The wars changed everything. I "lived" the Six Day War.* I was 17, and it is ironic that the war started the same day we had our big party at the youth movement. The Châtelet Theater—I remember that I had a part in the play and there were a lot of people there that night. I do not think we slept on any of the six days. We listened to the radio all the time. About 60 of us had planned to go to Israel in July 1967, but we went after the war.

In 1968, I was in Paris at the university. I was, of course, a Leftist like everyone, though a Leftist and a Zionist, as well. I considered myself a hard Leftist, a Trotskyite. At that age—18 or 20 years—we wanted to fight against injustice. Nowadays, I have changed my idea of politics. Nevertheless, I am still active.

People from my generation, the Jews from my generation, have this in their blood. Today, I have a different role in politics, but if I had the means, I would pursue the ideals I had at the time. I changed my views on Trotsky because they do not correspond to the reality we live in. It still represents something though. Back at the time, we had foreseen what would happen. We said it, but no one listened. For example, what happened here in Dijon? Factories shut down. The Hoover factory shut down. Salaries were cut by 30 per cent ... and everything was transferred to England, a major sore spot in 1993.

Today, I am more concerned with giving political power back to the citizens. Many of my Leftist ideas died. In France, Mitterrand was elected based on ideas from the Left. Then, he followed the politics of the Right. This is proof that is very hard to follow Leftist ideas in a European country. Now, in today's elections, there are no candidates for me.

The Yom Kippur War in 1973 was important for me. It was a difficult time because I was finishing my training. The war was going on in the middle of my exams. At that time, my involvement with the Jewish community was through music and the Yiddish classes at the University of Vincennes.

---

* Many Jews the world over interrupted normal activities during the early stage of the Six Day War, believing Israel's existence was at stake.

At the time of the war, I was older and living with my friends. During the war in 1956, we were too young. The 1967 war was the first one we "lived." We "lived" it as Jews. In 1973, we were intellectually prepared, and it was a destructive war.

I had put a lot of hope in that war. I had hoped that the media would declare that the Arabs were winning even though they had lost.[*] At the end of the war, I thought there would be peace. I hoped that there would be peace for everyone. It is also true that when we talked to people from Israel, they said they could not offer peace to the Arabs because the Arabs will accept and will use it against us. So, I did not know what the reality was there. I do not think that the people of Israel are ready for peace, for several reasons. First of all, for political reasons, obviously they are scared of the Arabs. The second reason is economic: Israel does not have the means for demobilization. Israel lives thanks to the money of the American Jews.[†]

I do not identify myself with any political group in Israel. It is difficult for a Frenchman to identify himself with a party in Israel. We have different perceptions. First of all, we are not the ones who live in Jerusalem. And if we listened to the Right in Israel, Israel would become a new Muslim country as a result of annexing Arab areas. We do not need that. In the case of the status of Jerusalem, I would use the example of Trieste. You know that Trieste is an open city. It is because of the Israeli administration that Jerusalem is not an open city.

It is hard to put yourself in the place of those who are responsible. But I would give back some occupied areas. We do not need Gaza. We do not need all that. That is not hard for Israel to accept. And also, now it is the United States who is in control. Before, there was an agreement between the United States and the Soviet Union. It was much easier to say that we would give back the territories and end everything.

If you are at peace with your enemies, it would not be a big deal. That is what I do not understand, though some Jews would not agree with that. A lot of friends, French Jews, think that they should keep everything, but they do not have to go through three years of military service. They are not the ones who would have to fight.

I married someone from Israel; I am in Israel three or four times a year. Those who never go find it easy to say that we should keep the land. And same for those who go there only on vacation, they think that everything is fine.

---

[*] Many believed the Arabs needed to regain their sense of dignity in order to make peace with Israel; in fact, this is partly what happened in Egypt.

[†] Israel was much less well-developed in 1993 than it is today.

Well, in the 1970s, after the war, after I finished my thesis, I accepted a job in the laboratory in Dijon with the condition that I be allowed to study and specialize for three years. I then moved to Dijon in 1980. By the time I left, I had changed more than had the [Jewish] community. Maybe the community remained the same, but I did not see it with the same eyes. So it is hard to tell. The question of how much the Paris community had changed is the kind of question a person who was an adult in the 1960s and the 1980s can answer. In the 1960s, I was ten years old and, in the 1980s, I was 30 years old. At the age of ten, I really had no idea about the community.

Between 1968 and 1980, I did see the community evolve. That is when all the synagogues emerged. Women are with men [during the services]; there are mixed marriages. I really appreciated the progress that was made within the Jewish community. However, there was a separation within the community because the Ashkenazim were more for progress and change. It was too new for the Sephardim who were new to the West. To this day, you see more Sephardim in the synagogue than you see Ashkenazim. It is like that now, but it will change.

Now, when did "Israélites" become "Jews"? When we were in high school, we would ask each other, "What is an Israélite"? We would say that an Israélite was a Jew who lived in the sixteenth [upper-class] district.

I had two friends who had made their aliyah, had moved to Haifa, and were very good friends of mine. I would visit them at least once a year, usually around Easter. At the time, I was a bachelor, and although I had girlfriends, there was nothing serious. So during Easter 1980, I went to visit my friends. One of them said that he wanted to get married and that he had met his future wife. They organized a little *soirée* and he invited his bride-to-be and her sister and husband. The sister of the husband also came along, and that was Gaby. I liked her, and we spent 15 days of the holidays together. When I left, I told her that I felt good with her and that I was coming back in July. After that, we started calling each other every other day. After about a month, she told me that there was a problem with her father. I did not know him, nor did I know her mother. She told me that her father did not trust me and that it was marriage or nothing for him. So that is how we got married. But before that she called telling me that she had problems organizing the wedding because her father did not believe it was going to happen. I asked her if a phone call from me would help. She said, "No." So, I asked my father to call him. When I arrived on the day of my wedding, I did not know anyone. To represent my side, I had only my parents and a friend. Fortunately, Gaby already knew French, like everyone else from Romania. I knew Yiddish, but her parents did not. My parents did not speak French very well because they came from Poland.

When we arrived in Dijon, it was important for Gaby to integrate. It was not that important for me. Thanks to my job, I did not need that. Everything was going well for me, but it was hard for Gaby. It came to a point where, when I had the opportunity to go to Australia, I was going to take it. But Gaby did not want to go; she said it would be a fourth language, a fourth culture. She has adapted, although she is not used to the Bourguignon [roughly, provincial middle-class] lifestyle. The Jews were even more Bourguignon than the real ones. Gaby was used to Romania, then to Israel, and to a different type of relationship among women [in which] you do not have to be very close in order to say, "Hi." This does not exist in the Jewish community.

Gaby told me some time ago, "Let's not call anyone for a month and see who calls us." Nobody called. I had to explain to her that we do not have anyone here and that she should not fall for fake smiles and invitations. I told her, "If you do not call, nobody is going to call you because we do not belong here, we are not from here."

I did not join the Jewish club [B'nai B'rith] because of my profession, because the majority of the members were doctors, dentists, or merchants. Therefore, the last 13 years, we have been by ourselves. We had our own family evolution, intellectual evolution, relationships with our kids. Everything in that sense went well, but if we were to leave, we will not feel sad because we would not leave anything behind. We do not belong here.

When I arrived in Dijon, I felt like I had moved a century back. I had a hard time understanding the Jews and the Gentiles. But it was harder to understand that a Jew here is stereotyped by other Jews, mostly by the Ashkenazim. The Sephardim set people in characterized norms too, but they have kept their Mediterranean personality, which I like a lot. I feel closer to a Sephardi who talks with his hands because I am a Jew and that is who Jews are. Do you understand? I have never hidden the fact that I am a Jew, even in my job where everyone else is a Gentile. In Paris, it was different, maybe because the community was bigger.

Sometimes when everything makes me angry, my Yiddish accent is stronger. I do it to show that I am a Jew. I cannot stand Jews who hide, even after the Shoah. It has not been a long time since the Shoah, and there are still people who try to look Gentile. It makes me laugh. And it is more present in Dijon than in Paris. All the Jews I know in Paris are happy to be Jews. Of course, there are some who try to hide. Now, I am not saying that in Dijon they deny being Jews, but that they act like Bourguignon. They have the same culture, but I do not. I am a Jew; I am not a Bourguignon.

Sometimes when we are at dinner at someone's house and hear Jews discussing about wine [a major French/Bourguignon subject], I wonder,

"Where am I? This is not kosher!" I do not eat kosher, but do you understand what I am trying to say?

I remember in Paris a discussion about Zionism. Now, it has been 13 years since I moved to Dijon and I never had that kind of conversation with anyone, because the Jews here are not ready, and that is because they are Bourguignon. Now, it is true that they are becoming more active. But there are other things in the background. I was asked to participate and I refused. I refused because it didn't have much to do with the concept of Israel. I tell you this: I read the first essay of Theodor Herzl [*The Jewish State*];* the essay was about the first aliyah, where he explained that the Jews should go to Israel. I started questioning Herzl, and later I read other things and realized it was all related to the nineteenth century. He thought, "We are going to rent a big ship with two levels of rooms, one for the rich and one for the poor, and then leave for Israel." I was kind of disturbed. And it was not my ideas from the Left, but my ideas as a Jew. I would say that when the Jews were living in Egypt—and I always remember this during **Pesach**—when the Jews crossed the desert, there were no classes. The invention of the classes comes from the Gentiles' perspective of the world. According to the Jewish ideal, there were no social classes in Judaism. And what Herzl wanted to do in Israel was create a little Europe, although Israel is not that.

I do not go to B'nai B'rith. It is a class phenomenon. I was asked, but I do not see why. And to do what? I do not know if this attitude is related only to Dijon. I do not know B'nai B'rith anywhere else. Here it is the organization of the *parvenu* [newly wealthy] Jews. I do not say that they are not good Jews. But I am sure that they would not allow a Jew who is a farmer to join B'nai B'rith.†

After I came to Dijon in 1980, a great guy, Roger Partouche, and I got together with others and established a community center for Jews [there]. Today, it is called the Jewish Cultural Center. We created it; it did not exist before. However, we were so annoyed by some people [in the community] that Partouche and I left. We had had enough.

When I came to Dijon I was still young and searching for direction. I still had ideas that belonged to the Left. Today I have a social position, but certain things do not change. I would always go into the factories looking for Jewish workers. My roots are within me. That is why I do not make my aliyah, because I could not work in Israel. They did not need people in my

---

* See Theodor Herzl, *The Jewish State, An Attempt at a Modern Solution of the Jewish Question*, ed. Jacob M. Alkow (New York, NY: American Zionist Emergency Council, 1946).

† This belief is probably incorrect.

field; Israel is too small to need people like me. I do medical research that is being done only in four countries right now.

Of course, I feel French, but I am not. I did not have a Romanian cultural background, either. I met Gaby; I married her; I learned Romanian. Today, I speak Romanian fluently, and this gives me a little bit of Romanian culture. And if you asked me today if I feel Romanian, my answer would be, "Sometimes, yes." That is because when you start understanding the humor, when you understand the history and things, you are no longer a foreigner.

I was born French, with a French culture. My interest has to do with French politics, not the politics of Israel. I have never understood the people who get involved with Israeli politics and live in France. If they want to get involved with Israeli politics, why don't they move to Israel?

Inside of me, I feel closer to the Israeli people. I often go there. And I do not feel like I am like the people who go there on vacation either. Half of my family is there. When I visit, I do not do so for vacation purposes. I go in order to take care of family affairs. But I both like being there and do not like it. People in Israel are very stressed, running after money in the American style. For me, as a European, it is hard to understand. There is no sign of intellectuality. But it is also true that I go to a small place in the countryside. Probably Jewish lifestyle is a lot different in Jerusalem. I feel at ease in Israel and safe as a Jew. I feel at home. I like the culture. There, everyone is open, and we can go to other people's houses and talk between Jews. Here I talk to Gentiles.

[In France] I have a different feeling about this new fascist movement* because I know a lot about history. They function as an anti-democratic party. The French people say that Le Pen would never get 50 per cent [of the vote]. But they do not know. It is true, but he does not need 50 per cent. Twenty-five per cent would be enough because the other 75 per cent are not strong enough. Taking over, they would need only 20 per cent [an exaggeration]. It was the same in Germany, in China, Argentina. But try telling them that it would be the same in France!

Le Pen gets his support because of immigration and also because of the Socialists with their false vision of the Third World. The problem is with respect to the illegal immigrants. There is a wonderful law in France, called the Family Law. If you come to work in France and find a job, you have the right to bring your family. For example, a Muslim person comes here looking for a job and finds one and then asks permission to bring his family. He gets the permission. Therefore, he brings his 17 wives [exaggerated], but

---

* The National Front party founded and led by Jean Marie Le Pen.

three-quarters of those women are not his wives. These women and their kids then want to work. What the Socialists did is that they created a whole class of immigrants against the French Constitution. That was a mistake.

I am not like Le Pen; I do not believe that all the family allocations should only go to French people. But when you see a man who has brought a couple of wives and their kids, that is not right. Family allocations for all the kids! Le Pen was created by Mitterrand in the 1980s.* I will never forgive him for that. French politics have not healed; this is not a healthy political society.

There is no anti-Semitic culture in the United States, but it has always existed in Europe. The Jew succeeded in the United States. In Europe, the image of the Jew is completely different. [The Europeans] don't realize what they are doing [in terms of excluding Jews socially and economically] and would not admit it if they did. [Because of that] we are Jews in the synagogue, but we hide when we are outside. We feel that we are French before being Jewish.

When I was young, about 20 years old, three friends and I got together and left for Strasbourg. We wrote to the Yeshiva there and stated that we did not believe in God but wanted to stay a couple of days. They told us to come. We lived there three months. I brought my kippa out of respect to the other people there. I always kept in on my head, even when I went down to the town to call my parents and things like that. I am not religious, but I walked around with my kippa, and they were more anti-Semitic in Strasbourg than they were in Dijon. The rabbi at the Yeshiva had explained to us that we are not in Jerusalem and that there are things that are hard to do, but that there is nothing that keeps you from wearing your kippa. He was right. You can understand the fact that you did not eat kosher when there was nothing else to eat [other than non-kosher food], but if you believe in God, you can wear your kippa.

---

* Elections were changed from a run-off system to proportional representation, allowing smaller parties to gain a place in Parliament.

Elie Sadigh

A widely published Iranian-born economist and university professor in Dijon with an international reputation, Dr. Elie Sadigh is a liberal Jew who had a very traditional education. He and his non-Jewish wife are active members of the Dijon community.

June 2006

I was born in Isfahan, Iran, into a traditional Jewish family, the third of eight children. When I was young, Jewish life was very good in Iran. We had a fine and well-organized Jewish community that got along well with the Muslims and the Armenians. We went to the Alliance Israélite School in Isfahan. My father was an important Jewish scholar and one of the major interpreters of Judaism in Iran; people came to ask him questions, and he translated and explained the Torah.

The community at one time numbered about 15,000. It was observant. For example, Jews ate kosher; it was self-evident. Everyone observed the Sabbath; it was the natural thing to do. On Friday evenings we all ate together at my paternal grandmother's house and sang songs. On Saturday mornings, we all went to the synagogue at five or six in the morning and finished around ten. Afterwards we all ate together again. In the afternoon, all the Jews strolled around in a public place near to where we lived. It was a place where nearly all Jews gathered.

After the Alliance Israélite School, I attended a public high school, a very good high school. We didn't have any problems except the type that occur between siblings or cousins. There was mutual respect, and also interesting is that on the second day of Passover, Jews exchanged short visits to each other's homes, and many Muslims also visited Jews, as well. We did the same on Muslim holidays, visiting Muslim homes, and this was a treat for us children because there were always good things to taste and to eat. Sometimes when an important person was buried, or there was some mourning experience, they attended our services or we went to their mosques. They gave us the best seats—the best seats reserved for Jews. This was during the 1950s and the early 1960s. Then, as circumstances changed, people left, for Teheran or Israel or other countries. By the time that I left, the community numbered about 5,000.

My father was an important carpet merchant, and every year for several weeks he visited his clients abroad, including Israel. El Al [Israel's airline] flew between Teheran and Tel Aviv several times a week. The trip was very easy. Immediately after Israel's independence my father, with a photograph of the five of us at that time, went to the Jewish Agency in Teheran to arrange for our departure to Israel. He was told that because of the young age of his children things would be too difficult there for them—not financially, because we were well off, but adapting to the culture. My mother's brother went anyway and did write that things were very difficult, very hard for him and his family for several years. Every year after that, my father would say, "If I can arrange my business affairs this year, we will go to Israel."

If we had left Iran at that time, it would have uprooted a family on my mother's side that had been there since the Babylonian expulsion from Israel 2,500 years ago. Meanwhile, my father's family, originally expelled from Spain in 1492, settled first in Turkey before finally being invited by the ruling sultan to come to Isfahan because my ancestor was a greatly respected rabbi.

In terms of Jewish studies, I think that I learned to read Hebrew before Persian. At four or five, we went to a Talmud Torah, but less organized than here in France: rabbis and sometimes women were the teachers. But I learned how to read and also studied history. On the Sabbath, before our walks, my father would talk about next week's Torah portion. Almost every night of the week, my father would tell us Bible stories. I did not, however, do any Talmud there, but here in France. Our family visited Israel, as well. I should have gone to Israel [for a long stay], but I directed a camp for young people in Iran for two years. At that time, I was 20. It was 1963.

I came to France for the first time when I was about ten. I always was very interested in the country, especially because of its human rights repu-tation. So, since I was a good student, I decided to start my legal studies in France. I had already completed my military service and begun my university studies in Iran. I could have continued in Iran because the times were good economically and new universities were opening, but I was set on France. I came and started at the university here in 1967. The first three days were difficult because I didn't know French well enough. It was then that I met Marie-Ange. She tutored me in French, and I fell for her quickly—though she responded a bit later. The fact that she was not Jewish mattered less than our family's beliefs that the most important thing was love for each other, above all.

In September 1978, when we and our two children were supposed to pack up and move to Iran, with all expenses paid by the central bank of Iran (my new employer), my mother said when I called home, "Don't come. The situ-ation is not good here. Wait for six months." And that's what we did.

After the Iranian Revolution [1979], there was a rather free period when my parents came to see us in France. This was very hard because before the revolution my sisters had suddenly left Iran, which was hard for my parents; my mother was very affected by her children's leaving. But they visited all their children living abroad. Upon returning to Iran, my mother died suddenly—from sadness, I suppose. When they returned, they were alone; all of their children were living abroad....

[After consolidating power] the revolutionary regime became very repressive, especially towards Jews; they were no longer able to leave Iran. My father was blocked from leaving for five years. I also had a brother who was living in the United States, and he returned to Iran right after the Revolution to visit our parents and was blocked from leaving again for ten years. When he and his wife finally departed, they had nothing left. He came to France and also visited his children in the United States, spent two years in Israel, and finally went to the United States to stay with his sons there.

When I first came to France, I lived in Besançon. The community there was very open, in particular several families that I came to know well. Dijon, however, was very, very different. At first I went to services here regularly, but for three months, from June to Yom Kippur, no one noticed me. I was transparent. No one said "Hello" to me. It was a very difficult period for me. Afterward it got better, but slowly. Now the community is more accepting.

January 2007

When I didn't go back to Iran after the revolution [1979], that is, when my parents told me not to go and I didn't, I asked for a job at the university in Dijon; the head of the university at that time contacted the Ministry [of Education], and they gave me a job that we call "associate." It was initially for a year, and I was told that this job would be renewed automatically. But after a year, I learned that my job was not renewed because I was Iranian. At that time, it was very hard for Iranians. The position was one that is nominated, and it is the prime minister who [technically] hires the individual. So another professor at the university who knew me quite well contacted the ministry again and said that I was needed there. And that is how my job was renewed, and then I was able to pursue my career.

I teach monetary macroeconomics and the history of economic analysis, and now I am mainly doing economic theory. That's the hardest one. I found out, through my books, which you are aware of, that there were a lot of mistakes and gaps [in the theory]. First I wrote critical works, and now I have been writing positive books for a while, that is, I construct my theory in relationship to others' works. Most of my books have been published recently, in the last 12 years. But I had also published many articles before. I worked, and [my writing] built up slowly until suddenly [my books] came out. All that I am saying [writing] is a product of what I had been doing for

30 years. Then suddenly [my publishing career] took off. Alone I wrote nine books, 12 or 13 in total co-authored or co-edited.[*]

On the subject of immigration: it has played a big role in France after World War II because there was a shortage of labor in France. Many people who are here now are the children of those immigrants. At that time, French industry, and European industry as well, created so many jobs that the existing labor [force] was unable to operate these machines. That is why we brought in foreign labor. But now, we can't. The economy doesn't allow it. There was a positive role played by foreign labor, and now it's France that has a high unemployment rate and that wants to create jobs for the country itself so it cannot accommodate the supply of labor that comes from abroad. At the same time, the French are not willing to do certain jobs, and these are the jobs that are taken by foreigners. The problem of immigration, is that we cannot solve this problem by laws or by closing the borders. Ten years ago, I wrote that there will come one day that there will be thousands of people who will come knock at our door and we won't be able to do anything [to prevent this]. We can already see what is happening in Spain and Italy. The only solution is for these underdeveloped countries to develop. That's the solution to immigration.

There are two things to consider if this happens. Is there a solution? Yes, there is one that I proposed in a book that I wrote on development [*Étude économique et géopolitique du développement*].[†] I talked about how it can be done. It is possible. At the same time, it is true that there is a sense of responsibility to help the people of these countries. That is very important. And now with the immigrants and the riots last year and the strikes—with all the urban problems in winter and last spring—everyone is telling me that the country is stagnant, that people don't want to work much. The state gives so much that it is not necessary to work. They say that it is impossible to reform this country.

If I went to Germany, I would find things working much better than here. What I would see there was that they are more energetic. When they have a problem, they don't have a perfect solution, but something is done. Here, as soon as we attempt to do something, we are stalled by reactions from the streets [large street demonstrations]. What can we do?

As far as last year's riots are concerned, it is a unique problem here that I think is a result of provocation. We said things about the youth living in those ghettos that were unfair.[‡] There are some elements that should be

* Several additional books have been published since 2007.
† Elie, Sadigh, *Étude économique et géopolitique du développement* (Paris : Ed. L'Harmattan, 2003).
‡ Interior Minister Sarkozy referred to the ghetto youth as "riff-raff."

understood. The youth there felt attacked—all youth, not only those who were responsible for the riots. This was hard. Secondly, unfortunately, we must admit that there is segregation in France. France is the country of human rights, but the French do not apply that. Even the French state does not apply this. For example, a job seeker from one of those ghettos is certain to be rejected even if he has a degree and is competent. His chances are very limited. All these problems accumulated along with the provocation, and this is the cause of the riots.

When you talked about the strikes, I think that you were talking about the strikes during the CPE.* This is yet another problem. We wanted to make all jobs become free. However, we do not create jobs with decrees and laws, the labor market being free or not. For example, the way they talk about liberalizing the labor market does not make any sense economically. If there are jobs, we employ people; if there are not, we don't. This is the problem. As we have seen with the problem of immigrants in the 1960s, there were much more restrictive measures than now. But, there was full employment because there were jobs available. Now we are saying that the cause of unemployment is attributed to the fact that the labor market is regulated. It's not true. We can liberalize all we want, but France does not have five million jobs to offer. This is the problem of employment and it is a problem faced by most industrialized countries, especially in France.

Regarding the comparison you made with Germany, it is a very interesting comparison because the difference between Germany and France is that the Germans consult with the unions. That is, before the strikes, they negotiate. In France, it's the opposite. Before we try to negotiate, we go on strike. This is a problem. The problem is that we have brought the issue of power struggles into social problems. We believe that we should always win through power struggles. I agree only because there are no economic principles being applied. Since there are arbitrary principles, it is the stronger one who wins. But if we apply economic laws, there is nothing arbitrary. There are rules to be respected. The Germans have understood this, but unfortunately the French haven't.

I think that when you talk about immigrants, you are referring to the Muslims. I lived in a Muslim country. I know about tolerance in Islam, of the true Islam. I think that I know the true Muslims and ... they are very tolerant. They are wonderful people. For example, with all that I have lost [Elie's family was quite wealthy before the revolution], I don't blame the Iranians. I do blame the leaders but not the Iranians because I know who

---

* Aborted law allowing workers to be fired during their first two years of work.

they are. I am currently working with three people at the university who are Muslim. There is a fantastic understanding. We talk about religion, but we respect each other. I call them. The other day they were celebrating Eid [Muslim holiday], and I called them to congratulate them. They call me for Rosh Hashanah to express their good wishes. But there is nevertheless a problem [and] that is fundamentalism. It is not the problem of Islam but of fundamentalism. It is fundamentalism that exploded and now is hard to contain. Some of the Muslims suffer from it. For example, I know one of those who worked with me who was saying that his father-in-law, who was not religious at all when he met his wife, became religious and now is demanding that my friend's wife wear the veil, and he is telling me that he doesn't want it. The father-in-law wants his daughter to wear the veil simply because the fundamentalists call her a prostitute.

But I need to be very clear. The radical Right in France scares me much more. There is the problem of fundamentalism, but I hope that this problem is only a passing one. I hope so. But I know that the Muslims that I know— because I know the Iranian Muslims, I know a lot of colleagues who are Muslims, I also know other Muslims who are not in my social circle—there is no problem. It is really a small number of people who are, unfortunately, very active.

I should say something about the imams. For a long time in France, the state did not provide funds to build a mosque and still does not, so it was the countries that provided the funds that imposed their imams here. Unfortunately, for a long time, it was Saudi Arabia that was funding this, and they sent imams who did not know anything about Western society, who had no philosophical or intellectual knowledge, and who are very close-minded; they are the main cause of this situation. And I think that in this case, it is Sarkozy who understood the situation. He understood that there was this problem, but I am not sure if his proposition* can indeed be the solution. But he did understand that the root of evil comes from the fact that there are imams who are fundamentalists and who preach fundamentalism. Since we are in a free country, [they] can say whatever [they] want. I think that the origin [of the problem] is here.

I do not want to relate what is happening in the Middle East to here. I think that there is no real relationship between the two except in cases where the television provokes it. Otherwise, I don't think so. For the majority of Muslims in France, the problem in the Middle East is a different issue. The problem in the Middle East is such that everyone is responsible. I would

---

* Establishment of a National Muslim Council in 2005, which seems to be working fairly well.

not want to establish any connection with Israel and what is happening in France between the Jews and Muslims. If there is such a link, it is very minimal. But they will find another excuse. I think that for these people this serves as an excuse, and they will find others. This is fundamentalism. Not the Muslims. It is not the majority of Muslims. There is fundamentalism in France and everywhere, and it is fundamentalists nowadays who find opportunities to implant themselves. These people use all kinds of excuses to further implant themselves.

To come back to what I said before, the radical Right scares me more than fundamentalism. Well, fundamentalism does scare me, but not the Muslims. It is really the Right that has the tools, the power, and a representative who speaks very well. We must admit that he [Le Pen] speaks impeccable French; he knows how to be manipulative. He is credible because he is French. Well, *he* believes he is credible because he is French. I think that there are a few who have a hatred for the Jews, but this is not new. Unfortunately, for 2,000 years we have lived in this situation [of dealing with anti-Semitism].

In general, however, I am not pessimistic about Dijon. But I am realistic. I know that in Paris, in certain places, there is great fear. For example, my brother in Paris tells me about it, and when I ask him if he has any example, he gives me small examples that we have all experienced in our youth. We cannot blame anyone until we know who it is. There are some fights between young Jews and young Muslims, but when we ask the parents, they wonder why this happened. If France applies its rules and its laws, I don't think that it will be any more dangerous than somewhere else.

I know those who want to leave or who have left. They are scared of integration leading to mixed marriages. This is a real problem, but more for the Jews. The fact is that we are very closed. Every time there is a mixed marriage, there is an exit. I think that reform has to come from inside. If we settle this problem, I think that a great part of this fear will disappear. I think that it is more a problem concerning Judaism itself and that what we say and apply today has nothing to do with the Torah because in the Torah there is the possibility of conversion. I know many who have done so. I, myself, presented two people. The problem is that it is not a solution. Since the normative Jewish community does not accept them, they do not consider them to be Jews. That is, they become Jewish without really being Jewish because they are not accepted within the community, so it is like they were never converted.

In France, there is still a big reluctance towards those who convert via liberal Judaism, not those who convert in a traditional way. Well, those who call it "normal." It is very hard. They have to meet certain conditions. I saw it with Marie-Ange [his wife], and [the conversion process] is very hard, so I think that there should be change. If we want Judaism to last, it has to go through this [allowing more conversions which] is not against the Torah. We have to open up and facilitate things. Also, I don't know if you have heard of it or not, I think that it is a form of racism not to accept the other who wants to be like you.

When I left Besançon to come to Dijon, the family that I knew in Besançon, the family who were like my adopted parents, told me that the president of the community is a dentist originally from Metz. When we came to Dijon at that time, I went to the synagogue very often. So for the first three months, from June to September, I went almost every Friday night and every Saturday morning to the synagogue. But I was "invisible." No one knew me, no one came to talk to me. So one day I wanted to say the blessing for the Torah and we were shown the president and I went to see him and told him that I was from Besançon and that I had been told that he was a dentist. And he said, "So what? What do you want me to do?"

I know him very well now. He is a great man, but he is sometimes curt. So now that I know him, I understand his reaction perfectly. But at that time, I didn't know him and I couldn't understand his reaction.... Even after [his rebuff], I still went [to the synagogue] but I saw that it was pretty closed and I had already been told in Besançon that the community of Dijon is pretty closed, so I started to go less [often]. But I always respected [the synagogue community]. When they had some difficulties, we organized a committee, and I was elected as a representative; and this is when we did a lot of things for the synagogue, a lot of work.... We started the work and then I saw a completely different community. I saw that they were people who did not take initiatives. We had to reach [out to] them. Once we knew them, it was fine. It was the first step that was very, very hard. Now, of course, I know a lot of people. Everything is fine. However, unfortunately, there is currently a very serious problem in Dijon. It is the division within the community. This division really scares me, and I am scared about the time when the rabbi will retire.

We will not be able to finance another rabbi. They will not be able to pay this salary. That's for sure. And the community cannot pay more. I know the finances. For six years, I was responsible for the finances and the treasury, and I know the situation of the community. It is an aging community. The young people do not stay in Dijon. They leave, and those who stay are divided. We don't have enough people to create two communities. This is the problem. And I am scared that when the rabbi will leave—because he will one day retire, I hope as late as possible because I love him and appreciate him on many levels—he is holding on for now. He is holding, but once he is not here, it will be hard. A lot of people I know will not want the Lubavitch as they are now. [They are] the complete opposite of what he [the rabbi] wants—he wants to be open and integrate everyone, and with them it is an elimination of the majority of people. This is a problem that is really worrying me. I am not the only one. There are several of us who are aware of this problem.

The problem comes from those who are accusing the rabbi of not being sufficiently kosher, etc. The rabbi does what he has to do and maybe he does not do it enough. I don't know, perhaps he can do more. We can all do more. But even if there are some who have a problem with the rabbi, these are personal problems. They cannot affect the community. This is what I don't understand. I tell them that even if they have a problem with the rabbi, it's their problem with the rabbi, but the community has nothing to do with it. They should not play against the community. They say "No, no. I won't be able to [go to the synagogue] as long as he is here." It is these people who are breaking the community apart and who say that they do not get along anymore. To be honest, I have gone less frequently to the synagogue during this tense period, the past 14 or 15 years. There were no longer prayers. There was a heavy atmosphere. I went to the synagogue to pray, to be relaxed, to see my friends, my brothers, and it was not like that anymore. There were groups that were on one side, others on the other side.

This was before 2000. I will tell you because here I have to say what I think because I am pretty honest. I think that the main person at fault is Mr. K. [who gave Talmud lessons] and who denigrated the rabbi. He believes himself to be Jewish, but for me, he is not. He can yell out whatever he wants, but he is not. He manipulated people who did not understand, who had no philosophical background, and with his interpretations, etc., he manipulated people into believing that the rabbi was not doing this or that. If you go to 36 communities, you will see 36 ways ... it is what makes up our strength as well. When I came to Besançon, I did not understand anything at all. But I tried, and I was happy. These are local customs. In other communities it might work better, but here there is a division. They tried to denigrate the rabbi, maybe to create a situation that would push him to leave. I don't know. It's really unfortunate.

I know Haim Slonim [Lubavitch leader] and I think that he is of good faith, but I think that unfortunately he is himself overwhelmed, and what's serious is that since he is overwhelmed, he cannot control anything. So, indirectly and maybe unconsciously, he contributes to this division. For example, even when there were women who were [seated] behind the men, when Slonim came to pray and there were prayers that he couldn't do in front of women, he retreated to a corner and said his prayers. He did not contest anything. He respected the situation. For example, when I was on the Board, we were told that we had to put a barrier [between men and women]. We did it. But it was not sufficient, they said. We asked how and said we would do it as they wanted. But it was not enough. We tried everything to satisfy their demands, but in the end there was only one person who was at fault and that's unfortunate. The main problem was a personal one. When there is good will, there is no bad thought; these problems can easily be solved.

My brother-in-law is in charge of a synagogue, a pretty religious one, I think. It is true that there is a partition, but you can see the women. They put a separation made of glass [through which] you can see the women. They didn't hide them. We can see them: we are on the same level, but we are separated by a glass pane. It is a very big synagogue, but there is a small separation. Here it was not possible.

For me, there is no distinction between man and woman. Society has evolved and we need to accept it. And we can understand the Torah along with this evolution because the Torah was itself an evolution from something else. The Torah brought wonderful things ... wonderful laws that are currently the foundation of human rights. There is also the evolution of the world. What matters is not that a person is Jewish, Christian, or Muslim, but that one is a human being. You asked me about Israel. I am going this summer, I hope. We are going for a wedding, the wedding of one of my nieces. It's a wonderful thing. It's our retreat. I haven't been there for a few years, but we used to go regularly, every two or three years. I also have a lot of commitments and there are a lot of people who come from other countries to work here with me. For example, there were Italians who came to work with me and they only came in the summer so I could not leave.

There are two levels. At the level of the community, I agree that we can be Jewish among ourselves, but when it comes to distinctions between Muslims, Christians, or atheists, on the philosophical and humane level, I cannot make this distinction. Someone who is Jewish, it's not his fault. He is a man like me. There are of course ties that have been woven among us for centuries, and that is Judaism. It is important for me, and I think that Israel has become a representation of this tie for us. And I have not forgotten it.

I think that present events [June 2009] are very difficult for the Iranians, very hard.[*] But nevertheless, they are full of hope. What is very important is that for the first time since the Revolution, people are contesting the

---

[*] A more moderate Iranian opposition contested the "re-election" of President Mahmoud Ahmadinejad, with extensive street demonstrations, thereby also contesting the position taken by Ayatollah Ali Khamenei, the supreme religious leader, or Guide.

Guide [supreme leader]. This is of considerable importance because since the Revolution what the Guide said, no one dared contradict, even if they disagreed. I think that this is a very important development. But of course, yes, the country where one was born is the country of one's heart, but I am more detached from Iran than I would have been years ago. The events in Iran touch me, but much less than before. I am a pacifist. I am for simplicity, peace, truth.

We lived well in Iran. There were neighborhoods that were almost entirely Jewish, but we were always open to non-Jews as well. Now, this is all gone.

The essence of Judaism is openness. When I visit the United States, "I live in Iran" with my family. There, they have reconstituted an Iranian community. I don't even have to speak any English. Once when I was visiting, a very distant cousin was getting married and we were invited to the wedding. We went directly from my sister's house to the marriage ceremony. It was like being in Iran!

Jennifer Taieb

Brooklyn-born Jennifer Taieb, who married and raised a family in France, has never lost her New York personality. Articulate, opinionated, open-minded, humorous—but caring and hard working, she added a spark to the Dijon community at a critical time. As an American who was raised in a near total Jewish environment, she provides a critical outside look from the inside at the French Jewish experience.

February 1993

Like most [American] Jews, I was born in Brooklyn. That's a French myth about Brooklyn. If you say that you're from there, they already know. You're either Black or Jewish.

My father is a retired baker, and my mother didn't have a professional activity because at the time it was an embarrassment for a married woman to work. She was very frustrated about this because she would have liked to work. She's a dynamic person. My father was born in Poland, my mother in New York. But her father was born in Poland, too, though his family was very "German." They spoke German, had a German culture. He was very Aryan looking: blue eyes, blond hair, a straight profile. But what saved him [from the Holocaust] was that he was in South America performing with a youth choir. He was the only one of his family of 13 to survive. After settling in New York, he married a Romanian girl, my grandmother, who had a terrible childhood there but had been taken in by an older brother who was living in New York.

The atmosphere that I grew up in was not what you would call intellectual, but it was still very open. There were books around, and we were constantly reading, including my parents. The Brooklyn library was fabulous; you never had to buy a book. I was a library mouse; I was there all the time. My childhood was really great, very secure. My father worked nights and slept during the day, so my mother was the major figure in my childhood. And she really was a fantastic mother. My sister was six years older than me, so I was the baby and got compensated. That's why I had no major problems. We were happy.

My sister's graduation present was a trip to Europe, and she took me along. I was 17. The following year we returned, and that's when I met my husband, Marc. It was at a family wedding where he was the groom's brother. I was 18; he was 21. He was in his first year of dental school. We didn't marry right away, of course, because I had just finished high school. We wrote letters back and forth for several years while I studied fashion design, worked for a year in New York as a fashion designer, became a strong Zionist, and worked another year in Israel as a designer. In 1971, Marc came to visit me there, and things got very serious. We got engaged, and after returning to New York to work for a year, I joined him in Paris in 1973. He was still in dental school, but I was fortunate in getting a job in France right away.

My Jewish identity came when I was growing up in a pervasive Jewish atmosphere. You didn't have to belong to a community. I didn't belong to a community. I didn't belong to a synagogue. My father only belonged to a little **schule** that was in the basement of a neighbor's house. There wasn't even a rabbi, but the men were all Polish Jews, and they just knew the prayers. I never went to Talmud Torah. I went to religion classes for two years during my school years, but I went to public schools where everybody except the teachers was Jewish.

I lived in a Jewish neighborhood in Brooklyn. It was our territory. We weren't, you know, in the United States. Later, when I went to the university and learned that the United States wasn't Jewish, I was amazed. But I always considered myself an American too. So my Jewish identity was part American. I would say, "First, I'm American; then, I'm Jewish." But during the Six Day War, I said, "First, I'm Jewish; then, I'm American."

I only encountered anti-Semitism when I attended the Fashion Institute of Design, part of the State University of New York, in New York City. There you had a mixed bag of people coming from all over the world. There was an incident when, for the first time, my identity was challenged by a non-Jew. That I didn't like at all. Of course, growing up, my parents told us there were anti-Semites, but before that incident I had never really felt it personally. I was aware of the Holocaust from about the age of 14. I started reading Wiesel[*] and things [other books about the Holocaust] and got very, very into it. These books were very important for my consciousness. I learned then that my mother had only one cousin who survived out of her entire family.

Politics in my family were sort of liberal Democrat. My father was more conservative than my mother, who was quite liberal. She was a strong supporter of the civil rights movement. My first personal experience with Blacks occurred in high school, when they were bussed to our school in order to desegregate. They were very hostile towards us. We wanted to get to know them and tried to be very open because most of us had liberal ideas and supported the civil rights movement. But there were incidents; things were stolen. They self-segregated within the school; there were almost no

---

[*] Elie Wiesel is a Holocaust survivor, author of more than 20 books, and a Nobel Prize winner. He is often considered the most important public voice of Jewish Holocaust victims.

crossings of the color line except occasionally boys and girls would talk to each other. Very few of them ever got involved in the school's activities.

My four years of high school were absolutely the most fantastic years. I was a good student, into everything. College, however, was totally blah. I was a commuting student, so there was no social life at all. There was no ambience, no atmosphere, few men, many of whom were homosexuals. It was really depressing. I think that maybe that was part of my wanting to go to Israel, to make a total change.

Let me tell you about Marc, my husband. He was born in Constantine, Algeria, and his parents came to France when he was two or three years old. He was born in 1948, so he came before most of the Algerian Jews, who arrived later, around the time of Algerian independence. Marc's only memories are of Paris. He is a Parisian, which means that he is a little like a New Yorker. The world is centered on Paris. It has everything. There is no reason to leave Paris. His culture is totally French.

He, like his family, is totally assimilated. When you see the Sephardim who came from North Africa in the 1960s, especially the Tunisians, they are much more religious and much more ethnic. His family, like mine, was assimilated; his father, like mine, went to the synagogue on holidays. His mother was a little more traditional, but we were all more interested in religion as expressed through food-type things, though his mother didn't keep kosher. Marc did have a bar mitzvah. He went to Talmud Torah and had a religious education. He had connections with Israel, but it would have been very easy for him to marry a non-Jew and forget about it, definitely. I think that we are the only side of his family that remained Jewish. His mother told me that he is still Jewish because of me. He doesn't have a commitment [to Judaism].

When we lived in Paris, we didn't have a particularly Jewish group of friends. There were Jews and non-Jews. We didn't belong to a Jewish community; in fact, we didn't belong to a Jewish community until our son Danny was born and we were already here in Dijon for a year. Since Marc and I were both from large cities, we didn't feel any real need to belong to a community before that. The first four years we were married we lived in Paris in a small studio apartment that I hated. But we had little money; Marc was working for other dentists in order to get experience. We then moved to a larger place in the suburbs, but it was no go, either. I said to him. "Look, neither you nor I are doing well, so let's go somewhere else." Well, this total Parisian panicked at the idea of leaving Paris. But I pushed and pushed, and we found something here and we took a chance.

We moved to Dijon because Marc had a fairly decent job offer. Neither of us wanted to ask our parents for money. We lived the way we did in Paris because we were very young and remained that way until we were in our mid-thirties and it didn't work anymore. After we settled in Dijon, Marc eventually established a practice in a small town about 30 kilometers away and commuted. I began teaching, something that I didn't want to do when I was young, but that my father wanted me to get into.

I don't know if people know that Marc is Jewish where he works. It was the same when I worked. Nobody discusses religion. It's different here than in the United States, where people come right out and ask if you're Jewish. It takes about five minutes to get to that question. In France, no. Nor do they ask about political affiliation, unless you become very close. In France, at work, nobody talks about his or her religion. They feel that it is not polite to do so or to ask. They don't [ask] because of the history of persecution [in France] of the Protestant Huguenots* in the seventeenth and eighteenth centuries and of the Jews throughout history. You know, when I first came to France, people would say "Israélite" for Jew because Jews were associated with persecution and racism. I hated that. Whenever someone would ask me if I was an Israélite, I would reply, "No. I'm Jewish." But now all that has changed. The word has ceased to be a dirty word, but people still won't talk about religion.

They won't talk about whom they voted for, either, or about money. People hide personal facts. They don't talk about them. The fact that traditional French houses are hidden behind high blank walls says much about French mentality. It stems from negativity, if you really think about it. When I get close to a person, for example, who comes to my house several times, they'll notice that my clock has Hebrew lettering and ask about it. I tell them it's from my family, and they'll ask where the family lives. When I tell them Israel and not New York, they're taken aback. Why is an American living in Israel? So I have to explain. Then they'll say that Taieb isn't a French name, and I tell them that my husband was born in Algeria.

All this tends to marginalize us. It puts a label on you. When I was married and moved to France, at the first job I had the head designer said to me right off that the name Taieb wasn't French. When I told her that my husband was born in Algeria, she said that he wasn't really French but Jewish. I said, "What do you mean, he's not really French? His grandfather fought at Verdun and was wounded in the First World War. His father was in the French Army during the Second World War. You don't know what you're talking about!" And she said, "No. To be French is to be Catholic."

---

* The Huguenots were Protestants who were expelled by Louis XIV in 1685, when the Edict of Nantes (1598), which established religious toleration, was repealed. Most fled to Prussia and Holland, but many remained underground in France until Protestants were emancipated in 1790 during the French Revolution.

The 1967 War [between Israel and Arab states] had a tremendous influence on Marc and his family, especially his mother. She was raised to always respect and adore France. But when de Gaulle turned against Israel, she was totally distraught. Now she speaks very harshly about the French. Her father was gassed by the Germans during World War I, never completely recovered, and died soon afterwards. But he taught her to respect France, and she took it very much to heart. She had tremendous love for her father. So she never forgave what she regarded as de Gaulle's betrayal of Israel and the Jews. Combining that with everything else that came out of the Holocaust, and the anti-Semitic collaborationist attitudes of so many French, she has become very anti-French. It's like a lover who has been betrayed. She carries a terrible hurt. And it gets worse as more of the history of the Vichy period is revealed. Her family that had felt very integrated and assimilated definitely was touched.

When my children were born, I began to become rooted in the Dijon community. We entered the community and made friends and contacts. When you have children, you meet other people with children at the same time, and so you have the same interests. That is what kept us here. We also have a lot of friends outside the community, as well. I think that we make friends very easily.

There are a lot of things to say about Dijon, but it is a very nice place to live. We know everybody in the community, and they're so nice, they really are. The Christians that we know are nice also, so we have a very good feeling, a fine rapport with Dijon.

For a long time I had wanted to return to the United States, but it's a pipe dream. And at one time I wanted to go to Israel where my sister and her family and my parents live, but when it came time to make a decision on a departure date, we couldn't decide. What was pushing me to go was my family, my Jewish identity, wanderlust, and my disgust with the French government's attitudes. Wanderlust? Yeah, I think that I was born with it, inherited from my grandfather. Identity-wise, I told myself that I didn't want to be French; I didn't want my children to be French. I was very negative, you know? But [deciding not to leave France] was the turning point. In the end, I told myself, "You might as well face the facts. You're going to be here until you die." I think that we're not prepared for the sacrifices that have to be made to live in Israel. I think that you have to be very serious about this; you have to be idealistically Zionist or you have to be very motivated religiously, which is not the case [for us]. We were not self-sacrificing; we were hedonistic. After years of struggling, we were beginning to be comfortable, and we didn't want to give that up.

I like going to Israel, but I really can't stand being there knowing that every bus I take is liable to be blown up. I mean, you can't live there without that fear, without dominating that fear—and I have it. During the Gulf War [1991] I was berserk, but I didn't go to Israel. My mother didn't want to leave, and my father who had heart trouble didn't want to leave without her. Finally, my sister insisted that they leave and come here. I went totally bananas during that period, I began organizing, raising money. I should have been there, but I wasn't, so I had to do something. I think that it was just expiation, you know? I started getting really involved, and people responded. I really got into it. We raised about 700,000 francs [US$120,000]. The French community is not known for that kind of generosity, but we really whipped them into shape then. I didn't do this single-handedly, of course. There were other people involved, but I was the one who insisted that this be done first.

In the beginning, when we first joined, much to my dismay the community seemed to be a lot sadder, a depressed community. I think that it was due to what happened during the war and the German Occupation. In contrast, the Tunisians who have come here relatively recently are very lively. I have found myself at dinners where I was the only Ashkenazi present, and I was told that I didn't act like an Ashkenazi. But being an American, I was totally isolated from what had happened. I had a good childhood. Nobody close to me suffered because of the Nazis. I'm a happy person and I've got a big mouth, so we sort of hit it off. I realized that it was true that the Ashkenazis here seem to be less lively, less joyful, and it is probably because of what their parents suffered.[*] It would be normal. I never noticed that in the United States because nothing happened to [Jews living there]. They may be sad because of what happened to their families, but it didn't happen to them, while here they had to hide or they were deported or they lost close family members. It's obvious that here they felt fearful or stressed and tried to keep a low profile.

Many Ashkenazim have assimilated but were saved from total assimilation by the Sephardim, who came and woke them up. The Sephardim may have been rejected in the beginning because they were noisy. The Ashkenazim feared that everyone would notice them and lump all Jews together and ridicule them. But the Sephardim were attractive; they wore Jewish symbols in public: in Paris, [you would see] big, dark, swarthy men with their hairy chests showing through open collars, wearing a big golden Star of David. They showed the Ashkenazim that you didn't have to hide, that you could be proud to be Jewish.

---

[*] Their behavior may have more to do with their assimilation into middle-class French norms of behavior, although the Holocaust certainly affected people as well.

When I first came to France, I had a fighting spirit that I had from Israel. Then, I went through sort of a mini-experience of what the Ashkenazim and some of the Sephardim who were here earlier went through. It was a tormenting sort of thing. You had waves of feelings, things happening to make you become more militant, and then you got back to where you wanted to be left alone. And I think that now, from where I am, it seems that I am coming out more because I am more involved with the community. But it's all so subjective.

Assimilation with a big A—I think that it's good. When my brother-in-law was getting married, he and his wife had a lot of problems because she was an Ashkenazi. The older generation of Ashkenazim who were here in France thought that they were being invaded by savages, people with no culture. The Sephardim suffered in their pride because they felt that they were being attacked. But I think that it is no longer an issue with my generation. We tease each other, but it's no longer an issue. There are so many marriages between the two groups that it just simply doesn't mean anything anymore. It certainly isn't an issue in this community.

I find that there are a lot of people who really don't know who Jews are. They ask you questions that are so ridiculous. Americans, unless you go to an area where they haven't seen a Jew for a hundred years, will know [about Jewish culture], and Yiddish has been adapted into English. "I'm a 'klutz'" [clumsy] is an example. They love such expressions there. There are Jewish expressions that have come into French, but French is totally defended as a language. They're very aggressive about the French language because they are in a position of inferiority, and about that the French have no sense of humor. That's one thing that is totally lacking from the French mentality: laughing at oneself. They don't have it, and Americans have been infused with it because of us. It's a Jewish trait.

There is no interchange [visits, joint services] between the different local religious communities that I know of, at least at the level of the membership. There are members of the community here who are not Jewish and do not intend to convert. They are Christians, and they come to all the functions and pay their membership dues. They're very interested and supportive of us, and I think it's great. One of them is a neighborhood priest who is a lovely man. He is very interested, and he comes to all the services and ceremonies. There is also the husband of one of the Jewish women in the community who always participates, though he does not intend to convert.

During the Gulf War, there was cooperation between the mufti [Islamic scholar], some priests, and the rabbi, in order to keep things cool in Dijon, but there is no formal organization. A man named Bernard David recently organized France-Israel, and his mission is getting more non-Jews interested and supportive of Israel. But as far as an interfaith organization, I don't know of any.

In France, Protestants are like Jews in that they've been persecuted, although that was an awfully long time ago. But they're exceedingly discreet. They are so very mainstream. Everything is ecumenical. They are very, very low key and low profile. That's the way they stay.

We joined the [Dijon] community 13 and a half years ago. We wanted to have a **bris** [for our son] and, obviously, we had to contact the Jewish community. Unfortunately, it was August, and in August nothing works, everybody's on vacation, nobody's around, and it was Saturday when he was born. Anyway, Marc contacted the only one who was here from the Board of Directors, Albert Huberfeld. Marc told him that we needed a **mohel**. So, the first thing that Albert asked was when did he come to Dijon and was he a member of the community. When Marc said that he had been here a year and wasn't a member, Albert told him that he owed a year's back dues. And Marc agreed to pay the back dues.

They arranged it. The mohel, I think, was the former rabbi's brother. The problem was to get a minyan because there was no one around. Finally, we did get everyone together, and that's how I met the butcher as well. He came directly from the butcher shop to the clinic wearing his apron, a white jacket, and a little hat, like the Good Humor ice cream man. So along with Marc, my father, and the eight men who came we had the minyan and the mohel. And that's how we entered the community in 1979.

Marc's former boss was Jewish, and though he was assimilated and wasn't a member of the community, he introduced us to others. Eventually, we got to meet more and more people, and our roots began to spread.

The community in the early 1980s wasn't active the way it is now, but that really is something that has happened recently. Before, there were certain functions. If you didn't go to the synagogue, they had trouble getting a minyan, you know, they had it for Friday night and Saturday morning. And that was it. We had Talmud Torah for a few kids. We started the kindergarten a few years after Danny was born, and the women with children who weren't working took it over. There was a community seder where I met people. But it was all very slow. Nothing much, just a little community with very few people who only went to synagogue on the holidays. Then, of course, the synagogue was full. There were a few other organizations; for example, the Scouts. But even they disbanded because there were no more young people and no adults to take care of it.

My children went to the Talmud Torah from the age of six. Sometimes they came home and said that the lesson wasn't interesting or that the rabbi was interrupted by the telephone or people coming to see him. But the rabbi was very good; he loves children, and I think that they realize that. Sometimes, a professional teacher came. From sitting in on her class, I could see that she really did know what she was doing, and did it very well. The rabbi taught in a more "rabbinic" way [more rote learning].

What stands out in my memory about that time, the 1980s, was Israel, especially the reaction of the French government. I remember the treatment of the First Intifada by the French press, the turn of public opinion here against Israel. The Lebanese War [1982] too was treated like an Israeli aggression. And nothing was said about Syria until Syria got in. They [the media] did say that the Syrians were kind of aggressive, but they and the government didn't attack them the way that they did Israel. So it was totally disproportionate and totally anti-Israeli.

Of course, there are how many—four million?—Arabs in France right now. They are not citizens the way Jews are, but France has been sucking up to the Arabs for many, many years, and their whole policy is based on that. So it's not going to turn around from one day to the next. Mitterrand came in [1981], and he sort of posed as a friend of Israel, but that lasted for only a few months or a year. Of course, French policy took over because they've invested so much in pro-Arab positions.

We demonstrated in protest. We marched down the streets with a lot of other groups, including the Communists, and maybe behind a banner of the LICRA. The problem is identifying yourself. You know, the Jews are really terrified of becoming a target, an easy target. In spite of everything that you want to do or say, there is still a fear of announcing that you are Jewish. There's the fear that you are still taking risks. And I don't think that it's the same way in the United States. But here there is the feeling of taking a risk, of being a target for extremists.

During the Gulf War [1991], a journalist called the rabbi at four o'clock in the morning, asking his reaction about the firing of Scud missiles from Iraq towards Israel. The rabbi has family in Israel, and this really woke him up. He responded with a gut reaction in a very strong way without trying to be, you know, diplomatic. And I thought that it was a good answer. But then, discussing this with other people, they said that this wasn't a good thing because we didn't want to stir up any excitement, that we've got to keep good relations with the Arab community here in Dijon. That's true, but it also was a trap set for the rabbi, and that also was the cause of discussion within our community.

I don't know if there's real danger, okay? There's the historical danger, I mean people were in hiding 40 or 50 years ago. It's very hard to distinguish between what's in your mind from what the reality is. It's just a feeling of malaise. And I don't know if it's a real danger or it isn't. I know that the Tunisians came in, and they didn't have that fear. Or, if they did, it didn't show at all. Nothing happened to them,* so they must be in the right. You know, it's a feeling of erosion, a sort of day-to-day erosion, and there are certain periods when you just don't feel a bit safe. It's the erosion of the feeling of comfort. It's a wearing away of your independence as a person.

Things began to change really recently, maybe a year ago. I don't know what happened, but all of a sudden there are many people who have become powerful [in the community]. Maybe it's because they have more money or because they have more energy—whatever. These people have gotten involved in things, and it really shows. When I first came to the community B'nai B'rith had maybe ten functions a year—and that's a large estimate— but now I find myself not able to do anything else. It's crazy; I've got three meetings a week. It's wonderful, but it's enough. There's the LICRA, the anti-racist organization, with several meetings a year. Then you have the Jewish Appeal. The Maccabees [youth sports club] have grown, and Danny goes to the gym with them once a week. There's also the radio and its programs.

I think that these changes happened for personal reasons. People are saying that there's a return to Judaism. More and more people are coming to services, and they are able to have minyans not only on Fridays and Saturdays, but also on Mondays and Thursdays. That is something. There are adults in post-bar mitzvah classes and expansion of the Talmud Torah as well. There may be a return to religion in general. It may be that some of these powerful people in the community had some awareness in their personal lives, like the death of a family member, which is coincidental with larger changes. This makes people aware, and often they are the right people.

There are people who can change and who don't have an impact on the community for various reasons. But then there are those who are willing to give their time and energy, who are very powerful and forceful, and who can impose a certain idea. This is what's happening; I can't explain it and I don't know why. Maybe it was the Gulf War; maybe it's a chance for peace.... I don't know. Maybe it's because certain of us have come of age. Our children are older so we have more time to give. There are people in the community who have been giving of their time and energy for 15, 20 years, and they're tired now. New people need to take over. Our generation, people in their

---

* Holocaust policies were enacted in Tunisia but not on the same level as in France or Algeria.

forties, still have the energy. We're more set up in life, and we're looking forward to other things. I think that this is going to be a time of transition. There are people who may not want control [in the community] but who are going to get it because they have been so active. And they're not going to be able to get out of it. The transition from the older group to the younger group may or may not go smoothly, but it is going to happen.

You know, there are a lot of people who come to Dijon and say that it's terrible. The Dijonnais are very, very cold. You can live here and never meet anybody. If you're not born here, you're not accepted easily. But I think that belonging to the Jewish community is a way in, a way to get contacts, to have friends. And I think that's a very important thing. If we hadn't had that, we would have had non-Jewish friends. We have our Christian friends, but maybe we wouldn't have stayed here as long. Maybe we wouldn't have put down roots here.

I think that the Jewish community here is very open. About that you're going to have conflicting opinions, and there are people who haven't been accepted, but that could be for a lot of different reasons.

Spring 2005

When I first came to France in 1973, I was extremely surprised and dismayed that the French Jewish leadership would always deny the fact that there was a Jewish lobby. I always thought that was tactically very stupid.... When people think that there's a lobby, whether there is or there isn't, at least then they think that there's some power behind it. If you have no power, if you don't represent anything or anyone, you're a negligible entity and have no power.... Because the Jews are such a small minority and because the memory of persecutions and the precariousness [of the Jews' situation is so pervasive], one doesn't want to call attention to one's difference and one is always trying to prove that one is a good citizen. A good citizen who is totally integrated and just like everybody else—except we're not.... [Thirty years later] I deplore the fact that when the French Jewish leaders are interviewed, they try to play down the differences and the fact that, yes, most of the Jewish people have a certain political point of view [especially with respect to Israel]. On the local front [in Dijon], I think we're blessed with people who are very political; they have a lot of political savvy, they know how to express themselves perfectly. They're not radical. They're measured. But when they have something to say, they say it and they say it well.

France is going through, Europe is going through, a religion of humanism, a humanism that is totally devoid of humanity. You know, it's victim worship. And whoever is perceived as victim can do no wrong.

Muslim and Arab populations were mostly born in France. They imported the Intifada, and of course it was anti-Semitic. We have heard about so many anti-Semitic acts and not in the media, might I add, not in the national media but in the specific Jewish media. So many anti-Semitic incidents. But, of course, the French people don't want outsiders to think anything bad of them. But the truth is, there is anti-Semitism. The truth is, the court system still doesn't do anything about it, or rarely. The truth is, police inspectors always label such acts to be other than anti-Semitic.* They reject the idea until they're forced to admit that there are some anti-Semitic acts. So, therefore, when the Jewish leadership says there's no anti-Semitism, it gets me very angry. When the leadership of the American Jewish community [institutes a boycott of a country's products because it allows anti-Semitic acts] that changes things. [For instance,] when Mexico voted that Zionism was racism [in the United Nations, 1975], there were no longer Jewish busloads of tourists going [there], and Mexico turned around and rescinded that remark.

Here [the French Jews] are out to prove that they are real French citizens, and I detest that because, again, having been brought up in Brooklyn, I feel entitled [to be called a Jew]. I can't tolerate people trying to prove that they're citizens [first, and not Jewish] when I feel there's no need for them to prove it [in spite of their history]. I can't stand it, but I'm tolerating it. I can't do anything about it anyway.

Stephanie [daughter] stopped wearing a Jewish star [during the Second Intifada] for the simple reason that we heard of people being molested on buses. There was a totally anti-Israeli atmosphere. There was graffiti. The conventional wisdom was that the Israelis were wrong, that they were aggressors, that they were Fascists or Nazis and the Palestinians were the victims, who only wanted peace. Not only could Stephanie not speak up in school,† I couldn't speak up either. We have Internet in the ministry where I work, and there would sometimes be comments or invitations to [pro-Palestinian] demonstrations in different parts of the country and petitions or boycotts. It was like swimming against a tidal wave. So after a while, I think what happened to all of us [Jews], we became numbed. I didn't say anything anymore because it was just impossible. I mean, you couldn't; Izy [Cemachovic, synagogue president; see p. 34] used to send me a newsletter

---

* This was especially true between 2000 and 2003. Thereafter, the police and even the courts became more concerned with anti-Semitism and effective in dealing with it, although problems remain.

† Stephanie had Israel-related problems at the University of Dijon, finished her BA in Canada, and now works in New York.

about all that [stories of anti-Semitic acts and protests against Israel]. I couldn't take it after a while. I was really getting depressed.[*]

I couldn't stand it anymore.... Serge Klarsfeld's son, Arnold Klarsfeld,[†] went to Israel because he said he had been sued for his comments, truthful comments, of course; he said that [the French media is] trying to make Jews political outcasts here in France, and it's true. It is totally true. It's calmed down now that the Intifada has calmed down, but if it flares up again, the same thing will happen.... The teaching profession is very Leftist, and therefore they're humanist, and therefore they're against Israel; even some of the more intellectual [professors] in the universities are against Israel. I was amazed to see that other people, in spite of all the propaganda—and it's not news here, it is propaganda— really are pro-Israel. I'm amazed to see that, and heartened.... This is especially true of our friends in France and Israel.

About the Lubavitch, there's a lot of misunderstanding on both sides. When they first came, there was a lot of fear that this [division] would happen, and I think that the fear and mistrust actually precipitated it. [Some] people weren't happy because our synagogue is conservative but very tolerant. In this day and age there is a lot of fundamentalism and a lot of people here who for some strange reason want to go back to something reactionary. Eighteenth-century, anti-feminist misogyny—that is where I draw the line. I would prefer a liberal synagogue if I could find one here. When I first came here, at least everyone tolerated the other. Maybe there was some grumbling, there were some rifts, okay, but there was one synagogue, one community, and we all gave a little. Then we had a group of people who desired something more. Maybe they wanted to be more religious, but if they are really more religious, then they have to be tolerant as well. Because without [tolerance], I don't see where they're going exactly. The misogyny is a problem, but it doesn't affect me directly because I don't go to synagogue that frequently. I don't care for the way the services are done here. But they also didn't care for the way it was done, they wanted things to be changed, tailor-made for themselves. Against all odds they opened up a school and have three kids, you know, they have a school for three kids.[‡]

But they are not tolerant. They won't make compromises. It's like dealing, unfortunately, with the Palestinians as well. They want what they want and nothing less. And any way they get it, by small steps or by confrontation, they'll do it. I'm not equating [the Lubavitch] with the Palestinians, but I am

---

* Author Robert Weiner receives these e-mails; they are depressing.

† Serge Klarsfeld is a famous postwar Nazi hunter and historian of the Holocaust. His activist son, Arnold, is an attorney involved in Holocaust-related legal cases.

‡ The EDEL Lubavitch school usually has about 12 students.

saying it's the same type of no win situation. Either you give everything, or you must build walls. And the problem is, that's what happened. Some of our very dear friends are very angry at the community and have just left the community, more or less, and I think that's terrible. I think it's just awful.

I have a relationship with the ones who've left the community because my family is very neutral. I mean, first of all, as I've said, we don't go frequently [to the synagogue]. I try to understand both sides. Each side thinks the other one [caused the rift] [intentionally]. I don't know; I tend to believe there was just a misunderstanding. I hope that. But the problem is, a line has to be drawn. You say, okay, you can't have any use of any of the halls or any of the facilities because apparently you don't pay dues. And [the community] needs the dues; otherwise, it will die. So, it's fair enough [to ask for dues for use of the facilities]. On their point of view, they think they're the ones who make the community live because they go to the synagogue. Yes and no. You need people in the synagogue, but that's not all. You also need people who go to activities, who give money. And I think [the Lubavitch and their supporters refuse] to see that.

All of our young kids, my kids' ages—in their twenties, post-high school— have gone away to get their higher education, and most of them haven't come back. They mostly went to Paris, a few of them to Strasbourg. We're going to be missing at least a generation. We've had some people come back, some with small children. I have no idea what's going to happen with them. [The Jews who leave will group together in] very big cities [where they will be faced with the] anti-Semitism of the Arab populations and Muslim populations. There's a danger of Islamization.... Maybe it's just a question of [the Muslims] feeling threatened, and so they hang on even tighter to their traditions. If it doesn't go away, the large Jewish communities in the big cities are going to be at risk and may have to leave. And there is no help from the French government. I still believe that the judiciary ... does not apply the laws [that the legislature makes], they don't enforce them. It's systemic practically.

My daughter is planning to leave.* She feels betrayed. She said, "I'll never trust France again." But this is an exception; after all, she's Franco-American. I don't know about the others. I know that parents my age think that there is no future; they would rather see their kids leave.

I think, I believe that our children would have a better future outside of France. I don't trust France—there has been periodic anti-Semitism always, always, always. It's a kind of paranoia here, psychosis ... not psychotic,

---

* Indeed, Stephanie Taieb now works in Manhattan.

schizophrenic. One day, no problem, the Jews are very good, great. They elect a Jew to the prime minister post. And then the next day they're deporting them. Those are two extremes, but I believe there's a real, deep-seated anti-Semitism all over Catholic Europe. Maybe Protestant Europe is different, I don't know. France was the elder daughter of the Church, there was a pope here,* and so there is ingrained anti-Semitism. The fact that [the French now are] anti-clerical has helped a lot, but I don't think you can wipe out 2,000 years of history. I just don't. It's part of their culture, like wine.

. . . There are people who feel that I exaggerate. I mean, it's not like pre-World War II. It's true, it's not. But I think it's been a big shock for our generation growing up after the war and thinking that this could never happen again, that anti-Semitism was totally unacceptable, [to find out] now it isn't.

I remember my mother telling me that in New York in the 1930s there was a period of anti-Semitism when people would say things with impunity and the Jews were rather frightened. The big turnabout came after the war, the second war, and we grew up then. So we had no knowledge of anything else. We took [the lack of anti-Semitism] to be normal. Well, it isn't normal; it was a parenthesis, it was a lovely little parenthesis in history—a period of 40, 50 years—and that period may come to an end—we have to be prepared for it. I don't think that it's the normalcy for Jews to be accepted completely and have the same opportunities and not be at risk. I think that if you look back since the first dispersions, Jews have had periods of sunshine and a lot of periods of storm. So I don't think that we can take [acceptance] for granted.

How do I feel about Israel? When I'm there, I hate the Jews [laughing]. I equate them with the American pioneers in the Wild West of the nineteenth century. They're not profane, the Israelis, on the contrary. What they are is—they're very much egocentric, each one of them. I guess the danger breeds that in you. It seems to me, from what I've read, that anybody who could survive the camps, the deportation, was very, very lucky and a survivor. I don't think you can be a survivor by being a nice, little, soft person. Those who came to build Israel were either the ones who were strong before the war, or the ones who gained strength after. I'm thinking about my family, my grandparents who left Poland [in the] 1920s. These people were tough, because the people who weren't tough stayed where they knew everything, where they had their family, where they weren't under threat. But my grandfather asked my grandmother to cut his toes off so he wouldn't have to go into

---

* From 1309–77, seven popes resided in Avignon, France—a period sometimes referred to as the "Babylonian Captivity" of the popes since their "captivity" lasted about as long as the Jewish exile in Babylon.

the Tsarist army. Now, that is tough. How many people would do that? He joined his brother in New York, and my father came in 1923 when his father had already been there for several years. These people were survivors....

I have three countries, I guess. The United States is always my country, although if I went back there, I don't know if I could make it again there. I don't know. In spite of everything, France is my country. There are a lot of nice things about it. There are a lot of nice people. The government is screwed up. The politics here are the worst—not the worst, but it's bad. There's no real democracy in Europe, I'm sorry. Maybe England, I don't know, but ... I think for me there are two real democracies that I know of. The United States is a real democracy, as far as I'm concerned. Israel is a real democracy, undoubtedly. Australia, I hope? Europe, no. In Europe, there are political bosses and the parties, the people who are in the parties vote the way the boss tells them, otherwise they are excluded.

I've been a French citizen since 1991. I think we need a new brand of politician. I heard, and I'm afraid to say I don't know who was speaking, a woman politician in the Socialist Party which I despair of, because I feel betrayed by the Socialist Party as well, who said that she feels that the politicians now should not vote according to party lines, that they should vote according to conscience. And I said, "Wow, that's new." That's a new thing. I like that.

I liked Sarkozy as the Interior Minister because he didn't pull punches and he didn't tolerate things and I think, I guess, in a way he was like a little Giuliani [former mayor of New York]. There was so much crime in France, so much violence in France, that was not admitted to, that he came and said there's a problem and we're going to do something about it. And he did. And I like him for that. I think we need no nonsense people.

First of all, politically France is tied up in knots. It's really tied up in knots. Since de Gaulle. De Gaulle created the Fifth Republic and I don't know if he's at the cause of this or not. But the rule of this country is ... it's divided into interest groups, economic interest groups, not lobbies the way we know it in the United States. But you have corporations and you have people who have certain privileges, acquired rights; the fact that you don't have the same retirement for every person in the country—that's crazy. The fact that people who are conductors of trains get to retire at 50 years old, their family gets to ride for free for the rest of their lives. That's crazy. And of course, those are the acquired rights. And they won't budge an inch. The teachers, my God, they have acquired rights, you can't touch them. As soon as you touch them, they go out on the streets. And the funniest thing is, the French public supports them. For the "nth" time, the metro was on strike, the people were stranded, and it's the metro for the suburbs so people have long treks and the people waiting on the platform say, "I support them. It's a problem for us but I support them." For Christ's sake, what are they supporting these people for? I mean there's no negotiation, there's just strike. There's negotiation via striking. I remember when the truckers ruined the economy for two years running, they ruined the economy. And the people were bringing them sandwiches. I would've taken a gun and shot them. And the French public is bringing them sandwiches. I don't know, I don't understand. I guess it's that humanism. They perceive them as being victims. But they're not victims. So you've got that problem and you've got the fact that everybody's working for the government, including me. And there's 25 per cent or 40 per cent of the working public. . . . I mean something crazy.*

It's crazy. And the fact that anybody who had his own business has to pay so much, so much [added social costs]. And you can't get rid of employees, so there's no flexibility. So everything's wrong. Everything's wrong, except that there's still national health insurance, which is going to go bankrupt, and a couple of other things that are good, but what I respect the most about France is the cheese [laughing]. The fact that people defend a quality of life. And one thing I say to myself, and it's totally selfish, is that had I been in the United States, I would've been very happy with my two weeks vacation. I work as much as I would've worked in the United States, that's for sure, because I'm just that way. That's me. And the free education—which is bad education, lousy education, because if Stephanie goes I'll be paying American prices basically—all of this was done in the '60s and it was great for a booming economy. Those things were wonderful. Today, it's just too expensive and it's a pity because there are things that are wonderful. As I said, free education, higher education, health insurance, national health insurance, the food, the quality of life. You sit down, you have a dinner, you can stay for two hours, three hours, talking. The fact that people take the time to speak. It may no longer be an art, conversation, but at least it exists still. I think that's wonderful. On the other hand, they don't have the Americans' *joie de vivre*, as paradoxical as that seems. Americans love to play, they know what entertainment means, they know what convenience is, they know what enjoyment is.

They [the French] depend on the government for everything. There's no initiative, and this is the big problem with France. I work with young people, people of high quality because they have to get accepted to these schools,

* In 2004–05, the Organization for Economic Co-operation and Development (OECD) found that 25 per cent of the French labor force was employed by the government, compared to 15 per cent in the United States.

but they're waiting for the government to give them jobs; you know, my own children, my own son is [waiting for a government job]; they all despair of anything because they're waiting for it to come, to fall to their laps. Maybe it's a generational thing.

Well, you know, the students who go to these business schools are those types of students [more independent]. But those who go to the universities, unfortunately, for the most part, aren't. And we, as parents of this generation, have been disgustingly protective. And the [kids] just don't know how to hustle. They haven't had jobs. There's no tradition of jobs. Not only is there no tradition of jobs, but there are no jobs to get, basically. You can be an intern and not be paid, that you can do. Slave labor is accepted, but working for money, working in a supermarket doesn't exist because you've got to be a certain age and they can't hire you because then they can't fire you. So there's no flexibility, and, therefore, the kids don't have the opportunities to work the way the American kids do.... And that's one thing I hate and that I'm worried about for the future.

At one point we had an opportunity to go back to the United States and I didn't push it. If I had to do it again, I would go back.

Synagogue centenary, 1979, front view; photo by Les Éditions de l'Est.

Synagogue centenary, 1979, front side view; photo by Les Éditions de l'Est.

Izy and Luna Cemachovic; date and photographer unknown.

Albert and Myrna Huberfeld at home, 2011; photo by Robert Weiner.

Michel and Cathie Bussidan at home, 2006; photo by Richard Sharpless.

Marcelle David (on right), daughter Corinne (middle), and sister Malou Dresler (on left), Marcelle's home, 2006; photo by Richard Sharpless.

Elie and Marie-Ange Sadigh at home, 2006; photo by Richard Sharpless.

Haim and Hannah Slonim with children, classroom, EDEL Lubavitch School, 2006; photo by Richard Sharpless.

Rabbi Simon Sibony (wearing kippa), Robert Weiner (center), and President Henri-Claude Bloch, in Albert Huberfeld's house, 1993; photo by Albert Huberfeld.

Maurice "Gislain" Bensoussan and Annie Edelman, at a birthday celebration, L'Hôtel Mercure, Dijon, 2006; photo by Sarah Bensoussan.

Deborah Bensoussan and her nephew Tolia, L'Hotel Mercure, Dijon, 2006; photo by Sarah Bensoussan.

Robert Weiner (second male on left) at a gathering of united community members, in Albert Huberfeld's house, 1993; photo by Albert Huberfeld.

Albert Huberfeld in his store *Albert*, the unofficial downtown synagogue "office," 2005; photo by Robert Weiner.

Nadia Jacobson Kaluski, lecturing about the life and death of her sister Louise in the classroom of her daughter, Cathie Bussidan, 2005; photo by Robert Weiner.

Radio Shalom's Dijon office and broadcasting center on the second floor of the community center attached to the synagogue, 2006; photo by Richard Sharpless.

Preparing for Patrimony Day Open House, the community center and chapel, 2006; photo by Richard Sharpless.

Students and teachers at the EDEL, the Lubavitch School just outside of Dijon; photo by Richard Sharpless.

The
LUBAVITCH GROUP

The Dijon Lubavitch leaders seek to revitalize Judaism according to the principles of their worldwide movement. Now consisting of about 15 families, the Lubavitch group practices a more Orthodox Judaism but also seeks to serve the needs of the widest number of Jews regardless of religious affiliation.

Haim Slonim and Hannah Slonim

This attractive, energetic, and committed Lubavitch couple arrived in Dijon in 1993 as missionaries with the purpose of rejuvenating Jewish life and practice. Their presence and activities caused a division in the community that continues to the present. However, their hard work building a school and a center for alternative religious practices and for Jewish study has provided a place for those in the community who seek a more orthodox religious experience.

September 2006

HAIM: I was born a Lubavitch in Israel in 1967. I lived there for 20 years, then studied in Brooklyn, New York for about five years. Then before our marriage I went to Russia for a year. The Lubavitch were the ones who opened a synagogue there. In the days of Gorbachev,* we opened a Yeshiva. The government gave us an old synagogue.

After [Hannah and I] got married, we stayed in New York for one year to study. Hannah was born near Paris. She's from an old Lubavitch community from after the war. .... Her father was a senior rabbi of the Lubavitch community in France and director of the main Lubavitch schools in Paris. There are 3,000 students in three schools.

Our fathers knew each other. At the time, my father was in New York representing the Russian community. He was director of **Habbad** activity in Russia.

In New York, we studied. We went to the **kolel**. Then, we started to help the community. We wrote. We had some opportunities. One was to go to Russia. My father-in-law said, "Why not France?" I asked the rabbi of the Lubavitch, and he said "no" to Russia and "yes" to France. So we came here. It was the rabbi who decided, and we realized that it was the best thing. He said that Russia was not the best place for us. We were, of course, close to [the rabbi]. Our two families, my wife's and mine, have been Lubavitch for generations.

HANNAH: We have seven children. The baby is this one [sitting on her lap]. He usually is the leader. But you asked how did we get to Dijon? Well, we were educated and from communities that were far away. We could have stayed in Paris and had good jobs. Yet, we know that there are areas where Jews are separated from each other, and we need to help. These are places where there are not many Jewish people, and this was why we looked for a

---

* Mikhail Gorbachev, the last leader of the Soviet Union.

place that was far away and difficult. We had agreed to go to Kazakhstan, which is hard, but the rabbi said it would not be good for us, and we got the offer of Dijon. My father-in-law said, "You want a challenge? There's Dijon, for example." There were others, too.

HAIM: We didn't know anyone here. A few weeks before we came, we were contacted by Dr. Gérard Hachmoun [dentist], but before that we didn't know anyone. We came not according to our personal needs but because we wanted to reunite the Jews through Judaism. Usually, it's not about what each individual person can do. For example, what we can do is to put up something besides a school that would be necessary for the Jews to retain their identities. Because nowadays, if we don't have a good foundation, there is nothing left.

In the beginning we set up some activities on various occasions. We sent out some reminders of the holidays, explaining what the holidays meant. We had some Hanukkah parties. With Françoise Tenenbaum, the assistant mayor, we have a menorah set up for Hanukkah in a main square of the city center. That is something new. And we have the Habbad house. We've been there 12 years. We teach the Talmud and the Torah. And we not only have activities in Dijon but in Besançon. We don't always go, but some people from here go to give classes.

The school we started after two years. Our first year was at the Beit Habbad, but it was not an appropriate place for a school. So then we eventually moved to this place [rue Jean Renaud]. It was hard at the beginning. It is always hard. But we are not afraid of adversity.

HANNAH: The school was a big achievement, even though there are not many children. We started with five, and now [after ten years] we have 20. I also teach in the school and teach teenagers at home. My husband also teaches teenagers. It is hard work, but we feel that it is very important for Judaism because even though the children go to other secular or private schools, they still have a good foundation that secures their adherence to the Jewish community. That is because they get to know their history and culture. Otherwise, they get to know the history and culture of others better than their own. So we do think that it is important. We feel involved in this community.

HAIM: We have done other activities in this community. We have classes for people who come from quite far, too, who don't have Yom Kippur. I have someone like that who comes from quite far, and he loves studying but doesn't celebrate. There are many people like that. So each one does what he can. And that's why we have the Beit Habbad—to give some classes.

HANNAH: The Lubavitch school also is like that. We teach Jewish culture even if the [students] don't practice religion at all or if they are very religious, of all races, from everywhere. We need to respect everyone because this is a principle of Judaism: to respect everyone. Even a fly needs respect. Even a leaf from a tree should not be plucked without reason.

HAIM: Although this is true, at times it is not well understood. The Jews suffered a lot; there was always some tension between Jews and non-Jews because there were a lot of problems. But this does not represent the Jewish viewpoint. Judaism offers a very positive point of view on everything. This is true in general. And this is what creates an opening—if we know that everyone has a positive aspect. Of course, we will not agree about everything. I remember there was someone, I don't remember his name, but he is known in the United States. He spoke during a meeting in New York in November [2005], and he expressed what he liked about the Lubavitch. He said that 90 per cent of the people are the same and 10 per cent are different. Most people tend to focus on that 10 per cent who are different, but the Lubavitch always say that they should focus on the 90 per cent who are similar. And it's true.

We have personal relations—not as an organization—with Catholics, Protestants, and Muslims in the area. We know people who work with us [instructors] who are Catholics, and there are some Muslims, too.

HANNAH: I want to add something to what I said previously. When we meet a Jew, or non-Jew for that matter, we really are concerned with what he needs. We will not ask him to do the Shabbat. If he needs to talk, if he needs moral support, or financial support, we start with this first. We are here to help people. And then, if they are willing, we offer more.

We want to make the practice of Judaism easier here in Dijon, because it isn't always easy. So we try to help them in their lives. For example, later my husband will go to Lyon and will bring back some kosher food and baked goods that people can prepare for themselves. We offer good fresh things. The synagogue takes care of offering meat, so we don't do that. When we bring the food, people can have something related to Judaism. For the major holidays, we try to add things that are missing.* It is one way we try to make things easier.

HAIM: There is in the Lubavitch a spirit of fun and celebration. In general, it's the same anywhere, but when we were in the United States, we celebrated according to the means there. We don't make the same jokes [here as there] because [humor is] adapted to each country, but the general idea is the same.

---

* Anything that would embellish the holiday spiritually or materially.

I don't really know if there is something unique among the Lubavitch in France as compared to Americans, Russians, or Germans, for that matter. I don't really know. Maybe my wife has another answer, but I don't think there is anything "typically French." I do think that people here in Dijon are different even from Parisians.

HANNAH: We have a friend who came to give a lecture. He told another friend that if he wanted to see what Paris looked like 30 years ago, he should go to Dijon.

HAIM: I think the fact that we are a very small community brings about a very special spirit, a family spirit. Maybe because it's small here and Paris is big. Here, the Beit Habbad is special, and people like it because of the family spirit. But it's hard to predict the future, because there are many people who leave. For example, we started our school with five students, and they all have moved somewhere else.

If they have the choice, some people choose to live in Paris rather than here. But there also are some people here who live among Gentiles. They have interracial [mixed] marriages, and there is no follow-up with them. But it's a responsibility to try. Yet, we can work for years with someone who in the end sends his children away. So, we can't really talk about the future because nothing is certain. People come and go. But we need to take care of the people who are here. Each person who comes to our school gets something out of it. He does not necessarily become very religious, but he gets something.

Of course, there are a lot of problems. We have nothing but problems. First of all, the biggest problem is money. But there are a lot of miracles. It's not logical, and I can't explain it. People don't understand anything here. We tried to tell them about the financial situation of the school, and we have someone who helps us a bit [Gaby Barda], but I don't understand. They say they don't have money, and they leave. Well, we just do what we have to do and leave the rest to God. But we find the money one way or another. This, too, is the Lubavitch spirit. Do what needs to be done, and as Hannah says, "God will help."

In regards to the Dijon community, to be honest I think that it was always bourgeois. And some things should have been done at the beginning. . . . In our modern society, we can't only speak with one voice because we don't progress in the same way. Some people need faith. We have a group of people who go to the mikveh regularly and to the synagogue during the week. Others don't want to. We don't agree with this, but we try to bring people to the synagogue for some things. Now some people do want to get more involved in Judaism, but it's like a highway. If someone is driving at 100 kilometers per hour, and I'm driving at 130, we have to help him overtake me.

HANNAH: The one who is driving at 100 will say everyone is free. We are in France. We have to look at things differently. We all have the right to do what we want. If some want to pray in a different synagogue, we need to go beyond that and still remain good friends. We are close friends with everyone.

HAIM: I personally think that we have to find the positive side of bad things. The fact that we lack something [spiritual or more strict religious practice] in the synagogue means that people have to put in some effort. Otherwise, we always have people at the synagogue who come and think that everything [as it is now] is fine. The Jewish lifestyle has always been about making efforts. It's true that the community is already doing some things, but we still want to help at the synagogue, and we try to. I think that having two or three people helping the synagogue will benefit everyone. Everyone needs to feel that they are together, and this is the hard part.

You asked about Israel and France, and this depends on how you view things. If you want to be blind, you won't see the problems of the world. If there is no problem, as France believes, then France is right. But if you look carefully, you do realize that there is a problem that needs to be fixed. It's true that nobody handles the media as badly as Israel. We don't attack just anybody like [the Hezbollah does]. You are in the United States. You know very well that the media in France is not accurate. Of course, we were for this war [Lebanon, 2006] even though there were problems. My sisters are there [in Israel]. And we don't know much. We follow the news like everyone else. We know that if there is a threat, it needs to be taken care of.

It's not very pleasant watching the French news, but I don't really feel angry. I did notice people staring at me during those times, but maybe I was imagining things, because no one ever said anything to me. But we felt it and we know that the average Frenchman is pro-Arab. And maybe it's not their fault because that's what they're told. But with time, people change.

Here in Dijon, if I dressed a bit differently, would I get looks from people? Well, to look is one thing. People look…yes, a little, but rarely. I personally think that Sarkozy did a good job; it seems to me that before Sarkozy we had more insults. But nowadays people are more careful. It's very rare that I get comments from people.

HANNAH: Thirteen years ago, when we first came, everybody stared at us when we walked [in the town].* Once I was in a store and my husband

---

* Haim dresses in traditional Lubavitch black garb, with a large black hat. Hannah wears a wig and long dresses, even in the summer months.

came to get me. The cashier said to her friend, "Look it's Rabbi Jacob!" [a movie character]. So I told her, "No. It's not Rabbi Jacob. It's my husband."

HAIM: Today a passerby will see me once and be shocked, but the second time he will be less shocked, and the third time even less so. Sometimes I see someone checking my license plate, so it means that not everyone knows me.

There are several thousand Lubavitch missionaries like me in the world, perhaps 100 in France. There are a lot in Paris. But there are Lubavitch who are not working as missionaries. Our strict form of dress is only regarding the *schlichim* [missionaries]. There are many more Lubavitch who are doctors, dentists, and so forth. So there are many Lubavitch or supporters of the Lubavitch in France, thousands, because they can be 100 per cent or 80 per cent Lubavitch.

HANNAH: There are some, of course, who are not supporters, but I think that they are a minority. Some people here tell us that they have heard things about the Lubavitch, that they are severe or intolerant and exacting, but then they meet us and see that those things are not true. In fact, the Lubavitch are very tolerant, very open. We try to do things completely according to the orthodox tradition, but we never tell people what they should do. If they are willing, we will help them. But we live as we want to and love others as they are.

David Laufer

David Laufer is a relatively young member of the Dijon community. His extensive religious education is rather rare; few young people today have either the opportunity or the inclination to pursue it. His experiences provide insights not only into the kinds of adjustments that were made between Ashkenazim and Sephardim but also how one comes to terms with one's Jewish identity. He left Dijon for a time to establish a business in Bordeaux but recently returned to the city with his family.

September 2006

I was born in September 1971 in Besançon, a provincial town not far from Dijon, where there was a large Jewish community with a rabbi, a synagogue, and a separate community center. I grew up there and did my bar mitzvah there when I was 13. I have two older brothers, one who recently moved to Israel and the other living in Besançon.

My father was a Jew from Poland, born there in 1927. My mother is a Jew from Alsace. They went to Switzerland during the war; afterwards, they came to Besançon. In Switzerland, my parents took refuge with an uncle who welcomed them in his house. My father did his studies in accounting and worked for a time in a factory. But as my grandfather got older, he asked my father to come work with him [selling clothes]. So he did. At first, they made the rounds of villages carrying clothing in their backpacks. Then my dad expanded and rented garages, where he displayed the clothes. We had three garages, and people came. It was the best time. There was no light, so people came with their cars and provided light with the headlights. It was great. So he worked that way for four or five years. My mother helped him, too. Now he's retired.

I grew up normally in Besançon. We were not very religious at home. We did the **Kiddish** on Friday nights. We celebrated the main festivals, Rosh Hashanah and Yom Kippur. Otherwise, we did not really receive a strict religious education. But at 13, something clicked in my mind, and I asked my dad to send me to a Jewish school in Strasbourg.

Why? Well, my second brother had married a Jewish girl, originally from Morocco but who lived in Strasbourg. I began to like this town and started seeing other Jews who were more religious. Besançon was a very traditional French town that was not very religious; when you live in the middle of that, you really don't see anything else. You live with it [assimilation], and you believe that this is what Judaism is all about. You don't think much more about it. So, seeing something else made me want to discover what true Judaism was, and after my bar mitzvah I asked my dad to send me to Strasbourg for a year. It was a Jewish school that was also a boarding school. I stayed there for more than a year, actually, five years. I discovered the big Jewish community of Strasbourg. Then, when I finished my studies, my dad asked me to come back and told me to decide what type of work I would do. So I came back to Besançon and worked for a year. He told me that I did good, and now that I knew the business, I could open my own shop. I decided to do it in Dijon because it was an hour from Besançon and also not that far from Paris. Moreover, I liked the community. I knew Dijon quite a bit because when we were young, we often had trips there, and the youth of the towns knew each other.

My father knew the religious world. His grandfather was a rabbi, so in Poland he lived it. With the war, he stopped everything. But I guess that he is proud that today one of his sons has had a purely religious education.

When I was in primary school in Besançon, we did not encounter any problems [with anti-Semitism] because we did not really stress our Jewish identity. For example, if I had to go to school on Saturdays, I did. I didn't have to face the problem. But I remember that when I was in high school, I was assaulted once because I was Jewish. At the time, I was 12 or 13. And it did hurt me. In fact, I think that it may have been one of the reasons that led me to leave. It was not the main reason, but you ask yourself: "What is it, exactly, to be a Jew?" You ruminate on that, and you tell yourself that you will learn what it means to be Jewish and why you are called "a damn Jew." You will learn your history, and it did help me.

In Strasbourg, I studied the religious subjects. We studied **Gemara**, **Rashi**, the **Mishna**, Chumash. I already knew how to read [Hebrew] since I had studied in the Talmud Torah. I was doing my prayers every day. I wore the **tephillin** regularly in Hebrew school. I was doing morning, afternoon, and evening prayers. So for five years I studied every day. It provided a foundation, made me acquire knowledge that I have now. Today I am **Shomer Shabbat**, and it is thanks to this education that I received. Of course, I also studied secular subjects. I did an economics Bac. So we did study economics and philosophy. None of those teachers were Jewish.

This Yeshiva [in Strasbourg] was opened in the early 1900s. It was a boarding school and an institution that welcomed all the Ashkenazim. Then there was the Moroccan immigration, so when I was there we were two Ashkenazim and 50 Moroccans. In the beginning, it was a problem being an Ashkenazi in this school. Because when you are in Besançon and you live in a small community, you do not feel the cleavage that exists between Ashkenazim and Sephardim. I wasn't aware of it at all. But when you arrive at the school, you are made to feel the difference. I remember that at the beginning, when I first arrived, I didn't say that I was Ashkenazi. I said that my dad was, but that my mother was Moroccan. I never had to defend myself physically, but when you first arrive you are alone, not knowing no one while the others all know each other, coming from the same country and the same towns like Meknès and Casablanca.

So I was alone. The other Ashkenazi was from Austria. I had two options in facing this environment: either I stay in my room alone, or I mingle with them and lie a little at the beginning about my origins and try to create some friendships. But after six months, in fact, I told them the truth, and it went very well. I stayed there for five years, and now those people are still my best friends.

We stayed there until we had our Bacs, until we were 18 or 19 years old. Then, some became [advanced religious] students. Not many, because we had not really gone there to study only the sacred texts. We were there to study the secular subjects, everything related to everyday life, and at the same time, sacred things. But the goal was to work, to get the Bac and go on to college. I went to college in Strasbourg. It was a non-Jewish environment, but the Jewish community was open [to newcomers], and I visited all the synagogues. My brother's family was there, and in the beginning I often went with them. I also went to the big synagogue of the great Ashkenazi Rabbi Gutval, who actually had been in Besançon. In college, I majored in marketing. Afterwards, I worked for a year there making commercials and for another two years in marketing.

I liked a lot of things about Strasbourg. First, being able to identify yourself as a Jew, then living as a Jew. You wear the kippa while taking a walk without being scared and not having to watch your back. There are a lot of Jews in Strasbourg, 16,000 [perhaps 12,000], and it is one of the biggest communities in France. So one is able to feel Jewish and also free. It was also possible to make friends there who were not Jewish. While studying at the Yeshiva, I didn't know any, but after the Bac, during college, I had some friends who were non-Jews. And it works out fine. When we had parties, we brought out friends and everyone got along really well. We would go to the library to study, or we went to have coffee, smoke a cigarette—Jews and non-Jews. And all the while I continued to wear the kippa.

Of course, there were protests at the university when there were problems with Israel. In France there always is a policy in favor of the Arabs that leads people to think that they are for the Arabs. You have to live with this. Even if you don't personally face it, you always feel the tension. There was a big movement called the UEJF [Union of Jewish Students of France] that was in my time there—the mid-1980s—very influential and very important in Strasbourg because the president of UEJF was from the city. So every time something was going on in Israel, we had protests in favor of Israel. For example, I remember that, led by the Strasbourg UEJF, which had gathered protesters from all over France, we marched and protested in front of the European Parliament.

Did I feel French? I didn't feel it at first. It's true that when you are in a religious environment, you think only about Judaism. You don't think about your nationality anymore. You study, and that's what you live. You don't ask yourself that question. Well, of course, I was young too. But it's true that even when I was 18, I didn't ask myself that question. I really started to feel French when I got my voter's card, and when I went to vote for the first time. [The choice for president] was between Mitterrand and Chirac. That was when I asked that question. You tell yourself, "OK, I have a good religious background, and now I will live this national fact of being French." So now when I am asked that question of feeling French, I feel French before anything else even though I follow Judaism thoroughly.

When I voted for the first time, it was for ideals. You are not economically affected because you are a student, but back then we had some problems with the Ministry of Education. We were questioning many things about the competitions, the exams. So you base your vote on that, and also on foreign policy—are they pro-Israeli or not? In choosing between Mitterrand and Chirac, we always heard that Mitterrand was a faithful friend and ally of Israel. And we didn't know Chirac very well. And the Jews always told you to vote for the Left. It's true that all the Jews in France always voted for the Left back then. Until Chirac. And now you will see that Jews vote for the Right.

I met my wife Yvette when I was at ORT [Organisation de Reconstruction et Travail], an institution for Jewish students to attend after the Bac. They teach all technology related subjects; and now in Strasbourg they even teach scientific subjects. Meeting her changed my life. She became my best friend back then when I was engaged to someone else who was from Nice. I was calling Yvette every day after I returned to Besançon. She even attended my engagement ceremony, and I realized at that time that I wasn't really in love with Céline, the girl I was engaged to. So I broke the engagement soon after and courted Yvette. I went to Strasbourg every weekend, and we eventually got engaged in August 1996. We were married in August 1997 in Morocco.

Yvette's father's family, the Wiseman family, is from Marrakesh, Morocco. They are very religious. Her grandfather was a rabbi but also was a spice merchant. On the other hand, her mother's family is Spanish, originally from Tangiers. In fact, my wife speaks Spanish. She and her siblings, a sister and two brothers, were born in Casablanca. All are traditional and religious. When we met, we didn't really mind the differences between the Ashkenazi and Sephardi cultures. I learned things their way; my prayers are the same as hers. But she is happy here. In fact, I was surprised that she adapted so quickly, because Casablanca is a large city with a big Jewish community. Dijon is much smaller, but she got used to it right away. Her parents and other members of her family, uncles and cousins, are still in Morocco. For those who have lived and worked in Morocco, it is hard to come to France. They have a lot of advantages there.

Her father is now retired. He was the manager for medical printing for a pharmaceutical company. He's not afraid to stay in Morocco. He's more afraid for us here in France. He believes that the Arabs in Morocco have more respect for the Jews than the French. Well, I don't really agree, but it's true that the King of Morocco needs the Jews. His right-hand men are Jews; one, an advisor to the King, was chosen both by him and by his father.[*] So Jews do have some power, and there is a lot of wealth that remains there. Although in the future.... There are not many Jews now: only 3,000, while before there were 250,000. But those remaining still have a political impact that is very important.

Historically, during World War II, Morocco was the only country that protected the Jews. When Hitler asked Mohammed V to give him the Jews, he refused. He told him, "You will not harm one hair of my Jews." So historically there is an important relationship between the Jews and the Moroccans.

Of course, with only 3,000 Jews in the country, if there is a war we never know what could happen. The Arab population could oust the king, and then you never know, with the fanaticism. And it can happen fast. Three thousand Jews is nothing. Some already have bought apartments in Israel and France and even in the United States.

But to return.... So I came to Dijon and the only thing on my mind was about business, to find out if I would be able to work and where I could open a shop. The only problem I faced when I started to work was whether to stay open during the Shabbat or not and, if yes, then how to do it. Well, fortunately, I found someone, and he worked Saturdays for me while I worked the weekdays.

Of course, as a Jew, one of the first things you do is find the synagogue. And back in those days there were families who were very welcoming when

---

[*] Serge Berdugo, a descendant of a family of Jewish royal advisors to the Moroccan throne, is the current Ambassador at Large.

I came and who invited me to their homes. I also met an old friend from Strasbourg whose name was Oliver Samuel. He and his wife lived across from the Barda family.* They were there too, and I did have friends here. So everything was fine. I was immediately well-integrated into the community in Dijon. I felt at ease right away.

But with the rabbi here, not really. There was no serious contact between us. His wife gets along very well with my wife. They call and talk to each other. When I see him, I greet him. I have a lot of respect for him as a man, but I think that he neglected his responsibilities as a rabbi. When you have religious people who arrive, you need to help them find their place in the synagogue. It's a place of worship, and when there is something wrong with the prayers—well, for example, the problem that we had was that the women were [seated] right behind the men, which was not done in Orthodox synagogues. Maybe it's not a tradition in the United States, but it is normally so here. And the presence of women there was creating some discomfort for us [the more religious Jews]. So, if you talk to the rabbi and tell him that things should be done in the normal way, and he says, "No, that is how the women want it, and that's it," then you tell yourself that you don't have a place there.

Well, that's how I felt. And there were other things, as well. But Haim [Slonim, the Lubavitch leader] never approached me. It was never his job to make people leave the synagogue. I remember that when we completely stopped going to the synagogue, Haim told us that he didn't want us to quit, that he wanted us to continue attending. And when he realized that we just didn't go to the synagogue, but were doing our prayers at home, that's when he offered us the use of Beit Habbad. But he kept going to the synagogue, until little by little he got the center established. And now he is always there [at the Lubavitch center].

I want it understood that I am not pointing fingers at anyone. I am talking about the rabbi, but it is also the institution [the Board of Directors]. The institution makes the decisions, but it makes the decisions with the advice of a religious authority, and the religious authority has the final say as to which way to go. I know why they didn't require the separation of the women. But now, during the Shabbat there isn't a minyan anymore, while before [at the beginning of the service] with us, there were enough. So what did they gain? In the Habbad center we have a minyan during the entire Shabbat.

In the beginning I was against the idea of leaving the synagogue. I told myself that we shouldn't leave. I have always had a synagogue in my life, and also I have my friends, whom I enjoy seeing. However, in the end I was

* The Bardas are a religious and influential family, now living in Paris.

alone in the synagogue, and I saw things that were really exasperating, so little by little I observed Shabbat here and there, and eventually I left, too. Some of my friends made the same choice. But Yvette still keeps in touch. She still tells me that it's a shame that we don't go to the synagogue. She has a lot of friends there, and she still goes. When there are conferences and things like that, she is the first to go. And I never tell her not to go. In fact, I like the fact that she goes and that she sees people.

But now I find it very hard to attend. I recently went for services in the morning, but when I saw that people looked at me in a disapproving way, I just left. But if I can work with the synagogue, if I am given the means to do what has to be done—and it does not have to be religious—but as long as there is a traditional aspect and we stay in touch with Judaism, then I am always for it. And it's not accidental that I live across from the synagogue, and that I stay there.

With the group [Lubavitch] what I like is that it is a big family. Tomorrow, if you need anything, they will be there for you. There are now about 20 [or 15] families, whole families with children at the school. My three children are there. We celebrate all the festivals together. Every time there is an activity, we are together. We invite each other for dinners. However, 20 families are not very many. Of course, it would be better if there were more. But, thanks to God, we have a person [Haim Slonim] who offers courses, so we can study. We have class every day. We also have the Jewish school, which is something great for a town like Dijon. Now my daughter, who is eight years old, can read Rashi.* It's fabulous. You tell yourself that thanks to these things, the tradition is maintained.

But my children are comfortable with others. During the week they play some sports outside the school with non-Jews. I want them to be French citizens who can freely practice Judaism. That is my whole idea. And I am comfortable with the standards of the secular classes taught at the school. They have good standards. All of the children who come out of the school and now got to secular schools are in the top 2 or 3 per cent of their classes. My children will go on, like the others, to secular schools. That is, for the time being. They are young yet, but when they turn 16 and 17 and start dating, I think that it is important that they date Jews. Also, they will leave one day. Dijon is a small town, and all the young people are leaving.

It's clear that I have to leave. I will try first of all to go back to Strasbourg, perhaps in four years at the most, when my oldest daughter must further [her secular and Jewish] studies. Of course, my business is doing great here.

---

* A great medieval rabbi and scholar who devised his own Hebrew-related script.

There aren't any problems. So if I go, I'll rent another shop [men's clothing store] and do the same thing. And keep this one, too. I already have people who can take charge. Yvette, too, has studied and become a lawyer. She also will work.

I feel safe in France. When we go to Israel and people tell us that we are in danger in France, as Jews living in provincial areas, we don't really feel the same as Jews living in Paris or other large cities. We don't really feel that we are in danger. But I don't really think about issues such as the large numbers of Arabs in France and their attitudes towards Israel and Jews. It's a very sensitive issue, and I don't ask myself such questions. I am a bit afraid to think about it: six million Arabs and half a million Jews in France. Will the Jew have his place in France in the future? I hope so. Historically, the Jews have a very long past in France. There has been a presence ever since the Middle Ages [in some regions], and I hope that there will always be Jews. It's true that we feel the threat, but we still practice our Judaism and have our synagogues, our religious places, our kosher restaurants, and nobody bothers us. So, right now, I think that Jews can fully practice their Judaism while being French citizens. But when the government takes anti-Israeli positions, this does create problems. And the media, too, especially the media, when you know that they are only showing one side of what is really happening, it is very annoying. You really want to call them and sometimes even insult them and tell them that they are liars. This is awful.

When I think about the United States, well, it's a good thing that Israel can count on American support. Now, there is always the fear we have of only having the support of one country, because if you lose that support in the future, to whom do you turn? That's why I sometimes criticize the policies of Israel. They should also turn toward Europe and have the same relationship that they have with Americans. I support the United States, and I am always concerned with what is happening there, because we are lucky to have them. But it's like holding only one joker. The day you play it, you have nothing else.

In Lebanon [2006] Israel was attacked and naturally responded. It had to be done. But I am critical of the way in which the government acted. I am not Israeli, but I do believe that they made a lot of mistakes, and I hope that these will be fixed. But they showed the world that they will defend themselves, because if they don't no one else will.

Of course, I do think that the French government is afraid of the Muslims who are here. And there are a lot of things that prove it. For example, in Dijon two Arabs in a car killed two young girls. I don't know how it happened. Anyway, the Arabs went to jail for four years. If they had been French, it would have been 15 years. But it was two Arabs, and the French are afraid of them. There was a riot here.

When I see Arabs in gangs, it is scary. This summer we went to the beach, and there were Arabs on the entire beach. We left immediately. Yesterday I went to the park to play ball with my children. I threw the ball, and four Arab kids came and just picked up the ball and started to play with it. They thought that my children were alone, and then they saw that I was there, too. Otherwise, they would have just taken the ball and left with it. We are constantly assaulted, not because we are Jews—we are all assaulted.

But I am proud of being French because I live here and take full advantage of the system. I am here and I respect the country. In our prayers, or in our Shabbat prayers, we have a prayer for the Republic of France. Why? Because as Jews we still feel that we are French citizens, and in the Torah, it is said that you have to first respect the country's laws.

Marcel and Leah Tobis

This professional couple of Ashkenazi and Sephardi backgrounds
was brought back to active involvement in religious practices and
traditions by Dijon's Lubavitch and the families who support them.
They express the uneasy and somewhat ambiguous relations between
the Lubavitch and Dijon's other Jews.

September 2006

MARCEL: I am Ashkenazi in origin. My parents came from Bessarabia, from Kishinev in Moldova. But I was born in Marseille. My father came to France in 1928 to study, then my mother followed in 1935 to get married to my father. They were cousins. My father studied at the École Supérieure de Commerce in Montpellier. He became an accountant and worked in Marseille. My mother was a housewife. I had a sister. The Jewish things that we did were [celebrating] Rosh Hashanah and Yom Kippur. Our orientation was pretty liberal. I went to study at the Talmud Torah, but I was never very religious.

I was born in 1951 in Marseille and went to the normal schools there. My Bac is in philosophy. That was in 1969. Then I studied dentistry at the university in Marseille. After spending a year in the military, I completed my thesis and started work in 1979. My practice was in Marseille.

I met my wife in Cannes. When I went on holiday, I met a woman from Dijon who told me she would introduce me to girls from there. The first two I met didn't work out. The third one called me and said that she was in Cannes, and if I wanted to meet her I should go there. I went, and that was it.

LEAH: Unlike Marcel, I am of Sephardic origins. I was born in Casablanca, Morocco, but I have very few memories of life there. We left when I was four or five years old. It was not safe. I do remember that on our way back from kindergarten, [Arab children] would throw stones at us, and we ran or our parents would have to pick us up at school by car.

I was born in 1958. We left in 1962 or 1963. We settled in Grenoble. It was nice there. There was my aunt and my uncle and their three children, all on my mother's side. They found an apartment [for us] close to them, and we started in France from there. My father remained in Morocco for a time before joining us. I was in school for a year in Grenoble, then we moved to a small village in the Drôme, called Saranbère. By coincidence, the mayor there was Jewish. My father was an accountant, and he had found a job there. We stayed for seven years, and there I attended primary school.

I had seven siblings, but it was great! I was the fourth one. My mother managed the house well. But the oldest one didn't help. She was a "princess."

The boys didn't help much either. My mother has always been very traditional. She is from the Cohen family where there were rabbis, so they are very traditional. My father was much more liberal until he retired. Now he has come back to religion. But at home it was our mom who chose our lifestyle, so she gave us good foundations in the traditions. However, when I left the house, I didn't do anything [about practicing her religion].

My mother taught the traditions but not Hebrew, not the history. She did the holidays, the cooking, the culture. Sometimes we sang the prayers. But she did only things assigned to women. However, the boys went to the Talmud Torah. I accompanied them, but I never went.

After finishing primary school, I left the village to attend junior high school, a boarding school in Romans, about 50 kilometers away.

Employment became difficult after 1968, and, as a result, my father moved to Dijon with the family to work. Eventually, he was transferred to Cannes, and I went with my parents while my older brothers remained in Dijon at the university there. I went to nursing school in Cannes and did my first year of work there. Then I moved back to Dijon for a number of reasons, including the fact that a sister lived there. By the time I was 33, I hadn't gotten married. I didn't want to get married. I didn't want children. I had no notion of time.

Then I met Marcel when on holiday in Cannes. We both married late; I was 33, as I said, and he was 40.

MARCEL: The civil marriage was at Marseille and the religious one at Cannes.

LEAH: He was a dentist practicing in Marseille, and I was a nurse in Dijon. We each stayed in our own city.

MARCEL: When my first son, Michael, was born in April 1992, I came to Dijon. A second son is now almost nine.

LEAH: Yes. He didn't want to come until there were kids.

MARCEL: It's not easy when you have first started. When I came to Dijon, I did two replacements [of other dentists]. Then, in September 1995, I settled in the medical center and brought my equipment from Marseille. So I started all over again, from scratch.

LEAH: I worked at a medical center that housed only doctors, paramedics, and nurses. I opened an office there in 1990 with a colleague. We worked as independents. That is, patients call me to provide nursing medical care either in their homes or in the office. I also work with doctors who do research, and I do everything that is related to paramedics.

When we came here, we didn't know anyone. When I started as an independent nurse, I had no contacts. I settled in an area that was under construction. As people moved in, they saw that I was there, and this allowed me little by little to become known. As I said, there were two of us [nurses]. At first, I would fill in somewhere to make some money while she managed the office; then she filled in while I managed the office. We did this until we became established. After a year, the business took off, and we didn't have to fill in anymore.

We had no problems as a couple in a mixed marriage. I didn't practice religion, and my husband only went to the synagogue for Yom Kippur. I knew about the Jewish community here in Dijon because this is where I grew up, spent my adolescence. When I lived with my parents, I went to the synagogue for all the holidays. So I knew members of the community. I was a leader of some of the youth groups. But I was not a believer, so I stopped practicing and was separated from the community. I just didn't want to go.

When we were first married, we had no contacts. Maybe Marcel did because he had some friends who were dentists and also Jewish, but I had no contacts. We decided to mix with the Jewish community after the Slonims contacted us several times. At first I didn't want to bother. And then Hannah [Slonim] asked me if I wanted to send my son to her school, and I said no because I didn't want my son to become a Lubavitch. She made several more attempts. She told me it was not a Lubavitch school. She told me that if I see something that bothers me, or that takes too much time, then just take him out. So that's how, little by little, we were brought together by a group of people who were not Lubavitch but who sent their children to the school. So we made friends with the parents of the children. And we found ourselves in a group that we mix with quite regularly.

It was the Lubavitch who brought us into the Jewish community; it was their kindness. They are nice. They don't ask for anything and they offer a lot.

Michael was eight years old when he started in the Lubavitch's school. That was in 2000. Now he is finished there, and he is in junior high. The second one is still at the school. The school lacks money, but the teaching is excellent.

MARCEL: Yes, that is true. But we are not Lubavitch.

LEAH: Well, you can't go to that school and go to the services, or to whatever they do, and then say that you are not a supporter. There's a limit. And, on top of that, you make donations.

My eldest son is a terrific student because he received a good foundation at the school. The teachers, both women, are non-Jews. They are very devoted, and we wonder what drives them because they are not well-paid and the parents are very demanding. But the teachers comply. I think they have faith in what they do. Young women travel from Strasbourg to teach Hebrew and Jewish history and traditions. They also are Lubavitch.

I think that the children are very happy at the school. They love their school, and they don't want to change it. My oldest son goes back regularly on Wednesdays, when he doesn't have school all day, to see his teachers and plunge back into that environment. It wasn't really hard for him to adapt to a new school after he left. However, he wants to go to a Jewish high school, but there are none here in Dijon. He did his bar mitzvah here with the Lubavitch. He isn't learning Jewish things now, but he goes to the Lubavitch services on Saturdays. I don't go, but his father does.

MARCEL: I go on Saturday mornings after work. I started going after my father died. When he died in 2000, I had to say the **Kaddish** in the synagogue. Then when the children went to the Jewish school, I followed to help them. I don't have anything against the synagogue or the rabbi. He was very good, very proper. And I always had good relations with others in the synagogue, but it was better for the family and the children to be in the school and to do services with the Lubavitch. There are about ten families who go now. There are prayers at the Slonims on Friday nights, and I often go.

LEAH: I don't go to the services because my beliefs haven't changed. I am not at ease singing the songs, for example. I feel like I'm cheating. However, I keep kosher, and I celebrate the holidays for the children. I started keeping kosher because I wanted to invite my family. It had to be kosher, otherwise, they couldn't visit. My parents only eat kosher, and so do my sister and her family who visit from the United States. Then I continued after Michael's bar mitzvah, though it's complicated to do.

MARCEL: What have the Lubavitch given us? Well, just the fact of opening the school. And they invite us often, without any problem. They are very friendly. When I need something [something specific or general advice], I ask and they find a way of resolving it. Both of the Slonims are very devoted, very involved in what they do, working for the community. They pray a lot, too. They believe a lot in their prayers. They believe a lot in God's help.

LEAH: And I like their dream. They don't ask for anything, but we feel obliged to give, because we see that they have needs. For the school, there are donors. Relative to what the school costs, what we give is the same amount as for any private school. We pay the same as if we put them in a Catholic school here, for example.

Sometimes they suggest changes of this or that. Once they said it would be nice if we put mezuzahs in the house. They wanted me to put one outside, but I refused. I put one on the inside of the door and another in the children's room. But I made a mistake when I placed the one on the door on the wrong side. When Haim came, he said that it was okay not to put it on the outside but at least place it correctly on the inside, so I changed it.

In general with the Lubavitch group, it's nice. We have a lot of friends.

MARCEL: I think that it would be good to have only one community—that is, where everyone prays together. It would be simple, more friendly, and it would create less problems, because now there are disagreements.

LEAH: I didn't really have any problems [with the larger community], but I didn't feel very comfortable. Once I had taken care of the children, I didn't expect anything from the community. ... It's a shame because the children will not meet the other [Jewish children in the wider community]. It is complicated to take them to the Talmud Torah classes when both parents work. There is nothing for adolescents now. And the Lubavitch really don't offer anything [for teenagers]. I don't even know if they can keep their school going because each year they have financial problems and each year they cut it close. Larger Jewish schools are financed by the state, but you have to have a certain number [of students per class—possibly eight or nine] to obtain that.

I do hope that the Lubavitch in Dijon will last because they make people who were far away [from practicing Judaism] want to come back. But I can't guarantee that they will last. The Slonims say that they are going to stay. They certainly want to.

On the larger question of French Jews, I'm not sure that it's not hard to be a Jew in France, despite what Marcel says about it. I think that if we want to be a Jew in France, and if we want things to be easy, we can't say anything. When we display [our culture], it makes people run away. And then we need to have the knowledge to be able to explain. Also, there is a culture in France that says that one must be wary of the Jew. Of course, some of my clients know that I am a Jew.

MARCEL: Some of my patients know that I am Jewish. In any case, I'm absent during Yom Kippur, so they should know. But, if people ask, I tell them.

LEAH: We don't hide it, but we don't display it.

MARCEL: Regarding Israel, I think that their government did well during the attack on Hezbollah in Lebanon [summer 2006]. It wasn't handled well militarily, but politically it was perhaps a unique opportunity to get close to Egypt, Saudi Arabia, Kuwait, and the Arab Emirates because these Arab states will be fatally opposed to the Persians [Iran]. During the war I listened to the radio every morning.

LEAH: I went on the Internet to read news that was not French.

MARCEL: I was not happy with the news in France or with the French government.

LEAH: They are traitors.

MARCEL: I wouldn't go that far.

LEAH: Oh, yes. That is just politics. The French government is better off making friends with the Arabs. The French policy is pro-Arab, and there is no doubt about it.

We have some friends who are not Jewish. They remained friends during the war because they don't care. It's not their problem. They don't realize that France is a country that also can be targeted. They think that they are safe because they are in France.

OTHERS

Consisting of as many as 50 families or households, the members of this group are Jewish but choose not to join any established community. Their reasons include indifference to religion, adherence to a more liberal form of Judaism unavailable in Dijon, or simply because they are in a transitional phase of life.

Jean-David and Arielle Attal

The Attals, French-born children of Algerian immigrants and a mixed marriage, are representative of a younger generation of French Jews: well-educated, professional, cosmopolitan, open-minded, widely traveled, conversant in several languages, and attuned to the emerging globalization of economy and culture. Though knowledgeable and proud of their heritage and traditions, the Attals find those roots remain part of their history and little of their current practice. Although they recently relocated to Paris, they were comfortable living in Dijon but did not find it necessary to be an active part of the Jewish community there. Their views, however, provide insights into the thinking and attitudes of this new generation.

September 2006

ARIELLE: I was born in 1963 in Meaux, in Seine-et-Marne, the first child of my family born in France. Both of my parents were born in Algeria, my father in a small village called Soukaras, my mother in a bigger town, near the coast. They came in 1962 during the repatriation of the French [following the Algerian War for Independence] and settled in a small village 40 kilometers from Paris. My father was a teacher, but things didn't go so well. He was 42 at the time; he had left his mother in Algeria because she hadn't wanted to leave. It was a difficult experience for him, and soon he fell into depression. According to my mother, this wasn't helped by the fact that he also had difficult students. Though he taught in a primary school, there apparently was anti-Semitism directed at him.

Eventually we moved to a larger town—Meaux, nearby—and there I grew up. And there were no problems. Eventually, the whole family from Algeria moved to this town. There, my maternal grandfather founded the first synagogue. He took care of it. From time to time, a rabbi came, then eventually settled there. So the community grew little by little.

The whole community came from Algeria, the rabbi, too. Unlike my husband's experience, we lived a sort of autonomous existence. We had a kosher butcher shop, the synagogue, a community that set the pace of our lives. My life was caught up in routines that included my grandparents, uncles and aunts, cousins. We all lived with a strong Judaism.

We followed tradition, such as the culinary. The girls didn't go to classes at the Talmud Torah, but the boys went. The boys also did their bar mitzvahs. In a way, it was liberal, too, but not in the modern meaning of the word. For example, in the synagogue, women sat in the back, but there was no barrier between men and women. The synagogue was a small villa that my grandfather and others had bought, and the entire community managed to fit inside.

There were no problems with the neighbors. The 50 or 60 people plus the rabbi in the community lived their own lives, observing the Shabbats and all the holidays. There were very important times when the entire family got together and when the women prepared traditional dishes. They gave me very powerful memories.

I worked in my hometown for a time, but after I was married at 26, we moved to Paris.

JEAN-DAVID: My father's father was born in Algeria into a modest family of people who worked in trade. They had a low level of education. He became the intellectual of the family because he learned to read and write. His son, my father, was the first to get a formal education; he went to engineering school in France. In 1962, however, the family was forced to go to France.

My father, who had just married my mother that year and was still in engineering school in Grenoble, had to take charge of his parents when they arrived without anything. They moved first to Paris, and eventually we moved to Lyon. There, we more or less became part of a Jewish community that was alternatively Sephardi and Ashkenazi.

We didn't have much religion, for that matter; let's say, the people were quite traditional but more in practice than in education. There certainly was belief, but it wasn't something that you discussed with them. You were in a community to practice [Judaism], and it shaped your life. I remember my grandmother making the big cleanup in her house before the holidays. It was her faith. It was her life. It was her community.

My grandfather worked in the community for a few years. Then we moved to Paris and lived very close to the liberal Jewish community of rue Copernic. We were very fond of it because we appreciated those people, especially the rabbi who came from England with a very broad and open cultured mind. His name was [Michael] Williams. And I must say that once you have started living in this [kind of community] and understanding what this is about, getting explanations—and with feelings of openness and understanding of the world around you—it is very powerful.* We still raise our children with, and keep the family in, the same spirit and traditions that are more or less the traditions that my parents had. However, we are fond of those practices that are quite open and provide a lot of cultural understanding.

---

* Author Robert Weiner agrees, having attended services at Copernic and having interviewed Rabbi Williams in 1980.

I must, by the way, say that my mother was converted to Judaism. She was a member of a French family that came from Brittany. They were Catholic in origin, although non-practicing. She converted in an Orthodox synagogue. That absolutely was not encouraged, but she went through the entire course and as a result probably knows Judaism better than many Jewish-born women.

So we had this climate and atmosphere of Jewish celebrations with the whole family, with the cousins and so on. We had a farmhouse in the country where we invited everybody. And at the same time, we were probably not as close to the Orthodox as many Sephardic Jews, for example.

By the memories collected in the family celebrations, we are able to go back in our genealogy to the roots, which was that of an Italian lady, probably originally coming from the Spanish Marranos and called Portuguese. To say something of her origins, she went to the Tripoli area, which was an Italian colony [in North Africa] at that time. There, the old family grew in that part of eastern Algeria. On the other side, my paternal grandfather was of Berber origin, probably originating in Egypt.

On my mother's side we have a family coming from a farm in Brittany. According to a family history written by my great-grandfather, the oldest son in each generation inherited the farm while the others got nothing and had to go into the police, the *gendarmerie*, or become teachers. One of those teachers left Brittany for southern France and formed a branch of the family there. That is the reason why my mother completed her studies in Grenoble.

I've heard mixed stories about how Arabs and Jews got along in Africa. There were family stories about a kind of segregation, with everybody living in their own communities, but there are also stories of a world where people lived side by side in peace and not troubled by each other. That's Arabs and Jews. The French, however, comprised a small class of people who were the wealthiest and who didn't mix at all with the Arabs and the Jews. They were probably the objects of hatred by the Arabs because they were the colonizers. But the Jews were citizens, and my family certainly considered themselves French. They were French Jews who resented extremely strongly the fact that they were bereft of French nationality during World War II.[*] But they were French and they always felt that way, even though they suffered a lot during the Vichy period.

ARIELLE: My father did not, but I know that my aunt—who died recently—told us that she was studying law and she was forced to stop her

---

[*] In October 1940, the Vichy regime abrogated the Crémieux Decree, which had given most Algerian Jews French citizenship in 1870.

studies because the laws of Vichy excluded Jews. The same happened to my mother's sister. She told me that her older sisters were excluded from primary school at that time.

JEAN-DAVID: My family never talked about it, although my brother told me that our father's grandfather, who was a big guy, suffered a lot when he had to leave the sidewalk when an Arab was passing. A Jew and an Arab could not walk on the same pavement; the Jew had to be down on the street while the Arab was above.

After the war and during the 1960s, I had not really heard anything specific about relations between Jews and Arabs, but my father was affected by the intolerance and absolute extremism of the Algerian independence fighters at that time. They refused any kind of discussion, negotiation, or compromise—but not especially towards Jews. It was a civil war against the French, against the colonizers.

When my family had to leave, they didn't have time to take anything with them. My father says that he talked to his own father and tried to explain to him that it was necessary to leave and that his father told him that he was wrong, that everyone would live in peace and there would be no problem. Then one day, people came to see them and told them that they had information that they would be slaughtered that night. So they left immediately and without anything. They left everything behind. I wasn't told about these facts as strongly related to being Jews but to being French.

When both families came here, they started with little. Arielle says that her parents came with one suitcase. They [were met] with contempt from the French. They were the people who were not accepted. They were slower, they were funny, they weren't elegant. They spoke loudly, and they were ridiculed.

My grandfather was granted a loan for opening a small store, and the same people who had given him the idea opened a supermarket across the street a year afterwards. So my grandfather went bankrupt, and my father had to pay back the loan. Until the last night of his life, my grandfather lived with the fear that someone would come looking for him.

Those first years of the Algerians in France were years of humiliation, years of denial. Yet these people worked harder than others and made their way through medical and engineering schools. They took on economic responsibilities and didn't do it because they were more accepted, but just the opposite.

ARIELLE: The conversations that I remember when I was small—the conversations of my uncles, aunts, and grandparents at home—were very nostalgic about what they left behind in Algeria. But I have no memories of accounts that reflected differences or conflicts that might have arisen between the Jewish community and the Arabs. Both communities lived together in harmony in Algeria. These are the memories of my grandfather and my father. They go far back.

But, yes, they did have to leave hastily, and it was a tearing experience for them. My entire family related what a terrible experience it was. I don't really know if it was hard for the family economically at first in France. My father worked in an office, so we always lived comfortably, but it was not much. We lived in cheap houses, but we lived comfortably.

Some time before they left Algeria, my maternal grandfather, who was the patriarch of the family, had a wish for the entire family to go to Israel. He went to live a bit in Israel with his two oldest sisters, who were married with children, and he tried to integrate. If it had worked, the whole family would have gone to Israel. But it was very hard. They were in a small town near the desert. I still have part of my family, cousins of my mother, who live there. I had one uncle who was a tailor who lived there. He had three or four children at the time. He was a small, fragile man, and he had to terrace land and labor as a mason. It didn't work. So everyone came to France.

The family left [Algeria] a little before 1962. They must have felt that something was going on, and they wanted to leave. Eventually, we all found ourselves on the outskirts of Paris.

JEAN-DAVID: I think that it has been equally difficult for these people to suffer economic difficulties as it was to suffer the fact of their rejection by the French.

As for the other Algerian Jews, I don't exactly know. They established different communities and stayed in these communities. They grouped in different parts of France, in some poor suburbs of Paris, as well as Marseille, for instance. They kept to themselves. I have a strong feeling that my children will do better.

I have heard that the repatriation of the Algerian Jews to France was the best immigration in Jewish history because so many Ashkenazim had been killed and this gave the newcomers the chance of a better future in France. The Ashkenazim were still suffering, were not sure that they had legitimate rights, were still shy and ashamed in their corners, and sad. And you had these people arriving without any shame, speaking loud, proud about what they were, and militant. It changed things.

I didn't experience difficulties because I didn't live in a city where there were a lot of Jews. But I remember that when I was seven years old my school was collecting money for Bangladesh. I had not brought my money soon enough, and the teacher said, "I'm not surprised because he's a Jew and Jews are cheap." My parents were scandalized, and they went to see the teacher and the director of the school to demand apologies. They [the apologies] were made in the class and that was it. Nobody spoke about it again. You still have that kind of behavior from people sometimes. But you also have Sephardim fighting very strongly and aggressively against that kind of behavior and anything that looks like it.

There is in France, as in many countries, a background of racism. It can be against Jews, against Muslims, against Africans. You always have in France 20 or 25 per cent of the population who are inclined to accuse others when their country is in trouble. Instead of saying, "Let's face our responsibilities," [they blame] the rich, the poor, the Arabs, the Jews, the Blacks, the Americans—who knows what? But it's never themselves who are to blame. And then you have a number of political parties who say, "You're right. It's not your fault. It's just the others, and they are ruining your life." Is it more against the Jews than the others? No. You have, for example, a large part of the population that believes that the African immigration in France is too large and is the root of their problems, and that if you had less Arabs, or if you had fewer Blacks, France would be better.

There also is a newer problem, which is that the second or third generation of Muslim North African immigrants have developed some groups who are openly anti-Semitic. About ten years or so ago, there were the bombings or fires in synagogues in Paris and Marseille in the suburbs where Jews and Muslims co-existed. This type of thing is decreasing rather than expanding right now. We have a situation that is a little bit more peaceful. So, we do not have anti-Semitic violence right now, but it is there, in the background, in the heads of many people. We have to face it. Also, this is a country that is strongly Catholic, where the Church has played a role for generations and generations. At the moment, [anti-Semitism] is regressing rather than expanding, but it is not disappearing.

Personally, I know that I can make a place for myself. It's just a question of will. I still have the feeling that I am not particularly protected, but if I want to do something somewhere else, I could. I do not fear things particularly. The quality of life in France and the living standards are very high. The quality of life here in Dijon is very high. I could certainly make more money somewhere else, but that doesn't mean that life would be better.

In recent years, we lived in other countries. We lived three years in Belgium; we lived in Germany. We enjoyed it a lot, so it's not that we don't know what other countries are like. We know what opportunities there could be. We wouldn't have an economic problem with moving to another country. My wife would be okay with it, my kids more than enthusiastic. So that isn't a problem. But there is nothing that is pushing us out of France. Of course, there is always the possibility of the development of hate feelings and behavior. And if they developed over time, we might say that we would be more comfortable somewhere else.

ARIELLE: I think that I agree with Jean-David's point of view, but I think that we are a bit different because we are not integrated into the community. As I described earlier, I was integrated into a community during my entire childhood. I was a living part of a community. I took care of the children; my brother took care of the adolescents. We were truly part of the community. After our marriage when we came back to the Parisian area, we were not really in the center of Paris. There was no community, and we never really tried to get close to one. Now, the community of Dijon is nearby, but we never go. I don't know why. It's because we don't want to go. That's the way it is.... We are Jewish, but internally. We are not Jewish externally.

JEAN-DAVID: Yes, we're not Jews within a community. That is because we have liked some open and enlightened communities so much that we don't feel at ease anywhere else but with them. We've experienced this in Paris, in Geneva, and we will not go to a community with narrow religious practices.

I work for an international company that supplies warehouses with software and automated conveyor systems. The few people in the company who have an in-depth knowledge of the company's know-how travel a lot. So I am in Belgium, the Netherlands, France, Germany, the United Kingdom, sometimes in China or the United States. I live in a circle of businessmen and try to convince them to acquire multimillion dollar installations for their warehouses.

We have never traveled to Israel together as a family. We both have been to Israel several times. We haven't in recent years. Neither of the children have been to Israel. There will come a time, certainly. We have nothing against this. It's just that it never came up. But when there are difficulties for Israel, we are especially concerned. We are in a country where the political parties—probably more those who claim to act for the poor in the world, and so on—after the Six Day War developed the idea that the despised and the poorest were the Arabs and the Jews were the despisers and the contemptuous and the aggressive party who represented capital and power. And they were to be fought.

France has a very long tradition of friendship with Arab countries. This has degenerated more than often into a pro-Arab and anti-Israeli political line. In the last few years, there has been a little more questioning from the media, although there are still a number of journalists who are the root of the [old] attitude and who are still in place. The French press has been particularly responsible, indeed, in the development of the Second Intifada by the images they have been showing and spreading across the media. At the same time, probably one part of the press has been trying to look at things with a more objective state of mind in the past few years.

An example is that the press was impressed by what happened when Israel left the Gaza Strip [2005]. They have a view of the Israeli army that was not one they had before. They were further impressed by what happened last summer [2006] with Hezbollah, by the fact that the party that Israel was facing was not at all a party with naked feet and living in misery but a party armed at a high level and with no openness at all in terms of negotiation. So, there are now a number of people saying that this is not as clear-cut as we have always been told.

France has always had to cope with Arab countries because Arab countries in North Africa, the Maghreb, are all ex-colonies, and this has had a major impact on the political attitude of France. Also, if you want votes, you have to consider minorities, and you have strong minorities here that you have to cope with. At the same time also, there was a development at the end of the 1980s and the beginning of the 1990s in the large suburbs of the big cities of an extremist form of Islam and a total rejection of everything that was connected to France. There were a number of bombings, for example, and France developed a total refusal of this kind of attitude and behavior. Then, in the past few years, Islam and its expression have been coordinated, and there has been a certain transformation. When the two French journalists were kidnapped in Iraq [2004], with the charge by the kidnappers that the French law against the wearing of the veil had to be revoked because it was an insult to Islam, suddenly the Muslims in France saw the real possibility of being totally rejected by the people as being associated with the Iraqi kidnappers. The Muslims here responded by saying, "Please, keep us out of this! We have our problems, but we cope. We don't want to be seen like this. And free them because they are not enemies of what you are doing." The Muslims saw the point where they were rejects of the national community, and that they don't want.

You know, at first, I didn't think that the French government worked reasonably well at trying to protect the Jewish community. They were surprised [by anti-Semitic activities], but then they acted. But, you know, I am quite sure that militant Islamic organizations were very infiltrated by the French police in the 1990s. There hasn't been anything like what happened in England. So even if the authorities were surprised when some teenagers or young adults who were not members of one of the militant organizations launched Molotov cocktails at a synagogue, the situation was easily mastered.

My children never had any difficulties at school and at other times. This is true whether in France or in Belgium. In Belgium, there is a law allowing religious instructors to come to school, and my kids were the only two Jews in the school. So a Jewish religious instructor came from Brussels once a week, a two-hour drive to and fro. There were some Catholics, some Protestants, some Muslims, and there were classes on morals and philosophy. Everybody knew everything, and it was very open. For example, "Raphael is not here today because he is having a celebration. Who knows anything about Yom Kippur?" Everything was open and even if, for instance, the Belgium press was strongly anti-Israeli, Jews didn't have to suffer from racism there.*

But we don't ever discuss our feelings about Israel or the United States at work or with our neighbors. These are subjects that we don't bring up.

My kids don't want to be seen as Jews. They are not ashamed to say that they are Jews if they have to say it, but they don't want to bring it up as an open subject. For instance, we had a discussion with Raphael [15-year-old son] a few years ago when we went to Yom Kippur [services], because he didn't want to tell the school he was going to a religious event. He wanted to say that he was going to be absent because of a family event. We said that it was religious and that everybody knows what it's about. We don't have any problem with it. We told him that you don't have to claim to be Jewish all the time, but you don't have to be ashamed of it either. Well, he was very uneasy about it, but finally he said, "Okay, let's do it like that." After that, he felt comfortable. The kids do stay home for Yom Kippur. They go to the synagogue. Actually, we only celebrate Yom Kippur.

You asked what I think about the United States and how I think the French view the United States. Well, the French admire the United States. They are sometimes a little bit bothered by the way it does things and by its attitude—that if something works well for them, it will work anywhere else the same way. The fact that there is no recognition [by Americans] that some people could be different and have their own way of thinking or doing is sometimes a problem. It is something that you can see in politics, for instance.

At some point, it is very important for the French to develop their own point of view, and the fact that the French are different from the United States is good in terms of independence. But I see very positive ways of living, thinking, and working of the French and the Americans, and I don't think that either side is totally correct or totally incorrect.

Of, course, American culture is very imposing. You can either accept it or refuse it. It's a little like the German [culture], by the way. The Germans tend to project a feeling of strength as something you cannot resist. It is difficult to find your own position when you are facing a culture that looks

---

* There have been a number of anti-Semitic acts in Belgium in recent years.

very strong. Facing the imposing American culture creates a certain way of acting and reacting among the French.

Personally, I have always had good connections with American colleagues, and I understand their way of working. This includes partners, clients, and competitors. I could live a few years in the United States. I wouldn't want to live there permanently because I would miss living in this old city and the France that is so familiar.

Alex Miles

New York-born Alex Miles, married to a French woman and a long-time resident of France, is the only American male interviewed in this book. An activist veteran of the culture-changing 1960s, he has been at various times a chef and baker, restaurateur, educator, radio personality, and author. He provides perceptive insights into French Jewry and, in fact, the French generally. He is particularly good at comparing French and American attitudes and behaviors on a variety of subjects: religion, race, politics, economics, and change. While not a full member of the Dijon community, he has the advantage of seeing it as a Jew and an outsider.

June 2005

From the viewpoint of being a Jew in the Bronx—oh, there were fights! Where we lived was a dividing line between our enclave of semi-detached houses on one side and the projects on the other side where Puerto Ricans, blacks, and poor whites lived. We moved there in the late 1950s when there were gang wars, big metal trash cans being thrown through house windows, that sort of thing.

There was a kid who called me a dirty Jew, so I beat him up.

The funniest thing that happened was in fifth grade when one of my best friends during the recreation period one day came up and punched me. When I asked him what that was for, he said that was because I killed Jesus. I asked, "Who was this Jesus guy?" Evidently, he had discovered that Jews were responsible for the death of Jesus. But that's what happened. Unfortunately, we're no longer friends.

What I really remember as a kid, we had a good time. I had a good childhood. I was born in Manhattan in 1947. My mother's family had come from Russia earlier in the century; my paternal grandparents came from Poland. We were a typical Jewish working-class family. My father used to take pride in saying that we were lower middle class, you know, with the emphasis on middle class. But he went through several businesses. He was a business failure, really. My mother kept the books, and when the businesses failed, she worked elsewhere.

What's interesting is that I always worked. I worked from when I was about ten years old, doing little things for neighbors for money. When I was 13, I got my first real job, in a pizzeria. I got paid $10 a week, and I was happy. Then, at Christmas season, we got a lot of work and sold a lot of pizza. Instead of $10, my pay was reduced to $8. So I said, "Fuck you!" and

"Good-bye." And that was it. The next year I became a plumber's assistant. The fellow I worked for was remarkable, a great philosopher. He said that if he stopped a leak, he had done his job. That's it. I think that our politicians could take something from that.

I went to high school in the Bronx and graduated in 1965. I have lots of stories, but something I can say with a lot of pride is that I wrote the senior play. It was a typical comedy-drama of good versus evil.

The first politically conscious thing I remember doing was when Nelson Rockefeller ran for governor and I had the pleasure of tearing his election signs down from telephone poles. But what was really significant from that time, and that still makes me cry, was 22 November 1963. I remember how, when the announcement came over the loudspeaker in school that [President John F.] Kennedy was shot, everything just stopped. People started walking around like sleepwalkers and crying, and teachers and no one knew what the hell to do. It was remarkable—all of a sudden we were at the same level: teachers, students. There were no differences anymore. We were all human beings touched by the same tragedy. What had I expected from Kennedy? Hope. Hope for something better. What he said made sense. You know, there was something about to happen in the United States. It was remarkable, but his death put an end to that dream.

As for being Jewish, in the home we did all the holidays. My grandfather went from store to store, buying the foods, bargaining for the best price. At one place, I remember, he bought something; the price was $10. Later, he said to me with sneaky pride that he gave the merchant eight $1 bills rolled up. It was his great lesson in doing business. But he also was a business failure, as well. It's sort of an interesting heritage.

I did go to Hebrew school as a kid. I went to about age 14. It was Orthodox, but nice. I was a member of a boys' scout troop there; I was actually a leader of the troop. I studied Hebrew all the time but without understanding what it meant. We never were told that. This gave a certain mystic aura, but still not how to say "Good morning. Can I have a cup of tea?" We never got that.

It was a kind of indoctrination, of course. I went through a very short period when I wanted to be completely kosher and become a rabbi and all that. And I am still an enthusiast, although not religiously. My bubble burst one Saturday morning when I went to the synagogue, which I thought was a good thing to do. And there was this Mister Levy who was always there. After services, he crossed the street and went into a candy store. When he came out and lit up a cigarette, I said, "Oh boy! What's this? Something is wrong here. He broke two very important rules on a Saturday [using money and smoking]." It was about that time that I began to become a man. I began to come of age, to think. And looking back, I certainly knew more then than I do now.

After high school, I went to community college. I got in by the skin of my teeth. Eventually, I transferred to City College, and that's when [politics] really started to get important. I'd gone to one of the peace marches [against the war in Vietnam] and to a couple of other things. I got involved in the politics of it, heavily, always on the non-violent end. And I became one of the leaders. It was a social cause, something important. Twenty years later, my brother and sister admitted that I was right in what I did.

We were vociferous. After the Kent State Massacre in 1970,* we took over the school. Two important things happened to me: I was interviewed on television as one of the people who had long hair and [the whole hippie get-up], and I thought that I said some very important, specific, and intelligent things about what was going on and what was wrong. Then when I saw myself on TV, it was totally different. I looked like an idiot. I told myself that I'd never do that again.

The other thing was that when we took over City College, we were invited over to Columbia University, which also had been occupied by their students. I was designated to speak because I was said to be a good public speaker. I said all the appropriate things, and since I was the last person to speak at the demonstration, I just invited everybody to join us at City College. I was totally unconscious of the effect this would have. Five thousand people got up and followed us through the city for a mile to the City College campus. That was something very exhilarating, but afterwards I said, "You know, these people will go anywhere if you get somebody to say the right words." And I just blanked out after that.

I had another experience that summer working with a group helping kids in Harlem. There was a former nun, a black woman, who was part of this association. We eventually understood that she was a fraud. She went on TV asking for donations, but the money went into her personal account rather than that of the group. So I said, "Screw this." You know, I just bowed out of everything. I realized that if I was going to change anything, it would have to be on a one-to-one basis, not by making speeches before thousands of people.

There are things you do growing up. I'm still an idealist, an enthusiast. And I still want to believe. But, you know, there are assholes everywhere, and we can't trust everybody, unfortunately.

---

* The National Guard shot several students, not all of them antiwar protesters, on the campus of Kent State University.

My being Jewish didn't really influence my actions, but there were links between Judaism and the causes I believed in. How can you dislike somebody because of his birth? And after you have been shut down for years, for thousands of years, you can't do that. It makes no sense. This made me think about religion. I always thought that religion was there to bind people together. Unfortunately, it creates a dividing line, in spite of the fact that you have Noah, Abraham, Moses, Jesus, Mohammed, and all that. It doesn't really bring us together as I would like. On 9/11, there was an ecumenical service of all the religious faiths here in Dijon at the Protestant church. I saw my doctor and asked what he was doing there. He said that he was representing the Orthodox [Christians] in Dijon. He was an Orthodox priest but had never spoken about it. He is a fervent believer, but ecumenical as well. I told him that I was Jewish, and [since then] we've had little discussions about religion. The way he believes, it's a personal faith. I told him that I would love to have his faith in knowing that there is an answer. But I have too many questions, you know, too many questions.

Anyway, I graduated from City College with a major degree in sociology and a minor in education. After working for a year, I went to Oregon, grew a beard and let my hair grow, smoked everything, screwed everything that walked, and just basically dropped out [of society]. Eventually, I made my way to San Francisco. While there, I learned something about homosexuality. While waiting for a friend in a gay bar, I was propositioned. It was the first time that I became a sexual object for other people. After that, I had a different approach to women. I didn't want to be treated that way, and I didn't want to treat women that way.

I returned to New York and started a plumbing and painting business. That lasted until I met a girl and followed her to California. The affair didn't last, and I had to work, so I got a job as a dishwasher in a restaurant. But I became a cook pretty quickly. That was 1974. I was 27. It was when the "New Cuisine" in France was happening. We heard about it in California, and we said, "Great. Let's do it!" And you know, without training, there were no inhibitions. We tried everything.

In 1979, I decided to go to France. I had been working as a pastry chef and a sous [assistant] chef, and I figured that if I were a rabbi, I'd go to Israel, and since I was going to cook, I'd go to France. I was lucky because I got a job right away, "under the table," and worked for two years without the proper papers.

During the first year, I met Babette. At first we were living together, so I decided to formalize my presence and work. I took a job with one of the leading bakers in the country who did a lot of the catering for the government, and they had my papers for me within days. During that time I also took cooking classes. Eventually, I became a chef in a one-star restaurant. Now, I was a pastry chef and a *chef de cuisine* [main chef].

Babette and I were married in February 1984 and decided to go to New York. We went without her two teenage daughters—who went with their father—because she said that she needed a break, and I was on the way to having a new life. For the next two years, I worked at Zaro's baking company in New York and then at a hotel next to the United Nations, where I did a lot of international stuff. But in 1986, two years after coming back, I opened my own restaurant in New Jersey. It was a lot of work. I was very much into doing high quality work, and it was very well-accepted. Nobody was cooking like we were.

When we came to the United States, I told Babette that I wanted to have a wedding with a rabbi and my family. I said that the reason I wanted to have one was because I wanted to break the glass. You know, chasing all the evil spirits.* We found a rabbi who was conservative [moderate], but really great, just brilliant and wonderful. We did the whole thing. I had a friend who was in the glassware business and had him get me the best crystal glass to crush. That was important. I thought having a traditional wedding was important, but I think that it was important for Babette, too.

See, she did not have any religious life at all. I did, but it vacillated over time. She comes from a different generation, born in 1942, during the war. Her father was captured in 1944, and was in the camps as a member of the Resistance, not as a Jew. Even though he was circumcised, he was able to deny that he was a Jew, and that saved his life. But obviously, when he came back, he was not the same person. *Babette didn't know that she was of Jewish origin until she was 16* [authors' emphasis]. The family never said anything about it. A family friend who was a priest had come to the house and baptized her and gave her communion because it was important to have certificates of them at that time.

When I was working in the kitchens in France, there were some anti-Semitic things said, but nothing really serious. When we came to New York, my identity as a Jew was less of a problem. New York was home. Being a Jew was nothing remarkable. In France, I don't say [that I'm a Jew] until I know the people. The first person I told in the school where I taught was a Moroccan friend, because he knew what it was like. We were, if you will, brothers within the same situation. I told him that I had come across many anti-Semitic remarks, and he said, "You know, I never heard anything said

---

* After the traditional wedding ceremony, the groom stamps on and breaks a glass. There are many interpretations for this ceremony, including the need, even at this joyous moment, to recognize responsibility to repair the broken world.

against the Arabs around you, because you look like one. It's obvious that no one is going to say anything in front of you." But I've heard comments. Once, in a teachers' meeting, jokes were made. It was the sixtieth anniversary of the Holocaust. Only one or two people in the room knew that I was Jewish. I could have been offended, but it would have been disastrous.

In 1992, we returned to France. The economy was not doing well in the United States; Babette's youngest daughter wanted to get married, so we said, "Okay, we're going back." Although the business [in New Jersey] was okay, we were just making a living, and, frankly, I was getting tired. Unfortunately, France also went into a recession not long after our return, and it was difficult finding a job. I eventually ended up in Dijon in 1995 managing a chain of croissant stores in the region.

I got into teaching in a peculiar way and because of an interesting event. I was at a café, people at the next table were speaking English, they were attempting to correct a letter, and I offered to help. Naturally, they asked if I spoke English, and when I told them that I was an American, I was asked if I would like a job teaching English. One thing led to another, and I ended up as an instructor at the École de Commerce [School of Commerce]. That was in the spring of 1998. By the end of the first year, I became a full-time faculty member and permanent teacher, which normally you have to wait some time for. It was because I had experience in business and could speak that language, and also because I could help the school with its international development efforts.

Eventually, I had the opportunity to teach at the university in Dijon in classes for food engineers. I thought that here was an opportunity to make a connection between the food business and my experience—biology, nutrition, and so forth. Then I read *The Omnivore* by Claude Fisher,[*] a top French sociologist, and I made the connection between sociology and food. That led me to further study. Sometime later I did a radio show on food and identity for a station in the Paris region. It was a big hit, and the result was [that I was asked to give] talks and classes on the subject at a variety of schools.

Did I have any difficulties as an American? No. But you know when I first came to France in 1980, the United States still at that time had a positive aura. My feeling then, as it is now in spite of all the problems with [President George W.] Bush and his stupidity, is that the French like Americans, they like American things, they like American culture: clothes, music, whatever it might be. They don't agree with American foreign policy simply because

[*] Claude Fisher, *The Omnivore* (New York, NY: Penguin, 2006).

it is too binary and there is no shading on the American side. And it's very difficult to be either with us or against us.

Being part of the problem or part of the solution is a very American way of looking at things. For the French, there is a lot of gray area, which disturbs Americans. I have talked about the United States in France quite a lot. We just have a different mode of thinking. But I have never been attacked as an American. I'm considered an American who is compatible. I am in an unusual situation here, particularly in Dijon. I am an American and I speak about food in the capital of food and wine. And I speak about food in French.

Right now, I'm on committees concerning health in Dijon and the region. I'll also eventually be presenting the film *Supersize Me*[*] to high schools in Burgundy and discuss it, not to show how diabolic McDonald's is, but to explain that in one sense McDonald's is a successful modernization of the restaurant system. They have been able to choose the right product at the right time for the right public. And, curiously enough, France has more McDonald's restaurants per capita than anywhere else in Europe. It's not that I like McDonald's. I don't. I'd rather make myself a meal than have a grilled chicken sandwich there. But I try to be informative, not to be polemical. I think that what I enjoy about sociology is that it puts things in context.

At the time of 9/11, I was just shocked—just shocked. But in the end, not surprised—if you will—when understanding the situation. It was a real awakening for the United States. I was very saddened because I knew what it meant when those buildings were hit and I watched them go down. At the school, there were Americans there and I wanted to protect them and let them know they were loved and understood. What's unfortunate is that Bush manipulated this situation and put it to his advantage. First, he destroyed the free press, and second he was able to validate the extreme Right of the Christian movement, which to me is just as dangerous as anything that is in Islam.

What spoiled the good will [after 9/11] was the invasion of Iraq. I think that any president, at least any American president, would have attacked Afghanistan and should have been satisfied with that and do it more completely without getting diverted to another situation. Obviously, attacking Iraq was for the oil. That didn't work, prices went up, and all the mistakes have been made. When the [then] French delegate to the United Nations, Dominique de Villepin, spoke about Iraq and American plans for it, what he said was absolutely beautiful, adequate, and perfect. He was 100 per cent right, and the United States was 100 per cent wrong.

---

[*] Morgan Spurlock, *Supersize Me,* a film directed by Morgan Spurlock (Kathbur Picture, 2004).

You know, the French understand the Arab world, and the French politicians understand the Arab world much better than Americans do. But on 9/11, the French president said that everybody is an American. That sentiment lasted through Afghanistan. Then with Iraq, it just turned sour.

Americans feel that the French are too haughty and independent. I think that all the things that the French are accused of by the Americans are what Americans are, as well. That is why there is difficulty in the relationship. I get along with my [French] wife because we are not the same. And each country, each person, has their patriotism, their pride, and so on. It's difficult to get through that, but countries have to get along just the same.

You say that most of your [Jewish] interviewees are more cynical and less trusting about French politicians, especially with respect to Jews, Israel, and the Arab world. Is the phrase "honest politician" an oxymoron? Probably. Anyway, our French politicians are different than anyplace else. They probably are different than Americans, but not any better or any worse. Yes, there is a history here. I'm very much aware of the past in France. My Jewish family in the United States was very concerned about me in France. "Watch yourself in the street," they said, "you're going to step into violence." But that's not happening. Yes, there is anti-Semitism here. Yes, there is anti-Semitism in the United States. But the point is that I think French society is changing.

In respect to the problems of Islam, the things that have happened here are horrible, but I'm not going to lose sleep over them. The only solution is to open the door to knowledge and communication. You have to have a dialogue. There are, of course, hard-core guys who are ready to blow everything up. You've got that. But getting to the students in schools is important, starting there, for example. The difficulty here is that they don't want to talk about religion. That's the problem. I think that if you can talk about problems, then you understand what the differences are.

There is a difference between what we consider secular in France and secular in the United States. And there is a great deal of misunderstanding in the United States about what it means to wear the [Muslim] scarf. Religious freedom there means that out in public you can display your religion and wear your star, cross, turban, whatever. It's part of American life. In France, secularism is different. Secularism here means that you practice your religion privately at home and in your church or temple and without government interference.

The United States is becoming more religiously oriented and religiously minded, whereas France is becoming less and less so. And France is a Catholic country. Here, the government is trying to work with Islam and organize it. That, you know, is antithetical to Islam. There is no central authority;

there are many groups: Sunni, Shia, and so on. Islam is in a phase now that is unfortunate, but we know from history that it was not always this way. I don't know what's going to happen, but if I were a minister of the interior here, I would certainly be concerned about it.

I don't want to condemn France for being intolerant, but being tolerant isn't enough. I think that there is a sense in the United States and France that there is a limit to toleration. We are less accepting [of difference], in France and in the United States, and this is what's creating the problems. The United States is building a wall around itself, and, my goodness, what can be more stupid? Israel, of course, has a wall, but I can understand that. Again, there are similarities between France and the United States that makes it so easy for one to criticize the other.

In economics, there are differences in attitude. In the United States, we believe that the pie is infinite; in France, they think it's finite. If I get a piece of the pie, there's less for you. If you got a big house and a big car—who did you screw to get them? That's the attitude here. And that has to change. In the United States, you got a big car, I say, "Well, good for you, I'll get mine one day." Of course, that's not always the case, and economists would say that I'm wrong. But it's a state of mind.

There are two commercials that I talk about in France if you want to go into business. They are about attitude and are quite important. In one you need to say to yourself, "I'm doing this because I'm worth it." The second commercial comes right from Nike: "Just do it!" And that's how you go into business and learn. You might have all the degrees in the world, but you may still screw up [if you don't have the right attitude] to get where you're going. But you have to try. I think that's a major problem here.

The other thing that I have often spoken about is that in France the past has great value. When we think of the future in France, we look at the past, what we did before. We analyze that, and then we construct the future. In the United States, the past has less importance. The past is "moldable," you know? We can choose the good things or the bad things from the past, but it has less significance for the American mind. We tear down a building that has some particular design or value, and we build another one that we think would be better. When we think of the future in the United States, we create a future with our minds. The French are a little timid about that. They say, "Take me step by step, step by step."

I think that there is more jealousy here than in the United States. And you know, in classes, when students tell me that the United States is great, it's fantastic, I tell them the opposite. And when they tell me France is terrible, I tell the opposite. There are a lot of great things going on here. They don't realize how fortunate they are. They don't put things into a global perspective, not in the sense of globalization, but in its entirety. They need to be a little more objective, a little more pragmatic, you know, to really understand how things function.

I have worked all my life. I have always done something, and I believe that work is a great training ground. I have often spoken about how in the United States I worked when I was young; I had my bakery with young girls working at the counter, high school students and young college students. This helps train people; they understand the value of work, the value of money. Kids in France don't have that, because the system is not open to that, and I think that it needs to be open. But that is not going to happen in five minutes, either. We are talking about 20 years' time. But if we had that [openness to opportunity], people would want to work more, because they would realize that if they work, they could get some benefits out of the work. They feel now that if they work, they will not get the benefits. And that is the problem. There is fear and caution with respect to any change. As human beings, we don't like change, but change here is more difficult to swallow because of the past.

As for living here in Dijon, I like it a lot. I never thought that I would be happy in a small city, but I really am. The city itself has about 150,000 people, and with its surrounding towns, administratively associated with Dijon in 2000, about 250,000. Positive things are happening. They are going to build a whole new commercial center. The mayor [François Rebsamen, Socialist] is a real human being, and this is very important. When the Jewish kid [Ilan Halimi] was tortured and killed in Paris, Rebsamen had a demonstration.... I think that he is very much aware of the problems that exist in French society. He is very concerned about keeping up the quota of housing for disadvantaged people. And I think that's essential. Everything that's done in the city is done with social consciousness. I have heard him speak and seen him do, and I believe that he's sincere. He understands the Jewish community that needs to be understood and reckoned with and dealt with. It's a diminishing community, you know, and there are fewer business people, but that's not problematical. He's just trying to do the best he can.

About the future of the Jews in France, I'm still somewhat positive. I know that people are leaving, but I don't think that's the answer. It gives the wrong signal. I believe that France is tolerant. I believe that the French government is tolerant and vigilant against anti-Semitism. It has become more so. I think that [anti-Semitic] incidents are reported here more than in the United States.

I don't minimize the problems that we face because of the radicalization in certain Islamic communities. Somebody has got a bomb, he's dangerous, and I don't care where he's from. It's a question of dialogue, of accepting the other person. If you are going to bring someone around to a way of thinking that is more humanistic, you cannot talk down to them. I found that the success that I had as a teacher is that I don't talk down to my students. I talk to them as equals. And I tell them that I can learn as much from them as they can from me. That is more of an American means of teaching, also.

Babette Miles

*Babette, wife of Alex Miles [see previous interview], didn't learn
that she was Jewish until she was a teenager. Born during World
War II into a family that assumed a false religious identity in order
to survive, and with a Resistance fighter father who lived through
Auschwitz because he convinced the Germans that he wasn't Jewish,
she grew up like many other Jewish children of that time in a world
of silence. Some survivors either rejected their religion entirely or, like
her family, simply denied it. Only as a mature woman did she come
to terms with her religious identity and find a comfortable home and
friends in the Dijon community.*

January 2007

I didn't realize that I was Jewish until I was 16 or 17. No one ever told me. It
was because of the war. When my father was arrested, in order to protect us,
[my parents] decided to have us baptized, my sister and me. At that time, my
sister was, perhaps, six or eight. There were priests who were willing to help
and who did not ask many questions. So we were baptized, and after the war
my father did not practice although he had a basic traditional religious education. My mother did not have any religious instruction at all. Later, when
I asked my mother why we didn't celebrate Hanukkah or the holidays, she
answered that it was because they never did in her family, so she didn't know
how. Her parents had wanted to start over in France and integrate into the
society. They didn't want to hear about anything [Jewish]. They were socialists.

After my father was arrested and sent to the camps, he realized that
there was danger in admitting to being Jewish and he turned his back on
it. When he survived and came back, he and my mother decided not to talk
about being Jewish. So, as children, my brother and I lived amid secrets
and silence. We didn't know. But even then we did not live like everyone
around us. We had family around who were basically secular, but a part
of the family, in particular one of my grandmother's brothers, was more
traditional without being excessively religious. When I was about seven,
one of his daughters was married in a synagogue. I had never attended a
wedding before, so for me all weddings were like that. Afterwards a bunch
of my cousins and I performed a short play. We enacted a wedding and we
broke the glass. I remember the embarrassed laughter from my parents and
aunts and uncles. I didn't understand why they had that reaction, as if we
had done something strange. That's how it was, and no one ever explained
anything to me.

My cousins weren't aware of anything. My two uncles were married to Catholic girls, so they did not practice anything. They went even farther than my mother, because they never told their children anything at all, which is even more incredible. My sister made her First Communion because my parents decided to go all the way. Then, when I was 12, everyone was studying catechism because at that time 98 per cent of the French population was Catholic. I didn't understand why I wasn't doing it like everyone else. So I asked, and my parents said that it was because they just didn't do it. But six months later, they enrolled me in a catechism class, and I also did my First Communion. It all was done very quickly. Later, I learned that my father's best friend was a priest who had escaped from the camps with him during the war. They were very close. It was this priest who had another priest who was teaching catechism take me in for instruction. I never knew why or all the details. At the time, I didn't ask any questions; now I regret not having done so. I did this thing and that was it. Unlike other families, we didn't go to Mass. The same thing happened with my brother, I think. He did his First Communion as well, and then it was forgotten. When my sister was married to a Catholic and had a church wedding, my mother told me that it had made her sick. But she said nothing because it was my sister's choice. My mother said that it was the price paid for what they [the parents] had done.

I don't know how it happened that my mother announced to me that we were Jews. But I think that I must have known. I already knew that there was something wrong. When I was told, I felt such a big relief, because all of a sudden everything seemed clearer. It cleared up a lot of things that I didn't understand, the silence, everything. Later on, when I asked why did they hide that we were Jewish, she told me not to say anything to anyone because it [persecution] might start again. She was in France before I was born, before the war, and she taught me this fear. For years until I met Alex [her Jewish second husband] I could not talk about my origins except to my very closest friends. Every time I said it, it was like this huge trust I was giving away because I was afraid. I can't even say that the feeling is completely gone. I barely talk about it, and every time that Alex says that he's Jewish I get this feeling, thinking why in the world does he have to say it, what will happen to us? It's like a sword hanging over my head. The anxiety is still here. I think that it's ingrained in me. I have to overcome it, but I find it hard to do.

I was born in 1942 at Thiers, in Auvergne, during the German Occupation. My parents were in hiding with an uncle who had a factory there. My parents went there with my grandparents and another aunt. My parents never declared themselves Jewish, so that they could live like everyone else. My family was atheist; they didn't practice any religion. My mother's name didn't have any particular meaning. My father's name originally was Kalinsky, but he shortened it.

My father was born in the Ukraine. He left with his family when the Communists came to power in 1918. My mother's family came from Lithuania. Her father, my grandfather, came to France in 1905 during the uprisings in Russia. He apparently was politically active and got into trouble. He had been a businessman and eventually left France for China seeking opportunities there. He left his family behind, and although he wanted them to join him, World War II came. He died there during the war.

During the war, I was too young to know what my father was doing, but I do know that he was in the Resistance. After he was arrested and deported, we remained in hiding, but my mother became even more cautious. My father was circumcised, and there were many questions, but he denied that he was Jewish. He held his ground and had a chance because he had married my mother in a civil ceremony. There was no proof that he was Jewish. His own papers had all been burned in Russia, so they couldn't prove anything. We assume that is what saved his life. He was sent first to Drancy, then to Auschwitz, where he was held for 15 months, but survived. When he was released, he came immediately to Paris to join us. He never completely healed. When my father left, I was a baby—15 months old. My mother told me that he was very joyful; he played with the children; he was always there. When he came back, he was someone else. I only knew him as someone who was reserved, quiet, who constantly had health problems. He had headaches, intestinal viruses. He never recovered, either physically or mentally.

When I went to primary school, I was a very good student. But when I got to high school, I didn't do anything. I was a daydreamer. I was an obedient student who didn't bother anybody, but I didn't do anything. I daydreamed. I drew. That was my thing. This actually made my mother despair. Both of [my parents] had been very athletic, but I wasn't interested. I just read a lot, and I drew.

I read everything that I found, though certainly not things related to school. I read things that were too advanced for me, and that I probably didn't understand. I read Camus, Sartre, and similar authors. I also saw a lot of movies. It was a time when there were a lot of war movies. They were really shocking. However, I did not look deeper into things. I was happy enough knowing who I was, where I came from. Things were already clearer. I don't know if it was because of the war or because of the family secrets, but I was someone who was very introverted. I did not communicate with others, and this lasted for a long time. My circle of friends was very small.

Certainly, I was not very social. I didn't do group activities. I was in my own world and absorbed by my own adolescent problems.

My studies were catastrophic, and so I failed the baccalaureate. For about a year afterwards, I was lazy and spent the time listening to my mother's threats to enroll me in a secretarial school if I didn't make a decision about what I wanted to do. I wanted to do art but was told that it wasn't a true profession. At the time, I was very passive; I let people decide for me. It happened that my best friend was studying physiotherapy. She said that it was fascinating, and that I should try it. I really didn't know what to do, and I was under pressure, so I studied for the entrance exams and passed. Then I got really passionate about it and eventually became first in class. It was really interesting for me. I studied for two years and finished when I was 21. It was new, and I left the old failures behind.

During this time, I got married and was pregnant. It was with a guy who was studying with me. He was a Catholic who didn't care much about [the religion], so we weren't married in a church. I received my degree but had to take care of the baby, so I worked part-time. My husband also did because he was still studying. So we didn't have any money. It got very complicated. Eventually, we both found work in a sports center.

My daughter Sandrine was born in February 1968 and in May [the Paris uprising] began. I remember that we were glued to the radio. I didn't get directly involved because I had the baby and was home, but we were not far from it at all. We were afraid that a civil war might break out. Fortunately, the troubles didn't last long.

Then when the Yom Kippur War happened in 1973, there was much talk about what to do. People were asking themselves how much to support Israel if a serious conflict broke out. That also involved the question of France and Israel. I would have been very upset if I had to take sides, but I was very much for Israel at that time. The existence of Israel was very important. I have memories of when Israel won its independence. I was very small, but there are things that are memorable. We must have talked about it at home. I remember how proud I was about how Israel defended itself. I had very positive feelings about it. My husband did understand, but I had the feeling that he never saw things the same way. He had his own perception. He saw things like that from the outside, while I felt them more from the inside. I really internalized being Jewish. I just didn't divulge it.

They were old memories, but that was one of our preoccupations. I don't know if it was like that in every French household, but that was the case in our house. These are things that made me realize that we did not react like everyone else. For example, when I was in high school there were Jews there and someone made some comments. It was a French teacher who was a racist and made a comment to a girl who was of Romanian origin. He told her that she was lucky that the French allowed her to live in France. That made me really angry. The girl's parents pressed charges. Things went further. I was really sensitive about racism and injustice. But racism wasn't discussed in school in the 1950s and 1960s. Those comments were by an individual teacher.

It's true that I always asked myself what it meant to be religious, since I was not religious myself. It is still an unanswered question because this sensitivity was developed over time when I heard racist comments. You know, when I heard things like, "Yes, he's like that because he's Jewish," I felt Jewish because of that. Otherwise, I felt like everybody else. I had French culture, and I didn't see what made me different except when I heard comments about Jews that I took personally. I did not like it either when de Gaulle said that Jews were "domineering."

There were always people who were saying things that I considered pretty racist and anti-Semitic. They said things without really knowing what it meant to others. I had a friend whom I admired a lot, and we talked frequently about the problems related to Judaism and anti-Semitism. She told me that people sometimes made comments in front of her, and she immediately said that she was Jewish, though of course she was not. It was interesting. On the one hand it was a powerful statement, but on the other it's easier to say it when you're not really Jewish. But I admire what she did. She had taken a stand.

When I heard comments about other minority groups, I became sensitive not only to anti-Semitism but to racism in general. I could not tolerate it. There's no reason to despise anyone because of his origins. When I was an adolescent during the Algerian War, there were Algerians among our group of friends. I clearly saw how people were arrested because they looked Algerian. The war became a reality for us.

In the late 1970s, my marriage began to deteriorate. This was a period of time that was very difficult. Both my brother and grandmother died. Then my mother became ill. My husband and I had difficult working hours. I worked until late at night, and we were raising two children. We had babysitter problems. We were fighting every day. It was a very agitated period. But it's also when I woke up. With all these things and with my marriage going down the drain, it was like a thunderbolt. All of this time I had lived in a bubble, in my little cocoon, living my routine life. All of a sudden, everything changed and was put into perspective. I realized that for 30 years I had been asleep. Things were very dynamic. Something was being set into motion.

Suddenly I was in total rebellion. It was a time when I began asking my mother a lot of questions. She was very defensive, and sometimes I was harsh. It took me a few years to understand that she had her reasons and that she had done what she could, but it took me a while to understand that. Then my father's sudden death left me with more questions that I never had a chance to ask. It was a lot to deal with.

In 1980, my husband and I separated. The children came with me because he didn't want to be bothered with them. Part of what happened, I think, was my involvement in the feminist movement. Everything that was wrong with my life.... I thought that I was the only one living it. Learning that there were other women who were living the same thing strengthened my own feelings. And, of course, this contributed to [the deterioration of the relationship]. Yes, it was hard to be married at that time. We did not accept the same things anymore, and naturally this created tension.

I was totally into it [the movement]. I met people in a women's group where we had discussions. There were people whom I respected and believed in more and who had ideas that I deemed valid. But I didn't go so far as having a hero. I was not that type. I was interested in ideas. The people with whom I was with were Leftists politically. But there were things that were shocking to me. Some were for violence, for violent revolution, and that wasn't really my thing. I started to become interested in ecology at that time. A group started to talk about it, and it was something that appealed to me because it seemed intelligent. If people had listened back then, we wouldn't be where we are now. What's being said about the environment and the earth now is what was being said back then. So what I was embracing was feminism and the emergence of environmentalism.

Well, then I met Alex. He was an American who couldn't speak French because he had been in the country only three months. He had sprained his wrist at work and was sent to our office for treatment, and my husband took care of him. Later, my husband invited Alex to our place and introduced him to our friends. In fact, Alex dated one of our friends for a while. After I separated, I was mad at all men in general, but I needed to get away and do other things so I went out with Alex as a friend for about a year. We really started dating in 1981. Then he returned to the United States for six months and underwent back surgery. When he came back to France, we began living together.

My children were with us and it was very hard for the youngest one. She could not tolerate Alex because she was convinced that he was responsible for the divorce. I thought perhaps that living together so soon had been a mistake. Years later, when we told her the story, she realized that she had always believed that he was responsible. But she made our lives difficult for several years until she grew older.

I'm not sure when Alex told me that he was Jewish. I wonder if he told me right away. I don't remember. I know that I didn't tell him right away, as usual. But since he was Jewish as well, I ended up telling him. I trusted him. So he learned about it quite soon. We weren't dating at that time. I guess that it was at the very beginning.

I continued working in the same office as my former husband, but I tried not to go there very often. I practiced in homes because [working in the office with him] was unbearable. He was so [verbally] violent. So when Alex decided to go back to the United States and wanted us to get married, I decided to go. At first I resisted, but I realized that it was an escape for me. It was a way to have a fresh start, because with my work and every-thing I couldn't see a way out. So we went to the United States. My eldest daughter, who was 20, decided to go out on her own. Sandrine, my young-est daughter, came to the United States and stayed with us for six months, but eventually she decided to return to France.

I left without really knowing for how long. I got married and told myself I'd see how long it would last, and if I would like living in the United States. It was pretty uncertain. We ended up living there from 1984 to 1992, eight long years.

It was interesting because meeting Alex and living in the United States was like finding a Jewish family again. At first, I really felt like I was coming home. There were things, for example, that I never could share with my ex-husband. I remember that when one of our neighbors was having us for tea she made a comment about Jews. When people said those kinds of things, I couldn't say anything back. I was so shocked. I was almost in tears when I left her house. And I couldn't share things like that with my ex-husband because even if he said that he understood, he couldn't. He didn't have the same feelings. Even if he understood intellectually, it was not the same.

With Alex, I really had the feeling that we were talking about the same thing, that there were similar feelings. On that level, the United States was quite a disappointment. I had not found what I was looking for among American Jews. I felt some mistrust and an inability to understand what it meant to be Jewish in France. I also felt that things were too clear-cut with them. One was either a good Jew or a bad one, either Jewish or not Jewish. It was a precarious situation. I felt like I was going nowhere. I did not feel like I was part of them. So I did not really find what I had wished to find there.

I also was very shocked—and this was because of what I had lived in the past—with the outright displays of people. It was almost the total opposite of what I had experienced and what French Jews were like. French Jews, except for the pieds noirs who had asserted themselves, never showed off, especially those from Europe. When people [in the United States] whom I didn't know asked me if I was Jewish, I looked at them thinking that it was none of their business. Or they would ask my daughter if she had a boyfriend. This straightforward and indiscreet attitude was shocking for me. For me, religion is private. Personal lives are private.

With Alex's family, it was a bit the same. His mother was absolutely adorable, but I didn't feel at home. I still felt like an outsider. I had felt that for a long time. For years, I felt as if I belonged nowhere. With time, I told myself that it was a good way to understand everyone. It can be positive. I could fully understand the predicament of immigrants, Jews, Arabs, and Blacks. At the same time, I was French and had the basic Christian education that helped me understand the others, as well. I can see it both ways. I can be an outsider everywhere, but it's never comfortable. Sometimes I would like to belong somewhere for a time.

We decided to come back to France because, even though Alex's business was good, he was working too much and was tired. He was working 20 hours a day, and it was crazy. He couldn't take it anymore. It was the early 1990s, the American economy wasn't doing well, and he couldn't find the capital to expand. Also, Sandrine, who had been living with her boyfriend for several years, decided to get married because she wanted to have children.

I asked myself what I was doing in the United States, especially if I would have grandchildren in France. And there was Alex, who couldn't take it anymore. So he decided to sell. And besides, he really liked France. So we decided to go back. But when we returned to France, the economy here started to go bad, as well. We just went the wrong way. It was difficult. We made mistakes, and it took us ten years to dig out.

I think that it was 1996 when we came to Dijon. We decided to come here because Dijon was a city. We realized that we felt better in a city than in the countryside, especially without children. After all, I was a Parisian and Alex was a New Yorker. So we chose Dijon because it was the main city in the region. But it was still difficult because at first we didn't have jobs. We found an apartment and started to look for work.

We quickly met people in an amusing way. It was because of our dog, a Labrador named Cowboy. Alex was walking the dog in the neighborhood when he met a young man who had the same breed of dog. They started to talk. He was an Italian, an opera singer who lived next door. He invited us to his house. The couple wasn't from Dijon, and they were younger than us, but they had us meet friends of theirs who were closer to our ages. Through their friends we met a lot of people. After that, Alex started to work at the School of Commerce. He talks to everyone, and so he knows everyone.

One of the people he met was an American woman who brings groups of American students to Dijon. She told us that she knew people whom she was sure we would get along well with. She knew Sarah Edelman [Bensoussan] very well. She was the one who gave us her parents' address. So we called and invited them over, and that's how we met Annie and Gislain and their family.

They are extraordinary people. When I am with Annie, I feel like I am with a member of my family. We can talk about anything. It feels natural. We connected, and it's a simple relationship. I found in Annie what I felt when I met this group of [Jewish] women. If we're in the neighborhood, we can call and say "hi." We don't have to dress up or do complicated things when we invite them over. We do whatever we are used to doing, just like I did in my family. It was like that at home. My friends came home, we set an extra plate, and everyone ate. It was very open, and that's not common within French families.

I can talk about things [with Annie] that I can't tell everyone. We talk more naturally. This doesn't mean that we always agree on everything, but they are very open people without prejudices. Yes, I remain within the community with a lot of friends who are part of it, but I am not at the heart of the community. I can't do that. But that's just me. I don't know about Alex; he has a different relationship with the community. He had a more traditional education. Personally, I still cannot go to the synagogue, but I think that's the religious aspect. I don't feel concerned at all. Even if I enjoy very much being with Jewish friends with whom I get along well because we are close, I still find it hard to be only around Jews. I feel closed up instead of being open to the world. I find it hard to tolerate closed communities in general. I like having friends from everywhere.

But for the first time I have found a place where I can be comfortable, more at ease. Yes, it's the first time.

Writing About Jewish Life in Dijon:
Mazal Tov

Introduction

The Dijon community's journal, Mazal Tov, has appeared almost continuously but under several different names since its first publication in the late 1970s. Its contents have varied little over the past three decades. It continues to provide a wealth of information on issues of concern to the community, plus material on history, other Jewish communities, the Holocaust, Israel, and anti-Semitism. It reports on communal business and recent events, and lists information on all of the holidays and religious ceremonies celebrated in the community. And, like all good local papers, it carries advertisements of upcoming events, humor, recipes, notices of weddings and celebrations, and obituaries. In short, Mazal Tov is an excellent source for learning about the Dijon community.

The journal technically is governed by a board of directors, but the views of the editor generally dominate, if for no other reason than the job requires a major commitment of time and energy. In addition to the usual editorial tasks, securing articles for publication from a relatively small but busy pool of local contributors is difficult. Yet long-time editor Cathie Bussidan, who has held the job since 1993, has done exceptionally well with limited resources. She has developed a talented group of contributors, maintained high quality, and increased readership, which now includes 60 per cent of Dijon's Jews as well as a number of Gentiles.

It is impossible here to provide examples from Mazal Tov spanning the entire period of the journal's existence. We have selected representative articles about current communal concerns that hopefully add substance and dimension to material presented in the interviews. Virtually every interview could be supported by a number of other articles to the same effect. Omitted here are the many articles describing Jewish holidays and observances, as well as items of personal and limited interest.

Collectively this selection presents a small-frame view of the mainstream Jewish community of Dijon; absent, for the most part, is its most recent Lubavitch component.

Opinions: Those who believe they have the right to demand

Mazal Tov 34 (March 2005): 19

Dear friends and fellow Jews,

Resident of Dijon for 70 years, member of this community for 55 years, president of the ACID[*] for 12 years, descendant of a family whose roots in Dijon go back 210 years and who were among those who built our temple, I have the right to be worried and to take, once and for all, a position opposing the critical and demanding minority, who believe they have the right to judge, to criticize, to decide, to claim, or to demand.

Certain people have hoped for years to take control of our community. Profiting from the presence in Dijon of a very likable orthodox religious couple, they have rebelled against the rabbi and the Consistory because the majority of the faithful are not sufficiently religious. Everything—the rituals and the community life—must change.

Indeed, some demands were granted, the change of rite (Moroccan instead of Algerian) and the removal of women from the [first] floor. All to maintain good relations and satisfy the minority, but without much consequence.

The Dijon Jews have for decades sustained this community, enduring the torments of Occupation. For 130 years, this community was traditional and unchanging. In this way, it maintained this beautiful synagogue, constructed with the effort of all, especially the Alsatians who came to France after their own province became a part of Prussia.

I venture to pose a question to all of you: would you like to maintain this community though it is far from "liberal"?

We have arrived at a moment in which it is necessary to make decisions: to maintain the service as it is, in accepting the modifications already cited, but in leaving to each his free will, to

---

[*] Religious Association of the Jews of Dijon

stop listening to all these discussions between those who [do]…
and those who do not want to accept anything.

We are all the same. We want all of our community to unite
under the same roof, including with those who believe they own
the "real truth."

I will stop with these critiques, these reproaches, and these
wishes, but I had to say it and I said it, perhaps displeasing the
minority who are not well behaved, who only know how to make
reproaches.

At the present time, we do not need to tear ourselves apart. To
all of you, dear friends, to all of you: pull yourselves together, form
a united community, for the good of all, especially for our children,
and leave out all jealousy.

Cordial shalom.
Henri-Claude Bloch

Journeys and Point of View: Jewish, born to a non-Jewish Mother

Mazal Tov 28 (September 2003): 23–24

Being Jewish, born to a non-Jewish mother, not circumcised, raised Christian, I joined the DROR [Zionist youth group, named Freedom] in my adolescence after the Six Day War, which, surely, awakened buried feelings in my father's heart.

Then, as a young adult, life kept me in France, and I lived as a "Frenchman of Jewish origin." I married the woman I loved; my children were brought into the French world, with French names, a republican baptism, and a Catholic welcome. But I had painted the word "shalom" on my house, as well as the three signs: the Star of David, the Cross, and the Crescent.

Later, in 1993, while living in the suburbs of the international city of Evry, I began a new path, not of **techouva**, but of consciousness, of clarification and development of my Judaism. It was a clumsy, winding, difficult path full of errors, of disillusions, but also of learning, of joys, and of personal growth.

In 1994, I think, I took part in a secular Seder organized by the young UJFP [Union of French Jewish Students for Peace]. One level boundary stage was closed this year, 2003, when I took part in the community of Dijon's Seder.

I know today that, as a member of the community, loyal and right, Jewish in my heart and spirit, I will be first and always a Frenchman, married to a Frenchwoman who I love above all else, and father to French children who will have their own families that they love with women or men whom they love as well.

I also know that I will always be a goy for numerous Jews and, in particular, for the religious institutions. Because, I'm sure, today I will never accept the caudal forks [circumcision] that the Consistory imposes on us.

Indeed, official Judaism is like this, in this country where the liberal and the secular Jews are minorities, and Judaism is the object of judgments where the criteria are, first, racial. What does the conscience of the individual matter, the faith of the believer or the principles of the secular person, his culture Jewish or not, his family's heritage, if Judaism is firstly a function of a racial criteria—"Is your mother Jewish?"

And on this basis, we'll ask the stranger for some difficult archaic and unjust guidance, where it suffices for the "automatic Jew" to make a **ketubah**. The conversion will require that the **guer** respect all sorts of **mitzvot** that the majority of automatic Jews mostly ignore. He will have to adhere to the most obscure concepts of Judaism (ah, the charm of angels, the pragmatism of

Paradise . . .) and above all else instill in his family the weight of timeless religious practices. This, regardless of the wishes of those he loves or even at the risk of their love.

There is, during the course of this conversation, a digest of all the things that eventually condemn the fundamentalist communities. And if one considers that 60 per cent of French Jews have mixed marriages, it seems suicidal to perpetuate the alternative Orthodox exclusion. On the other hand, the cultural heritage and religious Jews should incite the Consistory to overcome the racial barriers and to call into question the ancient practices. This questioning is not against the Law.

Indeed, archaeology [and] linguistics show us today at what point it is important not to stop at the letter of the texts but to take into account the conditions of their production: almost always in chronological disagreement with history, often inspired by the political necessities of the time period (in particular in the service of Judah's kingdom), generally produced and reproduced with the relative precision of a time when the bureaucracy left the job post to poetry and morals. Moreover, liberals, for many centuries, have been conducting numerous studies and research that shows how many texts themselves evolved.

Finally, it is evident that if there is something divine in our texts, the idea of a God who is the head clerk dictating the account [Book of Life] is as ridiculous and stupid as that of a God who is a grocer, marking in a huge book the number of commandments per client before readjusting his pencil between his ear and his mop of hair to divinely judge.[*]

The job of welcoming a stranger should include the warm and tolerant support of non-Jewish spouses in the discovery of Jewish culture.

Moreover, the respect due to the individual and to the family should inspire a relaxation of commandments to permit the non-Jewish spouses to share in the rituals without renouncing their religion. And the indestructible bond that exists between the religious and the secular should be revised in the light of generosity and intelligence to permit individual interpretation (and secular if the case arises) of the practices and rituals that give rhythm to Jewish life. Likewise, there is a certain cruelty in burdening the families with the heartbreak that results from the consequence of the alternative conversion.

---

[*] According to tradition and liturgy, between Rosh Hashanah and Yom Kippur, God judges each Jew, deciding on his/her fate for the next year; repentance, prayer, and charity can undermine the potentially evil decree, even at the end of Yom Kippur. For most Jews, this is a metaphorical, but still powerful moment in the High Holiday liturgy. However, for many (mostly) Orthodox and ultra-Orthodox Jews, it remains an article of faith, a living reality.

There exists today an individual conscience that makes the obligation of the woman to adhere to the will of the husband unacceptable. This is a violation of conscience. Likewise, the exclusion of children of non-Jewish mothers seems like an attitude full of inhumanity and contempt for the rest of humanity. This is contrary to the spirit of the Torah.

Thanks to the Orthodox education of children, [Orthodox Judaism] seems opposed to the ideals of individual liberty (like the requirement of sincerity that has to accompany all religious thought processes) insomuch as Judaism will weigh on the children like a racial destiny fatality instead of as an enlightened choice.

Finally, for the Jewish people living in France, the choices imposed by the orthodox majority finds expression in the exclusion of the secular Jews and even sometimes of those who might choose a more liberal path.

By Daniel

ACID: **A Word from the President**

Mazal Tov 32 (September 2004): 9

Dear Fellow Jews,
Dear Friends,

Just before the celebration of the holidays of Rosh Hashanah and
Yom Kippur, I would like, through this brief message, to wish you,
as well as your entire family, a new year full of happiness and of
simhot. We hope that the coming year will be a bearer of peace and
serenity for all the French and especially for the Jews of France, of
whom a certain number live in situations of tension and of threats
that one hoped were gone forever after the horror of the Shoah.

The unity of the Jews where they are, as is the case elsewhere
for all other humanity, constitutes one goal that has become more
and more urgent since the deterioration of the situation. Now,
on the one hand, there are Jews who take a very active part in
movements that are characterized by an aggressiveness against
Israel (actions which indirectly generate an aggressiveness against
us). On the other hand, the particularly Orthodox trends of
Judaism undermine unity within smaller communities.

The leaders of countries who have finally taken the
measurements of the problem of anti-Semitism (which is also—
and above all—a problem for the entire nation) are listening to
us in order to bring us their active assistance in order to suppress
the anti-Semitic acts and to promote, within the youth, with the
intercession of national education, the awareness necessary for a
total societal unity.

However, by their latest decisions, the judicial authorities,
independent of the legislative and executive powers, seem
somewhat less receptive to the dangers that threaten French
citizens of Jewish confession.

We hope that the future will see the risks, for all the civilian
populations of the world, progressively go away, even if one can
fear the contrary in seeing the taking of hostages, massive or not,
turn often to carnage.

I am delighted about the brilliant (and unexpected-for!) success
of the first European Day of Jewish Patrimony in Dijon which one
must attribute to the dedicated devotion of the team managed by

Jocelyne Azancot, helped by Henri-Claude Bloch, Simone Ayache, Cathie Bussidan, Monique Thébault, and about 30 other people of all ages (the list is too long). I would also like to thank the security team who, under the burning sun, took its role to heart under the direction of Michel Bussidan and Max Ayache; this team, which included some very motivated youth—like Raphael Huli and Estelle Girard-Ruben—will be able to, we hope, return "present" for the celebrations of Yom Kippur!

Cordial Shalom!
Chana tova [Happy New Year].
Israël Cemachovic

ACID: **A Word from the President**

Mazal Tov 33 (December 2004): 6

Dear Fellow Jews,
Dear Friends,

The dramatic developments in the Middle East drag us, very much against our will, into the spotlight of French news.

Some months ago, Ariel Sharon's "outburst" on "relentless anti-Semitism" supposedly pervading through France (that should have prompted the French Jews to leave for Israel), angered a good part of the crowd and French political class.

Today, the voices supported by this same political class, practically unanimous across party lines, are responsible for the assault on more Jewish citizens than since the end of World War II. These voices, therefore, create a definite uneasiness among Jews. And the history lessons recently taught in certain middle schools and high schools in France [following Yasser Arafat's death] concerning Arafat's life do not reassure us.

For the first time, also, anti-Semitic desecration took place at a Christian cemetery in the Côte d'Or [Dijon's Department]. All these events must prompt us to stay vigilant as much on the moral and intellectual level as the physical.

Again, regarding the speculations on the causes of the death of one of the greatest enemies of Israel, we see resurface the old hackneyed expressions on Jewish prisoners during the black plague. Jews, Israeli or not, will be implicated in all the shocking situations: the persistent rumors in Arab countries [that] attribute to them [Jews] the responsibility for the attacks of September 11 to Arafat's death. You would think that we have rather large shoulders!

With respect to our community, in several weeks a company will be chosen to carry out the renovation of the electricity of the synagogue, which is the next great site of restoration of our beautiful **schule**. Some subsidies were granted to us by all the local authorities with the exception of one for which we still await confirmation of the amount. These aids will not get us out of contracting a bank loan (which we hope will be the smallest possible so as not to burden our budget too seriously).

An extraordinary general meeting (which will probably immediately follow the annual customary meeting) will give its agreement for the contraction of this loan. Once again, your generosity will be employed to contribute to restricting the size of this loan to the minimum.

The first European Day of Jewish Patrimony in Dijon, which took place on September 5, was an unanticipated success. It certainly, through the interest it aroused for our religion, helped generate contributions for the renovation of our synagogue, which is certainly a part of Dijonnais and Bourguignon patrimony.

I hope that the coming year will bring more serenity than the preceding one for our Dijonnais community as well as for all the Jews and their friends in the world!

Cordial Shalom!
Israël Cemachovic

Security: Chronicle of ordinary days

Mazal Tov 33 (December 2004): 17

Responsible for the security of the community in Dijon, I receive each Friday, on my personal fax, the list of anti-Semitic or Judeophobic aggressions. This document is issued from the Service of Protection of the Jewish Community, which lists and monitors these incidents.

Maybe in order not to give in to security paranoia, I did not consider passing them on in *Mazal Tov*. But it seems to me that you must be informed.

These complaints are never published in the press either. Note for yourselves: the Minister of the Interior announced, at the end of June, a total of more than 180 acts (that is an aggression each day). That's the situation.

These acts are mainly committed in the Parisian region. To those who would be tempted to say to themselves that in Dijon "all is calm" or "in view of the foreign politics of France, we risk nothing" (remarks heard at the time of talks with the police), remember that sticking one's head in the sand does nothing to help or protect one from danger.

I am naturally keeping the original copies, at the disposition of those who want to consult them.

Michel Bussidan

Re-transcription of communicated material

Mazal Tov 33 (December 2004): 17–19

[Partial] List of hostile acts from October 5 to November 2, 2004 [32 acts occurred].

October 5, 2004
Nancy (54*): Two men of Maghrébin origin attacked a nurse at the home of a retired Israélite [Jew]. They made anti-Semitic remarks to their victim, molested her, stole her jewelry, and threatened her with reprisals if a complaint was registered.

October 7, 2004
Marseille (13): Some stones were thrown in the parking lot of the Synagogue of the thirteenth arrondissement, breaking the windshield of a parked vehicle.
Évry (91): Five youths of Maghrébin origin threw insults and stones at a rabbi who passed close to a high school.

October 8, 2004
Le Raincy (93): The mezuzah of a member of the Jewish community was stolen.

October 10, 2004
Paris XIX†: Four children of the same Jewish family who were on the first floor of their apartment building were struck and insulted—"Go back into your house, dirty Jews." A cell phone as well as some money was stolen from the eldest of the children (15 years). For fear of reprisals, the parents preferred not to file a complaint.

October 11, 2004
Paris XII: Leaving a bakery, a young boy of 12, not wearing any distinctive sign of religion, was knocked over by an adolescent boy. This boy called him a dirty Jew, threatened to kill him, attempted to drag him toward a parking lot, and finally stole his cell phone.

October 12, 2004
Montreuil (93): Following a dispute, a client made anti-Semitic comments to the person in charge at a pharmacy.

---

* Numbers denote French departments, of which there are 101, including Corsica.
† Roman numerals denote Parisian districts, of which there are now 20.

October 14, 2004
Boulogne-Billancourt (92): A young, adolescent female Jew was approached by two young girls, both of Maghrébin origin. They insulted her, slapped her, and pulled her hair.

October 17, 2004
Paris XVII: On the rue de l'Abbé Rousselot, a young man wearing a kippa was insulted, thrown to the ground, and struck by three individuals who hit him several times before stealing his cell phone.

October 20, 2004
Paris XV: At the approach to the Modigliani Middle School, a fight occurred between two students, one Jewish, provoked by anti-Semitic remarks.

October 21, 2004
Paris XI: A verbal altercation took place between a Jewish tenant and people responsible for maintenance, who felt that she was in the way. After kicking and ringing for a long time at the door, the maintenance people said to the woman: "You Jew, dirty rotten race, return to your country."

October 27, 2004
Strasbourg (67): The cellar of a Jewish family and that of one of their neighbors was riddled with anti-Semitic inscriptions.

October 29, 2004
Brumath (67): 92 graves of a Jewish cemetery were desecrated. Some stones were smeared with swastikas and with the tags "Heil Hitler," "White Power," and "SS."

October 30, 2004
Belfort (90): Some anti-Semitic inscriptions—"Down with the Jews; dirty Jew, we don't like you" were drawn on the exterior walls of a tobacco store. The owner of the store is not Jewish.

November 1, 2004
Genlis (21): About 30 tombstones were covered with Nazi and anti-Semitic inscriptions in the municipal cemetery. The graves were marked in graffiti with inscriptions such as "Death to the Jews," "Jewish cunts," as well as with swastikas and Nazi abbreviations.

NATIONAL BUREAU OF VIGILANCE AGAINST ANTI-SEMITISM
8 Boulevard Saint Simon 93700 Drancy

Speech for the Sixtieth Anniversary of the Liberation of the Auschwitz Camp

Mazal Tov 34 (March 2005): 25

Mr. Cabinet Director of the Prefect,
Dear Fellow Jews,
Dear Friends,

It is with great emotion that we participate, tonight, at this commemoration of the sixtieth anniversary of the liberation of the Auschwitz camp. This service should not be geared towards the Jewish community alone but, taking into account the breadth of the awareness of the event, at both national and international levels, we have decided to spread the information more widely.

But can we really speak of "liberation" to comprehend the title of commemorations that took place here in France and on the spot in Poland? Is that appropriate on the anniversary of the sad uncovering of the horror of extermination camps that for a long time we believed to be simple concentration or work camps?

This was a mass extermination of the Jewish people and Gypsies that, for the first time and in a unique manner in the history of humanity, took place on both an international and industrial level.

Because of all the genocides that preceded and, alas, followed this sad period, only the Shoah was carried out on such a grand scale and direction, by its simultaneous operation in a multitude of conquered countries and, on another hand, by the utilization of all the industrial methods known at the period (railroads, creation of vast regrouping camps, gassing, cremation).

This discovery, at the end of the war in January 1945, at a time when Paris had been liberated in August 1944 and Dijon in September of the same year, cast dismay among the armed allies who, after so many sacrifices on the battlefield, did not expect to find installations for putting to death large number of civilians, moreover partly destroyed by the dissembling, retreating Nazis.

Alas, for the millions of survivors facing brutal displacement, marching through Poland in the glacial cold, in a state of physical and moral dilapidation, the journey home was long and difficult— it had never been planned.

Those who made it back to their home countries still faced a lingering anti-Semitism in spite of their trials. Two-thirds of the Jewish population in Europe disappeared in the smoke of four crematories.

It is, however, in France, despite the active collaboration of the Vichy government, that the Jews have, proportionally, suffered the least: "only" a quarter of the Jewish population of France was deported. And this, thanks to the aid supplied by the French population who listened to their hearts more than to reason, which had prompted, for fear of death, a lack of opposition to the projects of the Nazis and their accomplices.

This belated discovery of extermination camps, hardly three months before the end of the war, raises the question that has now become commonplace: were the Allies aware of the extermination of Jews and Gypsies?

Alas, one must, today, respond to this question in the affirmative. Yes, the highest authorities of the Allied countries were well informed and did nothing to stop it. While some well-timed bombs could have seriously paralyzed the process of extermination, nothing was tried under the fallacious pretexts of preservation of forces with a view to the final offensive.

Yes, some arguments made at present refer to the problem that existed for Europe at the time: the presence of more than 11 million Jews, considered inassimilable, whose disappearance would not be entirely regrettable?

Today, at a time when the survivors are ever more rare, we, the children of survivors, soon must pass on the memory and testify to the future generations about the hell of the Holocaust, so that it never happens again.

Attacks against Jews in Western Europe and particularly in France (offshoots of the conflict in the Middle East) remind us that the situation always remains precarious for the Jewish people as long as anti-Semitism rages on. I would hope, dear fellow Jews and dear friends, that each of you will continue to preserve, in your hearts and in your spirits, the memory of our ancestors, gone forever in the torment of the twentieth century, a torment which was the outcome of 2,000 years of what historian Jules Isaac called the "teaching of contempt."

Is there anything worse than the systematic destruction of a people, taking away their pride, burning their holy books, stealing their dignity, their hair, their teeth, turning people into numbers, soap, ashes?

The response is yes, there is something worse: to perpetuate all of that and then to deny it. To perpetuate all of that and then to deny the victims—their children and grandchildren—a legitimacy to their sorrow.

And finally, these lessons are essential today because we are witnesses, again, to a violent assault against the fundamental principle of the sanctity of human life.

Maybe the greatest idea of foundation that the Bible has given to humanity is the simple truth that all men, women, and children are created in the divine image and, therefore, have an infinite worth. For the Nazis, the value of a human being was limited, indeed dispensable. The main thing to know was the amount of work a man could accomplish, how many teeth he had, what quantity of hair a woman could supply. For the Nazis, the destruction of a human being or of a hundred, a million, six million was irrelevant. He was nothing but a means for a perverse end.

At the same time, when we see what the survivors gave to humanity, we can only begin to imagine what could have been given to the world by the millions who did not survive. We mourn for their loss, even today. Each fiber of our being perceives their absence. Each family knows the suffering.

I thank you.
January 27, 2005
Israël Cemachovic

Israel, a World Problem?: Report on Liliane Missika's conference of 4 December 2005

Mazal Tov 37 (December 2005): 15–16

This conference was addressed primarily for what I call "BIMI," the people with good intentions but insufficient information.

In fact, Israel and the conflict in the Middle East in general, suffer from a culture of misinformation. According to a survey made several years ago, 60 per cent of French citizens see Israel as one of the countries most endangering world peace.

Moreover, the Israeli-Arab [conflict] plays a role in all cases, from the Gulf War to the riots in the suburbs (Intifada of the Suburbs) [November 2005]. This last expression might have appeared a little shocking at the beginning, but it is worth considering; why not use the same expression for these events since the Intifada in Israel was given that name by the Europeans. After all, the French rioters have the same motives as the Palestinians: motives of, "revolt," "injustice," "misery," and "frustration."

According to experts in this area, the same motives make the young British people of Pakistani origin blow themselves up in a bus in London.

Resolutions of the United Nations: in total, 322 resolutions have condemned Israel. Not a single one condemns an Arab country in spite of numerous human rights violations.

In Saudi Arabia one can be imprisoned for celebrating Christmas. In Jerusalem, the municipality distributes Christmas trees for free.

The Wall of Shame* [Protecting Israeli citizens from attack]

The people, who are against the building of this wall-border that is meant to separate two countries, remain silent about Ceuta or Melilla, the Spanish enclaves in Morocco. It is important to note that the latter enclaves exist only to protect the uncontrolled immigration of Europeans and [are] only a danger to the economy, while the Israeli barrier will become vital for the Israeli population constantly menaced by attacks.

How can the economy be considered more important than people's lives? This is exactly what the people, who protest against the building of the wall, try to do.

In Europe, those who fight against Israel are not anti-Semites, they are anti-Zionists. Anti-Zionism is seen as positive, especially by the left, because Zionism is considered synonymous with racism.

---

* Opponents to the Wall call it "The Wall of Shame."

On the contrary, Martin Luther King, incomparable in the fight against racism, because he succeeded in expanding the rights of the black people in America and paid for it with his life—even he said with certainty that "being anti-Zionist is being anti-Semitic," and he would never do this.

Is everything going to get better in the rest of the world if we do away with Israel?

The problems listed in the 2002–03 report of the United Nations reveal the illiteracy of the Arab countries, the inequality of men and women, the infant mortality rate, the low socioeconomic level, the terrible state of human rights, endemic corruption, the lack of openness to other cultures—would all these problems be resolved after the disappearance of Israel?

How to imagine that the Arab countries, having enormous wealth in the form of oil, would suddenly get better after "having gotten rid of the Jewish presence in the Holy Land?"

Isn't this just an attempt to hide their own insufficiencies or their lack of openness, their refusal to accept the democracy that Israel established, [instead calling it] "the one and the only troublemaker" in the region?

And of course, no one talks about eliminating Israel except the Iranian oligarchy and the "sympathetic" Hamas who have written down in their charter ["the throwing of the Jews into the sea"].

The soft approach is a binational state where the 5,000,000 Jews will rapidly become a minority among 3,750,000 Palestinians and 1,200,000 Israeli Arabs, according to a demographic report. Therefore the Jews will not be a majority, if they don't have their state anymore and return to their earlier status: the Jews will be persecuted, tortured, executed, even deported. Where would they go in this case? The 800,000 Jews deported from the Arab countries without any weapons or luggage—do you think someone will let them come back? Do you think that someone will let them celebrate their holidays in Poland, Russia, or Austria?

Certainly being anti-Zionist is calling into question the existence of the State of Israel and refusing the right of the Jewish people to a home country.

The secession of Gaza at this point is an affirmative example, because a non-negotiable greenhouse area that had been left by some "Jewish settlers" was destroyed after their departure, as if the only possible "victory" consists in the elimination of the Jews and not in the appropriation of the resources and the tools for production and economic prosperity that can be derived from there.

So, it is important to try to better understand the driving forces of this conflict and to admit that the media doesn't really understand the situation.

Daniel Lefebvre

The book by Liliane Missika and Fabien Ghez was published in January 2006: *The Impossible Peace*, Éditions l'Archipel.

Pauline Bebe

Mazal Tov 40 (October 2006): 24

Pauline Bebe, the only female rabbi in France, opens a House of Liberal Judaism in Paris.

The house, the first of its kind in the capital (where the Orthodox of Judaism dominates), will be inaugurated on 9 April, next to the Bastille. It is meant to be "a religious and cultural space open to everyone, Jews and non-Jews," explains Mrs. Bebe, 41, founder of the Liberal Jewish Community in Île-de-France in 1995.

Built in the old parking street Moufle, this bright modern center, designed by the architect Marc Fitoussi, maintains the memory of the Shoah.

"During the war, this was a metallurgy factory where, according to witnesses from the neighborhood, Jews worked and were deported," says Mrs. Bebe.

The center should be inaugurated by the Socialist Mayor of Paris, Bertrand Delanoë, by the Mayor of XIe urban district, Georges Sarré, and by the religious officers and the associations in the neighborhood. The religious part of the synagogue will be inaugurated in May.

The space, which is property of the Municipality of Paris, was leased at a very low price. The center has been bringing together Mrs. Bebe's community and Nitsa's cultural association for the last ten years. The project, with a total cost of €1.6 million, was financed by donations and aid from Jewish foundations as well as by grants from the Municipality of Paris and the region dealing with cultural development.

It has a polyvalent room with 300 seats, equipped with moving walls and illuminated by vaulting made of glass pavement; the room is back-to-back with another six classrooms and the rabbi's office. Stained glass windows, paintings, tapestries, mosaics, statues, and a special stone from Jerusalem adorn this "synagogue of the Arts."

Later on, they expect to expand the project to the basement, where a cafeteria, media library, [and] dance and art studios will be built, connected to the ritual bath (mikveh) supplied by rainwater collected on the roof and brought down by a special downpipe that doesn't contain any metal.

Liberal Judaism, born at the end of the eighteenth century, lauds adaptation to the modern period, particularly dealing with equality of rights and responsibilities among men and women. This movement, open to interreligious dialogue, has a big role in the world with more than 1,600,000 members.

In the new House, there will be dance, theater, and expositions, but also meals for the homeless. The services will be full of music: "Latin-American culture, since part of the community comes from Argentina, but also rock," explains Mrs. Bebe, a mother of four. Her husband, the American rabbi Tom Cohen, plays electric guitar.

"I have many fewer critics today, I don't feel excluded. I have good relationships with my Orthodox colleagues," Mrs. Bebe adds.

Her community, one of 15 liberal communities in France, has more than 300 families.

Ordained in 1990, she did her rabbinic studies at the Leo Baeck College in London, becoming one of the first female rabbis in Europe.

AFP— *5 April 2006*
Transmitted by Maurice Gislain Bensoussan

TESTIMONIES: An unprecedented or an eternally existing anti-Semitism?

Mazal Tov 50 (April 2009): 19–20

She and I

She is in her 60s. She arrived from an Eastern country when she was about 20 years old. She remained a practicing Communist, got married to a man from Burgundy, and adopted his style of living. She is fascinated by the Shoah. She does not miss any exhibition of Art, not a single film at Eldo (an arty movie theater). She becomes vehemently indignant to injustice and manifests her support of abused workers and victims. Still, she carries latent racism in her soul and a repressed anti-Semitism. The Jew she likes wears striped pajamas, is gassed, burned, chased, and is anti-Zionist. She is afraid of Islamic scarves, but fully supports the Palestinian extremists.

I

I am in my 60s too. My parents, who were born in France, have their origins in an Eastern country. I am often militant but never a member of a political party. I do not like any form of extremism, neither political nor religious. For a long time now, I have been demonstrating against social injustices and against racism, which offends me. I am a Jew, but I neither believe, nor practice. I love Israel, as I love France, without approving of everything; I have difficulty understanding how some Jews could wish for the defeat of this country. I call them suicidal. If I had the choice, I'd want the Jews to be free, and dignified rather than deported and abused. My ideals are democracy, freedom, and secularism. I avoid the exhibitions of Art and do not go to Eldo any more since it has been clearly supporting the movements of the extreme Left. I am afraid of Islamic veils and clothes, in general, since they demonstrate the convictions of the people who wear them.

We

We were meeting several times per week; we forced ourselves to put aside everything that pushed us apart and focused on the points of view we had in common. We used to take a walk around the lake, exchange secrets, protest from the bottom of our hearts against injustice, chatter on the phone, do each other favors, shop together, go to the theater several times, invite each other ... we did not wear any masks, we knew everything about each other. We were sworn to friendship and affection.

We loved each other "because it was her, because it was me."

At least I believed so....

When we felt like it was time for us to leave for Kenya, it was she who drove us to the station.

When I came back, I gave her a call. I got the cold shoulder.

She did not want to talk to me anymore because of Gaza, because, as a "non-suicidal" Jew, I was an accomplice of Israel, a monstrous country, which was responsible for the massacre of the Gaza population. It was the 25th of January [following the Israeli Cast Lead Operation][*].

I presume that her suppressed anti-Semitism came to the surface as a result of her anti-Zionism and that her activities within the Communist Party took on the spirit of a sect.

No doubt, I am not the only person who has had such an experience. I had to wait for 63 years to experience anti-Semitism, but I saw the same dismay in the faces of Arthur,[†] Michael Boujenah,[‡] Enrico Macias,[§] and other celebrities who were rejected because they were Jews and, therefore, accomplices of Israel—which was presented as a Nazi country.

All these good folks who exclude us, who throw us in the trash can, live with a clear conscience; they are not anti-Semites, just anti-Zionists.

Cathie: Selective Hospitality

Yes, I did have an experience of this type of reaction on the part of one of my very good Parisian friends. I am not a Jew, but I have become close to the Dijon [Jewish] community. For the last three years, I have studied Hebrew. I participate in difference reunions, and I am also a member of the Renanim choir. There was a planned concert in Paris on the 1st of February with the aforementioned choir.

My friend knew my sensitivity for the Jewish people and for the religion. She knows that I go to services and that I respect some mitzvot even though

---

[*] Israeli invasion of Gaza, December 2008-January 2009, in response to hundreds of Hamas rockets attacking Israeli.

[†] Stage name for Jacques Essebag, a well-known Moroccan-born television personality, especially known for hosting variety shows and one-man theater performances.

[‡] Well-known Tunisian-born Jewish comic who plays major roles in films and on stage (one-man productions especially).

[§] Famous Algerian-born Jewish folk/popular singer, especially known as a prime interpreter of Judeo-Arabic music and culture.

I am from a different faith. Every person has a right to choose his spiritual way, doesn't he? Am I not born in the country of liberty and human rights?

So, I had to spend two days in Paris to sing with the choir, and I just asked my friend to lodge me for this time.

I did not hear from her for several days. I tried to contact her again. She said she had not seen my message and invited me to stay, while asking me about the purpose of my visit.

When she understood the purpose of my visit, she told me that she had to work on that weekend and that her apartment was not heated. In short, I felt some reluctance ... until I read two pro-Palestinian pamphlets sent by her....

So, I could, by an exchange of messages (without the honesty of telling me) understand her reluctance to welcome me!

I put her in her place by reminding her of some events and real historical facts from the past, but I did not go to her house, and I severed our relationship. Her lack of sincerity hurt me as much as her propensity to keep her head down and give credit to media [bias] without looking for the truth.

On the other hand, I would like to clarify that it was out of the question that I hide my Star of David under my clothing even during this conflict. Provocation was not my thing, but I did not see why I should have hidden a medal of half a centimeter. My point is perhaps understood by some, but there was no negative reaction: thus, I like to think—and I hope I am not a naïve optimist—that the stigma of anti-Semitism characterizes only a small portion of the population.

Claudine Claves-Contet

CONCLUSION: AN UNCERTAIN FUTURE

The experience of the Jewish community of Dijon since the end of World War II can be described as an arc: restoration and recovery in the decade immediately following the war; slow, steady renewal into the 1960s; expansion, struggle, and assimilation into the 1980s; a decade of dynamic achievement and expansion; and, from the mid-1990s on, division and slow decline. It is a model that, unfortunately, characterizes many similar Jewish communities throughout France and, possibly, Europe as well.

In the years since the final interviews were conducted in 2007, trends noted earlier have continued. There is now a distinct feeling of pessimism, often openly expressed, among leading members of the community. This may, in part, be the natural response to aging and long labors. More likely, it is the reaction to a changing and less favorable reality.

France itself is undergoing changes similar to those afflicting much of the Western world in the new millennium. Unlike the United States and Britain, France was less affected by the economic crisis of 2007–08, but the 2011 euro-zone financial crisis of the Mediterranean countries, Portugal, and Ireland has exposed the underlying fragility of the European Union's economic structures. And now, at a time of intense global challenges from emerging economies in Asia and elsewhere, France's laudable social protective framework and capacity to compete are questioned.

The official unemployment rate in France hovers around 10 per cent and gross domestic product growth is about 2 per cent—hardly laudable numbers. What they do not reveal is that unemployment for youth and Muslims is much higher, while job growth is not significant. Additionally, the economic growth that does occur is mostly in large metropolitan areas such as Paris and Lyon. The phenomenon affecting much of the world of migration—often of the young, energetic, and brightest—from the countryside and peripheral regions to metropolitan centers, is present in France.

These developments have affected Dijon. As mentioned earlier, the city historically was a marketing and administrative center for the surrounding agricultural region. Industrialization was, and is, limited. Though retail and services have grown along with the population, especially in outlying areas from the city center, this has not been a sufficient driving force for sustained growth. Meanwhile, prices, even in Dijon, remain high, particularly for real estate. Simply stated, the city's economy is more static than dynamic. A much-heard demand is for more employment, particularly for the young.

The Dijon Jewish community, like many similar communities through-out France, continues to experience the loss of young families and people. As they leave for Paris, other European cities, Israel, or North America, the community left behind ages and shrinks. Religious services are less well attended, programs are eliminated, organizations disappear, and costs rise. Overall, what the community has to offer appears less appealing, especially for the young. Now, most of the adult children of the interviewees no longer reside in Dijon.

Along with the flight to more dynamic urban centers are increases in mixed marriages and assimilation into the larger non-Jewish society. This is due to secularization, ethnic and religious diversity, and the loosening of bonds after departure from a fairly tight-knit community. As young people leave Dijon for opportunities elsewhere, they are more likely to experience this. Dating and marriage with others of different religious and ethnic back-grounds are no longer exceptional, and most members of the community at least reluctantly accept it. On the other hand, however, other of Dijon's young urban exiles have become more traditional and, even, strictly Orthodox or Lubavitch. This is also true of those who have moved to Israel.

Although some of the more practicing young Jews have remained liberal and open-minded, others have clearly fallen prey to what the French refer to negatively as "communitarianism," a kind of self-segregation, partly in response to the growth of anti-Zionism and anti-Semitism in French public life. The fact that perhaps a third of French Jewish children now attend Jewish day schools, and not simply for reasons of religious identification, is representative of the same pattern of behavior. Perhaps another third now attend Catholic schools, where safety and discipline are also expected. These are the same reasons that non-Lubavitch couples in Dijon might decide to enroll their children in the Lubavitch school.

Additionally, the seemingly endless conflicts in the Middle East have taken a further toll of French attitudes towards Israel. The widely condemned attack by Israel on Hamas-dominated Gaza in 2008–09, the clumsy Israeli assault on the Turkish-led aid flotilla to Gaza in 2010, and the seeming reluc-tance by the Netanyahu administration to seriously negotiate a settlement with the Palestinians have all resulted in harsh criticism of Israel. In France, where the media are largely pro-Palestinian, Israel is seen as an aggressor state, with the Palestinian people as its foremost victims.

Large pro-Palestinian demonstrations have occurred in major French cities, even in Dijon. There the Jewish community countered with smaller pro-Israeli protests, including reminders to the public about Palestinians' rocket attacks against civilians and the Hamas-held Israeli hostage, Gilad

Shalit.[*] Especially during moments of Israel related crises in the Middle East, the atmosphere in France and Dijon has become increasingly toxic. Violent acts have increased, including attacks on Jewish individuals and property. To some extent the growing French antagonism in the general public towards its own Muslim population has also included Jews, who are somehow associated with the problems related to the country's large Arab minority. So-called Holocaust fatigue also has caused many French to be less sympathetic to Jewish causes, while others continue to be drawn to the Jewish community because of their increased awareness of the tragic history of French Jews.

The Arab Spring of 2011, in which oppressive regimes in Tunisia, Egypt, and Libya were overthrown and anti-government conflicts erupted through-out the Arab world, is viewed by the Dijon community, and by many Jews in general, with less good will and hope than they are in much of the Western world. The fear is that new, popular Arab governments may be more hostile to Israel than the former dictatorships with whom Israel had arrangements and that provided at least a "cold" peace.[†] In addition, a possible future nuclear-armed Iran, expanding its influence in Iraq, Syria, and Lebanon, and supporting Hezbollah and Hamas, is a growing cause for apprehension. Another reason for concern is that the Obama administration seems to be favoring the Arab world over Israel. The belief by many in the Dijon community that the United States will support Israel without reservations is no longer held.

Jews in Dijon, and France generally, already negatively impacted by global economic and political changes, have taken little relief from domes-tic developments. The majority of French Jews departed from their usual support for Socialist candidates and voted for the conservative Nicholas Sarkozy as president in May 2007. Sarkozy's Jewish maternal grandfather, his son's conversion and marriage into a prominent Jewish family, and his wife's partially Jewish background certainly were factors in the support he received. But French Jews also expected that policies towards Arab immi-grants and towards Israel would change under his presidency. Sarkozy has taken harder positions on internal security issues and Muslim immigration, and he has demonstrated greater sensitivity towards Israel and the United States. He played an activist role in European Union economic affairs and was a strong supporter in the NATO 2011 intervention in what had become the Libyan civil war.

---

[*] Shalit was finally released in November 2011, in return for over 1,000 Arab prisoners.

[†] Recent developments in Turkey and Egypt, including a mob assault on the Israeli Embassy in Cairo in September 2011, are negative portents for the future.

France's unsettled economic conditions, related to the global economy, and Sarkozy's drastic measures (at least to the French) to reduce fiscal deficits by curtailing entitlements, have undermined his popularity (which was also not helped by his erratic public personal behavior). His expulsion of illegal Roma (Gypsy) immigrants appalled many Jews, who were reminded of the Vichy and German deportations of French Jews during World War II. His sponsorship of discussions in 2009–10 in the Chamber of Deputies on the nature of French identity parallel with the deportations polarized public attitudes and were abruptly cancelled.

The re-emergence of the far-Right National Front, now under the leadership of the attractive and seemingly more moderate, media-savvy Marine Le Pen, daughter of the party's founder, has further alarmed Jews (several of whom in Dijon, however, look with favor on aspects of the Front's platform, especially in relation to immigration). She has repudiated anti-Semitism and has made pro-Israeli comments, demonstrating a change in attitude. The anticipated Socialist candidacy of Dominique Strauss-Kahn, a favored—and expected—winner in the 2012 presidential election, ended with his involvement in an alleged rape of a hotel maid in New York City in early 2011. Some French Jews wondered how far to the right Sarkozy would go in order to stop Le Pen, how much they could continue to support Sarkozy, and what other options they had. For most Jews, however, the "Sarkozy effect"—of sympathy toward Jews—was appreciated.

The defeat of Sarkozy by Socialist François Hollande in May 2012 likely darkened Jewish perceptions of their future in France. Hopefully, however, President Hollande can assuage Jewish concerns, while addressing major Muslim issues such as unemployment. The appointment of an interior minister who combines empathy with strength also would go a long way toward reassuring Jews as well as moderate Muslims. The swift government reaction to the murders of three Jewish children and a rabbi, among others, in Toulouse in March 2012, though under the Sarkozy administration, was supported by the Socialists. The anti-terrorist (and anti-immigrant) mood in France at this time cannot be ignored by even a Socialist administration.

Fortunately, in the management of Jewish-Muslim relations in Dijon the community has several excellent assets, including Rabbi Simon Sibony and Assistant Mayor Dr. Françoise Tenenbaum. Sibony, who had positive childhood experiences with Muslims in his native Morocco, has established solid relationships with Muslim leaders over the past two decades. He has been a force for moderation and understanding whenever a crisis has erupted.

Tenenbaum, a Socialist Party assistant mayor for almost a decade, and head of the municipality's health and social services, has played an important role in the growing Muslim population's welfare. As a strong believer in the need to integrate Muslims into the life of the city, she frequently meets with their leaders and ordinary citizens, including women. Her efforts have resulted in the establishment or enhancement of nursery schools, medical clinics, community centers, and cultural life in general. Though long a prominent member of the Jewish community and a strong advocate for Israel, she understands that creative and just policies, while also helpful for good relationships between Dijon's Muslims and Jews, are essential to France's republican mission.

Thus, the economic and political climate, so different from that of the previous decade, is a cause of deep concern for the Dijon community. It has been forced to adjust in various ways. Physical security is now a priority. During services, an occupied police car frequently parks on the street in front of the synagogue. The front gate, leading to the building's entrance, is frequently locked, except during services and community events. The doors and the locks of the synagogue have been repaired and reinforced. Television monitors have been installed, including in the sanctuary. Fortunately, the reinforced street barriers that front the entrances of some synagogues in Paris are not yet required, although there are a series of cement cylinders that prevent parking on the adjacent street, rue de la Synagogue.

Apart from its external concerns, the community faces ongoing problems. In the past several years a number of the community's leaders have died, while individuals capable of taking their place have moved from Dijon with their families. The remaining aging members find few young people to replace them, and attendance at religious services has declined. One prominent member of the community described the atmosphere in the synagogue as "lifeless." Synagogue President, Dr. Israël Cemachovic, who in 2011 had served in the office for 12 years, has complained that the community "is not doing well." He wants to retire, but there is no obvious candidate to replace him. Fortunately, for the Dijon community he, with his family's support, decided not to accept a lucrative position in Geneva, where there is a much larger Jewish population. That would have been a serious blow to the Dijon community, active members acknowledge.

Meanwhile, the 170–80 families who comprise the core of the community bear an increasing burden of mounting expenses to sustain the synagogue complex and its varied activities. Dues and other financial offerings have declined, placing an additional burden on the old families who have long been the financial backbone of the community. Some of these older families still contribute significantly, but they attend services perhaps only once or twice a year. Even Rabbi Sibony has been criticized by community members for frequently talking about the need for more financial support, especially from newer members, and during such occasions as funerals.

It is clear that the division in the community also has caused difficulties. The Lubavitch have a core group of about 12–15 families, but they have a school, activities for the young, and study groups for adults, and they sponsor numerous free events that sometimes draw as many as 100 people. Their new, expensive, state-of-the-art mikveh, inaugurated in the presence of the former Grand Rabbi of France, Joseph Sitruk, was a gala event and fundraiser. Though several members of the larger community joined with the Lubavitch in celebrating the widely publicized event, synagogue leaders were conspicuous by their absence, mirroring the lack of any participation by the Lubavitch in synagogue services and community activities. The new mikveh also means that the Lubavitch will no longer need the synagogue's older facility, thus removing one of the last ongoing contacts between the two groups. In further illustration of the division, in May 2011 when a visiting mixed-gender Israeli choir performed in the synagogue sanctuary and later socialized with the community, the Lubavitch refused to attend.

There was success in a number of areas, however. Expensive repairs on the synagogue's striking stained glass windows were completed and were marked by a visit by the present Grand Rabbi of France, Giles Bernheim. The community center was rededicated and named in honor of former synagogue president Henri-Claude Bloch. The community center has continued to offer many programs and a diversity of activities. On the annual Jewish Day of Patrimony, for example, the synagogue and its communal building with displays on view attract substantial numbers of the public.

A number of Christians who attend community events have become active in the choir and have assumed leadership roles in various aspects of community life, including *Mazal Tov*, Radio Shalom, and France-Israel. The choir could not function without their welcome participation; members of the community have said that the participation of Christians is literally necessary for the success of certain activities. In fact, the dance group recently disbanded owing to lack of sufficient interest.

One of these groups in which Christians participate is the France-Israel Association. Whether in the media, a public seminar, or in front of City Hall, the Jewish and Christian activists of this organization, numbering about 50–100 persons, demonstrate for fairness towards Israel. It is the community's arm, through public action, for confronting a hostile media and demands for boycotts, divestment, and sanctions against Israel. Of interest is the fact that it is one of the few remaining spaces in which the members of the Lubavitch group participate in the larger community's efforts, especially during public protests.

The cacophony of anti-Israeli voices, however, has clearly disturbed Jews, even in relatively calm, bourgeois Dijon. Numerous questions are on people's minds: Why is Israel always set apart for special attention in a world filled with many greater examples of human tragedy? What would the American leadership do, with its own people growing weary of Middle Eastern entanglements, in a crisis involving Israel? What about all the relatives and friends resident in Israel? And what future will Jewish children have in France? These questions have no certain answers. But over the centuries Jews have excelled in living with uncertainty, of making do, of getting by. At times, they even prevail. Will the future be any different?

Finally, however, the future of French Jews is inextricably linked to the future of democracy in France. If French Muslims become integrated into a more accepting and tolerant French culture, and if they embrace republican and democratic ideals, there will be ample space for Jews in France as well. If not, the Jews, always a bellwether, will be the first to know. Regardless, their voices will remain a source of fascination and lively interest in the years to come.

Meanwhile, many of the main streets of Dijon remain torn up as a result of the installation of a new tramway, a development that seems to have become *de rigueur* for many medium-sized French cities. Hundreds of jobs have been created locally, but a number of stores have also closed as a result of nasty traffic jams, parking quandaries, and ugly streets and sidewalks. It's a depressing sight that is finally supposed to get cleaned up by the end of 2012 but probably will linger somewhat longer. Sooner or later, however, the city will regain its classic bourgeois ambience, and a spirit of excitement and possibility will permeate Dijon once more.

Unfortunately, it may be easier to repair the ripped-up streets of Dijon than the ruptures that now exist in the Jewish community of the city. Each group can certainly exist separately and even thrive in some areas. Combined, however, they represented a real success story in Jewish living and respect for diversity. For now, as one old French adage has it, "if one can't have what one likes, one needs to like what one has." Hopefully, the divided community will eventually find some areas of common interest, so that the rupture will not become permanent. In such a small community as Dijon, a rupture serves no one's self-interest, especially not at this troubled moment in French Jewish life.

GLOSSARY AND ABBREVIATIONS

ACID: Religious Association of the Jews of Dijon.

aliyah: Immigration to Israel, literally *ascending* to Israel.

Amidah: Central component of all religious services, composed of a series of blessings which change somewhat as a result of which service (morning, afternoon, evening) is taking place.

Ashkenazim: Jews mainly from Germany who moved to Eastern or Western Europe during the Middle Ages, many then moving westward from the eighteenth century onwards.

baal techouva (also teshuvah and baalat teshuvah): A man or woman, respectively, who returns to strict religious practice, especially to Hasidism. See techouva.

bar mitzvah: Coming into manhood ceremony in which Jewish males, age 13, recite the blessings over a portion of the Torah and usually read a portion from the Torah and the Prophets; they may also conduct a wider portion of the Sabbath service, on which the bar mitzvah usually occurs. Literally means, son of a commandment. Thereafter such males may be counted in a minyan.

bat mitzvah: Similar to bar mitzvah for women at age 12 or 13. It originated in the United States in 1922, spreading thereafter worldwide, especially among more liberal and even conservative Jews, among whom women gained equal rights in the 1960s.

BBYO: B'nai B'rith Youth Organization.

Beit Din: Traditional rabbinical court that decides issues of Jewish law and supervises Orthodox conversions.

Beit Habbad: Lubavitch centers established worldwide since World War II.

B'nai B'rith: Largest international Jewish fraternal organization, founded in 1843 in the United States.

bris or bris milah: Ritual circumcision of Jewish male child on the eighth day following birth.

CCJD: Cultural Center of the Jews of Dijon.

Chumash: Hebrew Bible, with translations and commentaries used during Sabbath, Festival, High Holiday, and many other services, especially when portions of the Torah and Prophets are read.

diaspora: Jews the world over who live outside of Palestine/Israel, and who are, therefore, in exile from the Promised Land; a position no longer accepted by most non-orthodox Jews.

gan: Kindergarten class in Sunday schools or Talmud Torah schools.

Gemara: Rabbinic commentaries on the Mishna, part of the Talmud.

goy: A non-Jew or a Gentile, sometimes with a pejorative meaning. [goyim (plural).] The word literally means a nation or nations in Hebrew.

guer: Literally, a stranger, protected in the community according to Jewish law and custom, since the Jews were strangers in Egypt.

Habbad: Lubavitch Hasidism, see below.

haksharot: Varies, but usually about six months in an Israeli kibbutz, involving morning study (especially Hebrew) and afternoon work, especially on the land.

Hanukkah: Eight-day winter Jewish Festival of Lights, in which candles in a holder known as a menorah are lit on successive nights; it commemorates the Maccabi victory in ancient times against Syrian-Greeks. It is sometimes spelled Chanukah.

Hasidism: Mystical Jewish movement founded in eighteenth-century Poland by the Baal Shem Tov (master of a good name); there are many branches, the most important or well-known of which today is the Lubavitch movement.

Havurah: Small, autonomous Jewish prayer and observance groups developed in the late 1960s and thereafter in the United States, both within and outside of synagogue communities.

hazan (hazzanim) cantor(s): Learned singer who conducts services along with a rabbi.

High Holy Days: Refers to Rosh Hashanah and Yom Kippur.

Israélites: French name given to Jews after emancipation, signifying that they became an assimilated religious group, based upon individual choice, rather than members of an ascribed corporate ethnic community.

Kaddish: Prayer in memory of the dead, which sanctifies God's Name. It is said in other forms during services as well.

ketubah: Jewish marriage contract.

Kiddush, Kiddish: Prayers said over wine before dinner and lunch on the Sabbath and festivals.

kippa: Head covering worn by traditional Jewish men or by others during prayer.

kolel: Higher institute for Jewish learning among ultra-orthodox Jews.

kosher (kashrut): Jewish dietary laws, which include avoiding eating shellfish and pork; preparing and eating meat and dairy products separately; and only eating meat slaughtered in a ritual fashion. Products and restaurants are rabbinically supervised and given markings indicating the food is kosher.

LICRA (Ligue Internationale Contre le Racisme et l'Antisémitisme): Founded by Bernard Lacache in the late 1930s, originally just against anti-Semitism, but expanded to combat other racism in France and elsewhere.

Lubavitch: Lubavitch Hasidism or Habbad is a branch of Hasidism founded by Rabbi Shneur Zalman of Liadi, Poland in the late eighteenth century. Habbad stands for the Hebrew words wisdom, understanding, and knowledge. The Lubavitch now serve as missionaries to strengthen Judaism worldwide, in addition to maintaining large segregated communities.

mashgiach: Religious authority, normally a rabbi, who supervises Kashrut in restaurants, dining halls, etc.

mechitzah: A physical separation (partition) between men and women during prayers in traditional or Orthodox congregations and in social spaces among the ultra-Orthodox.

mezuzah: Amulet containing sacred prayers placed on the upper right door post of one's house or worn as jewelry around the neck.

mikveh: Ritual bath used for purification by traditional women before marriage and after menstruation, or by women and men as part of the conversion process.

mincha: Afternoon prayers recited by observant Jews daily.

minyan: Quorum of ten men needed for a traditional service; most non-Orthodox Jews count women in the quorum.

Mishna: Early Rabbinic commentaries on the Torah; the first part of the Talmud.

mitzvah: A commandment or good deed. Mitzvot is the plural. Observant Jews attempt to follow 613 commandments, the first ten of which have become universal in the Abrahamic religions—Judaism, Christianity, and Islam.

mitzvot: Commandments or good deeds observed by orthodox and some conservative Jews and by other Jews, according to choice.

mohel: Trained religious official who circumcises newborn males on their eighth day, as a sign of their covenant with God and the Jewish people.

ORT (Organisation de Reconstruction et Travail): Training institutes; now also teaches more advanced and technical studies needed for enhanced employment.

Passover (also called Pesah or Pesach): Eight-day spring festival commemorating the exodus from Egypt and involving special family or community services known as seders and the eating of motzoh or unleavened bread.

phylacteries (tephillin): Prayer aids, used by traditional Jews daily during morning services, except on the Sabbath, Festivals, and High Holy Days; composed of thin black straps worn around one's left arm and hand, with a small prayer box facing one's heart, and of a strap around the forehead, again with a prayer box, signifying total devotion of head and heart during prayer.

pieds noirs: French repatriates from Algeria in 1962, following Algeria's independence from France. Literally "black feet," referring to their original work as farmers, somewhat derogatory.

Rashi: Rabbi Shlomo ben Yitzchakh (1040–1105), a great French medieval commentator on the Torah and Talmud.

Rosh Hashanah: The first of the High Holy Days, celebrating the Jewish religious New Year, a.k.a. the Day of Judgment and the Day of Remembrance, and celebrated with awe and self-introspection.

Rosh Hodesh: Beginning of a new Hebrew month, with special prayers recited in synagogues.

schule: Sanctuary or synagogue. Also shul.

seder: Passover ceremony/meal during which Jews retell the story of their "deliverance" from Egyptian bondage, using a special prayer book, the haggadah, or the telling.

Sephardim: Refers to Jews whose customs and roots stem from medieval Spain (Sepharad) and the Near East; many came to France from North Africa in the 1950s and 1960s.

Sepher Torah: Torah scroll; literally, book of the Torah.

Shabbat: Sabbath day of rest and prayer, celebrated by Jews on Saturday.

shammes: Sexton, who takes care of the synagogue, including religious objects.

shiur: Lesson or analytical focused study of religious texts or concepts.

Sh'ma: Most important Jewish prayer, proclaiming the oneness of God and stressing the transmission of love for God/God's teachings to one's children; a part of all regular worship services.

Shoah: Hebrew word for the Holocaust, meaning purposeless destruction or catastrophe. Israelis and many other Jews prefer this to the word Holocaust, which implies a redemptive dimension.

Shomer Shabbat: Those Jews who observe (guard) the Sabbath in a traditional manner.

Simchat Torah: Last day of the Sukkot festival, marking the completed reading of the Torah, followed by beginning the cycle once again with the Book of Genesis.

simhot: Wonderful events, marriages, etc.

sukkah: Small wooden hut built especially for celebrating Sukkot.

Sukkot: Harvest festival, following Yom Kippur.

Talmud: Composed of multi-volume rabbinic commentaries found in the Mishna and Gemara, redacted in Babylonia about 500 CE and in Jerusalem around 350 CE; summarized and elucidated in several later rabbinical commentaries, the Talmud forms the basis of most traditional Jewish law and observance.

Talmud Torah: Weekday and Sunday school in which prayer, Bible, history, Israel, customs and holidays are taught.

Tanakh: Hebrew Bible composed of Torah, Prophets, and Writings.

techouva (teshuvah): Repentance, whether religious or secular in nature, if one harmed another person, or individual, one is supposed to request forgiveness from the one she or he harmed. Can be done anytime, but is especially necessary during the High Holy Days. Also a process in which a woman or a man hence known as a Baal techouva become observant, usually within a Lubavitch community.

tephillin: See phylacteries.

Torah: Five Books of Moses in scroll form, read weekly in synagogues. More broadly, Torah signifies religious Jewish learning.

Tosaphistes: Medieval rabbinic commentators who lived during Rashi's era and usually did not agree with him.

WIZO: Women's International Zionist Organization, founded by Henrietta Szold in the United States in 1912; also known as Hadassah.

Yeshiva: Traditional academies of advanced Jewish study and learning.

Yiddish: Mother tongue of much of Eastern European Jewry before the Holocaust; a combination of late medieval German and Hebrew, written in Hebrew letters, and brought westward during waves of migrations from the early modern era to modern times. Still spoken by ultra-Orthodox Jews today.

Yom Kippur: The Day of Atonement and fasting concludes the High Holy Days; it is the holiest day in the Jewish year, the sabbath of sabbaths.

Zionism: National liberation movement of the Jewish people, founded largely by assimilated Austrian journalist Theodor Herzl in the late nineteenth century, calling for the creation of a Jewish homeland/state in Palestine.

SUGGESTED READING

The following provide excellent overviews of Jewish history, historical and contemporary anti-Semitism, and the history of France.

Benbassa, Esther. *The Jews of France: A History From Antiquity to the Present.* Princeton, NJ: Princeton University Press, 1999.

Berenbaum, Michael. *Not Your Father's Antisemitism: Hatred of the Jews in the 21st Century.* St. Paul, MN: Paragon House, 2008.

Birnbaum, Pierre. *The Anti-Semitic Moment: A Tour of France in 1898.* Translated by Jane Marie Todd. New York, NY: Hill and Wang, 2003.

Birnbaum, Pierre. *Jewish Destinies: Citizenship, State, and Community in Modern France.* New York, NY: Hill and Wang, 2000.

Bowen, John R. *Can Islam Be French?* Princeton, NJ: Princeton University Press, 2010.

Brenner, Michael. *A Short History of the Jews.* Translated by Jeremiah Riemer. Princeton, NJ: Princeton University Press, 2010.

Byrnes, Robert. *Anti-Semitism in Modern France.* New Brunswick, NJ: Rutgers University Press, 1950.

Cohen, Erik H. *The Jews of France Today: Identity and Values.* Amsterdam. Brill, 2011.

Collins, James B. *From Tribes to Nation: The Making of France 500–1799.* Toronto: Wadsworth, Thomson Learning, 2002.

Conklin, Alice L., Sarah Fishman, and Robert Zaretsky. *France and its Empire Since 1870.* New York, NY; Oxford: Oxford University Press, 2011.

Dean, Carolyn J. *Aversion and Erasure: The Fate of the Victim after the Holocaust.* Ithaca, NY: Cornell University Press, 2010.

Efron, John, et al. *The Jews: A History.* Upper Saddle River, NJ: Pearson Education, 2009.

Fenby, Jonathan. *France on the Brink.* New York, NY: Arcade, 1998.

Freedman, Samuel G. *Jew vs. Jew: The Struggle for the Soul of American Jewry.* New York, NY: Simon and Schuster, 2000.

Friedlander, Judith. *Vilna on the Seine: Jewish Intellectuals in France since 1968.* New Haven, CT: Yale University Press, 1990.

Gartner, Lloyd P. *History of the Jews in Modern Times.* Oxford: Oxford University Press, 2001.

Graetz, Michael. *The Jews in Nineteenth-Century France: From the French Revolution to the Alliance Israélite Universelle.* Translated by Jane Marie Todd. Stanford, CA: Stanford University Press, 1996.

Hargreaves, Alec G. *Multi-Ethnic France: Immigration, Politics, Culture and Society.* 2nd ed., rev. New York, NY: Routledge, 2007.

Hyman, Paula E. *The Jews of Modern France*. Berkeley, CA: University of California Press, 1998.

Jenkins, Cecil. *A Brief History of France: People, History, and Culture*. Philadelphia, PA: Running Press, 2011.

Kedward, Rod. *France and the French: A Modern History*. Woodstock, NY; New York, NY: The Overlook Press, 2007.

Konner, Melvin. *Unsettled: An Anthropology of the Jews*. New York, NY: Viking Penguin, 2003.

Lindemann, Albert S., and Richard S. Levy, eds. *Antisemitism: A History*. New York, NY: Oxford University Press, 2010.

Marrus, Michael R., and Robert O. Paxton. *Vichy France and the Jew*. New York, NY: Schocken Books, 1983.

Mendes-Flohr, Paul, and Jehuda Reinharz. *The Jew in the Modern World: A Documentary History*. 3rd ed., rev. New York, NY: Oxford University Press, 2011.

Moynahan, Brian. *The French Century: An Illustrated History of Modern France*. Paris: Flammarion, 2007.

Perry, Marvin, and Frederick M. Schweitzer. *Antisemitism: Myth and Hate from Antiquity to the Present*. New York, NY: Palgrave Macmillan, 2002.

Poliakov, Léon. *The History of Anti-Semitism: From the Time of Christ to the Court Jews*. Vol I. Translated by Richard Howard. Paris: Calmann-Lévy, 1955.

Poliakov, Léon. *The History of Anti-Semitism: From Mohammed to the Marranos*. Vol II. Translated by Natalie Gerardi. Paris: Calmann-Lévy, 1961.

Poliakov, Léon. *The History of Anti-Semitism: From Voltaire to Wagner*. Vol III. Translated by Miriam Kochan. Paris: Calmann-Lévy, 1968.

Poliakov, Léon. *The History of Anti-Semitism: Suicidal Europe, 1870-1933*. Vol IV. Translated by George Klin. Paris: Calmann-Lévy, 1977.

Popkin, Jeremy D. *A History of Modern France*. 3rd ed. Englewood Cliffs, NJ: Prentice Hall, 2006.

Rousso, Henry. *The Vichy Syndrome: History and Memory in France since 1944*. Translated by Arthur Goldhammer. Cambridge, MA: Harvard University Press, 1991.

Sachar, Howard M. *The Course of Modern Jewish History*. New rev. ed. New York, NY: Vintage Books, 1990.

Van Creveld, Martin. *The Land of Blood and Honey: The Rise of Modern Israel*. New York, NY: Thomas Dunne Books St. Martin's Press, 2010.

Weidmer, Caroline. *The Claims of Memory: Representations of the Holocaust in Germany and France*. Ithaca, NY: Cornell University Press, 1999.

Wolf, Joan B. *Harnessing the Holocaust: The Politics of Memory in France*. Stanford, CA: Stanford University Press, 2004.

BIBLIOGRAPHY

Adler, Jacques. *The Jews of Paris and the Final Solution*. Oxford: Oxford University Press, 1987.

Aeschimann, Eric and Christophe Boltanski. *Chirac D'Arabie : Les mirages d'une politique française*. Paris: Bernard Grasset, 2006.

Albert, Phyllis Cohen. *The Modernization of French Jewry: Consistory and Community in Nineteenth-century France*. Waltham, MA: Brandeis University Press, 1977.

Aron, Raymond. *Mémoires*. New York, NY: Holmes and Meier, 1990.

Ascot, Roger. *Le sionisme trahi ou les Israéliens du dimanche*. Paris: Éditions Balland, 1991.

Astro, Alan, ed. *Discourses of Jewish Identity in Twentieth Century France*. Yale French Studies 85. New Haven, CT: Yale University Press, 1994.

Attali, Jacques, Pascal Boniface, Alain Houziaux, and Gérard Israel. *Israël, les juifs, l'antisémitisme*. Paris: Les Éditions de l'Atelier, 2005.

Azéma, Jean-Pierre. *From Munich to the Liberation, 1938–1944*. Cambridge: Cambridge University Press, 1984.

Badiou, Alain. *The Meaning of Sarkozy*. Translated by David Fernbach. London: Verso, 2008.

Barcellini, Serge, and Annette Wieviorka. *Passant, souviens-toi! Les Dieux du souvenir de la seconde guerre mondiale en France*. Paris: Graphein, 1999.

Barnavi, Élie. *Aujourd'hui, ou peut-être jamais*. Bruxelles: Mega Print-Turquie, 2008.

Barnavi, Élie. *Les religions meurtrières*. Paris: Flammarion, 2006.

Bazin, Jean-François. *Histoire du Département de la Côte-d'Or*. Paris: Éditions Gisserot, 2004.

Becker, Jean-Jacques, and Annette Wieviorka. *Les juifs de France : De la révolution française à nos jours*. Paris: Éditions Liana Levi, 1998.

Ben-Moshe, Danny, ed. *Israel and Diaspora Jewish Identity*. Sussex, UK: Sussex Academic Press, 2007.

Benayoun, Allouche, and Doris Bensimon. *Juifs d'Algérie, hier et aujourd'hui : Mémoires et identités*. Paris: Éditions Privat, 1989.

Benbassa, Esther. *Être juif après Gaza*. Paris: CNRS Éditions, 2009.

Benbassa, Esther, and Jean-Christophe Attisas, eds. *Juifs et musulmans : Une histoire partagée, un dialogue à construire*. Paris: La Découverte, 2006.

Bensimon, Doris. *Les juifs de France et leurs relations avec Israël (1945–1988)*. Paris: L'Harmattan, 1989.

Bensimon, Doris, and Sergio Della Pergola. *La population juive de France : Socio-démographie et identité*. Jerusalem: Hebrew University of Jerusalem, 1984.

Bensoussan, Georges. "Antisemitism in French Schools: Turmoil of a Republic." Analysis of Current Trends in Antisemitism 24 (2004).

Bernheim, Gilles. *N'oublions pas de penser la France*. Paris: Stock, 2012.

Birnbaum, Pierre. *Face au pouvoir*. Paris: Éditions Galilée, 2010.

Birnbaum, Pierre. *Les fous de la république : Histoire politique des juifs d'état, de Gambetta à Vichy*. Paris: Éditions du Seuil, 1994.

Birnbaum, Pierre. *La France et les juifs : De 1789 à nos jours*. Paris: Éditions du Seuil, 2004.

Birnbaum, Pierre. *Histoire politique des juifs de France*. Paris: Presses de la Fondation nationale des sciences politiques, 1990.

Birnbaum, Pierre. *The Idea of France*. Translated by M.B. De Besoise. New York, NY: Hill and Wang, 2001.

Birnbaum, Pierre. *La libération du juif*. Paris: Gallimard, 1966.

Birnbaum, Pierre. *Un mythe politique, la « république juive »: De Léon Blum à Pierre Mendès France*. Paris: Fayard, 1988.

Birnbaum, Pierre. *Prier pour l'état : Les juifs, l'alliance royale et la démocratie*. Paris: Calmann-Lévy, 2005.

Birnbaum, Pierre, and Ira Katznelson, eds. *Paths of Emancipation: Jews, States and Citizenship*. Princeton, NJ: Princeton University Press, 1995.

Birnbaum, Pierre, et al. *Les intellectuels français et Israël*. Paris: Éditions de l'éclat, 2009.

Bitton, Michèle, and Lionel Panafit. *Être juif en France aujourd'hui*. Paris: Hachette, 1997.

Bloch, Henri-Claude. *Histoire des juifs bourguignons*. Dijon: Ed. Erem, 1989.

Bolacre, Orimont. *J'y crois pas! : Une réponse à Stéphane Hessel*. Paris: Éditions David Reinharc, 2011.

Boniface, Pascal. *Est-il permis de critiquer Israël?* Paris: Laffont, 2003.

Bourdrel, Philippe. *De la Shoah à nos jours. Vol. II: Histoire des juifs de France*. Paris: Albin Michel, 2004.

Brauman, Rony, and Alain Finkielkraut. *La Discorde : Israël-Palestine, les juifs, la France*. Paris: Mille et Une Nuits, 2006.

Brenner, Emmanuel, ed. *Les territoires perdus de la république : Antisémitisme, racisme, et sexisme en milieu scolaire*. Paris: Mille et Une Nuits, 2002.

Brenner, Michael, Vicki Caron, and Uri R. Kaufmann. *Jewish Emancipation Reconsidered: The French and German Models*. London: Leo Baeck Institute, 2003.

Brown, Frederick. *The Soul of France: Culture Wars in the Age of Dreyfus*. New York, NY: Alfred A. Knopf, 2010.

Caron, Vicki. *Between France and Germany: The Jews of Alsace-Lorraine, 1871–1918*. Stanford, CA: Stanford University Press, 1988.

Caron, Vicki. *Uneasy Asylum: France and the Jewish Refugee Crisis, 1933–1942*. Stanford, CA: Stanford University Press, 2002.

Celestin, Roger, and Eliane DalMolin. *France from 1851 to the Present*. New York, NY: Palgrave MacMillan, 2007.

Cesarani, David, ed. *After Eichmann: Collective Memory and the Holocaust since 1961*. New York, NY: Routledge, 2005.

Charbit, Denis. *Les intellectuels français et Israël*. Paris: Éditions de l'éclat, 2009.

Chevallier, Jean-Jacques, Guy Carcassonne, and Olivier Duhamel. *Histoire de la Vᵉ République 1958–2009*. Paris: Aubin Imprimeur, 2009.

Clendinnen, Inga. *Reading the Holocaust*. New York, NY: Cambridge University Press, 1999.

Cohen, Asher. *Persécutions et sauvetages: Juifs et Français sous l'Occupation et sous Vichy*. Paris: Cerf, 1993.

Cohen, Erik H. *L'étude et l'éducation juive en France*. Paris: Editions du Cerf, 1991.

Cohen, Erik H. *Heureux comme Juifs en France? Etude sociologique*. Paris, Jerusalem: Akadem—Elkana Editions, 2007.

Conan, Eric, and Henry Rousso. *Vichy: An Ever-Present Past*. Hanover, NH: University Press of New England, 1998.

Cohen, Jeremy. *Christ Killers: The Jews and the Passion from the Bible to the Big Screen*. New York, NY: Oxford University Press, 2007.

Cohen, Richard I. *The Burden of Conscience*. Bloomington, IN: Indiana University Press, 1987.

Commission nationale consultative des droits de l'homme. *La lutte contre le racisme, l'antisémitisme et la xénophobie, 2008*. Paris: La documentation française, 2009.

Controverses: L'identité Nationale Face au Postmodernisme 3 (October 2006).

Controverses: Les Alterjuifs 4 (February 2007).

Controverses: Le signe juif de la politique française 10 (March 2009).

Controverses: Post colonialisme et sionisme 11 (May 2009).

Controverses: Gaza une critique du rapport Goldstone 13 (March 2010).

Controverses: Raison Garder : Un tournant de l'opinion 15 (November 2010).

Controverses: L'avenir de Jérusalem 17 (June 2011).

Cukierman, Roger. *Ni fiers ni dominateurs*. Paris: Éditions du Moment, 2008.

Delatte, Rémi. *Un deputé à vos côtés*. Dijon: Presses de l'Imprimerie ICO, 2011.

Dieckhoff, Alain. *L'état d'Israël*. Paris: Librairie Arthème Fayard et Centre d'études et de recherches internationales, 2008.

Downs, Laura Lee, and Stéphane Gerson, eds. *Why France? American Historians Reflect on an Enduring Fascination*. Ithaca, NY: Cornell University Press, 2007.

Dreyfus, Michel. *L'antisémitisme à gauche : Histoire d'un paradoxe, de 1830 à nos jours*. Paris: La Découverte, 2009.

Drouout, Henri. *Notes d'un dijonnais pendant l'occupation allemande 1940–1944*. Dijon: Éditions Universitaires de Dijon, 1998.

Dugourd, François-Xavier. *Dijon demain : Lettre ouverte aux Dijonnaises et aux Dijonnais*. Dijon: Éditions de Bourgogne, 2005.

Epstein, Simon. *L'Antisémitisme français aujourd'hui et demain*. Paris: Pierre Belfond, 1984.

Epstein, Simon. *Un paradoxe français : Antiracistes dans la Collaboration, anti-Sémites dans la Résistance*. Paris: Éditions Albin Michel, 2008.

Eskenazi, Frank, and Édouard Waintrop. *Le Talmud et la République : Enquête sur les juifs français à l'heure des renouveaux religieux*. Paris: Grasset, 1991.

Éytan, Freddy. *David et Marianne : La France, les juifs et Israël*. Paris: Éditions Alain Moreau, 1986.

Éytan, Freddy. *Sarkozy, le monde juif et Israël*. Paris: Éditions Alphée, 2009.

Farhi, Daniel. *Profession rabbin : De la communauté à l'universel*. Paris: Albin Michel, 2006.

Farmer, Sarah. *Martyred Village: Commemorating the 1944 Massacre at Oradour-sur-Glane*. Berkeley, CA: University of California Press, 1999.

Finkielkraut, Alain. *Au nom de l'Autre : Réflexions sur l'antisémitisme qui vient*. Paris: Gallimard, 2003.

Finkielkraut, Alain. *L'humanité perdue : Essai sur le XXᵉ siècle*. Paris: Seuil, 1996.

Finkielkraut, Alain. *The Imaginary Jew*. Translated by Kevin O'Neill and David Suholl. Lincoln, NE: University of Nebraska Press, 1994.

Finkielkraut, Alain. *L'imparfait du présent : Pièces brèves*. Paris: Gallimard, 2002.

Finkielkraut, Alain. *L'interminable écriture de l'extermination*. Paris: Éditions Stock, 2010.

Finkielkraut, Alain. *Nous autres, modernes. Quatre leçons*. France: Ellipses/École Polytechnique, 2005.

Finkielkraut, Alain. *Qu'est-ce que la France?* Paris: Éditions Stock, 2007.

Finkielkraut, Alain. *Remembering in Vain: The Klaus Barbie Trial and Crimes against Humanity*. New York, NY: Columbia University Press, 1992.

Fisher, Claude. *The Omnivore*. New York, NY: Penguin, 2006.

Fishman, Sarah, Laura Lee Downs, Ioannis Sinanoglou, Leonard V. Smith, and Robert Zaretsky, eds. *France at War: Vichy and the Historians*. New York, NY: Berg, 2000.

Frank, Anne. *The Diary of Anne Frank*. New York, NY: Random House, 1956.

Frankel, Jonathan, and Steven J. Zipperstein, eds. *Assimilation and Community: The Jews in Nineteenth-Century Europe*. Cambridge: Cambridge University Press, 1992.

Geisser, Vincent, and Aziz Zemouri. *Marianne and Allah : Les politiques française face à la « question musulmane »*. Paris: Éditions La Découverte, 2007.

Gensburger, Sarah. *Les Justes de France : Politiques publiques de la mémoire*. France: Presses de la Fondation Nationale des Sciences Politiques, 2010.

Ghiles-Meilhac, Samuel. *Le CRIF : De la résistance juive à la tentation du lobby de 1943 à nos jours*. Paris: Robert Laffont, 2011.

Giesbert, Franz-Olivier. *M. Le President : Scènes de la vie politique 2005–2011*. Paris: Flammarion, 2011.

Girard, Patrick. *Les juifs de France*. Paris: Éditions Bruno Huisman, 1983.

Girard, Patrick. *La Révolution française et les juifs*. Paris: Robert Laffont, 1989.

Glucksmann, André. *La République, la pantoufle et les petits lapins*. Paris: Desclée de Brouwer, 2011.

Goldstein, Phyllis. *A Convenient Hatred: The History of Antisemistism*. Brookline, MA: Facing History and Ourselves, 2012.

Gounand, Pierre. *Dijon 1940–1944: Du désespoir à l'espoir*. Dijon: Éditions de l'Armaçon, 2004.

Gras, Pierre. *Histoire de Dijon : Univers de la France*. Toulouse: Éditions Privat, 1987.

Green, Nancy. *The Pletzl of Paris: Jewish Immigrant Workers in the "Belle Époque."* New York, NY: Holmes and Meier, 1986.

Guland, Olivier, and Michel Zerbib, eds. *Nous les juifs de France*. Paris: Bayard, 2000.

Gurfinkiel, Michel. *Israël peut-il survivre? La nouvelle règle du jeu*. Paris: Hugo&Cie, 2011.

Halioua, Bruno. *Blouses blanches, étoiles jaunes : L'exclusion des médecins juifs en France sous l'Occupation*. Paris: Liana Levi, 2002.

Halperin, Jean and Nelly Hansson. *Comment vivre ensemble? : Actes du XXXVIIe Colloque des intellectuels juifs de langue française*. Paris: Albin Michel, 2001.

Harris, André, and Alain de Sédouy. *Juifs et Français*. Paris: Grasset, 1979.

Hecker, Marc. *La Défense des intérêts de l'état d'Israël en France*. Paris: L'Harmattan, 2005.

Heilman, Samuel C. *Defenders of the Faith: Inside Ultra-Orthodox Jewry*. Berkeley, CA: University of California Press, 2000.

Heilman, Samuel C. *Sliding to the Right: The Contest for the Future of American Jewish Orthodoxy*. Berkeley, CA: University of California Press, 2006.

Henry-Lévy, Bernard. *L'idéologie française*. Paris: Bernard Grasset, 1981.

Héran, François. *Le Temps des immigrés : Essai sur le destin de la population française*. Paris: Éditions du Seuil, 2007.

Herf, Jeffrey. *Holocaust Rememberance: The Shapes of Memory*. Cambridge: Basil Blackwell, 1994.

Hertzberg, Arthur. *The French Enlightenment and the Jews: The Origins of Modern Anti-Semitism*. New York, NY: Columbia University Press, 1968.

Herzl, Theodor. *The Jewish State: Attempt at a Modern Solution of the Jewish Question*. New York, NY: Maccabaean Publishing Co., 1904.

Herzl, Theodor. *The Jewish State, An Attempt at a Modern Solution of the Jewish Question*. Ed. Jacob M. Alkow. New York, NY: American Zionist Emergency Council, 1946.

Histoire: Les juifs en France 3 (November 1979).

Hollifield, James F., and George Ross, eds. *Searching for the New France*. London: Routledge, 1991.

Hutton, Patrick H. *History as an Art of Memory*. Hanover, NH: University Press of New England, 1993.

Hyman, Paula. *From Dreyfus to Vichy*. New York, NY: Columbia University Press, 1979.

JCall. *Les raisons d'un appel*. Paris: Éditions Liana Levi, 2011.

Jordan, William Chester. *The French Monarchy and the Jews: From Philip Augustus to the last Capetians*. Philadelphia, PA: University of Pennsylvania Press, 1989.

Jouanneau, Bernard. *La justice et l'histoire face au négationnisme*. France: Éditions Fayard, 2008.

Judaken, Jonathan. *Jean-Paul Sartre and the Jewish Question*. Lincoln, NE: University of Nebraska Press, 2006.

Juza-Rosinski, Philippe, et al. *Pourquoi un état juif*. Paris: Les Éditions de Passy, 2010.

Kahn, Jean-François. *Ce que Marianne en pense*. Louvre, Paris: Mille et Une Nuits, 2002.

Kaluski-Jacobon, Nadia. *Les lettres de Louise Jacobson et de ses proches, Fresnes, Drancy 1942–1943*. Paris: Robert Laffont, 1997.

Kessler, Edward. *An Introduction to Jewish-Christian Relations*. New York, NY: Cambridge University Press, 2010.

Killian, Caitlin. *North African Women in France: Gender, Culture and Identity*. Stanford University Press, 2006.

Knobel, Mark. *L'internet de la haine : racistes, antisémites, néonazis, intégristes, islamistes, terroristes, et xénophobes à l'assaut du web*. Paris: Berg International, 2012.

Kriegel, Annie. *Reflexion sur les questions juives*. Paris: Hachette, 1984.

LaCapra, Dominick. *History and Memory after Auschwitz*. Ithaca, NY: Cornell University Press, 1998.

Langer, Lawrence L. *Preempting the Holocaust*. New Haven, CT: Yale University Press, 1998.

Laqueur, Walter. *The Changing Face of Antisemitism: From Ancient Times to the Present Day*. Oxford: Oxford University Press, 2006.

Laskier, Michael. *North African Jewry in the Twentieth Century: The Jews of Morocco, Tunisia and Algeria*. New York, NY: New York University Press, 1994.

Lasry, Jean-Claude, and Claude Tapia, eds. *Les juifs du Maghreb : diasporas contemporaines*. Paris: Éditions l'Harmattan, 1989.

Latour, Anny. *The Jewish Resistance in France (1940–1944)*. Translated by Irene R. Ilton. New York, NY: Holocaust Publications, 1981.

Laurence, Jonathan. *The Emancipation of Europe's Muslims: The State's Role in Minority Integration*. Princeton, NJ: Princeton University Press, 2012.

Lévêque, Pierre. *La Bourgogne de Lamartine à nos jours*. Dijon: Éditions Universitaires de Dijon, 2006.

Lévy, Élisabeth, and Robert Ménard. *Les français sont-ils antisémites?* Paris: Mordicus, 2009.

Lignes: Les extrêmes-droits en France et en Europe 4 (October 1988).

Lignes 1989: Nouvel antisémitisme 9 (March 1990).

Lucassen, Leo. *The Immigrant Threat: The Integration of Old and New Migrants in Western Europe since 1850*. Urbana, IL: University of Illinois Press, 2005.

Maeck, Julie. *Montrer la Shoah à la télévision, de 1960 à nos jours*. Paris: Nouveau monde éditions, 2009.

Mak, Geert. *In Europe: Travels through the Twentieth Century*. Translated by Sam Garrett. New York, NY: Pantheon Books, 2007.

Malino, Francis, and Bernard Wasserstein, eds. *The Jews in Modern France*. Hanover, NH: University Press of New England, 1985.

Mandel, Arnold. *Nous autres juifs*. Paris: Hachette, 1978.

Marcus, J. *Social and Political History of the Jews in Poland, 1919–1939*. Berlin: Walter de Gruyter, 1983.

Marrus, Michael R. *The Politics of Assimilation: The French Jewish Community at the Time of the Dreyfus Affair*. Oxford: Clarendon Press, 1971.

MacCulloch, Diarmaid. *Christianity: The First Three Thousand Years*. New York, NY: Viking, 2009.

Meilhac, Samuel Ghiles. *Le CRIF: De la résistance juive à la tentation du lobby*. Paris: Éditions Robert Laffont, 2011.

Meilhac, Samuel Ghiles. *Le monde diplomatique et Israël 1954–2005*. Paris: Éditions Le Manuscrit, 2006.

Memmi, Albert. *La libération d'un juif*. Paris: Gallimard, 1966.

Memmi, Albert. *Portrait du colonisé, précédé du portrait du colonisateur*. Paris: Buchet-Chastel, 1957.

Memmi, Albert. *Portrait d'un juif*. Paris: Gallimard, 1962.

Miller, Judith. *One, by One, by One: Facing the Holocaust*. New York, NY: Simon and Schuster, 1990.

Morin, Edgar. *Le monde moderne et la question juive*. Paris: Éditions du Seuil, 2006.

Mosse, George L. *Toward the Final Solution: A History of European Racism*. Madison, WI: University of Wisconsin Press, 1985.

Moyn, Samuel. *A Holocaust Controversy: The Treblinka Affair in Postwar France*. Lebanon, NH: University Press of New England, 2005.

Nahum, André. *Juifs de France : La tentation assimilation*. Paris: Les Éditions de Passy, 2007.

Nicault, Catherine. *La France et le sionisme, 1897–1948 : Une rencontre manquée?* Paris: Calmann-Lévy, 1992.

Noiriel, Gérard. *Immigration, antisémitisme et racisme en France (XIXᵉ–XXᵉ siècle)*. Paris: Librairie Arthéme Fayard, 2007.

Paris, Erna. *Unhealed Wounds: France and the Klaus Barbie Affair*. New York, NY: Grove Press, 1985.

Paugam, Serge, ed. *Repenser la solidarité : L'apport des sciences sociales*. Paris: Presses Universitaires de France, 2007.

Paxton, Robert O. *Vichy France: Old Guard and New Order, 1940–1944*. New York, NY: Colombia University Press, 1972.

Perchenet, Annie. *Histoire des juifs de France*. Paris: Les Éditions du Cerf, 1988.

Pernet, Rachel. "La communauté juive de Dijon." Masters Thesis under the direction of Serge Wolikow, University of Burgundy, 1998.

Philippe, Béatrice. *Être juif dans la société française*. Paris: Éditions Montalba, 1979.

Podselver, Laurence. *Fragmentation et recomposition du judaïsme : Le cas français*. Genève: Éditions Labor et Fides, 2004.

Podselver, Laurence. *Retour au judaïsme? Les Lubavitch en France*. Paris: Odile Jacob, 2010.

Podselver, Laurence, and Annette Wieviorka, eds. *Pardes : Histoire contemporaine et sociologie des juifs de France* 14 (Paris: Cerf, 1991).

Pomson, Alex, and Deitcher Howard, eds. *Jewish Day Schools, Jewish Communities: A Reconsideration*. Oxford, UK: Littman Library of Jewish Civilization, 2009.

Pra, Marie. *Synagogue Morne Plaine : Comment je me suis convertie au judaïsme*. Paris: Luc Pire, 2008.

Rajsfus, Maurice. *Identité à la carte : le judaïsme français en questions, rapport sur l'antisémitisme en France*. Paris: CRDA, 1993.

Ramadan, Tariq, and Alain Gresh. *L'Islam en questions*. Arles: Actes Sud, 2002.

Rayski, Adam. *Le choix des juifs sous Vichy*. Paris: La Découverte, 1992.

Revue d'histoire de la Shoah : Catholiques et protestants français après la Shoah 192 (Janunary/June 2010).

Revue d'histoire de la Shoah : Enseigner l'histoire de la Shoah en France 1950–2010 193 (July/December 2010).

Revue d'histoire de la Shoah : Spoliations en Europe 186 (January/June 2007).

Rioux, Jean-Pierre. *The Fourth Republic, 1944–1958*. Cambridge: Cambridge University Press, 1987.

Rosenzweig, Luc. *La jeune France juive : Conversations avec des juifs d'aujourd'hui*. Paris: Éditions Libres-Hallier, 1980.

Roudinesco, Élisabeth. *Retour sur la question juive*. Paris: Éditions Albin Michel, 2009.

Sadigh, Élie. *Étude économique et géopolitique du développement*. Paris: Éditions L'Harmattan, 2003.

Sarkozy, Nicholas. *Témoignage*. Paris: XO Éditions, 2006.

Schnapper, Dominique, Chantal Bordes-Benayoun, and Freddy Raphaël. *La condition juive en France : La tentation de l'entre-soi*. Paris: Presses Universitaires de France, 2009.

Schechter, Ronald. *Obstinate Hebrews: Representations of Jews in France, 1715–1815*. Berkeley, CA: University of California Press, 2003.

Schor, Ralph. *L'antisémitisme en France pendant les années trente*. Brussels: Éditions Complexe, 1992.

Schor, Ralph. *L'étrange procès*. Paris: Fayard, 1998.

Schwartz, Vera. *Bridge Across Broken Time: Chinese and Jewish Cultural Memory*. New Haven, CT: Yale University Press, 1998.

Schwartz-Bart, André. *Le dernier des justes*. New York, NY: Artheneum, 1960.

Schwarzfuchs, Simon. *Du juif à l'israélite : Histoire d'une mutation, 1770–1870*. Paris: Fayard, 1989.

Servan-Schreiber, Jean-Jacques. *Le choix des juifs*. Paris: Grasset, 1988.

Shapira, David. *Les antisémitismes français : De la Révolution à nos jours*. Lormont: Éditions Le Bord de l'Eau, 2011.

Sieffert, Denis. *Israël-Palestine : Une passion française*. Paris: La Découverte, 2004.

Simonnot, Philippe. *Enquête sur l'antisémitisme musulman*. Paris: Éditions Michalon, 2010.

Slama, Alain-Gérard. *La société d'indifférence*. Paris: Perrin, 1994.

Spurlock, Morgan. *Supersize Me*. Film. Directed by Morgan Spurlock. USA: Kathbur Picture, 2004.

Sternhell, Zeëv. *Neither Right nor Left: Fascist Ideology in France*. Berkeley, CA: University of California Press, 1986.

Stow, Kenneth R. *Alienated Minority: The Jews of Medieval Latin Europe*. Cambridge, MA: Harvard University Press, 1992.

Strudel, Sylvie. *Votes juifs : Itinéraires migratoires, religieux et politiques*. Paris: Presses de Sciences Po, 1996.

Sweets, John F. *Choices in Vichy France*. Oxford: Oxford University Press, 1986.

Szafran, Maurice. "Les Juifs." In *La politique française : De 1945 à nos jours*. Paris: Flammarion, 1990.

Szafran, Maurice, and Simone Veil. *Destin*. Paris: Flammarion, 1994.

Szajkowski, Zosa. *The Economic Status of the Jews in Alsace, Metz and Lorraine, 1648–1789*. New York, NY: Éditions historiques franco-juives, 1954.

Szajkowski, Zosa. *Poverty and Social Welfare among French Jews, 1800–1880*. New York, NY: Éditions historiques franco-juives, 1954.

Szajkowski, Zosa. *Relations among Sephardim, Ashkenazim and Avignonese Jews in France: From the 16th to the 20th Centuries*. New York, NY: Yivo Institute for Jewish Research, 1955.

Szlamowicz, Jean. *Détrompez vous! Les étranges indignations de Stéphane Hessel décryptées*. Paris: Éditions Intervalles, 2011.

Taguieff, Pierre-André. "La nouvelle judéophobie : Antisionisme, antiracisme, et anti-imperialisme." *Les Temps Modernes* (November, 1989).

Taguieff, Pierre-André. *La judéophobie des modernes. Des Lumières au Jihad mondial*. Paris: Odile Jacob, 2008.

Taguieff, Pierre-André. *La nouvelle propagande antijuive*. Paris: Presses Universitaires de France, 2010.

Tapia, Claude. *Les juifs sépharades en France, 1965–1985*. Paris: Éditions L'Harmattan, 1986.

Thalmann, Rita. *Tout commença à Nuremberg : Entre histoire et mémoire*. Paris: Berg International Éditeurs, 2004.

Tiersky, Ronald. *François Mitterrand: The Last French President*. New York, NY: St. Martin's Press, 2000.

Trigano, Shmuel. *L'avenir des juifs de France*. Paris: Bernard Grasset, 2007.

Trigano, Shmuel. *La démission de la république : Juifs et musulmans en France*. Paris: Presses Universitaires de France, 2003.

Trigano, Shmuel. *L'énigme juive*. France: Éditions in Press, 2009.

Trigano, Shmuel. *Face à l'universel : la pensée juive*. France: Éditions in Press, 2011.

Trom, Danny. *Promesse et l'obstacle : La gauche radical et le problem juif*. Paris: Le Cerf, 2007.

Uris, Leon. *Mila 18*. New York, NY: Doubleday, 1961.

Valensi, Lucette, and Nathan Wachtel. *Jewish Memories*. Berkeley, CA: University of California Press, 1991.

Venner, Fiametta. *Extrême France*. Paris: Grasset & Fasquelle, 2006.

Vidal, David. *A People Apart: The Jews in Europe 1789–1939*. Oxford: Oxford University Press, 1999.

Vidal-Naquet, Pierre. *Assassins de la mémoire*. New York, NY: Colombia University Press, 1992.

Vigoureux, Elsa. *L'affaire du gang des barbares*. Paris: Flammarion, 2010.

Valentine, Mitchell. *Aspects of French Jewry*. London: n.p. 1969.

Wasserstein, Bernard. *Vanishing Diaspora: The Jews in Europe since 1945*. Cambridge, MA: Harvard University Press, 1996.

Weil, Patrick. *How to be French: Nationality in the Making since 1789*. Translated by Catherine Porter. Durham, NC: Duke University Press, 2008.

Weill-Raynal, Guillaume. *Une haine imaginaire? Contre-enquête sur le « nouvel anti-sémitisme »*. Paris: Armand Colin, 2005.

Weinberg, David. *A Community on Trial: The Jews of Paris in the 1930s*. Chicago, IL: University of Chicago Press, 1977.

Weinberg, David H. "The Reconstruction of the French Jewish Community after World War II." *She'erit Hapletah 1944–48* (1990): 167–86.

Weinberg, Henry. *The Myth of the Jew in France, 1967–1982*. New York, NY: Mosaic Press, 1987.

Weiner, Robert I. "The Evolution of French Jewry since World War II: An Analysis," *Proceedings of the Ninth Annual Meeting of the Western Society for French History*. The University of Kansas, IX (1982): 402–13.

Weiner, Robert I. "French Jewish Images of America: The Case of Dijon," *Proceedings of the Western Society for French History: Selected Papers of the Annual Meeting* XXV (1998), 79–87.

Weiner, Robert I. "On Interviewing French Jews: The Case for Oral History," *Proceedings of the Ninth Annual Meeting of the Western Society for French History*. The University of Kansas, XVI (1989): 316–25.

Weiner, Robert I. *The Long 19th Century: European History from 1789 to 1917*. 3 vols. Chantilly, VA: The Teaching Company, 2005.

Weiner, Robert I. "Perspectives on French Jewry in the 1980s: Crisis and Renewal," *Proceedings of the Ninth Annual Meeting of the Western Society for French History*. The University of Kansas, XIII (1986): 251–59.

Weiner, Robert I. "Pour le meilleur ou pour le pire : The Jews of Dijon in the 1990s, A Memoir," *Proceedings of the Western Society for French History: Selected Papers of the Annual Meeting* XXVIII (2002), 68–75.

Wettstein, Howard, ed. *Diaporas and Exiles: Varieties of Jewish Identity*, Berkeley, CA: University of California Press, 2002.

Wiesel, Elie. *Night*. New York, NY: Hill and Yang, 2006.

Wieviorka, Annette. *Déportation et génocide : Entre la mémoire et l'oubli*. Paris: Plon, 1992.

Wieviorka, Michel. *La tentation anti-sémite : Haine des juifs dans la France d'aujourd'hui*. Paris: Robert Laffont, 2005.

Wieviorka, Olivier. *La mémoire désunie*. Paris: Éditions du Seuil, 2010.

Wilson, Stephen. *Ideology and Experience: Antisemitism in France at the Time of the Dreyfus Affair*. Rutherford, NJ: Fairleigh Dickinson University Press, 1982.

Winock Michel, ed. *Histoire de l'extrême droite en France*. Paris: Seuil, 1990.

Winock, Michel. *Parlez-moi de la France*. Paris: Plon, 1995.

Wolitz, Seth. "Imagining the Jew in France: From 1945 to the Present." *Yale French Studies* 85, 85 (1994): 119–34. http://dx.doi.org/10.2307/2930070.

Yerushalmi, Yosef, and Zakhor Hayim. *Jewish History and Jewish Memory*. Seattle, WA: University of Washington Press, 1982.

Zaoui, Michel, Noëlle Herrenschmidt, and Antoine Garapon. *Mémoires de justice : Les procès Barbie, Touvier, Papon*. Paris: Éditions du Seuil, 2009.

Zuccotti, Susan. *The Holocaust, the French, and the Jews*. New York, NY: Basic Books, 1993.

Zuccotti, Susan. *The Italians and the Holocaust: Persecution, Rescue, Survival*. New York, NY: Basic Books, 1987.

INDEX

Cabrini Medical Center in Manhattan, 35
campus radio, 160
Canada, xxx
Carnavalet Museum, 65
Casablanca, 5, 234, 239
Catholic Church, 139
Catholic schools
  French Jewish children in, 302
Catholics
  anti-Semitism, 40–41
CCJD. *See* Cultural Center of the Jews of
  Dijon (CCJD)
celebrities rejected because they were Jews
  (accomplices of Israel), 299
Cemachovic, Israel (Izy), xxix, 34–47, 125,
  130, 285, 287, 293
  anger at public menorah during Hanukkah,
    129
  early life and family, 34–35
  Jewish education, 35–36
  marriage, 38
  medical degree, 35
  medical practice, 39
  moved to Dijon, 39, 41
  not interested in France-Israel Association,
    128
  philosophically more European than
    American, 37
  president of synagogue board, 41–42, 305
  Zionist, 47
Cemachovic, Luna, 38, 120–30
  family background, 120
  in Israel to study languages, 122
  on Judaism, 127
  marriage, 125
  move to Dijon, 125
  parents did not talk about Hitler years, 123
  training as interpreter, 124
Center for Documentation of The
  Agricultural Industry, 177
Ceuta (Spanish enclave in Morocco), 294
Chalkida, 38, 121–22
Chalons-sur-Saône, 23–24, 105
child-care centers, 77–78
  rules for gaining acceptance, 81
children of non-Jewish mothers, 12, 43, 60,
  140
China, 252
Chinese students, 163
Chirac, Jacques, 151–52, 171
Chirac government, 58
choirs, xxii, 70, 197, 306
  Christian participation in Dijon, 306
choral concerts, 28
Christian Right
  validated by 9/11, 262
Christianity, 115, 174
Christmas, 109, 294
Chumash, 9, 231
circumcision, 281
City College, 258–59
civil rights movement, 198

class (social class and hierarchy), 131–32,
  183, 248
  comes from the Gentiles' perspective of the
    world, 183
  middle class, xix, 182
  in Paris and Israel, 178
  Polish Jews, 49
  working class, xviii, xix
classes for adults, 8. *See also* conversion
  post-bar mitzvah classes, 206
  study groups for adults, 306
Claves-Contet, Claudine, 300
Cluny, 95
Cohen, Albert, 164
Cohen, Tom, 297
Cohen family, 240
Colonie, Michael, 10
Columbia University, 258
Communism, 108, 149, 178
Communists, 101, 108
"communitarianism" (or self-segregation),
  302
community centers, 305. *See also* Cultural
  Center of the Jews of Dijon (CCJD)
Conservative Catholics, xix
Consistorial standards, 53
Consistorial synagogues, xiii
Consistorial system, xviii, xix, 13, 43, 56, 141,
  281–82
  conversion and, 60
Consistory Council, xii
contraception, 74
conversion, 12, 60
  alternative conversion, 282
  Isabelle Danino, 133, 138–40
  Jean-David Attal's mother converted in an
    Orthodox synagogue, 248
  not accepted in the Jewish community,
    192–93
  requires respect for mitzvot that the
    automatic Jews ignore, 281
  in Torah there is the possibility of
    conversion, 192
Copernic liberal Jewish community, 247
Crusades, xviii
Cultural Center of the Jews of Dijon (CCJD),
  xxv, xxix, 8, 15, 54, 183
  open to everyone, 16, 28, 55
cultural life, 305
Cyper, Élie, xxi

dance (in synagogues), 297
dance (Jewish dancing), 28–29
Danino, Alain, 131–36
Danino, Isabelle, 137–45
  Catholic childhood, 137
  classic dance and piano, 137
  conversion, 133, 138–40
  expected to go to North America, 143
  fear of showing signs of wealth in France,
    145
  on future of France, 144
  veterinary medicine, 137–38